XML BASICS

LICENSE, DISCLAIMER OF LIABILITY, AND LIMITED WARRANTY

XML BASICS

Shashi Banzal

Mercury Learning and Information
Dulles, Virginia
Boston, Massachusetts
New Delhi

Original title and copyright: *Learning XML.*

Publisher: David Pallai
Mercury Learning and Information
22841 Quicksilver Drive
Dulles, VA 20166
info@merclearning.com
www.merclearning.com
1-800-232-0223

S. Banzal. *XML Basics.*
ISBN: 978-1-68392-546-0

Library of Congress Control Number: 2020942355

202122321 Printed on acid-free paper in the United States of America.

CONTENTS

PREFACE

This book focuses on standards that are relevant to almost all developers working with XML. We investigate XML technologies that span a wide range of XML applications, not just those that are relevant only within a few restricted domains. XML is not a programming language. It is a markup language; but it is successfully used by many programmers. The book also covers generic supporting technologies that have been layered on top of XML and are used across a wide range of XML applications. These technologies include XLinks, XSLT, Namespaces, Schemas, XHTML, RDDL, XPointers, XPath, SAX, and DOM.

S. Banzal
August 2020

CHAPTER 1

UNDERSTANDING XML

MARKUP LANGUAGES

The term *Markup* is a concatenation of the words "mark up." This refers to the traditional way of marking up a document in the print and design worlds.

Markup is used to modify the look and formatting of text or to establish the structure and meaning of the document for output to some medium, such as the printer or the World Wide Web. Markup consists of codes, or tags, that are added to text to change the look or meaning of the tagged text. The tagged text for a document is usually called the *source code* for that document. Most word processors use some sort of markup languages to produce formatted text. There are two types of Markup languages: Specific Markup Languages and Generalized Markup Languages.

SPECIFIC MARKUP LANGUAGES

Specific markup languages were developed for specific purposes. These markup languages cannot be used for any other purpose other than that for what it was developed for. Hypertext Markup Language, or HTML, was designed for simplicity and it has a flexible structure. It allows text and graphics to be displayed in any Web browser.

Many markup languages have served quite well as document formatting tools for printing on the Web. However, they do not perform well in describing the data they contain or at providing contextual information for the data. For example, Hyper Text Markup Language describes how the text should be formatted, but conveys nothing about the kind of text data included in the document.

When using specific markup languages, the authors are limited to a particular set of tags. If a set of tags does not meet a need, authors must find an alternative way to meet those needs. A document might not be portable to other applications, as the data is not self-describing. It cannot be used for any other purpose than that for which it was originally intended. The language probably has a proprietary way of marking up text that is not compatible with other markup languages. This can create confusion and additional work for authors who must use several languages to accommodate different applications.

GENERALIZED MARKUP LANGUAGE

In the 1970s, Dr. C. F. Goldfarb and two of his colleagues proposed a method of describing text that was not specific to an application or a device. The method had two suggestions:

- The markup should describe the structure of a document and not its formatting or style characteristics.
- The syntax of the markup should be strictly enforced so that the code can clearly be read by a software program or by a human being.

The result of these suggestions was the Standardized General Markup Language (SGML) that was adopted as a standard by the International Organization for Standardization in 1986.

SGML - A METALANGUAGE

SGML has added provisions for identifying the characters to be used in a document. This makes it easier to ensure that a processor can understand everything in a document by allowing a document to specify the character set that it uses.

SGML provides a way to identify objects that will be used throughout a document. These objects, called *entities*, are convenient to use when a text fragment or any other data appears in several places in a document. If an entity is declared in one place of the document, any changes to that declaration will be reflected in all occurrences of the entity throughout the document.

SGML – Example

```
<!DOCTYPE CARS PUBLIC "//EXT/DTD CATALOG//EN">
<CAR>
<COLOR> Red
<PRICE> $20,000
</CAR>
```

The code snippet shown is an example of an SGML document. We can see that the content is the same as that of the HTML document. These similarities exist because HTML is an application of SGML. HTML was created using SGML standards. The main difference between SGML and HTML is that SGML is extensible, which means that it allows an author to define a particular structure by defining the parts that fit that structure. HTML is not extensible, which means that HTML cannot be used to create another markup language with its own rules and purposes.

WHY IS XML SO ADAPTABLE?

If XML is a new generation, then SGML is its mother. SGML is likely one of the most adaptable languages of all time, allowing the use of constructs that even XML won't allow. Unfortunately, SGML is more complex and not as universally supported as XML, so the use of SGML instead of XML isn't really recommended.

XML has inherited many of the key features of SGML, however, and puts them to good use; in many cases, the ways that it differs from its predecessor are inconsequential. While you may occasionally run across strange circumstances that would work better with SGML, it's best to focus on XML since that's where most of the support and interest lies.

XML OVER SGML

Even though XML is a subset of Standard Generalized Markup Language (SGML), XML is optimized for use on the World Wide Web. XML is designed in such a way that it has some benefits that are not found in SGML. XML is a smaller language than SGML. The designers of XML removed some specifications in SGML that were not needed for Web delivery.

XML includes a specification for the hyperlinking scheme, which is described as a separate language called eXtensible Linking Language (XLL).

XML supports the basic hyperlinking found in HTML as well as extended linking. XML includes specification for a style sheet language called eXtensible Stylesheet Language (XSL). XSL provides support for a style sheet mechanism, which allows an author to create a template of various styles.

XML documents are self-describing documents. That is, each document contains a set of rules to which its data must conform. Since the same set of rules can be reused in another document, other authors can easily create the same class of document, if necessary.

XML can be used as the data interchange format. Many legacy systems can contain data in disparate forms, and developers are doing a lot of work to connect these legacy systems using the Internet. Since the XML text format is standards-based, data can be converted to XML and then easily read by another system or application.

XML can be used for Web data. For example, the content is stored in an XML file and the HTML page is used simply for formatting and display. So, the content can be updated and translated into another language without modifying anything in the HTML code.

INTRODUCTION TO XML

XML (eXtensible Markup Language) was invented for the purpose of having a standard and powerful way of describing any kind of data. XML offers a widely adopted standard way of representing text and data in a format that can be processed without much human or machine intelligence. Information formatted in XML can be exchanged across platforms, languages, and applications, and can be used with a wide range of development tools and utilities.

XML is a *meta-language*; that is, it is a language in which other languages are created. In XML, data is "marked up" with tags similar to HTML tags. In fact, the latest version of HTML, called XHTML, is an XML-based language, which means that XHTML follows the syntax rules of XML.

XML is used to store data or information. This data might be intended to be by read by people or by machines. It can be highly structured data, such as data typically stored in databases or spreadsheets, or loosely structured data, such as data stored in letters or manuals.

XML is all about preserving useful information—information that computers can use to be more intelligent about what they do with our data. The best part of XML is that it liberates information from the shackles of a fixed-tag set.

XML provides a standard approach for describing, capturing, processing, and publishing information. It is a language that has significant benefits over HTML.

Unlike most markup languages, XML is a flexible framework in which you can create your own customized markup languages. All XML-based languages share the same look and feel, and they share a common basic syntax. The essence of XML is in its name: Extensible Markup Language.

- Markup – It is a collection of tags.
- XML Tags – Identify the content of the data
- Extensible – User-defined tags

EXTENSIBLE

XML is extensible. It lets you define your own tags, the order in which they occur, and how they should be processed or displayed. Another way to think about extensibility is to consider that XML allows us to extend our notion of what a document is: it can be a file that lives on a file server, or it can be a transient piece of data that flows between two computer systems (as in the case of Web Services).

MARKUP

The most recognizable feature of XML is its tags, or *elements* (to be more accurate). In fact, the elements you'll create in XML will be very similar to the elements you've already been creating in your HTML documents. However, XML allows you to define your own set of tags.

LANGUAGE

XML is a language that's very similar to HTML. It's much more flexible than HTML because it allows you to create your own custom tags. However, it's important to realize that XML is not just a language. XML is a meta-language: a language that allows us to create or define other languages. For example, with XML we can create other languages, such as RSS, MathML (a mathematical markup language), and even tools like XSLT.

HISTORY OF XML

In 1970, IBM introduced SGML (Standard Generalized Markup Language). SGML was developed out of the General Markup Language (GML), which was developed by IBM in the late 1960s. SGML is a semantic and structural language for text documents, but it is very complicated. HTML is a subset of SGML.

In 1996, XML Working Group was formed under W3C. The World Wide Web Consortium (W3C) is an international consortium where Member organizations, a full-time staff, and the public work together to develop Web standards. W3C was created by Tim Berners-Lee in 1994 who also invented the World Wide Web in 1989. In 1998, W3C introduced XML 1.0.

XML (Extensible Markup Language) is a dialect of SGML. XML is not a programming language. Rather, it is a set of rules that allows you to represent data in a structured manner. Since the rules are standard, the XML documents can be automatically generated and processed.

XML was designed to describe data and is a cross-platform, software- and hardware-independent tool for transmitting or exchanging information. It is an open-standards-based technology which is both human and machine readable. XML is best suited for use in documents that are similar. In future Web development, it is most likely that XML will be used to describe the data, while HTML will be used to format and display the same data. The XML specification includes the syntax and grammar of XML documents as well as DTD.

Website creation is a fast-growing sector. In the early days, Website design consisted primarily of creating fancy graphics and nice-looking, easy-to-read Web pages.

As today's Websites are interactive, the steps in Website design have changed. Although creating a pleasant-looking Website is still important, the primary focus has shifted from graphical design to programmatic design.

Consider a company wanting to sell its product on the Web. In such cases, the Webpages will collect and store a user's billing information. This calls for storing and manipulating such data in a database. This is where XML comes into the picture.

XML is the solution for the problems that arise when using database Webpages.

HTML AND XML

HTML and XML were designed with different purposes in mind. XML is similar to HTML—they are both closely related to the SGML markup definition language that has been an ISO standard since 1986. SGML is an early attempt to combine the metadata (data about the data) with the data and it was used primarily in large document management systems. Because SGML is a very complex language, it has limited mass appeal.

HTML is the most recognized application of SGML and it allows any Web browser or application which understands HTML to display information in a consistent form. A HTML document is effective when it comes to laying out and displaying data, but it is a fixed set of tags, and it does not have the flexibility to describe different document and data types. HTML, in conjunction with Cascading Style Sheets (CSS), is reasonably good at displaying data, but it is not as good as XML at transporting data that is meant to be viewed or parsed in dozens of different ways by a variety of devices. In essence, where HTML is a presentation language, we require a richer communication means that can help with exchanging information from one computer to another.

The need to extract data and put a structure around information led to the creation of XML. Since it was released in 1997, XML use has been growing rapidly. There are two major fundamental differences between HTML and XML:

- Separation of form and content—HTML mostly consists of tags defining the appearance of text; in XML, the tags generally define the structure and content of the data, with the actual appearance specified by a specific application or associated stylesheet.
- XML is extensible—tags can be defined by individuals or organisations for some specific application, whereas the HTML standard tagset is defined by the World Wide Web Consortium (W3C).

XML is not intended as a replacement for HTML and both are complementary technologies. XML is a more general and better solution to the problem of sharing data on the Web than extending HTML.

XML STRUCTURE

One of XML's best features is its ability to provide structure to a document. Every XML document includes both a logical and a physical structure. The logical structure is like a template that details the elements to be included in a document and the order in which they have to be included. The physical structure contains the actual data used in a document.

LOGICAL STRUCTURE

Logical Structure refers to the organization of the different parts of a document. It indicates how a document is built, as opposed to what a document contains. The first structural element in an XML document is an optional prolog element. The prolog is the base for the logical structure of an XML document. The prolog consists of two basic components, the XML Declaration and the Document Type Declaration. These two components are also optional.

XML DECLARATION

The XML Declaration identifies the version of the XML specification to which the document conforms. Although the XML declaration is an optional element, we should always include it in the XML document.

The code snippet here gives an example of basic XML declaration. Here, the line of code must use only lowercase letters.

```
<?xml version="1.0"?>
```

An XML declaration can also contain an encoding declaration and a standalone document declaration.

The encoding declaration identifies the character-encoding scheme, such as UTF-8 or EUC-JP. Different encoding schemas map to different character formats or languages. For example, UTF-8, the default scheme, includes representations for most of the characters in the English Language.

XML SYNTAX

The first thing that you'll need to do is open up your text editor of choice. At this point, your document is going to look something like this (if you're using XML version 1.0):

```
<?xml version="1.0"?>
```

Once you've typed your directive, it's time to start adding some content to the page. Information on an XML page is handled in a very precise and structured format, using tags to define your data. White space can be included in the document to make it more easily readable, though you should be careful not to use that white space inside of your tags, as it can create problems when being read by a browser.

Let's say that you've decided to create a new XML document to tell the world about your two favorite cats. You want to use the tag <cats>. Your document now looks a little something like this:

```
<?xml version="1.0"?>
<cats>Tooter and Shade are the best cats in the world!</cats>
```

Note the white space in between the directive and the first tags. You could also have put both of the tags on their own line, with the content of the tags between them, as long as you don't add additional white space within the tags.

Of course, the <cats> tags don't do anything. If you load this page into a Web browser, you'll end up with more or less a copy of the file contents displayed on the screen with the tags in some pretty colors. You'll have to define the tags, which can be done in 1 of 4 ways:

- Using Cascading Style Sheets (CSS)
- Using the eXtensible Style Language (XSL) Style Sheets
- Using a Data Island plus Script
- Using a Data Object Model plus Script or Client-Side Program

All of this might sound complicated, but it's really not. It does involve creating and referencing other pages, though for now we're still working on just the basic structure of XML. Save the document (in Text-Only mode) under the name cats.xml (making sure to use the .xml extension).

HOW DO I STRUCTURE MY XML DOCUMENTS?

Structure in an XML document is very important. Small errors in the structure of your document can have large effects on the overall outcome; pieces may not be displayed correctly, or might not appear at all. If the structure is too damaged, then the entire document might fail to work.

As previously mentioned, all XML documents begin with the XML directive. Open up the previously-saved file, cats.xml, and you'll find your directive already in place.

```
<?xml version="1.0"?>
<cats>Tooter and Shade are the best cats in the world!</cats>
```

Unfortunately, your file is still missing a few vital elements. The <cats> tags don't work, and the browser has no idea how to make them work. If you load it up in a browser, you'll just see a copy of the file, with the various elements in different colors. This is actually useful, however; as long as you see this, then your code is good. The browser doesn't know what else to do with it, in this case because some of the elements are missing, but the lack of definitive error codes tells you that it's at least well-coded.

Go into the file, between your directive and the content, and get ready to add another vital element to your page. Type the following:

```
<?xml-stylesheet type="text/css" href="cats.css"?>
```

Of course, this doesn't mean much to you right now. In time, though, it's going to be a vital part of your page. What you just typed is the directions that the browser needs to find the XML processor, or the file that tells it how it should handle the information in the XML document. The line that you just typed tells the browser to find the file called cats.css, and that the file is a Cascading Style Sheet. It also tells it that it's the stylesheet that it needs for this page. Now your cats.xml file should look like the following, which looks a lot more like an XML file.

```
<?xml version="1.0"?>
<?xml-stylesheet type="text/css" href="cats.css"?>
<cats>Tooter and Shade are the best cats in the world!</cats>
```

NEED FOR XML-BASED LANGUAGES

The main advantage of being able to define your own markup language is that it gives you the freedom to capture and publish useful information about what your data is and how it is structured. To show the difference, consider a company wanting to sell books on the Web. If they want to publish the information about the books on a Webpage, then we need to write an HTML document like the one shown.

The original data has been formed into HTML for publishing purposes. In the course of that transformation, useful information about what the information really is has been lost. If the same content were written in XML, it would look like the following code snippet.

```
<!-Book Snippet in HTML —>
<h1> Books for Sale </h1>
<table border=1>
<tr>
<td>Title</td><td>Paradise Lost</td>
</tr>
<tr>
```

```
<td>Author</td><td>John Milton</td>
</tr></table>
<!-Book snippet in XML ->
<BooksForSale>
<Title>Paradise Lost</Title>
<Author>John Milton</Author>
</BooksForSale>
```

If this code were to be published on the Web, this representation opens up some interesting possibilities. No image is shown.

XML BENEFITS

Initially, XML received a lot of excitement, but that has now died down some. This isn't because XML is not as useful, but rather because it doesn't provide the "Wow! factor" that other technologies, such as HTML, do. When you write an HTML document, you see a nicely formatted page in a browser—instant gratification. When you write an XML document, you see an XML document—not so exciting. However, with a little more effort, you can make that XML document sing.

XML is Everywhere

XML is now as important for the Web as HTML was to the foundation of the Web. XML is the most common tool for data transmissions between all sorts of applications. XML is used in many aspects of Web development, often to simplify data storage and sharing.

XML Separates Data from HTML

If you need to display dynamic data in your HTML document, it will take a lot of work to edit the HTML each time the data changes. With XML, data can be stored in separate XML files. This way you can concentrate on using HTML for layout and display and be sure that changes in the underlying data will not require any changes to the HTML. With a few lines of JavaScript code, you can read an external XML file and update the data content of Webpage.

XML Simplifies Data Sharing

In the real world, computer systems and databases contain data in incompatible formats. XML data is stored in plain text format. This provides a software- and hardware-independent way of storing data. This makes it much easier to create data that can be shared by different applications.

XML Simplifies Data Transport

One of the most time-consuming challenges for developers is to exchange data between incompatible systems over the Internet. Exchanging data as XML greatly reduces this complexity, since the data can be read by different incompatible applications.

XML Simplifies Platform Changes

Upgrading to new systems (hardware or software platforms) is always time consuming. Large amounts of data must be converted and incompatible data is often lost.

XML data is stored in text format. This makes it easier to expand or upgrade to new operating systems, new applications, or new browsers without losing data.

XML Makes Your Data More Readily Available

Different applications can access your data, not only from HTML pages, but also from XML data sources. With XML, your data can be available to all kinds of "reading machines" (handheld computers, voice machines, and news feeds), and make it available for blind people or people with other disabilities.

XML is Used to Create New Internet Languages

New Internet languages are created with XML. Here are some examples:

- XHTML
- WSDL for describing the available Webservices
- WAP and WML as markup languages for handheld devices
- RSS languages for news feeds
- RDF and OWL for describing resources and ontology
- SMIL for describing multimedia for the Web

The future might give us word processors, spreadsheet applications, and databases that can read each other's data in XML format, without any conversion utilities in between. XML documents form a tree structure that starts at the "root" and branches to the "leaves."

XML DISADVANTAGES

XML is useful for developing future Web applications, and it almost defines the future of Web development. However, XML also has some drawbacks. One of the biggest drawbacks of XML is that it lacks adequate applications for processing.

LACK OF APPLICATION PROCESSING

XML needs an application processing system. There are no browsers yet that can read XML. For HTML, anyone can write up a program that can be read using any browser anywhere in the world. To be able to be read in a browser, XML still depends on HTML and is not independent of it. XML documents have to be converted to HTML before they are deployed. The most common method is to write the parsing routes in either DHTML or Java applications and parse them through the XML document. The formatting rules can be applied by the style sheet to convert the entire document into HTML.

Other disadvantages of XML include the fact that it is more difficult, more demanding, and more precise when compared to HTML. XML does not have any browser support and does not have anything to support the end user applications.

XML is very flexible, but its flexibility can potentially become one of its disadvantages, since there may be disagreements in its tags. If an XML object has too many constraints, it might become very difficult to construct the file. While just describing tags and building a system sounds easy, it may not be that easy in reality. For example, a business or professional organization may have hundreds of functions related to one set of documents. XML does not have the capability to synthesize all the information related to the document.

GENERAL WEAKNESSES OF XML

Since XML is a verbose language, it is dependent on who is writing it. A verbose language may pose problems for other users. XML is not specific to any platform and has a neutral platform requirement that may be a disadvantage in a few circumstances. All the standards of XML are not yet fully compliant. Users have reported problems with the parser and there are problems with XML and HTTP that are still being resolved.

XML documents can be difficult and expensive to set up. A freelancer, for example, can sit at his home and at his own pace create, write, and format a document or a manuscript using any of the free software available. However, the moment he introduces XML, the whole process becomes more complicated.

XML AND UNICODE DISADVANTAGES

Implementing multiple programs that are incompatible can be challenging. When XML is tied closely to Unicode, the Unicode changes XML's attributes, which might result in a file that is totally different from the original.

The XML parsers, when used along with the RSS and the component called next, cannot disable the external entities. Instead they recognize them as their own, which can prove to be a major disadvantage. XML by itself cannot work along with Netscape, which makes it dependent on HTML. XML is not a super efficient model, it is not platform independent, and it cannot be deployed on every operating system. The limitation here is also very basic since it cannot talk to the browsers.

There are sample codes that belong to HTML and XHTML which contain a doctype and point to a DTD. The common belief is that this actually works, but browsers do not actually retrieve these DTDs. Whenever the DTD is unavailable, then the entire application breaks down. This is a problem because the DTD can be unavailable for other reasons, and it doesn't mean that the service itself has to become unavailable.

XML creates an abundant amount of dependency on single factors that can create problems for programs. DTD, when available, is totally not useful, and an outside program has to be used to create a backup system, so users and developers might as well use an outside program made from scratch, which has the back up at intermediary levels.

External entities pose a problem, which is a major disadvantage for XML. The best way to fix the external entities' problems with XML DTD is to not to use them at all, or if you have to use them, then don't use them on the producer side. Do not attempt to retrieve them on the client's side.

When you write the specifications for an XML document, do not mention the specifications for DTD in the vocabulary. There is a need for the programs to run their parsers for XML by disabling the external entity resolution. Otherwise, the external entities' problem will invariably crop up, triggering a series of problems that cannot be solved by the XML environment alone.

While layering the specifications, it is against the rules to disable or ban certain document types, which is allowed in SOAP.

If your job is to implement a Web application which is based on XML, you may need to configure the parser not to perform the DTD-based validations, and also not to try and resolve the external entities. This could be an answer to some problems, so taking precautionary measures is worthwhile. Publishing documents on the Web requires the same precautions; the document types should not be included.

A document may not be valid in the way XML describes it to be, and some people even believe that document validation in XML is overrated. Document data types are not very powerful when it comes to validation and it has been forgotten that the document has its own language and grammar which are not efficient for getting validated. There is also the problem of other programs not trusting the XML DTD. The doctype in HTML is much different from the doctype in XML. You may not be able to use the doctype in XML as an indicator, which helps programs understand what type of document it is dealing with.

If there is an application which exists that can handle multiple vocabularies of XML, and also knows to dispatch the respective documents to the concerned handlers by checking the namespace at the root of the element, then you can consider yourself lucky. If the vocabularies are not mentioned in the namespace, then you can look for them in the mime type. In some cases, the vocabularies are not present in the name space, nor are they specific to the mime. Such language is certainly a bad example and will create problems because you will have to use the root element name.

XML specifications define three kinds of file processing. The first one is DTD based validations which do not perform or retrieve external entities. The second one is the DTD based validation, which does not perform or retrieve external entities so that the information set and the reference library can be expanded. The third one is to perform the DTD-based validation by retrieving the external entities so that the information set and the entity reference can be expanded.

The point of having many profiles is so that the application has a choice and it chooses the right one. Character entities are considered unsafe for Web applications. It is a disadvantage because there will be a problem with the input and its editor. On the World Wide Web, there may be other options available when there is such a problem. The situation need not be so unfortunate because there may be a solution which exists, and there is an input method which can solve the problem with the editor. If the XHTML entities were pre-defined, then there wouldn't be many problems.

CHARACTERISTICS OF AN XML DOCUMENT

There are a range of characteristics associated with XML.

Simplicity

Information coded in XML is easy to read and understand, and it can be processed easily by computers.

Self-Describing

Unlike records in traditional database systems, XML data does not require relational schemata, file description tables, or external data type definitions because the data itself contains this information. XML also guarantees the total usability of data, which is imperative for business applications whose tasks extend beyond the mere presentation of content.

XML documents use a self-describing and simple syntax:

```
<?xml version="1.0" encoding="ISO-8859-1"?>
<note>
<to>Susan</to>
<from>Sullivan</from>
<heading>Reminder</heading>
<body>Don't forget me this weekend!</body>
</note>
```

The first line is the XML declaration. It defines the XML version (1.0) and the encoding used (ISO-8859-1 = Latin-1/West European character set).

The next line describes the root element of the document (like saying: "this document is a note"):

```
<note>
```

The next 4 lines describe 4 child elements of the root (to, from, heading, and body):

```
<to>Susan</to>
<from>Sullivan</from>
<heading>Reminder</heading>
<body>Don't forget me this weekend!</body>
```

And finally the last line defines the end of the root element:

```
</note>
```

OPEN AND EXTENSIBLE

XML allows you to add other elements when needed. This means you can always adapt your system to address specification modifications.

APPLICATION INDEPENDENCE

Using XML, data is no longer dependent on a specific application for creation, viewing or editing. In this sense, XML is to data what Java is to applications. Java allows programs to run anywhere—XML allows data to be used by any application.

DATA FORMAT INTEGRATION

XML documents can contain any imaginable data type—from classical data like text and numbers, or multimedia objects such as sounds and video, or active components like Applets.

ONE DATA SOURCE, MULTIPLE VIEWS

By formatting our data in a markup language, we allow computer applications to process and present this data to us in different ways. In contrast, HTML presents data in one fixed way.

DATA PRESENTATION MODIFICATION

You can change the look and feel of documents, or even entire Websites, with XSL Style Sheets without manipulating the data itself.

INTERNATIONALIZATION

Internationalization is important for electronic worldwide business applications. XML supports multilingual documents and the Unicode standard.

FUTURE-ORIENTED

XML is the endorsed industry standard of the World Wide Web Consortium (W3C) and is supported by all leading software providers. Furthermore, XML is also the standard today in an increasing number of other industries, such as health care.

IMPROVED DATA SEARCHES

Tags, attributes, and element structure provide context information that can be used to interpret the meaning of content, opening up new possibilities for highly efficient search engines, and intelligent data mining. An intelligent search engine for a body of XML-compliant markup languages would search both the content and the metadata, which would drastically improve the accuracy of searches. This will obviously cause an increase in the relevant and accessible data on a global basis.

ENABLES E-COMMERCE TRANSACTIONS

An ecommerce transaction requires instant cooperation between a host of agents involved in a single purchase. For example, a customer ordering an item from a supplier involves a number of transactions, including those with the customer ("B2C ecommerce"), businesses in a supply chain ("B2B ecommerce"), and banks ("B2B"), and between systems ("enterprise integration"). The initial reaction of most companies was to integrate these diverse operations by building or buying software that employed protocols, such as DCOM or CORBA, to perform such integrations. However, XML offers the option of performing the necessary integration by exchanging standardized data.

XML DOCUMENTS FORM A TREE STRUCTURE

XML documents must contain a root element. This element is the parent of all other elements. The elements in an XML document form a document tree. The tree starts at the root and branches to the lowest level of the tree. All elements can have sub-elements (child elements):

```
<root>
<child>
<subchild>.....</subchild>
</child>
</root>
```

The terms *parent*, *child*, and *sibling* are used to describe the relationships between elements. Parent elements have children. Children on the same level are called siblings (brothers or sisters). All elements can have text content and attributes (just like in HTML).

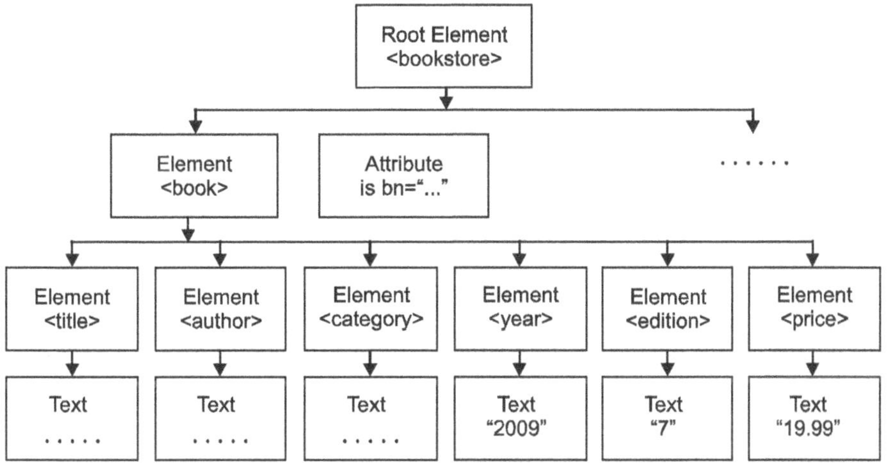

FIGURE 1.1 Tree structure of an XML document

The image above represents one book in the XML below:

```
<bookstore>
<book category="COOKING">
<title lang="en">Indian Food</title>
<author>Swati Jain</author>
<year>2011</year>
<price>200.00</price>
</book>
<book category="CHILDREN">
<title lang="en">Dolls</title>
<author>J K Jain </author>
<year>2010</year>
<price>29.95</price>
</book>
```

```
<book category="WEB">
<title lang="en">Learning XML</title>
<author>G.Ram</author>
<year>2009</year>
<price>13.95</price>
</book>
</bookstore>
```

The root element in the example is <bookstore>. All <book> elements in the document are contained within <bookstore>.

The syntax rules of XML are very simple and logical. The rules are easy to learn and easy to use.

ALL XML ELEMENTS MUST HAVE A CLOSING TAG

In HTML, elements do not have to have a closing tag:

```
<p>This is a paragraph
<p>This is another paragraph
```

In XML, it is illegal to omit the closing tag. All elements must have a closing tag:

```
<p>This is a paragraph</p>
<p>This is another paragraph</p>
```

You might have noticed from the previous example that the XML declaration did not have a closing tag. This is not an error. The declaration is not a part of the XML document itself, and it has no closing tag.

XML TAGS ARE CASE SENSITIVE

XML tags are case sensitive. The tag <Letter> is different from the tag <letter>. Opening and closing tags must be written with the same case:

```
<Message>This is incorrect</message>
<message>This is correct</message>
```

Opening and closing tags are often referred to as *Start* and *end tags*. Use whatever terms you prefer.

XML ELEMENTS MUST BE PROPERLY NESTED

In HTML, you might see improperly nested elements:

```
<b><i>This text is bold and italic</b></i>
```

In XML, all elements must be properly nested within each other:

```
<b><i>This text is bold and italic</i></b>
```

In the example above, “properly nested” simply means that since the <i> element is opened inside the <b> element, it must be closed inside the <b> element.

XML DOCUMENTS MUST HAVE A ROOT ELEMENT

XML documents must contain one element that is the parent of all other elements. This element is called the *root element*.

```
<root>
<child>
<subchild>.....</subchild>
</child>
</root>
```

XML ATTRIBUTE VALUES MUST BE QUOTED

XML elements can have attributes in name/value pairs just like in HTML.

In XML, the attribute values must always be quoted. Study the two XML documents below. The first one is incorrect, and the second is correct:

```
<note date=12/11/2019>
<to>Tonu</to>
<from>John</from>
</note>
<note date="12/11/2019">
<to>Tonu</to>
<from>John</from>
</note>
```

The error in the first document is that the date attribute in the note element is not quoted.

XML IS FREE

XML doesn't cost anything to use. It can be written with a simple text editor or one of the many freely available XML authoring tools, such as XML Notepad. In addition, many Web development tools, such as Dream-weaver and Visual Studio .NET, have built-in XML support. There are also many free XML parsers, such as Microsoft's MSXML (downloadable from *microsoft.com*) and Xerces (downloadable at *apache.org*).

XML TECHNOLOGY

The structured data is contained in an XML document, a text file with .xml as the extension. You can use CSS as in HTML to provide style sheets for XML data display. For more advanced features, power, and flexibility for the presentations, you could use XSL (XML Style sheet Language) to build the style sheets.

To enforce the structural constraints and rules on the data contained in an XML document, you could code a DTD (Document Type Definition). Due to certain limitations that were inherent in DTDs, the W3C came up with a specification to serve the same purpose as DTDs—the schemas. The schemas are contained in a .xsd file, and DTDs in a .dtd file. XML schema is an XML-based alternative to DTD.

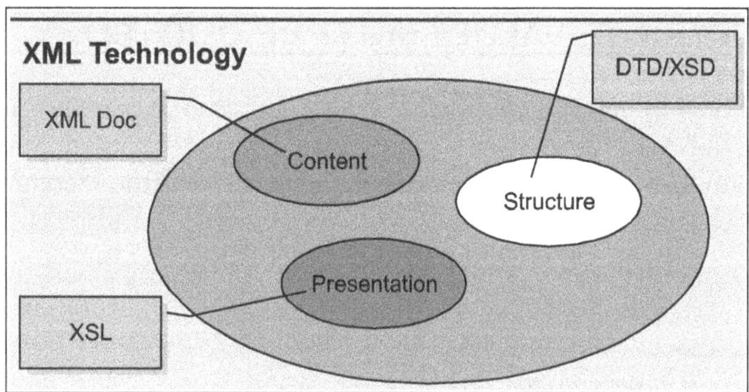

FIGURE 1.2 XML Technology

```
XSD - XML Schema Definition
DTD - Document Type Definition
XSL - Extensible Stylesheet Language
```

USES

XML is widely used for the following purposes.

- Storing configuration information—typically data in an application which is not stored in a database. Most server software has configuration files in XML formats.
- XML documents can also be used as a mini data store. This data can be used to present it on a variety of targets including browsers, and print media.
- Transmitting data between applications—overcomes problems in client server applications which are cross-platform in nature. Ex: A Windows program talking to a mainframe, Little and Big Endian problems, and data type size variations across platforms.

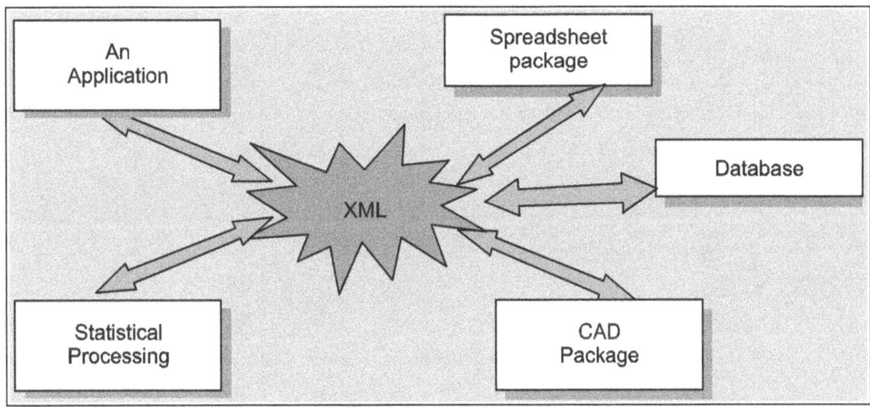

FIGURE 1.3 Variant uses of XML

When XML data is transferred across different systems, the data contained in an XML document can be read using a software entity called a *parser*. Most of the popular databases (Oracle, MS SQL Server, Sybase, and DB2) provide their own mechanisms to store and retrieve data as XML. Some of them also provide parsers to work with the XML documents programmatically. XML is a key technology when it comes to Web Services. .NET uses XML extensively. It is used as a data format for everything—configuration files, metadata, RPC, and object serialization.

SAMPLE XML DOCUMENT

The following is a sample section from a possible XML document. It is *not* a full XML document—we will discuss the structure of XML documents shortly and you will notice that we need a few extra lines to consider it to be a full document.

```
<employee>
 <ident>3348498</ident>
  <name>
   <lastname>Peterson</lastname>
   <firstname>Sam</firstname>
<title>Dr.</title>
</name>
<phonedetails>
  <extension>8221</extension>
  <companyprefix>700</companyprefix>
  <regionprefix>1</regionprefix>
  <intprefix>+353</intprefix>
</phonedetails>
<department>
   <title>Software Development</title>
   <depid>8</depid>
</department>
<location>
  <building>Aston Quay</building>
  <room>A142</room>
</location>
</employee>
```

While not necessarily the optimum structure for information such as above, it illustrates a major point of XML. The tags are defined by individuals, rather than some predefined standard structure. There are two different kinds of information in the above example:

- markup - such as <department> and <firstname>
- text/character data - such as "Peterson" and "+353"

XML documents mix markup and text together into a single file: the markup describes the structure of the document, while the text is the document's content.

XML IN PRACTICAL WORLD

Content Management

Almost all of the leading content management systems use XML in one way or another. A typical use would be to store a company's marketing content in one or more XML documents. These XML documents could then be transformed for output on the Web as Word documents, as PowerPoint slides, in plain text, or audio format. The content can also easily be shared with partners who can then output the content in their own formats. Storing the content in XML makes it much easier to manage content for two reasons.

Content changes, additions, and deletions are made in a central location and the changes will cascade out to all formats of presentation. There is no need to be concerned about keeping the Word documents in sync with the Website, because the content itself is managed in one place and then transformed for each output medium.

Formatting changes are made in a central location. To illustrate, suppose a company had many marketing Web pages, all of which were produced from XML content being transformed to HTML. The format for all of these pages could be controlled from a single XSLT and a sitewide formatting change could be made modifying that XSLT.

WEB Services

XML Web services are small applications or pieces of applications that are made accessible on the Internet using open standards based on XML. Web services generally consist of three components:

- **SOAP**—an XML-based protocol used to transfer Web services over the Internet.
- **WSDL (Web Services Description Language)**—an XML-based language for describing a Web service and how to call it.
- **Universal Discovery Description and Integration (UDDI)**—The yellow pages of Web services. UDDI directory entries are XML documents that describe the Web services a group offers. This is how people find available Web services.

It might be a bit easier to list what you can't use it for! In addition to making simple Webpages about your cats, you can use XML to create more complex applications such as online databases, custom-built pages, and more. By combining XML with Style Sheets and dynamic elements, you can even create a storefront for online shopping! The possibilities are nearly endless.

XML Web services are a relatively new development, designed to become the fundamental building block in distributed computing on the Internet. In other words, Web services allow business and personal users to interface online without the need for a third-party program.

Imagine having an application running on your computer. You enter information into that application, while a business partner in another part of the country does the same in an application they're working with. Instead of you having to use an Instant Messenger or some other third-party program so that you can communicate with your partner (even simple email is considered a third party in this example), the applications that the two of you are using share the information directly, providing both of you with the results. Now imagine that the applications that the two of you are using are simply built into a Webpage. That's the integration of Web services with XML.

When it comes down to it, all that Web services are is a new way for users to interface with applications. The Web services application uses an XML messaging system to make itself available over the Internet, and because the core of the communications is XML, it doesn't have to communicate with the systems that it would normally be compatible with. Windows can communicate with Unix, and Java can send messages to Perl. Web services use XML as a sort of "universal translator."

Web services are still a relatively new technology, with new Web services being developed by programmers everyday. Some of the Web services that have already been created, though, are nothing short of amazing. Examples of these Web services are

- News syndication services that present the most recent headlines to users
- Stock market analysis, with up-to-date tickers of the ups and downs of the market
- Weather reports giving current information for the users area
- Shipping systems, giving up-to-date tracking information
- Traffic reports for different localities
- Interactive sites offering products
- Up-to-date currency exchanges
- Applications that need to be used by large numbers of users, some of whom are behind firewalls

More Web services are being developed every day. It's still a growing technology, so advances that are made which might seem minor at first stand a chance of becoming ground-breaking work.

RDF/RSS Feeds

RDF (Resource Description Framework) is a framework for writing XML-based languages to describe information on the Web (e.g., Web pages). RSS (RDF Site Summary) is an implementation of this framework; it is a language that adheres to RDF and is used to describe Web content. Website publishers can use RSS to make content available as a "feed," so that Web users can access some of their content without actually visiting their site. Often, RSS is used to provide summaries with links to the company's Website for additional information.

Limitations

Not surprisingly, there are limits to what you can do with style sheets. Languages for style sheets are optimized for different purposes. You need to be aware of how a style sheet language works to use it most effectively.

CSS, for example, is designed to be compact and efficient. Documents have to be rendered quickly because people don't want to wait a long time for something to read. The style sheet processor is on the client end, and doesn't have a lot of computing power at its disposal. So the algorithm for applying styles needs to be very simple. Each rule that matches an element can only apply a set of styles. There is no other processing allowed, no looking backward or forward in the document for extra information. You have only one pass through the document to get it right.

Sometimes, information is stored in an order other than the way you want it to be rendered. If that is the case, then you need something more powerful than CSS. XSLT works on a tree representation of the document. It provides the luxury of looking ahead or behind to pull together all the data you need to generate output. This freedom comes at the price of increased computational requirements. Although some browsers support client-side XSLT processing (e.g., Internet Explorer), it's more likely you'll want transformations to be done on the server side, where you have more control and can cache the results.

Property sets are finite, so no matter how many features are built into a style sheet language, there will always be something lacking, some effect you want to achieve but can't. When that happens, you should be open to other options, such as post-processing with custom software.

Unquestionably, implementation among clients has been the biggest obstacle. The pace of standards development was much faster than actual implementation. Browsers either didn't support them or had buggy and incomplete implementations. This is quite frustrating for designers who want to support multiple platforms but are stymied by differing behaviors among user agents. Not only does behavior vary among vendors, but among versions and platforms, too. Internet Explorer, for example, behaves very differently on a Macintosh than it does on Windows for versions that came out at the same time.

The CSS Specification

The goal of a CSS specification was to create a simple yet expressive language that could combine style descriptions from different sources. Another style description language, DSSSL, was already being used to format SGML documents. Though very powerful, DSSSL was too big and complex to be practical for the Web. It is a full programming language, capable of more precision and logical expression than CSS, which is a simple language, and focused on the basic needs of small documents.

While other style sheet languages existed when CSS was proposed, none offered the ability to combine multiple sources into one style description set. CSS makes the Web truly accessible and flexible by allowing a reader to override the author's styles to adapt a document to the reader's particular requirements and applications.

The W3C put forward the first CSS recommendation (later called CSS1) in 1996. A short time later, a W3C working group formed around the subject of "Cascading Style Sheets and Formatting Properties" to add the missing functionality.

Syntax

Below is a sample CSS style sheet:

```
/* A simple example */
addressbook {
 display-type: block;
 font-family: sans-serif;
 font-size: 12pt;
 background-color: white;
 color: blue;
}
entry {
 display-type: block;
 border: thin solid black;
 padding: 5em;
```

```
 margin: 5em;
}
name, phone, email, address {
 display-type: block;
 margin-top: 2em;
 margin-bottom: 2em;
}
```

This style sheet has three rules. The first matches any addressbook element. The name to the left of the open bracket is a selector, which tells the processor what element this rule matches. The items inside the brackets are the property declaration, a list of properties to apply.

CSS also has a syntax for comments. Anything inside a comment is ignored by the processor. The start delimiter is /* and the end delimiter is */. A comment can span multiple lines and may be used to enclose CSS rules to remove them from consideration:

```
/* this part will be ignored
gurble { color: red }
burgle { color: blue; font-size: 12pt; }
*/
```

White space is generally ignored and provides a nice way to make style sheets more readable. The exception is when spaces act as delimiters in lists. Some properties take multiple arguments separated with spaces like border below:

```
sidebar {
 border: thin solid black
}
```

Matching Properties to Elements

Let's look more closely at this rule:

```
addressbook {
 display-type: block;
 font-family: sans-serif;
 font-size: 12pt;
 background-color: white;
 color: blue;
}
```

Qualitatively, this rule is like saying, "for every addressbook element, display it like a block, set the font family to any sans serif typeface with size

12 point, set the background color to white, and make the foreground (text) blue." Whenever the CSS processor encounters an addressbook element, it will set apply these properties to the current formatting context.

To understand how it works, think of painting-by-numbers. In front of you is a canvas with outlines of shapes and numbers inside the shapes. Each number corresponds to a paint color. You go to each shape, find the paint that corresponds to the number inside it, and fill it in with that color. In an hour or so, you'll have a lovely stylized pastoral scene with a barn and wildflowers. In this analogy, the rule is a paint can with a numbered label. The color is the property and the number is the selector.

The selector can be more complex than just one element name. It can be a comma-separated list of elements. It could be qualified with an attribute, as in this example, which matches a foo element with class="flubber":

```
foo.flubber { color: green; }
```

This dot-qualified selector matches an element with a class attribute, which is supported in HTML and SVG.

The CSS processor tries to find the best rule (or rules) for each element. In a stylesheet, several rules may apply. For example:

```
p.big {
 font-size: 18pt;
}
p {
 font-family: garamond, serif;
 font-size: 12pt;
}
* {
 color: black;
 font-size: 10pt;
}
```

The first rule matches a p with attribute class="big." The second matches any p regardless of attributes, and the last matches any element at all. Suppose the next element to process is a p with the attribute class="big." All three rules match this element.

How does CSS decide which properties to apply? The solution to this dilemma has two parts. The first is that all rules that match are used. It's as if the property declarations for all the applicable rules were merged into one set. That means all of these properties potentially apply to the element:

```
font-size: 18pt;
font-family: garamond, serif;
```

```
font-size: 12pt;
color: black;
font-size: 10pt;
```

The second part is that redundant property settings are resolved according to an algorithm. As you can see, there are three different font-size property settings. Only one of the settings can be used, so the CSS processor has to weed out the worst two using a property clash resolution system. As a rule of thumb, you can assume that the property from the rule with the most specific selector will win out. The first font-size property originates from the rule with selector p.big, which is more descriptive than p or *, so it's the winner.

In the final analysis, these three properties will apply:

```
font-size: 18pt;
font-family: garamond, serif;
color: black;
```

PROPERTY INHERITANCE

XML documents have a hierarchy of elements. CSS uses that hierarchy to pass along properties in a process called inheritance. Going back to our DocBook example, a sect1 contains a para. Consider the following style sheet:

```
sect1 {
 margin-left: 25pt;
 margin-right: 25pt;
 font-size: 18pt;
 color: navy;
}
para {
 margin-top: 10pt;
 margin-bottom: 10pt;
 font-size: 12pt;
}
```

The para's set of properties is a combination of those explicitly declared for it and those it inherits from the elements in its ancestry. Not all properties are inherited. Margins are never inheritable, so in the above example, only font size and color may be inherited. However, the font-size property is not inherited by para because it is redefined there. So the para's properties include those specifically defined for it, plus the one it inherited, color: navy.

COMBINING STYLESHEETS

A very powerful feature of CSS is its ability to combine multiple style sheets by importing one into another. This lets you borrow predefined style definitions so you don't have to continuously reinvent the wheel. Any style settings that you want to redefine or don't need can be overridden in the local style sheet.

One reason to combine style sheets is modularity. It may be more manageable to break up a large style sheet into several smaller files. For example, we could store all the styles pertaining to math equations in math.css and all the styles for regular text in text.css. The command @import links the current style sheet to another and causes the style settings in the target to be imported:

```
@import url(http://www.example.org/mystyles/math.css);
@import url(http://www.example.org/mystyles/text.css);
```

Some of the imported style rules may not suit your taste, or they may not fit the presentation. You can override those rules by redefining them in your own style sheet. Here, we've decided that the rule for h1 elements defined in text.css needs to be changed:

```
@import url(http://www.example.org/mystyles/text.css);
h1: { font-size: 3em; } /* redefinition */
```

QUESTIONS FOR DISCUSSION

1. What is XML?
2. What is a markup language?
3. Where should we use XML?
4. Why is XML such an important development?
5. Describe the differences between XML and HTML.
6. What is SGML?
7. Aren't XML, SGML, and HTML all the same thing?
8. Who is responsible for XML?
9. Give a few examples of types of applications that can benefit from using XML.
10. Why not just carry on extending HTML?

11. Can you walk us through the steps necessary to parse XML documents?
12. What is the difference between XML and C or C++ or Java?
13. Does XML replace HTML?
14. Is it necessary to know HTML or SGML before learning XML?
15. What does an XML document actually look like (inside)?
16. How can XML data be displayed using HTML?
17. How you define the tree structure in XML?
18. What are the disadvantage of XML?
19. What are the advantages of XML?
20. Why is XML referred to as having self-describing data?
21. How we define an empty XML element?
22. How we use xml.onload?
23. Where data is stored in XML?
24. How we can say that XML is extensible?
25. How do you create an XML document? Explain it with an example.

CHAPTER 2

XML SYNTAX

THE WELL-FORMED DOCUMENT

XML is a tool used to generate markup languages in a general, rather than a specific, markup language. Thus, rather than pre-defining a set of tags, XML defines a methodology for tag creation. Once defined, tags are mixed with plain text to form an "XML document."

It is worth mentioning that the word "document" can be a little misleading because although XML markup can certainly be contained in a file, (as the word document would imply), it can also be sent as a data stream, a database result set, or be dynamically-generated by one application and sent to another. More correctly, an XML document can be thought of as a "data object," but for simplicity, document will work just fine.

However, though you are free to be as innovative as you want with the tag sets you create, you must follow the constraints of the XML tag set generation standards exactly. When an XML document is presented to an XML-processor, in order for the XML processor to understand how to process it, the XML must follow the XML standard. Specifically, the document must be "well-formed." If the document is not well-formed the processor will stop, complaining about a "fatal error."

Well-formedness has an exact meaning in XML. Specifically, a well-formed document adheres to the syntax rules specified by the XML 1.0 specification in that it must satisfy both the physical and logical structures.

XML DOCUMENT STRUCTURE

XML documents are intended to store data, not necessarily to be viewed. They follow a layout very similar to HTML. In HTML, there are two main sections in a document defined by the HEAD and BODY tags. An XML document also contains two sections: the document prolog at the head of the document and the instance or the body.

XML documents have a logical structure and a physical structure. Logically, documents are composed of declarations, elements, comments, character references, and processing instructions, all of which are indicated in the document by explicit markup.

All XML documents may be understood in terms of the data they contain and the markup that describes that data. Data is typically "character data" (letters, numbers, punctuation—anything within the boundaries of valid Unicode), but can also be binary data. Markup includes tags, comments, processing instructions, DTDs, and references.

A simple example of character data and markup is as follows:

```
<NAME>Selena Sol</NAME>
```

In this case, the <NAME> and </NAME> tags comprise the markup and "Selena Sol" comprises the character data. As you can imagine, there are few rules that manage your data (content) other than what type of data is allowed (binary or ASCII, for example). On the other hand, there are many rules that define how you must code your markup.

To begin an XML document, it is a good idea to include the XML declaration as the very first line of the document. I say "good idea" because, though the XML declaration is optional, it is suggested by the W3C specification.

Essentially, the XML declaration is a processing instruction that notifies the processing agent that the following document has been marked up as an XML document. It will look something like the following:

```
<?xml version = "1.0"?>
```

We'll talk more about the details of processing instructions later, but we can at least explain how the XML declaration works.

All processing instructions, including the XML declaration, begin with <? and end with ?>. Following the initial <?, you will find the name of the processing instruction, which in this case is "xml."

The XML processing instruction, requires that you specify a "version" attribute and allows you to specify optional "standalone" and "encoding" attributes.

In its full regalia, the XML declaration might look like the following:

```
<?xml version = "1.0" standalone = "yes" encoding = "UTF-8"?>
```

As we said before, if you do decide to use the optional XML declaration, you must define the "version" attribute. As of this writing, the current version of XML is 1.0. Note that if you include the optional attributes, "version" must be specified first.

PROLOG SECTION

The document prolog must be the first thing in an XML document—it is the introduction to the document. Here is a sample prolog of an XML document:

```
<?xml version="1.0"?>
<!DOCTYPE book SYSTEM "DTD/book.dtd">
```

The specification states that both parts of the prolog are optional. The first part is called the XML declaration and the second part the Document Type Definition. A Document Type Definition (DTD) sets all the rules for the document regarding elements, attributes, and other components. This DTD may be either an external DTD or Internal DTD.

- Internal DTD—An internal DTD document is contained completely within the XML document.
- External DTD—An external DTD document is a separate document, referenced from within the XML document.

The example prolog above refers to an external DTD that can be found in the local system path "DTD/book.dtd." Any time you use a relative or absolute file path or a URL, you must use the SYSTEM keyword. The other option is using the PUBLIC keyword, and follow it with a public identifier. This means that the W3C or another consortium has defined a standard DTD that is associated with that public identifier. For example,

```
<!DOCTYPE html PUBLIC "-//W3C//DTD XHTML 1.0 Transitional//EN"
"http://www.w3.org/TR/xhtml1/DTD/xhtml1-transitional.dtd">
```

THE STANDALONE ATTRIBUTE

The *standalone* attribute specifies whether the document has any markup declarations that are defined in a separate document. Thus, if standalone is set to "yes," there will be no markup declarations in external DTD's. Setting it to "no" leaves the issue open. The document may or may not access external DTD's.

THE ENCODING ATTRIBUTE

All XML parsers must support 8-bit and 16-bit Unicode encoding corresponding to ASCII. However, XML parsers may support a larger set.

Once you have written your XML declaration, you are ready to begin coding your XML document. To do so, you should understand the concept of elements.

Elements are the basic unit of XML content. Syntactically, an element consists of a start tag, an end tag, and everything in between. For example, consider the following element:

```
<NAME>Frank Lee</NAME>
```

XML defines the text between the start and end tags to be "character data" and the text within the tags to be "markup."

INSTANCE SECTION

The *instance* contains the remaining parts of the XML document, including the actual contents of the document, such as characters, paragraphs, pages, and graphics.

ELEMENTS

Elements are the most important part of an XML document. An element consists of content enclosed in an opening tag and a closing tag. An element can contain several different types of content:

- **Element Content**—Contains only other elements. Example: the <name> element in <name><firstname>Tom</firstname><lastname>Smith</lastname></name>
- **Mixed Content**—Contains both text and other elements. Example: the <para> element in <para>This point is a <emphasis>very important</emphasis> point.</para>

- **Simple Content**—Contains only text. Example: <lastname>Molloy</lastname>
- **Empty Content**—Does not contain information. Example: <image src="test.jpg"></image>

XML element names are case-sensitive, meaning that opening and closing tags must be written in the same case. XML documents require both a begin and an end tag. Although you can frequently omit the closing tags with some elements in HTML (such as <BR>), all XML elements must include an end tag. Otherwise, the XML would not be properly structured and would result in an error. For example, the following is incorrect:

```
<title>Introduction to XML
```

The correct format would be

```
<title>Introduction to XML</title>
```

When dealing with elements such as empty elements it is possible to specify them using the following shorthand:

```
<image src="test.jpg"></image>
 <image src="test.jpg" />
```

XML documents must be well-formed. First, this means that you must follow the rules regarding case-sensitivity and always include closing tags. Additionally, you cannot mix the order of the nested tags: the first opened element must always be the last closed element. If any of the rules for XML syntax are not followed in an XML document, the document is not well-formed. The following is an example of an XML fragment that is not well-formed:

```
<tag1>
<tag2>
</tag1>
</tag2>
```

A well-formed document is not necessarily valid. Valid XML must additionally follow the constraints set upon an XML document by its Document Type Definition or schema.

In XML, you can only have a single root element. That root element has sub-elements which may also further have sub-elements. The structure of an XML document is a tree of elements. So if you think of an element as a container, an XML document becomes a container of containers. Containers have a name associated with them (the element name) and possible additional characteristics (called *attributes*). The containers hold the content (or data) of the document. The start and end tags define the boundaries of the container.

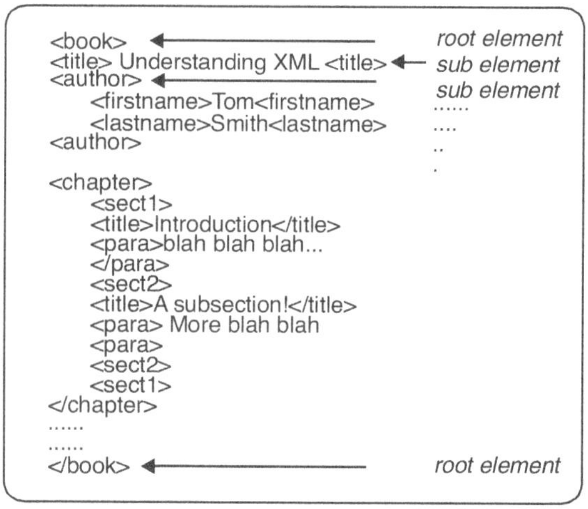

```
<book>  ←――――――――――――――――――――――――――――――   root element
<title> Understanding XML <title> ←――   sub element
<author> ←―――――――――――――――――――――――――――   sub element
    <firstname>Tom<firstname>           ......
    <lastname>Smith<lastname>           ....
<author>                                ..
                                        .
<chapter>
    <sect1>
    <title>Introduction</title>
    <para>blah blah blah...
    </para>
    <sect2>
    <title>A subsection!</title>
    <para> More blah blah
    <para>
    <sect2>
    <sect1>
</chapter>
......
......
</book> ←――――――――――――――――――――――――――――   root element
```

FIGURE 2.1 XML element structure

CHARACTER DATA

Character data may be any legal (Unicode) character with the exception of "<." The "<" character is reserved for the start of a tag. XML also provides useful entity references that you can use so as not to create any doubt whether you are specifying character data versus markup. Table 2.1 shows the entity references in XML.

Table 2.1 Character Data and its Entity References

Character	Entity Reference
>	>
<	<
&	&
"	"
'	'

Note that all values are not typed. That is, they are considered strings. Thus, if you were to process the tag

```
<ROOM_SIZE RADIUS = "10" DEPTH = "13">
```

you would have to convert “10” and “13” to their numeric values outside of the XML environment.

CDATA

It is a pretty good rule of thumb to consider anything outside of tags to be character data and anything inside of tags to be considered markup. But alas, in one case this is not true. In the special case of CDATA blocks, all tags and entity references are ignored by an XML processor that treats them just like character data.

CDATA blocks serve as a convenience measure when you want to include large blocks of special characters a character data, but you do not want to have to use entity references all the time. What if you wanted to write about an XML document in XML? Consider the following example in which you would have an example tag in your XML Guide written in XML:

```
<EXAMPLE>
&lt;DOCUMENT&gt;
&lt;NAME&gt;Coleen Merriman&lt;/NAME&gt;
&lt;EMAIL&gt;cm@mydomain.com&lt;/EMAIL&gt;
&lt;/DOCUMENT&gt;
</EXAMPLE>
```

As you can see, you would be forced to use entity references for all the tags.

To avoid the inconvenience of translating all special characters, you can use a CDATA block to specify that all character data should be considered character data whether or not it “looks” like a tag or entity reference.

Consider the following example:

```
<EXAMPLE>
<![CDATA[
<DOCUMENT>
<NAME>Coleen Merriman</NAME>
<EMAIL>cm@mydomain.com</EMAIL>
</DOCUMENT>
]]>
</EXAMPLE>
```

COMMENT

Not only will you sometimes want to include tags in your XML document that you want the XML processor will ignore (display as character data), but sometimes you will want to put character data in your document that you want the XML processor to ignore (not display at all). This type of text is called *comment* text.

You will be familiar with comments from HTML. In HTML, you specified comments using the <!-- and --> syntax. In XML, comments are done in just the same way. So the following would be a valid XML comment:

```
<!-- Begin the Names -->
<NAME>Jim Nelson</NAME>
<NAME>Jim Sanger</NAME>
<NAME>Les Moore</NAME>
<!-- End the names -->
```

When using comments in your XML documents, however, you should keep in mind a couple of rules.

First, you should never have "-" or "--" within the text of your comment as it might be confusing to the XML processor.

Second, never place a comment within a tag. Thus, the following code would be poorly-formed XML:

```
<NAME <!--The name --> >Peter Williams</NAME>
```

Likewise, never place a comment inside of an entity declaration and never place a comment before the XML declaration that must always be the first line in any XML document.

PROCESSING INSTRUCTION

We have already seen a processing instruction. The XML declaration is a processing instruction. And if you recall, when we introduced the XML declaration, we promised to return to the concept of processing instructions to explain them as a category.

A processing instruction is a bit of information meant for the application using the XML document. That is, they are not really of interest to the XML parser. Instead, the instructions are passed intact straight to the application using the parser.

The application can then pass this on to another application or interpret it itself.

All processing instructions follow the generic format of:

```
<?NAME_OF_APPLICATION_INSTRUCTION_IS_FOR INSTRUCTIONS?>
```

As you might imagine, you cannot use any combination of "xml" as the NAME_OF_APPLICATION_INSTRUCTION_IS_FOR since "xml" is reserved. However, you might have something like

```
<?JAVA_OBJECT JAR_FILE = "/java/myjar.jar"?>
```

ENTITIES

To a large, degree much of the discussion of entities is more relevant in the next section, writing "valid" documents, rather than in this section, writing "well-formed" documents.

Entities are essentially aliases that allow you to refer to large sections of text without having to type them out every time you want to use them.

Suppose you have your letterhead saved as an entity in a shared file. Then, every time you write a letter in XML, you might say something like

```
<LETTER>
 &letterhead;
 <TO>Bobby Rosy</TO>
 <BODY>
 blah blah blah
 </BODY>
 <FROM>Shashi Banzal</FROM>
</LETTER>
```

Notice that the letterhead might expand out to:

```
S & B Company
 37,I G Nagar
 Indore,MP
```

However, instead of typing that out in every letter, you just use & letterhead;

There are two types of entities, general and parameter entities and each entity has two parts, the declaration and the entity reference.

GENERAL ENTITIES

General entities look something like

```
<!ENTITY NAME "text that you want to be represented by the entity">
```

which might look like the following in the real world:

```
<!ENTITY full_name "Shashi Banzal">
```

PARAMETER ENTITIES

Parameter entities, that can also be either internal or external, are only used within the DTD that we will discus in the next section so we will defer a serious discussion until then. However, we will mention that a well-formed parameter entity will look the same as a general entity except that it will include the "%" specifier. Consider the following example:

```
<!ENTITY % NAME "text that you want to be represented by the entity">
```

If you want to declare entities, you MUST do so within the document DOCTYPE declaration that always follows the prolog (DTD and xml Declaration).

```
<?xml version="1.0"?>
 <!DOCTYPE myDocument [
 ...here is where you declare your entities....
 ]>
 <myDocument>
 ...here is the body of your document....
 </myDocument>
```

Thus, you might have something like the following (Consider how much easier changing office addresses is when you use entities!):

```
<?xml version="1.0"?>
<!DOCTYPE CLIENTS [
<!ENTITY ninthFloorAddress "2345 Broadway St Floor 9">
<!ENTITY eighthFloorAddress "2345 Broadway St Floor 8">
<!ENTITY seventhFloorAddress "2345 Broadway St Floor 7">
]>
<CLIENTS>
<CLIENT>
```

```
<NAME>Fred Jenkins</NAME>
<ADDRESS>&ninthFloorAddress;</ADDRESS>
<PHONE>x345</PHONE>
</CLIENT>
<CLIENT>
<NAME>Ravi Gupta</NAME>
<ADDRESS>&ninthFloorAddress;</ADDRESS>
<PHONE>x111</PHONE>
</CLIENT>
<CLIENT>
<NAME>Natalia Kinski</NAME>
<ADDRESS>&ninthFloorAddress;</ADDRESS>
<PHONE>x346</PHONE>
</CLIENT>
<CLIENT>
<NAME>Mary Smith</NAME>
<ADDRESS>&seventhFloorAddress;</ADDRESS>
<PHONE>x289</PHONE>
</CLIENT>
<CLIENT>
<NAME>Kristin Mancuso</NAME>
<ADDRESS>&eighthFloorAddress;</ADDRESS>
<PHONE>x945</PHONE>
</CLIENT>
</CLIENTS>
```

ENTITY REFERENCES

Entity references refer to the key that unlocks an entity which has been declared in an entity declaration. Entity references follow the simple syntax of

```
&ENTITY_NAME;
such as
&letterhead;
```

Parameter entity references work much like general entity references. In this case, we use a "%" sign instead of a "&."

```
%PARAMETER_ENTITY_NAME;
```

Now, you have already seen that entity references can take the place of regular character data and you have seen how useful that is. You could also use entity references within tag attributes. For example, consider the following:

```
<INVOICE CLIENT = "&IBM;" PRODUCT = "&PRODUCT_ID_8762;" QUANTITY = "5">
```

ATTRIBUTES

In additional to content, elements may have attributes. XML attributes are identical to HTML attributes, allowing you to attach characteristics to an element. For example, in HTML:

```
<IMG SRC="images/test.jpg">
and XML
 <image src="images/test.jpg" />
```

Attributes have a name and a value and are placed within the start tag. In the document type definition (DTD), you define the legal attributes for an element and what values are legal for that attribute.

An element can have multiple attributes. While you can get away with omitting quotes for attributes in HTML, in XML the value must be surrounded by single or double quotes. When you use one type of quotes, the other type is legal within the quotes - for example

```
<topic name=" Brian O'Sullivan">
```

or

```
<topic name=' The Use of "s in Popular Literature '>
```

In addition to learning how to use attributes, there is an issue of when to use attributes. Because XML allows such a variety of data formatting, it is rare that an attribute cannot be represented by an element, or that an element could not be easily converted to an attribute.

Although there's no specification or widely accepted standard for determining when to use an attribute and when to use an element, there is a good rule of thumb: use elements for multiple-valued data and attributes for single-valued data. If data can have multiple values, or is very lengthy, the data most likely belongs in an element. To understand this, let us consider two formats for storing phone information:

```
<phone number="+35318008583" />
```

and

```
<phone>
        <intcode>+353</intcode>
        <localcode>1</localcode>
        <prefix>800</prefix>
        <extension>8583</extension>
</phone>
```

Using attributes in this case is obviously far simpler to write and less verbose. However, it would make searching our data for all phone numbers with an 800 prefix quite difficult. Equally, the multiple element format would make it easy to generate an internal phone book only showing the local extensions.

Both formats are correct data formats. Essentially, which you use comes down to your own preference.

ENTITIES' REFERENCES AND CONSTANTS

Let us consider a XML file where we wish to include the data <HTML>.

```
<chapter>
    <sect1>
    <title>Using HTML</title>
     <para>
    HTML is defined using tags, such as <HTML> and <BODY> .....
            </para>
          </sect1>
</chapter>
```

The problem here is that XML parsers will attempt to handle this data as an XML tag, and then generate an error because there is no closing tag. This is a common problem, as any use of angle brackets results in this behavior. Entity references provide a way to overcome this problem. An entity reference is a special data type in XML used to refer to another piece of data. The entity reference consists of a unique name, preceded by an ampersand and followed by a semicolon: &[entityname];. When an XML parser sees an entity reference, the specified substitution value is inserted and no processing of that value occurs. XML defines five special entities to address this problem: < for <, > for >, & for &, " for "and ' for". Using these entities, it is possible to define the above example:

```
<chapter>
<sect1>
<title>Using HTML</title>
<para>
HTML uses tags, such as &lt;HTML&gt; and &lt;BODY&gt.
  </para>
 </sect1>
</chapter>
```

Once this document is parsed, the data is interpreted as "<HTML> and <BODY>" and the document is still considered well-formed.

Using entities is not restricted to simply handling difficult escape characters within data. It is possible to use entities to effectively define variables or constants within your XML data. Consider the case where we repeatedly use the data "Royal Society for the Prevention of Cruelty to Animals (RSPCA)" in our XML document. Rather than repeatedly type this every time, in our XML document (or root XML document, if we use multiple subdocs) we define the following:

```
<!ENTITY rspca "Royal Soc. for the Prevention of Cruelty to Animals">
```

Then, when we wish to use this text within our XML document at any subsequent stage, we simply use the entity: &rspca; to represent our constant. Likewise, the variable representing the author's current email could be defined as an entity and referenced throughout the rest of the document. If the author's email address changes at a later date, then a simple change to the entity would modify the data throughout the rest of the document.

UNPARSED DATA

In XML, there are three kinds of data that are ignored by the parser: comments, processing instructions (PIs), and character data (CDATA). When the parser encounters one of these, normal operation is suspended while the parser looks for the end marker.

Comments in XML are exactly like comments in HTML. Typically, they are ignored by most XML parsers.

```
<!-- this is a comment -->
```

CHARACTER DATA (CDATA)

Sections allow you to put information that might be recognised as markup anywhere characters may occur. CDATA sections begin with <![CDATA[and end with]]>. The parser ignore everything within the CDATA section. CDATA is also used when a significant amount of data should be passed to the calling application without any XML parsing or when spacing must be preserved. Throughout these notes, CDATA is almost always used when it comes to displaying listings of programs or samples of XML and HTML where brackets and ampersands are frequently used. It would not be practical in these situations to also use entity references repeatedly (although it could be done) so we just use CDATA to display the block of unparsed code. Additionally, when it comes to program listings, it allows us to preserve the spacing and layout of our sample code. So for example,

```
   <para>
<![CDATA[
   <HTML>
   <HEAD>
  <TITLE>Test HTML Page</TITLE>
 </HEAD>
  <BODY>
         <H1>Hello World!</H1>
 </BODY>
 </HTML>
    ]]>
 </para>
```

PROCESSING INSTRUCTIONS (PIS)

Processing instructions (PIs) allow XML documents to contain instructions for applications. Like comments, they are not part of the document's character data, so they are of little interest to the XML processor. However, they must be passed through to the proper application. The PI begins with <? and ends with ?>. The only PI we have encountered so far has been in the prolog:

```
<?xml version="1.0"?>
```

QUESTIONS FOR DISSCUSSION

1. Give examples of XML editors.
2. Define the syntax rules in XML in brief.
3. Define XML elements and attributes with examples.
4. What are the basic problems with using Attributes?
5. What are the basic problems with using Attributes?
6. In XML, elements have to be nested properly. Explain.
7. How does XML handle white-space in documents?
8. Which parts of an XML document are case-sensitive?
9. How would you build a search engine for large volumes of XML data?
10. What is a well-formed XML document?
11. What is a valid XML document?
12. What is the structure of an XML document?
13. What is a processing instruction in XML?
14. How is the XML structure defined?
15. What do you know about the XML parser?
16. How does XML support UNICODE characters?
17. Write some basic rules of XML.
18. How is XML element defined?
19. How do you define attributes in XML?
20. How do you define an XML entity?
21. How can you write comments in XML?
22. How you define DTD in XML?
23. What is the XML prolog?
24. What you understand with document validity?
25. What is the CDATA section in HTML?

26. “<?xml version=”1.0 “encoding=”UTF-8“standalone=”no“?>” in brief.
27. Explain \“<!doctype document system \”R4R.dtd\“>\”.
28. Explain <!-- Here is a comment -->.
29. Explain <?xml-stylesheet type=“text/css” href=“myStyles.css”?>.
30. Explain Child Elements and Content in any XML Program.
31. In XML, elements have to be nested properly. Explain.
32. What are some terms used when naming an element in XML?
33. What essential components of security do the XML Signatures provide?
34. What is a validating parser?
35. What is URN?

CHAPTER 3

DOCUMENT TYPE DEFINITION (DTD)

PHYSICAL STRUCTURE IN XML

The physical structure of an XML document is composed of all the content used in that document. The storage units, called *entities*, can be part of the document or external to the document. Each entity is identified by a unique name and contains its own content, from a single character inside the document to a large file that exists outside the document.

In terms of the logical structure of an XML document, entities declared in the prolog and referenced in the document element, an entity directs the processor to retrieve the content of the entity, as declared in the entity declaration, and use it in the document.

Entities in an XML document can be handled in the following ways. Entities may either be parsed or unparsed, may be predefined entities, or the entities may be an external or an internal entity.

PARSED AND UNPARSED ENTITIES

An entity can be either parsed or unparsed. A *parsed entity*, also called a *text entity*, contains text data that becomes part of the XML document once that data is processed. An *unparsed entity* is a container whose contents may or may not be text. If the content is text, the content is not parsable XML.

A parsed entity is intended to be read by the XML processor, which will extract the content. After the content is extracted, a parsed entity's content appears as part of the document at the location of the entity reference. For example, in our Book document, a publisher information entity may be declared as shown in the following code snippet. Whenever this entity declaration is referenced in the document, it will be replaced by its content. So, if we need to change it in only one place, the declaration, the change will be reflected wherever the entity is used in the document.

```
<!ENTITY Publisher1 "McGrawHill Publishing Company.">
```

An unparsed entity is sometimes referred to as a *binary entity* because its content is often a binary file (such as an image) that is not directly interpreted by the XML processor. An unparsed entity requires a notation. A notation identifies the format, or type, of resource to which the entity is declared. The following code snippet shows the declaration of an unparsed entity.

```
<!NOTATION GIF SYSTEM "/Utils/Gifview.exe">
```

PREDEFINED ENTITIES

In XML, certain characters are used specifically for marking up the document. For example, in the following element, the angle brackets (< >) and forward slash (/) are interpreted as markup and not as actual character data.

The characters that are reserved for markup cannot be used as content. If we intend to use these characters as displayed data, they must be escaped. To *escape* a character, we must use an entity to insert the character into a document. So, if the text <bookname> is entered in the document, we use the following sequence.

```
&lt;BOOKNAME&gt;
```

INTERNAL AND EXTERNAL ENTITY

An *internal entity* is one in which no separate physical storage exists. The content of the entity is provided in its declaration as shown in the following piece of code.

```
<! ENTITY Publisher1 "Fireworks publishing">
```

An *external entity* refers to a storage unit in its declaration by using a system or public identifier. The system identifier provides a pointer to a location at which the entity content can be found, such as the URI (Uniform Resource Identifier). The following code snippet gives an example of how the file book1.gif is used by the XML processor to read and retrieve the content of this entity.

```
<ENTITY FirstImg SYSTEM "www.books.com/images/book1.gif" NDATA GIF>
```

XML GENERAL SYNTAX

In HTML code, an element usually contains an opening tag and an optional closing tag. XML, unlike HTML, requires a closing tag for every element.

HTML is based on a predefined structure that allows processors to assume where certain tags should be located in a document. Since a paragraph in HTML cannot be nested inside another paragraph, the processor can read an opening paragraph tag and assume that it also marks the end of the preceding paragraph. Such minimization techniques are not allowed in XML.

Although XML requires the usage of a closing tag, it supports a shortcut for empty elements called the *empty-element tag*. The empty-element tag effectively combines the opening and closing tags for an element containing no content. It uses a special format: `<TAGNAME/>`. In this format, the forward slash follows the tag name, which is not supported in HTML.

ATTRIBUTES

Attributes provide a method of associating values to an element without making the attributes a part of the content of that element.

```
<PRICE CURRENCY="USD">315.00</PRICE>
```

The code snippet provides an example. Here, we can see that a currency attribute can be added to the price element of the book document instead of adding a separate currency element to the document.

The attribute in XML is used in the same way as an HTML attribute, but we can define our own attribute names. One important point is that the value of the attribute must be within single or double quotes.

VALID DOCUMENTS

The DTD (Document Type Definition) specified in the prolog outlines all the rules for the document. A valid document must obey the rules specified in the DTD. A valid document also obeys all the validity constraints identified in the XML specification.

The processor must understand the validity constraints of the XML specification and check the document for possible violations. If the processor finds any errors, it must report them to the XML application. The processor must also read the DTD, validate the documents against it, and again report any violations to the XML application.

As all the above-mentioned processing and checking take time, and because validation might not always be necessary, XML supports the concept of a well-formed document.

WELL-FORMED DOCUMENTS

A document is described as well-formed if it meets the well-formedness constraints of the XML recommendation. Principally, this means it must have a single root element and all the other elements must be correctly nested. If a document is well formed, it can be correctly parsed by a computer program.

Well-formedness can reduce the amount of work a client has to do. For example, if the server has already validated a document, it is not necessary to burden the client with validating the document again. As a result, well-formedness can save download time because the client does not need to download the DTD, and it can save processing time as the DTD need not be processed again.

In many cases, authoring a DTD or validating a document is unnecessary. For example, someone at a small company might want to use XML to provide structure to a departmental Website, but all the features that validation provides are not needed for the site.

According to the XML specifications, a well-formed document must meet the following criteria:

- A well-formed document must match the definition of a document. The definition of a document is that it should contain one or more elements. It contains exactly one root element, also called the *document element*, and all other elements must be properly nested.

- All of the parsed entities referenced in the document are well-formed. Since parsed entities become part of the document once the XML processor parses them, they must satisfy the well-formedness constraints for the document to be considered well-formed.
- A well-formed document must observe the constraints for a well-formed document as defined by the XML specifications.

The data objects, also referred to as documents that conform to the syntax specification in XML, are called well-formed XML documents. These documents describe the structure, and are also known as standalone XML documents.

These documents are not dependent on external declarations, and the attribute values receive no special processing or default values.

A well-formed XML document contains one or more elements in it that are delimited by the start and end tags. There is one element, the document element, that contains all the other elements within the document. All the elements are in the form of a hierarchical tree, thus, the relationship between the elements is in the form of a parent-child relationship. So, to summarize, data objects are well-formed documents if

- The syntax conforms to the XML specifications,
- elements are in the form of a simple hierarchical tree with a single node
- there are no external references to entities

An XML parser that encounters a construct in XML and finds the construct not to be well-formed will report an error to the application as a "fatal" error. This approach to error handling is the result of the compact design of XML and the intention that XML is to be used for much more than document display.

WELL-FORMED XML DOCUMENTS

A well-formed XML document has the correct XML syntax. The syntax rules were described in the previous chapters:

- XML documents must have a root element
- XML elements must have a closing tag
- XML tags are case sensitive
- XML elements must be properly nested
- XML attribute values must be quoted

```
<?xml version="1.0" encoding="ISO-8859-1"?>
<note>
<to>Tonu</to>
<from>Jani</from>
<heading>Reminder</heading>
<body>Don't forget me this weekend!</body>
</note>
```

XML DOCUMENTS

An XML document is made up of the following parts:

- An optional prolog
- A document element, usually containing nested elements
- Optional comments or processing instructions

The Prolog

The prolog of an XML document can contain the following items:

- An XML declaration
- Processing instructions
- Comments
- A Document Type Declaration

THE XML DECLARATION

The XML declaration, if it appears at all, must appear on the very first line of the document with no preceding white space. It looks like this:

```
<?xml version="1.0" encoding="UTF-8"standalone="yes"?>
```

This declares that the document is an XML document. The version attribute is required, but the encoding and standalone attributes are not. If the XML document uses any markup declarations that set defaults for attributes or declare entities then standalone must be set to "no."

PROCESSING INSTRUCTIONS

Processing instructions are used to pass parameters to an application. These parameters tell the application how to process the XML document. For example, the following processing instruction tells the application that it should transform the XML document using the XSL stylesheet beatles.xsl.

```
<?xml-stylesheet href="beatles.xsl"type="text/xsl"?>
```

As shown above, processing instructions begin with `<?` and end with `?>`.

COMMENTS

Comments can appear throughout an XML document. Like in HTML, they begin with <!— and end with—>.

```
<!—This is a comment—>
```

DOCUMENT TYPE DECLARATION

The Document Type Declaration consists of markup code that indicates the grammar rules, or Document Type Definition (DTD), for the particular class of the document. The document type declaration can also point to an external file that contains all or part of the DTD.

```
<?xml version="1.0"?>
<!DOCTYPE Book SYSTEM "Book.dtd">
```

The code snippet here conveys to the XML processor that the document is of the class Catalog and conforms to the rules formed in the DTD file named "book.dtd."

The second structural element in an XML document is the document element, where the actual content lies. Each XML document must have only one root element, and all other elements must be completely enclosed in that element. The document element contains all the data in an XML document. This element can comprise any number of nested sub-elements and external entities.

```
<?xml version="1.0"?>
<!DOCTYPE Book SYSTEM "Book.dtd">
<Book>
```

```
<Bookname>Paradise Lost</Bookname>
<Authorname>John Milton</Authorname>
</Book>
```

The code snippet given here shows the book element in Book.dtd. Here, we can see that the element tags can include one or more optional or mandatory attributes that give further information about the elements they delimit. Attributes can only be specified in the start tag.

```
<element.type.name attribute.name="attribute value">
```

The code snippet here gives the syntax for specifying an attribute. In direct contrast to SGML and HTML, in which multiple declarations are considered as errors, XML deals with multiple declarations of attributes in a unique manner. If an element appears once with one set of attributes and then appears again with a different set of attributes, the two sets of attributes are merged. The first declaration for a particular element is the only one that counts, and any other declarations are ignored.

XML APPLICATION CLASSIFICATION

The following two broad categories of XML applications are expected:

XML Applications without a DTD. This can be considered as the simplest case. The author creates his/her own elements to be used with the content, and may or may not decide to provide a corresponding DTD. Without appropriate documentation, these elements are "meaningless" and without a formal DTD, the use of the elements is limited to that XML document instance.

XML Applications with a DTD. The DTD could be internal, where it is embedded in the XML document. This is usually recommeded for small DTDs. The DTD can also be external as a "standalone" or available "publicly." In the latter case, it can be referenced via an FPI (Formal Public Identifier).

PARSERS

The W3C Recommendation has also described the behavior of parsers or the XML processor, or the lower tier of the XML's architecture. This has been defined with the objective of easing the burden on the applications that handle the XML data.

There are two types of parsers: non-validating and validating.

The non-validating type of parser merely ensures that a data object is in well-formed XML.

In the validating type, the parser uses a DTD to ensure the validity of a well-formed data object's form and content. Some parsers support both types along with configuration switches that determine the validation of the document.

The behavior of XML parsers has been defined with the purpose of easing the burden on the application's handling of the XML data. For example, the sequences of characters that are used as delimiters of the end of texts are operating system specific.

Nevertheless, the XML application need not be concerned about this, as the parser will normalize all the delimiters to a single line-feed character. White spaces are another area where the parsers are constrained, as unlike HTML or SGML all white spaces must be passed from the document to the application. The general entity strings are expanded by the parser as defined by the internal or external DTD subset.

XML PROCESSING-ATTRIBUTE VALUES

XML parsers are required to normalize the attribute values (AttValue) before passing them to the XML application. The table shows how the parsers handle the characters and references.

Table 3.1 Handling of Characters and References by Parsers

Reference	Handling
Character Reference	Append referenced character to AttValue.
Entity Reference	Expand the replacement text of that entity, appending it to the AttValue.
White Space Characters	Replace any carriage return/line-feed pairs that are a part of an external parsed entity or the literal entity value of an internal parsed entity, or any single white space character with the space character and then append the space of the AttValue.
Other Characters	Append the character to the AttValue.

XML PROCESSING

The AttValue is then processed by removing any leading or trailing spaces and converting the multiple spaces into single spaces. The exception to this rule arises if the attribute value is declared as CDATA in the DTD and a validating parser is used.

There are two approaches in implementing an XML parser. They are the event-driven parsers and the tree-based parsers.

EVENT-DRIVEN PARSERS

In this approach of XML processing, namely the event-driven parser—the model which is familiar to the programmers of modern GUIs and operating systems—the parser executes a call-back to the application for each class of XML data that includes an element with attributes, character data, processing instructions, notation, or comments.

Data handling in XML depends on the application as data is provided through the call-backs. The XML parser does not maintain the element tree structure or any of the data after it has been parsed.

TREE-BASED PARSERS

The most widely used structure in software engineering is the simple hierarchical tree.

In this approach, the well-formed documents are defined as a tree, and common and mature algorithms are used to traverse the nodes of an XML document.

This approach conforms to the Document Object Model as specified by W3C. The DOM is a platform and language neutral interface that allows manipulation of tree-structured documents.

MSXML, a Java-based XML, was developed by Microsoft. XML was later included as a part of the Internet Explorer 5 with a different parser.

XML PARSER

All modern browsers have a built-in XML parser. An XML parser converts an XML document into an XML DOM object—which can then be manipulated with JavaScript.

PARSE AN XML DOCUMENT

The following code fragment parses an XML document into an XML DOM object:

```
if (window.XMLHttpRequest)
{// code for IE7+, Firefox, Chrome, Opera, Safari
xmlhttp=new XMLHttpRequest();
}
else
{// code for IE6, IE5
xmlhttp=new ActiveXObject("Microsoft.XMLHTTP");
}
xmlhttp.open("GET","books.xml",false);
xmlhttp.send();
xmlDoc=xmlhttp.responseXML;
```

PARSE AN XML STRING

The following code fragment parses an XML string into an XML DOM object:

```
txt="<bookstore><book>";
txt=txt+"<title>Everyday Italian</title>";
txt=txt+"<author>Giada De Laurentiis</author>";
txt=txt+"<year>2005</year>";
txt=txt+"</book></bookstore>";
if (window.DOMParser)
{
parser=new DOMParser();
xmlDoc=parser.parseFromString(txt,"text/xml");
}
else // Internet Explorer
{
xmlDoc=new ActiveXObject("Microsoft.XMLDOM");
xmlDoc.async="false";
xmlDoc.loadXML(txt);
}
```

Internet Explorer uses the loadXML() method to parse an XML string, while other browsers use the DOMParser object.

DOCUMENT TYPE DEFINITIONS (DTDS)

DTD stands for Document Type Definition. A DTD allows you to create rules for the elements within your XML documents. Although XML itself has rules, the rules defined in a DTD are specific to your own needs.

So, for an XML document to be well-formed, it needs to use correct XML syntax, and it needs to conform to its DTD or schema.

The DTD is declared at the top of your XML document. The actual contents of the DTD can be included within your XML document or included in another document and linked to (or both).

A DTD uses a formal grammar to specify the structure and permissible values of XML documents. The well-formed XML just conforms to the basic syntactic rules in XML. With DTD, we are going to create valid XML: XML that conforms to the syntactic rules of XML as well as the vocabulary we create.

There are several benefits when a DTD is used. A DTD created in a formal and precise manner identifies the vocabulary. The rules of the vocabulary are contained in the DTD.

The parsers could also use the DTD to validate an instance of the document. A simple declaration in the document instance allows the parser to retrieve the DTD and compare the document instance to the rules in the DTD.

The DTD must have a formal structure. A question arises regarding the need for a formal structure. The answer is a clear, precise set of syntactic rules that capture everything permitted in the vocabulary. There are encoded rules in the vocabulary in the source code. The code enforces a certain structure: when the structure changes, the code must also change. This helps the designer to convey the information he wants to and the user understands what the programmer wants him to know.

The XML document is a snapshot of the data structures in a program. The XML documents communicate with one another. The DTD, on the other hand, captures the information in the vocabulary by definition. Everything learned that went into the design of the vocabulary must be in the DTD.

EXAMPLE DTD

The following example demonstrates what a DTD could look like:

```
<!ELEMENT tutorials (tutorial)+>
<!ELEMENT tutorial (name, url)>
<!ELEMENT name (#PCDATA)>
<!ELEMENT url (#PCDATA)>
<!ATTLIST tutorials type CDATA #REQUIRED>
```

DTD <!DOCTYPE>

If you've had the opportunity to view some XML documents, you may have noticed a line starting with <!DOCTYPE appearing near the top of the document. For example, if you've viewed the source code of a (valid) XHTML file, you may have seen a line like this:

```
<!DOCTYPE html PUBLIC "-//W3C//DTD XHTML 1.0 Transitional//EN" "http://
www.abc.org/TR/xhtml1/DTD/xhtml1-transitional.dtd">
```

The purpose of this line is to declare the Document Type Definition (DTD). Actually, we even use the DOCTYPE declaration in a previous lesson to define an entity.

DOCTYPE SYNTAX

To use a DTD within your XML document, you need to declare it. The DTD can either be internal or external (located in another document).You declare a DTD at the top of your XML document (in the prolog) using the <!DOCTYPE declaration. The basic syntax is

```
<!DOCTYPE rootname [DTD]>
```

where, rootname is the root element, and [DTD] is the actual definition.

Actually, there are slight variations depending on whether your DTD is internal or external (or both), public or private.

Table 3.2 DOCTYPE Declaration Syntax

DOCTYPE Variation	Example	Description
<!DOCTYPE rootname [DTD]>	<!DOCTYPE tutorials [<!ELEMENT tutorials (tutorial)+> <!ELEMENT tutorial (name,url)> <!ELEMENT name (#PCDATA)> <!ELEMENT url (#PCDATA)> <!ATTLIST tutorials type CDATA #REQUIRED>]>	This is an internal DTD (the DTD is defined between the square brackets within the XML document).

(continued)

(continued)

DOCTYPE Variation	Example	Description
<!DOCTYPE rootname SYSTEM URL>	<!DOCTYPE tutorials SYSTEM "abcd.dtd">	The keyword SYSTEM indicates that it's a private DTD (not for public distribution). The presence of a URL indicates that this is an external DTD (the DTD is defined in a document located at the URL).
<!DOCTYPE rootname SYSTEM URL [DTD]>	<!DOCTYPE tutorials SYSTEM "abcd. dtd" [<!ELEMENT tutorial (summary)> <!ELEMENT summary (#PCDATA)>]>	The keyword SYSTEM indicates that it's a private DTD (not for public distribution). The presence of the URL and [DTD] together indicates that this is both an external and internal DTD (part of the DTD is defined in a document located at the URL, and the other part is defined within the XML document).
<!DOCTYPE rootname PUBLIC identifier URL>	<!DOCTYPE html PUBLIC "-//W3C// DTD XHTML 1.0 Transitional//EN" "http://www.abc.org/TR/xhtml1/DTD/ xhtml1-transitional.dtd">	The keyword PUBLIC indicates that it's a public DTD (for public distribution). The presence of the URL indicates that this is an external DTD (the DTD is defined in a document located at the URL). The identifier indicates the formal public identifier and is required when using a public DTD.

(continued)

DOCTYPE Variation	Example	Description
<!DOCTYPE rootname PUBLIC identifier URL [DTD]>	<!DOCTYPE html PUBLIC "-//W3C// DTD XHTML 1.0 Transitional//EN" "http://www.abc.org/TR/xhtml1/DTD/xhtml1-transitional.dtd" [<!ELEMENT abcd (tutorial)+> <!ELEMENT xyz (name,url)> <!ELEMENT name (#PCDATA)> <!ELEMENT url (#PCDATA)> <!ATTLIST abcd type CDATA #REQUIRED>]>	The keyword PUBLIC indicates that it"s a public DTD (for public distribution). The presence of the URL and [DTD] together indicates that this is both an external and internal DTD (part of the DTD is defined in a document located at the URL, the other part is defined within the XML document). The identifier indicates the formal public identifier and is required when using a public DTD.

XML SYNTAX RULES

XML has relatively straightforward, but very strict, syntax rules. A document that follows these syntax rules is said to be well-formed.

- There must be one, and only one, document element.
- Every open tag must be closed.
- If an element is empty, it still must be closed.

  Poorly-formed: <tag>

  Well-formed: <tag></tag>

  Also well-formed: <tag />
- Elements must be properly nested.

  Poorly-formed: <a><b></a></b>

  Well-formed: <a><b></b></a>
- Tag and attribute names are case sensitive.
- Attribute values must be enclosed in single or double quotes.

DTDS(WELL-FORMED VS. VALID)

A well-formed XML document is one that follows the syntax rules described in the XML Syntax Rules. A valid XML document is one that conforms to a specified structure. For an XML document to be validated, it must be checked against a schema, which is a document that defines the structure for a class of XML documents. XML documents that are not intended to conform to a schema can be well-formed, but they cannot be valid.

GENERAL PRINCIPLES IN WRITING DTDS

XML documents consist of elements and their attributes. There are some other items, but documents support only the above two main concepts. In addition, an element's content is defined in terms of other elements or some basic concepts defined in the XML standard. A DTD, therefore, must define all the elements in a document and the relationship between elements.

DTDs are associated with documents. When a validating parser reads the instruction by which documents are associated with a DTD, that tells the parser to get the DTD and validate the document according to the rules provided therein. We will now see how to tie DTDs to document instances.

XML provides the DOCTYPE tag to connect the DTD declarations to a document instance. The DOCTYPE declaration must follow the XML declaration and precede any elements in the document. However, comments and processing instructions may appear between the XML declaration and the DOCTYPE declaration.

The DOCTYPE declaration must contain the keyword DOCTYPE followed by the name of the root element of the document, followed by a construction that brings in the content declaration.

DOCUMENT VALIDATION

A well-formed document written using implicit rules cannot be checked for errors. We rely on the integrity of the applications that create and consume the XML for the integrity of the overall system. Errors in the code cannot be caught. They could either cause the program to break or cause bad errors. This is the reason that the W3C specifies the behavior of a validating parser. If an XML document refers a DTD, a validating parser is required to retrieve the DTD and ensure that the document conforms to the grammar that the DTD describes.

To check errors, simply use DTDs and a validating parser. The parser will check for errors in the document syntax, vocabulary, and any specified values.

After the parser has validated the document, the document can be passed on to the application logic. The application logic does protect the document from faulty application logic but filters the bad data. This is particularly important in case of Internet applications.

One cannot assume that the quality control over the application subject and the codes written are the same. A programming team working for one organization might be implementing a public XML vocabulary for a particular business. Their interpretation of the vocabulary may not be the same. The same case applies for the testing as well. But, with a DTD and a validating parser, we can have an immediate and effective check of the document's integrity. This check depends on the DTD. With this in mind, we now delve into the principles needed to write effective DTDs.

VALIDATING AN XML DOCUMENT WITH A DTD

The DOCTYPE declaration in an XML document specifies the DTD to which it should conform. In the code sample below, the DOCTYPE declaration indicates the file should be validated against Beatles.dtd in the same directory.

Code Sample: DTDs/Demos/Beatles.xml

```
<?xml version="1.0"?>
<!DOCTYPE beatles SYSTEM "Beatles.dtd">
<beatles>
 <beatle link="http://www.paulmccartney.com">
 <name>
 <firstname>Paul</firstname>
 <lastname>McCartney</lastname>
 </name>
 </beatle>
 <beatle link="http://www.johnlennon.com">
 <name>
 <firstname>John</firstname>
 <lastname>Lennon</lastname>
 </name>
 </beatle>
 <beatle link="http://www.georgeharrison.com">
```

```
 <name>
 <firstname>George</firstname>
 <lastname>Harrison</lastname>
 </name>
 </beatle>
 <beatle link="http://www.ringostarr.com">
 <name>
 <firstname>Ringo</firstname>
 <lastname>Starr</lastname>
 </name>
 </beatle>
 <beatle link="http://www.webucator.com" real="no">
 <name>
 <firstname>Nat</firstname>
 <lastname>Dunn</lastname>
 </name>
 </beatle>
</beatles>
```

THE PURPOSE OF DTDS

The purpose of a DTD is to define the structure of an XML document. It defines the structure with a list of legal elements:

```
<!DOCTYPE note
[
<!ELEMENT note (to,from,heading,body)>
<!ELEMENT to (#PCDATA)>
<!ELEMENT from (#PCDATA)>
<!ELEMENT heading (#PCDATA)>
<!ELEMENT body (#PCDATA)>
]>
```

A Document Type Definition (DTD) is a type of schema. The purpose of DTDs is to provide a framework for validating XML documents. By defining a structure that XML documents must conform to, DTDs allow different organizations to create share able data files.

Imagine, for example, a company that creates technical courseware and sells it to technical training companies. Those companies may want to display the outlines for that courseware on their Websites, but they do not want to display it in the same way as every other company who buys the courseware.

By providing the course outlines in a predefined XML format, the courseware vendor makes it possible for the training companies to write programs to read those XML files and transform them into HTML pages with their own formatting styles (perhaps using XSLT or CSS). If the XML files had no predefined structure, it would be very difficult to write such programs.

CREATING DTDS

DTDs are simple text files that can be created with any basic text editor. Although they look a little cryptic at first, they are not terribly complicated once you get used to them.

A DTD outlines what elements can be in an XML document and the attributes and sub-elements that they can take. Let's start by taking a look at a complete DTD and then dissecting it.

CODE SAMPLE: DTDS/DEMOS/BEATLES.DTD

```
<!ELEMENT beatles (beatle+)>
<!ELEMENT beatle (name)>
<!ATTLIST beatle
 link CDATA #IMPLIED
 real (yes|no) "yes">
<!ELEMENT name (firstname, lastname)>
<!ELEMENT firstname (#PCDATA)>
<!ELEMENT lastname (#PCDATA)>
```

INTERNAL DTD

Whether you use an external or internal DTD, the actual syntax for the DTD is the same—the same code could just as easily be part of an internal DTD or an external one. The only difference between internal and external is in the way it's declared with DOCTYPE.

Using an internal DTD, the code is placed between the DOCTYPE tags (i.e., <!DOCTYPE tutorials [and]>.

EXAMPLE INTERNAL DTD

This is an example of an internal DTD. It's internal because the DTD is included in the target XML document:

```
<?xml version="1.0" standalone="yes"?>
<!DOCTYPE tutorials [
<!ELEMENT tutorials (tutorial)+>
<!ELEMENT tutorial (name,url)>
<!ELEMENT name (#PCDATA)>
<!ELEMENT url (#PCDATA)>
<!ATTLIST tutorials type CDATA #REQUIRED>
]>
<tutorials>
 <tutorial>
 <name>XML Tutorial</name>
 <url>http://www.abc.com/xml/tutorial</url>
 </tutorial>
 <tutorial>
 <name>HTML Tutorial</name>
 <url>http://www.abc.com/html/tutorial</url>
 </tutorial>
</tutorials>
```

EXTERNAL DTD

An external DTD is one that resides in a separate document. To use the DTD, you need to link to it from your XML document by providing the URI of the DTD file. This URI is typically in the form of a URL. The URL can point to a local file using a relative reference or a remote one (i.e., using HTTP) using an absolute reference.

EXAMPLE EXTERNAL DTD

Here's an example of an XML document that uses an external DTD. Note that the "standalone" attribute is set to "no." This is because the document relies on an external resource (the DTD):

```
<?xml version="1.0" standalone="no"?>
<!DOCTYPE tutorials SYSTEM "tutorials.dtd">
```

```
<tutorials>
 <tutorial>
 <name>XML Tutorial</name>
 <url>http://www.abc.com/xml/tutorial</url>
 </tutorial>
 <tutorial>
 <name>HTML Tutorial</name>
 <url>http://www.abc.com/html/tutorial</url>
 </tutorial>
</tutorials>
```

And, using the above XML document as an example, here's an example of what "tutorials.dtd" (the external DTD file) could look like. Note that the external DTD file doesn't need the DOCTYPE declaration—it is already on the XML file that is using this DTD:

```
<!ELEMENT tutorials (tutorial)+>
<!ELEMENT tutorial (name,url)>
<!ELEMENT name (#PCDATA)>
<!ELEMENT url (#PCDATA)>
<!ATTLIST tutorials type CDATA #REQUIRED>
```

COMBINED DTD

You can use both an internal DTD and an external one at the same time. This could be useful if you need to adhere to a common DTD, but also need to define your own definitions locally.

Example

This is an example of using both an external DTD and an internal one for the same XML document. The external DTD resides in "tutorials.dtd" and is called first in the DOCTYPE declaration. The internal DTD follows the external one, but still resides within the DOCTYPE declaration:

```
<?xml version="1.0" standalone="no"?>
<!DOCTYPE tutorials SYSTEM "tutorials.dtd" [
<!ELEMENT tutorial (summary)>
<!ELEMENT summary (#PCDATA)>
]>
<tutorials>
 <tutorial>
 <name>XML Tutorial</name>
```

```
<url>http://www.abc.com/xml/tutorial</url>
<summary>Best XML tutorial on the web!</summary>
</tutorial>
<tutorial>
<name>HTML Tutorial</name>
<url>http://www.abc.com/html/tutorial</url>
<summary>Best HTML tutorial on the web!</summary>
</tutorial>
</tutorials>
```

DTD ELEMENTS

Creating a DTD is straight forward. It's really just a matter of defining your elements, attributes, and/or entities.

To define an element in your DTD, you use the `<!ELEMENT>` declaration. The actual contents of your `<!ELEMENT>` declaration will depend on the syntax rules you need to apply to your element.

BASIC SYNTAX

The `<!ELEMENT>` declaration has the following syntax:

```
<!ELEMENT element_name content_model>
```

Here, element_name is the name of the element you're defining. The content model could indicate a specific rule, data or another element.

If it specifies a rule, it will be set to either ANY or EMPTY.

If specifies data or another element, the data type/element name needs to be surrounded by brackets (i.e. (tutorial) or (#PCDATA)).

The following examples show you how to use this syntax for defining your elements.

PLAIN TEXT

If an element should contain plain text, you define the element using #PCDATA. PCDATA stands for Parsed Character Data and it is the way you specify non-markup text in your DTDs.

Using this example - `<name>XML Tutorial</name>` - the "XML Tutorial" part is the PCDATA. The other part consists of the markup.

Syntax

```
<!ELEMENT element_name (#PCDATA)>
```

Example

```
<!ELEMENT name (#PCDATA)>
```

The above line in your DTD allows the "name" element to contain non-markup data in your XML document:

```
<name>XML Tutorial</name>
```

UNRESTRICTED ELEMENTS

If it doesn't matter what your element contains, you can create an element using the content_model of ANY. Note that doing this removes all syntax checking, so you should avoid using this if possible. You're better off defining a specific content model.

Syntax

```
<!ELEMENT element_name ANY>
```

Example

```
<!ELEMENT tutorials ANY>
```

EMPTY ELEMENTS

You might remember that an empty element is one without a closing tag. For example, in XHTML, the <br/> and <img/> tags are empty elements. Here's how you define an empty element:

Syntax

```
<!ELEMENT element_name EMPTY>
```

Example

```
<!ELEMENT header EMPTY>
```

The above line in your DTD defines the following empty element for your XML document:

```
<header/>
```

CHILD ELEMENTS

You can specify that an element must contain another element by providing the name of the element it must contain. Here's how you do that:

Syntax

```
<!ELEMENT element_name (child_element_name)>
```

Example

```
<!ELEMENT tutorials (tutorial)>
```

The above line in your DTD allows the "tutorials" element to contain one instance of the"tutorial" element in your XML document:

```
<tutorials>
 <tutorial></tutorial>
</tutorials>
```

When defining child elements in DTDs, you can specify how many times those elements can appear by adding a modifier after the element name. If no modifier is added, the element must appear once and only once. The other options are shown in the table below.

Table 3.3 List of Modifiers

Modifier	Description
?	Zero or one times.
+	One or more times.
*	Zero or more times.

It is not possible to specify a range of times that an element may appear (e.g., 2-4 appearances).

OTHER ELEMENTS

The other elements are declared in the same way as the document element—with the <!ELEMENT> declaration. The Beatles DTD declares four additional elements.

Each beatle element must contain a child element name, which must appear once and only once.

```
<!ELEMENT beatle (name)>
```

Each name element must contain a firstname and lastname element, which each must appear once and only once and in that order.

```
<!ELEMENT name (firstname, lastname)>
```

Some elements contain only text. This is declared in a DTD as #PCDATA. The data will be parsed for XML tags and entities. The firstname and lastname elements contain only text.

```
<!ELEMENT firstname (#PCDATA)>
<!ELEMENT lastname (#PCDATA)>
```

CHOICE OF ELEMENTS

It is also possible to indicate that one of several elements may appear as a child element. For example, the declaration below indicates that an img element may have a child element name or a child element id, but not both.

```
<!ELEMENT img (name|id)>
```

EMPTY ELEMENTS

Empty elements are declared as follows.

```
<!ELEMENT img EMPTY>
```

MIXED CONTENT

Sometimes elements can have elements and text intermingled. For example, the following declaration is for a body element that may contain text in addition to any number of link and img elements.

```
<!ELEMENT body (#PCDATA | link | img)*>
```

MULTIPLE CHILD ELEMENTS (SEQUENCES)

You can also provide a comma-separated list of elements if it needs to contain more than one element. This is referred to as a *sequence*. The XML document must contain the tags in the same order that they're specified in the sequence.

Syntax

```
<!ELEMENT element_name (child_element_name, child_element_name,...)>
```

Example

```
<!ELEMENT tutorial (name, url)>
```

The above line in your DTD allows the "tutorial" element to contain one instance of the "name" element and one instance of the "url" element in your XML document:

```
<tutorials>
 <tutorial>
 <name></name>
 <url></url>
 </tutorial>
</tutorials>
```

AN XML APPLICATION WITHOUT A DTD

The following is a simple XML fragment:

```
<?xml version="1.0" standalone="yes"encoding="UTF-8"?>
<quote>
 <title>
The quick brown fox jumps over the lazy dog
 </title>
 <comment>
This quote has <property>all the alphabets</property> of the English
language.
 </comment>
</quote>
```

To display this fragment in a document-like fashion, we must first declare which elements are inline-level (i.e., do not cause line breaks) and which are block-level (i.e., cause line breaks). After that, we can "decorate" the rest of the content. Here is a sample CSS stylesheet:

```
property {display: inline; font-style: italic; color: rgb(000,000,128);}
quote, title, comment {display: block; margin: 0.5em;}
title {font-size: 1.5em;}
```

The first rule declares property to be inline, in italic, and navy; the second rule, with its comma-separated list of selectors, declares all the other elements to be block-level (with a bit of a margin added in the end).

Finally, the title is given a larger font size than the rest of the text. The presentation of the document can be further improved by adding more rules to the stylesheet.

DTD ELEMENT OPERATORS

One of the examples in the previous lesson demonstrated how to specify that an element ("tutorials") must contain one instance of another element ("tutorial").

This is fine if there only needs one instance of "tutorial," but what if we didn't want a limit? What if the "tutorials" element should be able to contain any number of "tutorial" instances? Fortunately, we can do that using DTD operators.

Table 3.4 List of Operators/Syntax Rules

Operator	Syntax	Description
+	a+	One or more occurences of a
*	a*	Zero or more occurences of a
?	a?	Either a or nothing
,	a, b	a followed by b
|	a | b	a followed by b
()	(expression)	An expression surrounded by parentheses is treated as a unit and could have any one of the following suffixes?, *, or +.

Examples of usage follow.

Zero or More

To allow zero or more of the same child element, use an asterisk (*).

Syntax

```
<!ELEMENT element_name (child_element_name*)>
```

Example

```
<!ELEMENT tutorials(tutorial*)>
```

One or More

To allow one or more of the same child element, use a plus sign (+).

Syntax

```
<!ELEMENT element_name (child_element_name+)>
```

Example

```
<!ELEMENT tutorials (tutorial+)>
```

Zero or One

To allow either zero or one of the same child element, use a question mark (?).

Syntax

```
<!ELEMENT element_name (child_element_name?)>
```

Example

```
<!ELEMENT tutorials (tutorial?)>
```

Choices

You can define a choice between one or another element by using the pipe (|) operator. For example, if the "tutorial" element requires a child called either "name", "title," or "subject" (but only one of these), you can do the following document type definition (DTD).

Syntax

```
<!ELEMENT element_name (choice_1|choice_2|choice_3)>
```

Example

```
<!ELEMENT tutorial (name|title|subject)>
```

Mixed Content

You can use the pipe (|) operator to specify that an element can contain both PCDATA and other elements.

Syntax

```
<!ELEMENT element_name (#PCDATA | child_element_name)>
```

Example

```
<!ELEMENT tutorial (#PCDATA|name|title|subject)*>
```

DTD OPERATORS WITH SEQUENCES

You can apply any of the DTD operators to a sequence.

Syntax

```
<!ELEMENT element_name (child_element_name dtd_operator, child_
element_name dtd_operator,...)>
```

Example

```
<!ELEMENT tutorial (name+, url?)>
```

The above example allows the "tutorial" element to contain one or more instances of the "name" element, and zero or one instance of the "url" element.

SUBSEQUENCES

You can use parentheses to create a subsequence (i.e., a sequence within a sequence). This enables you to apply DTD operators to a subsequence.

Syntax

```
<!ELEMENT element_name ((sequence) dtd_operator sequence)>
```

Example

```
<!ELEMENT tutorial ((author,rating?)+ name, url*)>
```

The above example specifies that the "tutorial" element can contain one or more "author" elements, with each occurence having an optional "rating" element.

THE DOCUMENT ELEMENT

When creating a DTD, the first step is to define the document element.

```
<!ELEMENT beatles (beatle+)>
```

The element declaration above states that the "beatles" element must contain one or more "beatles" elements.

LOCATION OF MODIFIER

The location of modifiers in a declaration is important. If the modifier is outside of a set of parentheses, it applies to the group; if the modifier is immediately next to an element name, it applies only to that element. The following examples illustrate.

In the example below, the body element can have any number of interspersed child link and img elements.

```
<!ELEMENT body (link|img)*>
```

In the example below, the body element can have any number of child link elements or any number of child img elements, but it cannot have both link and img elements.

```
<!ELEMENT body (link*|img*)>
```

In the example below, the body element can have any number of child link and img elements, but they must come in pairs, with the link element preceding the img element.

```
<!ELEMENT body (link, img)*>
```

In the example below, the body element can have any number of child link elements followed by any number of child img elements.

```
<!ELEMENT body (link*, img*)>
```

USING PARENTHESES FOR COMPLEX DECLARATIONS

Element declarations can be more complex than the examples above. For example, you can specify that a person element either contains a single name element or a firstname and lastname element. To group elements, wrap them in parentheses as shown below.

```
<!ELEMENT person (name|(firstname,lastname))>
```

XML CDATA

All text in an XML document is parsed by the parser, but text inside a CDATA section is ignored by the parser.

PCDATA-PARSED CHARACTER DATA

XML parsers normally parse all the text in an XML document. When an XML element is parsed, the text between the XML tags is also parsed:

```
<message>This text is also parsed</message>
```

The parser does this because XML elements can contain other elements, as in this example, where the <name> element contains two other elements (first and last):

```
<name><first>Bill</first><last>Gates</last></name>
```

and the parser will break it up into sub-elements:

```
<name>
 <first>Bill</first>
 <last>Gates</last>
</name>
```

This term is defined earlier.

CDATA-(UNPARSED) CHARACTER DATA

The term CDATA is used about text data that should not be parsed by the XML parser. Characters like "<" and "&" are illegal in XML elements. "<"

will generate an error because the parser interprets it as the start of a new element. "&" will generate an error because the parser interprets it as the start of a character entity.

Some text, like JavaScript code, contains a lot of "<" or "&" characters. To avoid errors, script code can be defined as CDATA. Everything inside a CDATA section is ignored by the parser. A CDATA section starts with `"<![CDATA["` and ends with `"]]>"`:

```
<script>
<![CDATA[
function matchwo(a,b)
{
if (a < b && a < 0) then
 {
 return 1;
 }
else
 {
 return 0;
 }
}
]]>
</script>
```

In the example above, everything inside the CDATA section is ignored by the parser.

NOTES ON CDATA SECTIONS

A CDATA section cannot contain the string "]]>". Nested CDATA sections are not allowed. The "]]>" that marks the end of the CDATA section.

INTERNAL & EXTERNAL SUBSETS

```
<?xml version="1.0?>
<!DOCTYPE Catalog...>
<Catalog>...
```

Before we discuss the DOCTYPE tag, we need an example of the position of the DOCTYPE declaration in a document instance. Shown in the image are the three lines of an XML document. The first line states that this document conforms to the syntax of XML 1.0. This is done by using the XML declaration at the top. We have declared that this document falls under the CATALOG vocabulary.

This is done by specifying the word CATALOG after the document type "CATALOG". The first element, the root of the document, must be CATALOG or the parser will return an error.

The ellipsis concealing the DOCTYPE declaration is not very satisfying. Where are the declarations? There are two ways to provide declarations. There can be an external subset of declarations in a separate DTD file or include an internal subset within the body of a DOCTYPE declaration or both.

In the instance of mixing the external and internal subsets, the internal DTD may add declarations or override declarations found in the external DTD. Parsers, generally, read the internal subset first, and the declarations therein take priority, because of the XML specifications.

STANDALONE ATTRIBUTE

There is one further variation to be considered before we further discuss how to provide declarations. The XML declaration can have a standalone attribute. The standalone attribute is, however, seldom seen in practice. The figure shows the declaration of the standalone attribute.

```
<?xml version="1.0" standalone="YES" ?>
<!DOCTYPE Catalog…
```

This attribute can have two values: YES and NO.

If the value of the attribute is YES, then there are no declarations external to the document instance that would affect the information in the document passed to the application using it. The presence of the attribute with the value YES does not guarantee that the document does not have external dependencies of any type. It merely states that the document has no external dependencies that if not included in the processing would make the document erroneous as far as the receiving application is concerned.

A value of NO indicates that there are external declarations that contain values that are necessary to properly define the document content. The standalone attribute serves as a flag for parsers and other applications to indicate whether they need to retrieve external content.

DOCTYPE DECLARATION

The DOCTYPE declaration formally consists of the keyword followed by the name of the document's root element's root element in our example the word CATALOG. This is followed by an optional external identifier, which is again followed by an optional block of markup characters.

The external identifier locates the external DTD (external subset).The markup declaration block actually contains markup declarations (internal subset).

INTERNAL DTD SUBSET DECLARATIONS

Declarations, such as entity references, can be declared in the internal subset. This markup declaration block is delimited within the DOCTYPE declaration using square brackets ([……]). A list of declarations is declared within these brackets. An example of the declaration is shown below.

```
<!DOCTYPE Catalog […internal subset declaration here…]>
```

Internal DTDs are very useful. An internal DTD, however, adds a substantial size to the document. The declarations must be transmitted with the document even if the consumer of the document does not intend to verify the document. Internal DTDs are very useful for simple vocabularies when using prototypes of a markup.

Sometimes, programmers might feel the need to use both the internal as well as external DTD. In such cases, the internal DTD adds declarations. Nonetheless, when an internal DTD declares some item that is also declared in the external DTD, the internal DTD supersedes the external DTD. This permits some fine-tuning of the declarations for a particular document's needs, but enough care must be taken, as, if we override the external DTD, it starts to loose relevance, which is a sign of poor initial design.

EXTERNAL DTDS

An external DTD is more flexible in certain aspects. In this case, the DOCTYPE declaration comprises the usual keyword and the root element name, followed by another keyword denoting the source of the external DTD, which is then followed by the location of that DTD.

The keyword can either be SYSTEM or PUBLIC.

In case, the keyword is SYSTEM, and a URL directly and explicitly locates the DTD. Thus, the parser should be able to find the DTD given the URL alone. Hence, what follows SYSTEM is a URL naming the DTD file. The URLs used to locate DTDs should not contain fragment identifiers, that is, the character # followed by a name, as XML 1.0 indicates that parsers may signal an error if the URL contains such an identifier.

```
<DOCTYPE Catalog SYSTEM http://myserver/Catalog.dtd>
<DOCTYPE Catalog SYSTEM http://www.universallibrary.org/Catalog.dtd>
```

The image shows an example of the DOCTYPE declaration using the SYSTEM keyword. All the declarations needed to validate the document containing the first DOCTYPE declaration will be found in the file Catalog.dtd. In the second case, the DTD file is found on a Web server that is operated by a hypothetical universal library organization. In both cases, an element declaration for the CATALOG element is to be found within the Catalog.dtd file.

The PUBLIC keyword is used for well-known vocabularies. Going back to our CATALOG example, let us suppose considerable consensus has been built upon the catalog DTD in the publishing industry. In that case, an application parsing a document from this vocabulary might employ some strategy for locating the DTD. If possible, the application might have a local copy. Hence, using it would be preferable to making a roundabout trip to a Web server.

Using the PUBLIC keyword with a Uniform Resource Identifier (URI), applications are given the opportunity to locate the DTD using their own algorithms. The URI could be a URL or simply a unique name.

If the URI universal/Book is well known to the application processing documents of this type, the application can go and find the DTD on its own. It might even have a local copy of the DTD, or it might access a DTD maintained on a local database server. Thus, it can be inferred that the means of finding the DTD is left primarily to the application processing the DOCTYPE declaration.

The term "well known" is normally relative. XML 1.0, however, it permits a PUBLIC declaration to have both a public URI and a system identifier. If the application or parser consuming the document cannot locate a DTD from the URI provided with the PUBLIC keyword, it must use the system identifier. In the example shown, the author of the document gave the receiving application a chance to find the DTD based on the public URI. If that fails, which can expected from a general-purpose parser with no knowledge of our publishing domain, the application would be expected to request the name from the Web server at *www.universallibrary.org*.

BASIC MARKUP DECLARATIONS

The content of an XML document is defined in terms of four kinds of markup declarations used in the DTD.

Table 3.5 List of DTD Constructs and Meanings

DTD Construct	Meaning
ELEMENT	Declaration of an XML element type
ATTLIST	Declaration of the attributes that may be assigned to a specific element type and the permissible values of those attributes
ENTITY	Declaration of reusable content
NOTATION	Format declaration for external content not meant to be parsed and the external application that handles the content

The keywords associated with these declarations and their meanings are shown in the table. The first two declarations deal with the information found in an XML document element, namely ELEMENTS and ATTRIBUTES. The last two types could be considered supporting players. Entities in particular are designed to make an XML vocabulary designer's life easier. They normally consist of content that recurs in the DTD or document to warrant creating a special declaration. Notations deal with content other than XML. A notation is used to declare a particular class of data and associate it with an external program. That external program becomes the handler for the declared class of data.

FORMAL DTD STRUCTURE-ENTITIES

XML provides a facility for declaring chunks of content and referencing them as many times as we like where they are needed, saving space and sparing document authors a lot of typing. With the declaration of an entity in the DTD, we can define a name and the content it refers to. When needed, we can refer to it by name with a particular syntax that the name is an entity reference.

An entity used within the content of a document is called as a *general entity*.

A parsed entity is an XML document. The value of the entity is known as the replacement text. In contrast, an unparsed entity need not even be text. If it is text, it need not be XML. If the replacement content is not XML, there is no need in using a parser on it. On the other hand, a parsed entity is XML that is pasted into the document content, so it must be passed through the parser.

PREDEFINED ENTITIES

XML reserves some characters, such as the angle brackets, for its own use.

In addition, some characters are unprintable. XML therefore provides some predefined entities so that authors can use these characters in their documents without conflict. Hence, in the text content of an element, for example, certain characters can be referred to without using them and may be confused with the markup by the document processor during parsing.

Any character can be referred to by a numeric reference. This is done by writing the characters followed immediately by the numeric value of the character and a semicolon. For example, the "greater than" symbol is written as >.

Some characters are so prevalent in XML that XML provides some predefined entities.

GENERAL ENTITIES

General entities allow us to declare a piece of parsed text associated with a name by which we shall refer to the text. The entity is declared with the keyword ENTITY, a name, and a replacement value.

With this declaration in place, we can plug in the copyright text anywhere in a document's content when we need it simply by referring to the name "copyright." Of course, the parser needs to be told when we are making an entity reference so that it will not confuse the entity name with the markup text. To signal this intent, we delimit the name with an ampersand in front of the name and a semicolon following. There cannot be a white space between the name and its delimiters.

The ampersand character is reserved for this role in XML. If we need to use an ampersand for something else in a document, we must use the predefined entity for the character.

```
<!ENTITY Entity1 SYSTEM http://www.vvco.com/boilerplate/copyrighttext.txt>
```

General entities also have an external form, where the replacement text is given in an external file. The declaration takes the form as shown in the figure.

The keyword SYSTEM is used to indicate an external source followed by the URL for the file.

Lastly, entities must not contain references to themselves, directly or indirectly.

PARAMETER ENTITIES

Parsed entities that are used solely within the DTD are called *parameter entities*.

Parameter entities allow the user to easily reference or change commonly used constructs in the DTD by keeping them in one place.

This is easier than changing a construct everywhere it appears in a DTD, but it still must be edited when a construct is extended.

The keyword CDATA refers to character data. The replacement text is a part of an attribute list declaration containing three common attributes. This is processed as if it had been written into the DTD. Whenever this set of attributes turns up in the DTD, we can simply refer to the entity people-Parameters.

All the parameter entities must be declared before they are referred to in the DTD.

This means that the parameter entity declared in the external subset of the DTD cannot be referred to in the internal subset as the latter is read first by the parser, thus, the reference will be seen before the declaration.

A parameter entity reference consists of the name delimited by a percent sign in front of the name and a semicolon following. There cannot be any white space between the delimiters and the name.

```
<!ATTLIST InsuredPerson
age CDATA # IMPLIED
weight CDATA #IMPLIED
height CDATA #REQUIRED
carrier CDATA #REQUIRED
```

Thus, the reference for the example would be as shown. For the moment, the InsuredPerson element is declared to have four attributes: one carrier, which is explicitly declared, and the other three, namely age, weight and height, that appeared in the parameter entity and have already been declared when the replacement text is substituted for the entity reference by the parser.

The above example is thus equivalent to the following:

```
<ATTLIST InsuredPerson
%peopleParameters;
carrier CDATA #REQUIRED>
```

All the rules for well-formed documents apply to parameter entities. The document must be well-formed after the replacement text has been substituted for the entity reference.

Just as in the case of general entities, parameter entities can also have a replacement text that resides in an external file.

FORMAL DTD STRUCTURE-ELEMENTS

Element types are declared in DTDs using the ELEMENT tag. In addition to the keyword, the tag provides a name for the declared type and a content specification.

The element type names have some restrictions that apply to names throughout XML. Names may use letters, digits, and punctuation marks (colon, underscore, hyphen, and period). Names may not begin with a digit. They may only begin with a letter, underscore or colon. The element content can be classified into four categories: empty, element, mixed, and any.

An empty element neither has text nor child elements contained in it. It may, however, have attributes. The empty element is denoted by the keyword EMPTY.

Element content is the condition where the element contains child elements but no text. Mixed content is a mix of elements and parsed character data (#PCDATA) or content.

Element and mixed are the two types where we can use structure to express meaning. Mixed and element content is indicated with a content model.

If we wish to leave the content of an element open to any content that does not violate XML well-formed syntax, we declare it using the keyword ANY.

CONTENT MODEL

A *content model* is a specification of the internal structure of an element's content.

A content model consists of a set of parentheses enclosing some combination of child element names, operators, and the #PCDATA keyword. The operators denote the cardinality and indicate how elements and character data can be combined. The table shows the operators and their meaning.

Table 3.6 List of Order Operators

Order Operators	Meaning
,	(comma) strict sequence
|	(pipe) choice

Taking the first of these, the elements may be combined in a sequence using a comma delimiting the list. The figure shows the declaration for a PersonName element and FruitBasket element. The elements First, Middle, and Last must appear in the order specified. The declaration for FruitBasket element type could contain Apple or Cherry, but not both.

```
<!ELEMENT PersonName (First, Middle,Last)>
<!ELEMENT FruitBasket (Apple | Cherry)>
```

CARDINALITY OPERATORS

The operators seen so far lack something important—cardinality, such as how many instances of an element type are permitted? The table shows the cardinality operators.

Table 3.7 List of Cardinality Operators

Cardinality Operators	Meaning
?	Optional; may or may not appear
*	Zero or more
+	One or more

If no cardinality operator is used, then the cardinality is one. These operators can be used with elements or content model groups to form very complicated structures. Let us now see an example using the FruitBasket element type declaration.

```
<!ELEMENT FruitBasket (Cherry+, (Apple | Orange)*>
```

This content model group says that the basket contains one or more instances of the element type Cherry, followed by zero or more instances of the choice between Apple and Orange. Note that all the elements must appear together. This would lead to an instance as shown.

```
<FruitBasket>
<Cherry>…</Cherry>
<Cherry>…</Cherry>
<Apple>…</Apple>
<Orange>…</Orange>
<Orange>…</Orange>
</FruitBasket>
```

To indicate mixed content, one must include #PCDATA in the content model. The elements in the content model must be separated by the pipe (|) operator and the whole group as a whole declared as having zero or more cardinality.

When using mixed content model, the #PCDATA keyword must be the first choice in the model. This would indicate zero or more choices from ItemA, ItemB, and #PCDATA. This could lead to an instance as shown.

```
<MixedBag>
<ItemA>…</ItemA>
```

This is the text that we wanted to include as PCDATA:

```
<ItemA>…</ItemA>
<ItemB>…</ItemB>
</MixedBag>
```

ATTRIBUTES

Attributes complement and modify elements by means of associating simple properties with elements. Attributes are a rich feature in XML that allows us to include a significant amount of information.

In HTML, SRC is an attribute in the IMG tag. Attributes are declared in XML using the ATTLIST tag. Each element that has attributes declared for it will have at least one ATTLIST that declares the attribute for the element.

The ATTLIST declaration consists of the ATTLIST keyword followed by the element to which the attribute applies, followed by zero or more attribute definitions. For readability purposes, it is better to place the attribute definition on a separate line.

Each attribute definition consists of the name of the attribute, its type, and a default definition.

```
<!ATTLIST ourElement AttributeName CDATA #REQUIRED>
```

Here, we are declaring a single attribute AttributeName that must occur in the start-tag of every instance of ourElement element, and that the value of the attribute is a character data string (CDATA) #REQUIRED is the default definition.

An attribute can have one of the several different defaults that define the way the attribute appears in the document.

DEFAULT VALUES

There are four defaults for attribute declarations. They are shown in the table.

Table 3.8 List of a Default Attributes

Attribute Defaults	Meaning
#REQUIRED	Attributes must appear on every instance of element.
#IMPLIED	Attribute may optionally appear on an instance of an element.
#FIXED plus default value	Attribute must have default value; if attribute does not appear, value is assumed by the parser.
Default value only	If attribute does not appear, default value assumed by parser. If attribute appears it may have another value.

If the default attribute value is provided in the ATTLIST and omitted in the instance of the element in a document, an XML parser behaves as though the attribute appeared with the default value. Thus, for the example, both instances are the same.

```
<!ATTLIST SomeCol color "blue">
<SomeCol color="blue">...</SomeCol>
<SomeCol>…</SomeCol>
```

From the example, we can see that the declaration of the color attribute gave us a default value that is blue. In the first instance, this has been explicitly declared, but left off in the second instance of the element. A parser would treat both as having a value of blue for the attribute color.

ATTRIBUTE TYPES

The attribute type specifies whether the attribute is needed. The table shows the various types of the attributes and their meanings.

Table 3.9 List of Attribute Types and Meanings

Attribute Types	Meaning
CDATA	Character data (String)
ID	Name unique within a given document
IDREF	Reference of some element bearing an ID attribute possessing the same value as the IDREF attribute
IDREFS	Series of IDREFs delimited by whitespaces
ENTITY	Name of a predefined external entity
ENTITIES	Series of ENTITY names delimited by whitespaces
NMTOKEN	A Name
NMTOKENS	A series of NMTOKENS delimited by whitespaces
NOTATION	Accepts one of a set of names indicating notation types declared in the DTD
[Enumerated Value]	Accepts one of a series of explicitly user-defined values that the attributes can take on

CDATA

Eventually, all the content turns up as text. When there is an attribute type whose value consists of just text, it may be declared as CDATA.

The value of the attribute could be any character data string of any length. The only restriction is that the attribute value cannot contain markup. An example is shown. As long as the attribute value is simple text, the parser will declare it valid.

```
<!ATTLIST SomeCol someText CDATA #IMPLIED
<SomeCol someText= "This is a validtext">…</SomeCol>
```

ID

The ID attribute type will have a value that is a unique identifying name. The value of the ID attribute must be unique throughout the document. This allows us to uniquely name an element. No element can have more than one ID for an element.

The attribute type must be #IMPLIED or #REQUIRED but never #FIXED or defaulted. It makes no sense if the default value is provided, especially the fixed default for an ID, as that would violate the uniqueness constraint.

What can we do with an ID type attribute to make it useful? Refer to it, of course. It can be used to model a one-to-one relationship between two objects modeled by elements in our vocabulary. As the example shows, the declaration attaches a personal identification number to their details within a file as a unique identifier.

```
<!ATTLIST Person
PIN ID #REQUIRED>
```

IDREF

The IDREF allows us to create links and cross references within the document. The values of IDREF must meet the same conditions as ID. They must also be the same as the value of some ID attribute value within the document.

We cannot use an IDREF to point to a document that is not within the document. In such a case, we can use ID and IDREF to cross reference information instead of repeating it. If a document contained the declaration as the Person element, we can have the declarations as shown elsewhere in the DTD.

```
<!ELEMENT AccountHolder EMPTY>
<!ATTLIST AccountHolder
id IDREF #REQUIRED>
```

In such cases, we have to know implicitly that the attribute id refers to the PIN attribute in Person. Instead of duplicating the entire Person element within the AccountHolder, we have an empty element with an IDREF. Whenever we need the Person information, the application searches for a Person element with the PIN attribute whose value matches the id attribute in a specified AccountHolder.

```
<Person PIN= "405060">
<Name>…</Name>
```

```
...
</Person>
...
<AccountHolder>
```

The IDREFS type is used when we want to link to many other elements. It allows us to model one-to-many relationships. The value of this attribute is a series of ID values separated by white space. The individual Ids must meet the ID type constraints and must match up with ID attribute values elsewhere in the document.

ENTITY

Entities are used within the declarations of the attributes for efficiency and reuse. If there is a construction that appears many times, we can declare an entity representing the construction and then refer to it, whenever the construction is needed. ENTITY is therefore referred to as *replaceable content.*

Entities may also be used to include unparsed entities as valid attribute values. This is exactly the mechanism by which a document's author can point to data other than the XML markup.

For example, if we want to include some XML data, we can do this with an entity as shown. We start by declaring the attribute to be of type ENTITY.

```
<!ENTITY Turnover_chart SYSTEM "Turnover_chart.gif" NDATAgif>
```

Elsewhere in the DTD we declare the entity.
We can refer to the image through the attribute.

```
<ATTLIST MonthlyTurnover
Month_graph ENTITY #IMPLIED>
```

ENTITY, ENTITIES

To use an ENTITY as an attribute type, four things need to be done. Of these four, three are declarations in the DTD. The fourth involves a specific document instance. They are declaring a notation, declaring one or more entities for use with the attribute, declaring an attribute of type ENTITY for some element, and creating an instance of the element type in a document, and providing the attribute and an entity name as the value.

Just as we were able to use multiple IDREF values as a single attribute value, we can also do the same with entities. This type is called as ENTITIES. This works similarly to IDREFS.

Each name in the attribute value must conform to the rules of the ENTITY type, and individual entity names are separated by white space.

NMTOKEN, NMTOKENS

Sometimes we might want to treat the value of an attribute as a distinct token rather than text and want to leave the list of values imprecise. In such a case, we can use name token, which is abbreviated as NMTOKEN and NMTOKENS.

Similar to IDREFS and ENTITIES, attributes of type NMTOKENS can be declared, and they have values comprised of multiple name tokens. Each name must be a valid name token and items must be separated by white space.

Although, they must conform to the rules for names that were discussed for elements, they are free of one restriction. They are to be comprised of letters, digits, and punctuation marks like colon, underscore, period, and hyphen, unlike element and attribute names; any of these can be used as the first character of an NMTOKEN. The following shows an example of an NMTOKEN attribute.

```
<!ATTLIST Employee
security_level NMTOKEN #REQUIRED>
<employee security_level="trusted">…
```

The example says that an Employee element may have an attribute named security level whose level conforms to the rules for XML name tokens. We could use this to control access to confidential information. By choosing NMTOKEN, the document authors will be able to accommodate new security level designations as they are created without editing the DTD every time. Any value that conforms to the rules for comprising NMTOKEN values will be accepted as the value for this attribute.

NOTATION

An XML parser is not set to deal with binary data formats. To overcome this problem, notations are used which identify the format of external data items that we would want to link to XML documents.

We need the notation declaration to declare a name for the notation and associate the name with an external handler. The parser refers the foreign data to the handler for processing.

The handler declaration works in same manner as DTD locating files in the DOCTYPE declaration. It can be PUBLIC or STATIC, and it must include the name of the external handler. The figure shows an example of NOTATION declaration.

With notations, XML documents can be used as the unifying document of a collection of dissimilar data types. This is useful for legal reports, medical reports, and multimedia presentations. XML, however, only provides the minimal set of tools. Considerable effort is needed to build the proper presentation semantics into an application.

```
<!ATTLIST Imager type NOTATION (gif | jpg) "gif">
<Image type="jpg">…
```

An attribute can be typed as a notation name using the keyword NOTATION as shown. The above declaration says that an Image that is a notation. The acceptable values of the attribute are gif and jpg. On leaving the attribute without an instance, the parser would assume that the attribute appeared with the default value, gif. In the instance shown, however, the value jpg overrides the default.

ENUMERATIONS

Name tokens are open ended. The format of values of NMTOKEN and NMTOKENS are restricted by name rules; otherwise, the set of permissible values are open. In many cases, we have a small set of character string values that we want to be permitted, such as YES or NO. These are the useful enumerations for decision-making.

The enumeration attribute is declared by placing a group of values where the type keyword appears. The group consists of parentheses enclosing the permitted values separated by the pipe symbol (|). The values are not enclosed by quotation marks, but like names as in XML, are case sensitive.

The instance of an attribute in the document must include only one of the permitted values as it appears in the attribute declaration. Like any other attribute value, the enumerated value should be enclosed by quotation marks.

```
<!ATTLIST Employee
manager (yes|no) #REQUIRED>
```

```
<!ATTLIST ClassifiedDoc
security_level (unclassified | secret | Top_secret) #REQUIRED>
```

In the first case, only the values YES and NO are allowed. YES, NO, and MAYBE will all be rejected as invalid. It is important to respect case sensitivity, as it is to emphasize the values provided in the enumeration declaration. When composing an enumeration for values that may be manually entered by a user, all the variations produced by modifying the case of the values must be considered.

DECLARING ATTRIBUTES

Attributes are declared using the <!ATTLIST > declaration. The syntax is shown below.

```
<!ATTLIST ElementName
AttributeName AttributeType State DefaultValue?>
```

ElementName is the name of the element taking the attributes.

AttributeName is the name of the attribute.

AttributeType is the type of data that the attribute value may hold. Although there are many types, the most common are CDATA (unparsed character data) and ID (a unique identifier). A list of options can also be given for the attribute type.

DefaultValue is the value of the attribute if it is not included in the element.

State can be one of three values: #REQUIRED, #FIXED (set value), and #IMPLIED (optional).

The beatle element has two possible attributes: link, which is optional and may contain any valid XML text, and real, which defaults to yes if it is not included.

```
<!ATTLIST beatle
 link CDATA #IMPLIED
 real (yes|no) "yes">
```

CONDITIONAL SECTIONS

Conditional sections are those statements that are parsed by the compiler only if certain conditions are met. But in DTDs, this feature is restricted; there is no conditional expression to be evaluated at runtime. DTDs include conditional sections that instruct the parser to include or ignore a section of declarations. These are useful for controlling blocks of declarations in a DTD. The conditional sections are, however, not allowed in the internal subset of the DTD.

The declaration of conditional sections consists of exclamation mark, square left bracket, and a keyword followed by a block of declarations delimited by square brackets. If the keyword is INCLUDE, the declarations in the block are considered a part of the DTD for validation. On the other hand, the DTD declarations in the block are read but passed by the parser if the keyword is IGNORE.

LIMITATIONS OF DTDS

DTDs have propelled XML through its early adoption phase. However, they suffer from a few limitations. They use a syntax all of their own, distinct from that of document instances. Importantly, it would be beneficial if XML parsers could give an application easy access to the declarations in DTDs they process. We cannot use parsers to build dynamic DTDs.

DTDs are closed constructs. The rules of an XML are wholly contained in the DTD. The DTD contains only the vocabulary and nothing else. There is no simple and clear way to promote extensibility in DTDs.

DTDs also lack datatype information. The only tool that is provided is the notation. This does little to allow us define our own types based on existing types.

DESIGNING XML DOCUMENTS

While discussing data flow models, we saw that there are two kinds of data in the system, data stores and message flows. XML is useful for both kinds of data, but the design considerations are rather different. One is the XML for messages, and one is the XML for persistent data.

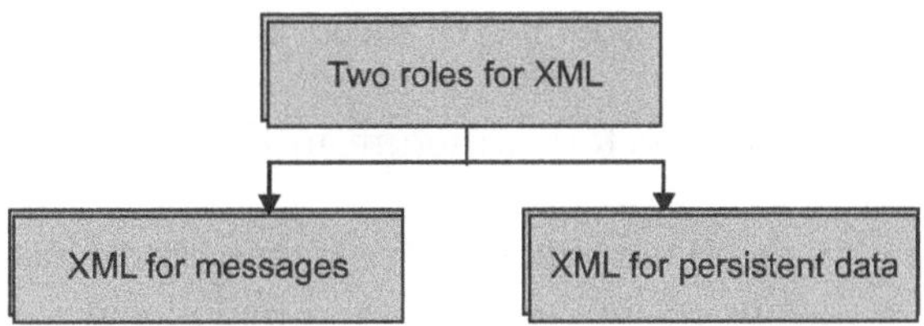

FIGURE 3.1 Data flow models for XML roles

XML FOR MESSAGES

Using XML for messages in systems poses fewer design problems than it does for persistent data.

This is mainly because each message is fairly self-contained, and the question of what to include in a message usually falls out naturally from the process model. The term *message* is usually used in a very general sense, which might be an EDI-style message sent between organizations to represent a transaction.

There are some general rules that are to be applied to all XML messages whatever their precise role might be. The design must reflect the information and not the intended use. This means that the use of the information may change over time, whereas the information content is more likely to remain stable. This applies particularly to presentation details.

The design must foresee change. The design of XML itself gives an advantage to this area, by avoiding traditional drawbacks such as fixed sized fields and fixed column ordering. But the document designer also has the responsibility to structure information in a way that foresees change.

XML FOR PERSISTENT DATA

The dynamic information model determines the design of messages. By contrast, for persistent data, it is the static model that is important.

The first thing that is to be decided is the vastness of the document. The most difficult part of the design is to decide what the granularity of data should be and what needs to get into the document. There are some applications where it makes sense to have a single XML document run into gigabytes of data. In such a case, it will be necessary to parse the whole document, which might take hours. On the opposite extreme, having a large number of documents is usually not ideal either.

When document XML persistent data is used, finding information is always a two-part operation. First, find the right document, then the facts interested in the information. To locate the right document, there are four options.

First, use the directory structure in the operating system to locate the documents.

Second, index the documents from each other, like in a traditional Website where documents are always found by following links, but typically in a more structured manner.

Third, index the documents from a relational database. In this case, we have the choice of holding the XML documents in files referenced from the database or holding them in the database itself.

Fourth, index the documents using a free-text search engine. A large number of search engines offer native support for XML.

Another option would be to use the XML server. An XML server not only holds the XML data in a raw unparsed form, but in the form of a persistent DOM, that is, it stores the nodes of the Document Object Model as objects in an object database.

MAPPING THE INFORMATION MODEL TO XML

This basically deals with how to map the different parts of the information model to an XML document structure. One of the ways is through representation of object types. Generally, an object type in the information model will translate into an element type in the XML structure. We can use the name of the object type as the element name or abbreviate it.

Most people use short names as their elements not to save space, but because XML seems to be more readable that way, and perhaps to avoid the tags distracting too much from the content. The advantage of using a specific type is that the DTD can define more precisely exactly attributes and child elements are associated with this element.

Nested elements in the XML document structure can used to represent some of the relationships in the model. The obvious ones to represent this way are the "contains" relationships.

There are several ways to represent a link from one element to another in XML. We can use ID, IDREF attributes, and Xpointer references that are equivalent to the HREF tag in HTML. We can also use application-defined primary keys and foreign keys in XML documents.

All the three approaches have their own merit. The main advantage of using ID, IDREF is that the validation is done by the XML parser.

Xpointer references are much more flexible than ID, IDREF, but they are not yet fully standardized.

The option of handling relationships through primary and foreign key is a perfectly viable approach, but the XML parser does not give any help in this matter.

When we have identified a property in the information model, a dilemma arises whether we represent it in the XML document using an XML attribute or using a nested element. In this case, there are no rules and we are free to choose the way we want either using an attribute or using a nested element. The table gives the pros and cons of each approach.

Table 3.10 Pros and Cons of Using an Attribute or Using a Nested Element

	Advantages	Disadvantages
XML Attributes	DTD can constrain the values; useful when there is a small set of allowed values, such as "yes" or "no."	Simple string values. No support for metadata (or attributes of attributes).
	DTD can define a default value	Unordered
	ID and IDREF Validation	
	Lower source overhead (makes a difference when sending gigabytes of data over the network)	
	White space normalization available for certain data types that save application some parsing effort	
	Easier to process DOM and SAX interfaces	
Child elements	Support arbitrarily complex values and repeating values	Slightly higher space usage. More complex programming
	Ordered	
	Support "attributes of attributes"	
	Extensible when data model changes	

To represent the properties of an object using elements or attributes, we have to make a decision on how to encode their values. Some of the common situations that are encountered are quantities such as height, width, and weight, Yes/No values, dates and times, property names, and binary data.

A DOCUMENT TYPE DECLARATION

The Document Type Declaration (or DOCTYPE Declaration) has three roles.

- It specifies the name of the document element.
- It may point to an external Document Type Definition (DTD).
- It may contain an internal DTD.

The DOCTYPE Declaration shown below simply states that the document element of the XML document is beatles.

```
<!DOCTYPE beatles>
```

If a DOCTYPE Declaration points to an external DTD, it must either specify that the DTD is on the same system as the XML document itself or that it is in some public location. To do so, it uses the keywords SYSTEM and PUBLIC. It then points to the location of the DTD using a relative Uniform Resource Indicator (URI) or an absolute URI. Here are a couple of examples.

Syntax

```
<!--DTD is on the same system as the XML document-->
<!DOCTYPE beatles SYSTEM "dtds/beatles.dtd">
```

Syntax

```
<!--DTD is publicly available-->
<!DOCTYPE beatles PUBLIC "-//Webucator//DTD Beatles 1.0//EN"
"http://www.webucator.com/beatles/DTD/beatles.dtd">
```

As shown in the second declaration above, public identifiers are divided into three parts:

- An organization (e.g., Webucator)
- A name for the DTD (e.g., Beatles 1.0)
- A language (e.g., EN for English)

ELEMENTS

Every XML document must have at least one element, called the document element. The document element usually contains other elements, which contain other elements, and so on. Elements are denoted with tags. Let's look again at the Paul.xml.

```
Code Sample: XMLBasics/Demos/Paul.xml
<?xml version="1.0"?>
<person>
 <name>
 <firstname>Paul</firstname>
 <lastname>McCartney</lastname>
 </name>
 <job>Singer</job>
 <gender>Male</gender>
</person>
```

The document element is person. It contains three elements: name, job, and gender. Further, the name element contains two elements of its own: firstname and lastname. As you can see, XML elements are denoted with tags, just as in HTML. Elements that are nested within another element are said to be children of that element.

EMPTY ELEMENTS

Not all elements contain other elements or text. For example, in XHTML, there is an img element that is used to display an image. It does not contain any text or elements within it, so it is called an empty element. In XML, empty elements must be closed, but they do not require a separate close tag. Instead, they can be closed with a forward slash at the end of the open tag as shown below.

```
<img src="images/paul.jpg"/>
```

The above code is identical in function to the code below.

```
<img src="images/paul.jpg"></img>
```

ATTRIBUTES

XML elements can be further defined with attributes, which appear inside of the element's open tag as shown below.

Syntax

```
<name title="Sir">
 <firstname>Paul</firstname>
```

```
 <lastname>McCartney</lastname>
</name>
```

CDATA

Sometimes it is necessary to include sections in an XML document that should not be parsed by the XML parser. These sections might contain content that will confuse the XML parser, perhaps because it contains content that appears to be XML, but is not meant to be interpreted as XML. Such content must be nested in CDATA sections. The syntax for CDATA sections is shown below.

Syntax

```
<![CDATA[
```

This section will not get parsed by the XML parser.

```
]]>
```

WHITE SPACE

In XML data, there are only four white space characters.

- Tab
- Line feed
- Carriage return
- Single space

There are several important rules to remember with regards to white space in XML.

White space within the content of an element is significant; that is, the XML processor will pass these characters to the application or user agent.

White space in attributes is normalized; that is, neighboring white spaces are condensed to a single space. White space in between elements is ignored.

```
xml:space Attribute
```

The xml:space attribute is a special attribute in XML. It can only take one of two values: default and preserve. This attribute instructs the application how to treat white space within the content of the element. Note that the application is not required to respect this instruction.

SPECIAL CHARACTERS

There are five special characters that can not be included in XML documents. These characters are replaced with predefined entity references as shown in the table below.

Table 3.11 List of Special Characters

Special Characters	
Character	**Entity Reference**
<	<
>	>
&	&
"	"
'	'

QUESTIONS FOR DISCUSSION

1. What is DTD?
2. How do we declare DTD?
3. Give the main reasons to use DTD.
4. How you define building blocks in an XML document?
5. How you define DTD elements?
6. How you define attributes in DTD?
7. How we can store data in both child elements and attributes?
8. How you define entities in DTD?
9. How is validation performed in DTD?
10. What are the differences between DTDs and schema?
11. What is a simple element?
12. What is a complex element?

13. What is the relevance of the Element Form Default attribute in the schema?
14. What is the XML parser?
15. Give some examples of XML DTDs or schemas that you have worked with.
16. When constructing an XML DTD, how do you create an external entity reference in an attribute value?
17. Can you use an attribute default in a DTD to declare an XML namespace?
18. Do the default values of xmlns attributes declared in the DTD apply to the DTD?
19. Does the scope of an XML namespace declaration ever include the DTD?
20. Can you use XML namespaces in DTDs?
21. Do XML namespace declarations apply to DTDs?
22. Can you use qualified names in DTDs?
23. What are the limitations of DTD?
24. Give some examples of XML DTDs or schemas.
25. Using dynamic DOCTYPE generation, we want to generate an XML document using JAXP parsers. We want to include a DOCTYPE tag that references a DTD. How is this accomplished?
26. Can you use a arbitrary defined DTD to generate all possible XML templates?
27. Defining SQL statements in the DTD: How can we declare XML embedded SQL statements in the DTD?

CHAPTER 4

NAMESPACES

NAMESPACES

A namespace is a collection of names that is identified by a Uniform Resource Identifier (URI). Namespaces is a methodology for creating universally unique names in an XML document by identifying element names with a unique external resource.

Namespaces help XML vocabulary designers to break complex problems into smaller pieces. Namespaces mix multiple vocabularies as needed to fully describe a problem in a single XML document.

A URI is a unique name for resource that resides on a network. A Uniform Resource Locator (URL) locates the resource using an access protocol and network location.

Namespaces are used to group elements and attributes that relate to each other in some special way. Namespaces are held in a unique URI. Note that, although it is possible that an XML schema is kept at this URI, it is not required. This can be a bit confusing. It is important to understand that a namespace is a set of rules that can be enforced by an application in whatever way the application wishes.

It is unlikely that these editors ever visit the URI that holds the XHTML namespace. Instead, these applications have built-in functionality to support the namespace. The main reason a URI is used is to provide a unique variable name to hold the namespace. Namespace authors should use URIs that they own to prevent conflicts with each other.

PURPOSE OF NAMESPACES

As described above, one purpose of namespaces is to provide a unique identifier for a group of elements and attribute declarations.

Another purpose is to allow instance documents to be made up of a combination of such groups without having name conflicts. For example, we could hold the book schema and song schema we have worked on in separate namespaces. Now suppose you wanted to use both schemas to create a book of songs. Both songs and books can have Title elements. This could potentially be a source of confusion as an application might not understand which Title element to apply. By specifying which namespace the Title elements come from, the confusion is removed.

DECLARING A NAMESPACE

Two XML documents might contain elements with the same names but different meanings. If both the documents need to be used in a single environment, there will be confusion about the overlapping elements. For example, consider the following XML code.

```
<CUSTOMER>
     <NAME>Shashi</NAME>
</CUSTOMER>
<BOOK>
      <NAME>Yashasvi</Name>
</BOOK>
<BILL>
   <CUSTOMER>
        <NAME>Shashi</NAME>
   </CUSTOMER>
   <BOOK>
        <NAME>Yashasvi</NAME>
   </BOOK>
</BILL>
```

Here, the CUSTOMER element and the BOOK element have NAME element, but the NAME element has different meanings in each case. If these elements are combined into a single document as shown in the following code, the NAME elements will lose their meaning.

This is a very big problem and the solution is XML namespaces, which offer a way to create names that remain unique no matter where the elements are used.

A namespace can be qualified or unqualified. It does us no good to declare a namespace if we can't tie it to a specific name we want to use. This is done through the use of qualified names.

The two parts of qualified name are the namespace and local part. The namespace name is a URI and selects the namespace. The local part is the local document element or attribute name. To use a namespace in an XML document, a namespace declaration in the prolog of the document must be included. A namespace prefix can also be included in the declaration. The prefix with a colon can be attached to local part to associate the local part with the namespace name. The following code declares two namespaces with prefixes and then uses those namespaces in the document.

Here cust:NAME and book:NAME are fully qualified names and they are unique no matter where they are used.

```
<xmlns version = "1 . 0"?>
<xmlns : namespace ns="http://books/schema/ns" prefix = "books"?>
<xmlns : namespace ns="http://customer/schema/ns" prefix = "cust"?>
<BILL>
  <CUSTOMER>
        <cust:NAME>Shashi</cust:NAME>
  </CUSTOMER>
  <BOOK>
        <books:NAME>Yashasvi</books:NAME>
  </BOOK>
</BILL>
```

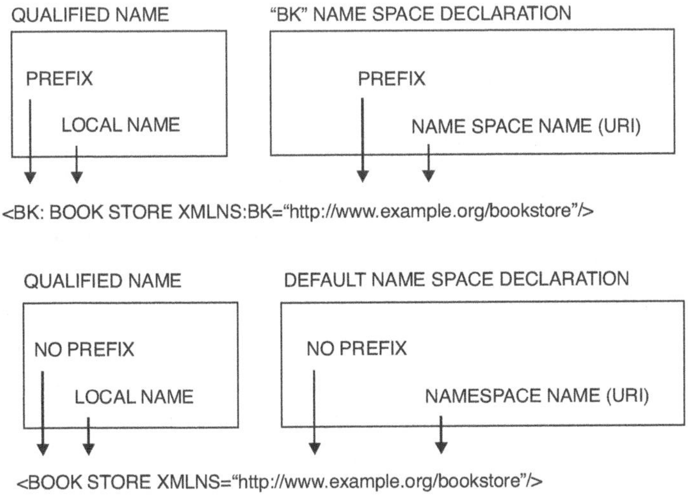

QUALIFIED NAME

PREFIX

LOCAL NAME

"BK" NAME SPACE DECLARATION

PREFIX

NAME SPACE NAME (URI)

<BK: BOOK STORE XMLNS:BK="http://www.example.org/bookstore"/>

QUALIFIED NAME

NO PREFIX

LOCAL NAME

DEFAULT NAME SPACE DECLARATION

NO PREFIX

NAMESPACE NAME (URI)

<BOOK STORE XMLNS="http://www.example.org/bookstore"/>

FIGURE 4.1 Namespace declaration representation

One of our prime motivations for using namespaces is to be able to mix name from different sources. It might be useful for you to be able to provide an alias you could use throughout a document that would refer to the declaration. You do this by appending a colon and your alias to xmlns.

SCOPE

Namespace declarations have scope in the same way that variable declarations do in the programming. This is important because it is not always the case that namespaces are declared at the beginning as XML document; they can be included within a later section of the document.

A name can refer to a namespace only if it is used within the scope of the namespace declaration. However, we will also need to mix namespaces where elements would otherwise inherit the scope of a namespace, so there are two ways in which scope can be declared. It can be either *default* or *qualified.*

To use namespaces, we need to prefix every name in a document; this could be tiresome when we have many namespaces in the document.

By introducing the concept of name scope to our tool set, we can dispense with a lot of prefixes. If we define a default namespace, all unqualified names within the scope of the declaration are presumed to belong to that default. So, if you declare a default namespace in the root element, it is treated as default namespace for the whole document, and can only be overridden by more specific namespace declared within the document.

QUALIFIED

Though we clearly separate the various namespaces, sometimes we need to sprinkle names from foreign namespaces through a document. For this, a finer degree of granularity is needed. Hence, we can make use of qualified names instead of declaring namespaces all over the space. The namespaces are to be declared at the beginning of the document and then qualified at the point of use.

```
<Measurements xmlns="urn:mydecs-science-measurements">
     xmlns:units="urn:mydecs-science-unitsofmeasure"
     xmlns:prop="urn:mydecs-science-thingsmeasured"
    <OutsideAir units:units="Fahrenheit">86</OutsideAir>
    <FuelTank>
```

```
        <prop:Volume units:units="liters">120</prop:Volume>
        <prop:Temperature units:units="Celsius">20</prop:Temperature>
    </FuelTank>
</Measurements>
```

In the root element, Measurements, we have declared three namespaces. The default takes care of the elements <OutsideAir>, <FuelTank>, and <Measurements>. However, we need to qualify some readings with units of measure, which we have done with the units namespace and the attribute units: units drawn from that namespace. Finally, we need to differentiate between some types of measurements, prop:Volume and prop:Temperature.

XML NAMESPACE

In XML, a namespace is used to prevent any conflicts with element names.

Because XML allows you to create your own element names, there's always the possibility of naming an element exactly the same as one in another XML document.

This might be OK if you never use both documents together. But what if you need to combine the content of both documents? You would have a name conflict. You would have two different elements, with different purposes, both with the same name.

Imagine we have an XML document containing a list of books.

```
<books>
  <book>
    <title>XML Programming</title>
    <author>Shashi Banzal</author>
  </book>
  ...
</books>
```

And imagine we want to combine it with the following HTML page:

```
<html>
  <head>
    <title>Cool Books</title>
</head>
<body>
<p>Here's a list of cool books...</p>
```

```
(XML content goes here)
 </body>
</html>
```

We will encounter a problem if we try to combine the above documents. This is because they both have an element called title. One is the title of the book, and the other is the title of the HTML page.

EXAMPLE NAMESPACE

Using the above example, we could change the XML document to look something like this:

```
<bk:books xmlns:bk="http://somebooksite.com/book_spec">
  <bk:book>
    <bk:title>XML Programming</bk:title>
    <bk:author>Shashi Banzal</bk:author>
  </bk:book>
  ...
</bk:books>
```

We have added the xmlns:{prefix} attribute to the root element. We have assigned this attribute a unique value. This unique value is usually in the form of a URI. This defines the namespace.

And, now that the namespace has been defined, we have added a bk prefix to our element names.

Now, when we combine the two documents, the XML processor will see two different element names: bk:title (from the XML document) and title (from the HTML document).

If you have defined your tags and attributes in a DTD, you need to update your DTD in order to make the new element names legal.

XML LOCAL NAMESPACE

In the previous lesson, we created a namespace to avoid a name conflict between the elements of two documents we wanted to combine. When we defined the namespace, we defined it against the root element. This meant that the namespace was to be used for the whole document, and we prefixed all child elements with the same namespace.

You can also define namespaces against a child node. This way, you could use multiple namespaces within the same document, if required.

EXAMPLE LOCAL NAMESPACE

Here, we apply the namespace against the title element only:

```
<books>
  <book>
    <bk:title xmlns:bk="http://somebooksite.com/book_spec">
      XML Programming
    </bk:title>
    <author>Shashi Banzal</author>
  </book>
  ...
</books>
```

MULTIPLE NAMESPACES

You could also have multiple namespaces within your XML document. For example, you could define one namespace against the root element, and another against a child element.

Example

```
<bk:books xmlns:bk="http://somebooksite.com/book_spec">
  <bk:book>
    <bk:title>XML Programming</bk:title>
    <bk:author>Shashi Banzal</bk:author>
    <pub:name xmlns:pub="http://somepublishingsite.com/spec">
      Sid Harta Publishers
    </pub:name>
    <pub:email>author@shashi .com.au</pub:email>
  </bk:book>
  ...
</bk:books>
```

XML DEFAULT NAMESPACE

The namespaces we created in the previous two lessons involved applying a prefix. We applied the prefix when we defined the namespace, and we applied a prefix to each element that referred to the namespace.

You can also use what is known as a default namespace within your XML documents. The only difference between a default namespace and the namespaces we covered in the previous two lessons is a default namespace is one where you don't apply a prefix.

You can also define namespaces against a child node. This way, you could use multiple namespaces within the same document if required.

Here, we define the namespace without a prefix:

```
<books xmlns="http://somebooksite.com/book_spec">
  <book>
    <title>XML Programming</title>
    <author>Shashi Banzal</author>
  </book>
  ...
</books>
```

When you define the namespace without a prefix, all descendant elements are assumed to belong to that namespace, unless specified otherwise (i.e., with a local namespace).

UNDERSTANDING NAMESPACES

In XML, when different markup languages have elements and attributes that are named the same, the XML problem is much more severe, however, because XML applications aren't smart enough to judge the difference between the context of elements from different markup languages that share the same name. For example, a tag named <goal> would have a very different meaning in a sports markup language than the same tag in a markup language for a daily planner. If you ever used these two markup languages within the same application, it would be very important for the application to know when you're talking about a goal in hockey and when you're talking about a personal goal. The responsibility falls on the XML developer to ensure that uniqueness abounds when it comes to the elements and attributes used in documents.

Fortunately, namespaces make it possible to enforce such uniqueness without too much of a hassle.

A namespace is a collection of element and attribute names that can be used in an XML document. To draw a comparison between an XML namespace and the real world, if you considered the first names of all the people in your immediate family, they would belong to a namespace that encompasses your last name. When I call my brother by his first name, Steve, it is implied that his last name is Morrison because he is within the Morrison namespace. XML namespaces are similar because they represent groups of names for related elements and attributes. Most of the time an individual namespace corresponds directly to a custom markup language, but that doesn't necessarily have to be the case. You also know that namespaces aren't a strict requirement of XML documents, as you haven't really used them throughout the book thus far.

The purpose of namespaces is to eliminate name conflicts between elements and attributes. To better understand how this type of name clash might occur in your own XML documents, consider an XML document that contains information about a video and music collection. You might use a custom markup language unique to each type of information (video and music), which means that each language would have its own elements and attributes. However, you are using both languages within the context of a single XML document, which is where the potential for problems arises. If both markup languages include an element named "title" that represents the title of a video or music compilation, there is no way for an XML application to know which language you intended to use for the element. The solution to this problem is to assign a namespace to each of the markup languages, which will then provide a clear distinction between the elements and attributes of each language when they are used.

"Defining Data with DTD Schemas" is used to demonstrate how an XML document consists of a hierarchical tree of elements. Each node in the tree of an XML document has its own scope, and can therefore have its own namespace.

Scope is important to namespaces because it's possible to use a namespace within a given scope, which means it affects only elements and attributes beneath a particular node. Contrast this with a namespace that has global scope, which means the namespace applies to the entire document.

NAMING NAMESPACES

The whole point of namespaces is that they provide a means of establishing unique identifiers for elements and attributes. It is therefore imperative that each and every namespace have a unique name. Obviously, there would be no way to enforce this rule if everyone was allowed to make up their own names, so a clever naming scheme was established that tied namespaces to URIs. URIs usually reference physical resources on the Internet and are guaranteed to be unique. So, a namespace is essentially the name of a URI. For example, consider the Website *http://www.michaelmorrison.com*. To help guarantee name uniqueness in any XML documents that created, we could associate the documents with the namespace:

```
<mediacollection xmlns:mov="http://www.michaelmorrison.com/ns/movies">
```

The ns in the namespace name *http://www.michaelmorrison.com/ns/movies* stands for "namespace" and is often used in URL namespace names. It isn't a necessity, but it's not a bad idea in terms of being able to quickly identify namespaces. If you don't want to use a URI as the basis for a namespace name, you could also use the URN (Universal Resource Name) of a Web resource to guarantee uniqueness. URNs are slightly different from URLs and define a unique location-independent name for a resource that maps to one or more URLs. The following is an example of using a URN to specify a namespace for a Website:

```
<mediacollection xmlns:mov="urn:michaelmorrison.com:ns:movies">
```

Keep in mind that a namespace doesn't actually point to a physical resource, even if its URI does. In other words, the only reason namespaces are named after URIs is because URIs are guaranteed to be unique. They could just as easily be named after social security numbers. This means that within a domain name, you can create URIs that don't actually reference physical resources.

DECLARING AND USING NAMESPACES

Namespaces are associated with documents by way of elements, which means that you declare a namespace for a particular element with the scope you want for the namespace. More specifically, you use a namespace declaration, which looks a lot like an attribute of the element. In many cases, you want a namespace to apply to an entire document, which means you'll use the namespace declaration with the root element. A namespace declaration takes the following form:

```
xmlns:Prefix="NameSpace"
```

The xmlns attribute is what notifies an XML processor that a namespace is being declared. The NameSpace portion of the namespace declaration is where the namespace itself is identified. This portion of the declaration identifies a URI that guarantees the uniqueness for elements and attributes used within the scope of the namespace declaration.

The Prefix part of the namespace declaration allows you to set a prefix that will serve as a shorthand reference for the namespace throughout the scope of the element in which the namespace is declared. The prefix of a namespace is optional and ultimately depends on whether you want to use qualified or unqualified element and attribute names throughout a document. A qualified name includes the Prefix portion of the namespace declaration and consists of two parts: the prefix and the local portion of the name. Examples of qualified names include mov:title, mov:director, and mov:rating. To use qualified names, you must provide Prefix in the namespace declaration. The following is a simple example of a qualified name:

```
<mov:title>Raising Arizona</mov:title>
```

Declaring a namespace in an XML document is a little like declaring a variable in a programming language. The declared namespace is available for use, but doesn't actually enter the picture until you specify an element with a qualified name.

In this example, the prefix is mov and the local portion of the name is title. Unqualified names don't include a prefix and are either associated with a default namespace or no namespace at all. The prefix of the namespace declaration isn't required when declaring a default namespace. Examples of unqualified names are title, director, and rating. Unqualified names in a document look no different than if you weren't using namespaces at all. The following code shows how the movie example would be coded using unqualified names:

```
<title>Raising Arizona</title>
```

Notice that in this example, the <title> and </title> tags are used so that you would never know a namespace was involved. In this case, you are either assuming a default namespace is in use or that there is no namespace at all.

It's important to clarify why you would use qualified or unqualified names because the decision to use one or the other determines the manner in which you declare a namespace. There are two different approaches to declaring namespaces:

- Default declaration: The namespace is declared without a prefix; all element and attribute names within its scope are referenced using unqualified names and are assumed to be in the namespace.
- Explicit declaration: The namespace is declared with a prefix; all element and attribute names associated with the namespace must use the prefix as part of their qualified names or else they are not considered part of the namespace.

  The next sections dig a little deeper into these namespace declarations.

DEFAULT NAMESPACES

Default namespaces represent the simpler of the two approaches to namespace declaration. A default namespace declaration is useful when you want to apply a namespace to an entire document or section of a document. When declaring a default namespace, you don't use a prefix with the xmlns attribute. Instead, elements are specified with unqualified names and are therefore assumed to be part of the default namespace. In other words, a default namespace declaration applies to all unqualified elements within the scope in which the namespace is declared. The following is an example of a default namespace declaration for a movie collection document:

```
<mediacollection xmlns="http://www.michaelmorrison.com/ns/movies">
  <movie type="comedy" rating="PG-13" review="5" year="1987">
    <title>Raising Arizona</title>
    <comments>A classic one-of-a-kind screwball love story.</comments>
  </movie>
    <movie type="comedy" rating="R" review="5" year="1988">
    <title>Midnight Run</title>
    <comments>The quintessential road comedy.</comments>
  </movie>
</mediacollection>
```

In this example, the *http://www.michaelmorrison.com/ns/movies* namespace is declared as the default namespace for the movie document. This means that all the unqualified elements in the document (mediacollection, movie, title, and so on) are assumed to be part of the namespace. A default namespace can also be set for any other element in a document, in which case it applies only to that element and its children. For example, you could set a namespace for one of the title elements, which would override the default namespace that is set in the mediacollection element. The following is an example of how this is done:

```
<mediacollection xmlns="http://www.michaelmorrison.com/ns/movies">
  <movie type="comedy" rating="PG-13" review="5" year="1987">
    <title>Raising Arizona</title>
    <comments>A classic one-of-a-kind screwball love story.</comments>
  </movie>
  <movie type="comedy" rating="R" review="5" year="1988">
    <title xmlns="http://www.michaelmorrison.com/ns/title">Midnight Run</title>
    <comments>The quintessential road comedy.</comments>
  </movie>
</mediacollection>
```

Notice in the title element for the second movie element that a different namespace is specified. This namespace applies only to the title element and overrides the namespace declared in the mediacollection element. Although this admittedly simple example doesn't necessarily make a good argument for why you would override a namespace, it can be a bigger issue in documents where you mix different XML languages.

EXPLICIT NAMESPACES

An explicit namespace is useful whenever you want exacting control over the elements and attributes that are associated with a namespace. This is often necessary in documents that rely on multiple schemas because there is a chance of having a name clash between elements and attributes defined in the two schemas. Explicit namespace declarations require a prefix that is used to distinguish elements and attributes that belong to the namespace being declared. The prefix in an explicit declaration is used as a shorthand notation for the namespace throughout the scope in which the namespace is declared. More specifically, the prefix is paired with the local element or attribute name to form a qualified name of the form Prefix:Local. The following is the movie example with qualified element and attribute names:

```
<mediacollection xmlns:mov="http://www.michaelmorrison.com/ns/movies">
  <mov:movie mov:type="comedy" mov:rating="PG-13" mov:review="5" mov:year="1987">
    <mov:title>Raising Arizona</mov:title>
    <mov:comments>A classic one-of-a-kind screwball love story.</mov:comments>
```

```
  </mov:movie>
  <mov:movie mov:type="comedy" mov:rating="R" mov:review="5" mov:year="1988">
    <mov:title>Midnight Run</mov:title>
    <mov:comments>The quintessential road comedy.</mov:comments>
  </mov:movie>
</mediacollection>
```

The namespace in this code is explicitly declared by the shorthand name mov in the namespace declaration; this is evident in the fact that the name mov is specified after the xmlns keyword. Once the namespace is declared, you can use it with any element and attribute names that belong in the namespace, which in this case is all of them.

Listing 4.1: The Media Collection Example Document

```
<?xml version="1.0"?>

<mediacollection xmlns:mov="http://www.michaelmorrison.com/ns/movies"
  xmlns:mus="http://www.michaelmorrison.com/ns/music">
  <mov:movie mov:type="comedy" mov:rating="PG-13" mov:review="5"
    mov:year="1987">
    <mov:title>Raising Arizona</mov:title>
    <mov:comments>A classic one-of-a-kind screwball love story.
    </mov:comments>
  </mov:movie>

  <mov:movie mov:type="comedy" mov:rating="R" mov:review="5" mov:year="1988">
    <mov:title>Midnight Run</mov:title>
    <mov:comments>The quintessential road comedy.</mov:comments>
  </mov:movie>

  <mus:music mus:type="indy" mus:review="5" mus:year="1990">
    <mus:title>Cake</mus:title>
    <mus:artist>The Trash Can Sinatras</mus:artist>
    <mus:label>Polygram Records</mus:label>
    <mus:comments>Excellent acoustical instruments and extremely witty
      lyrics.</mus:comments>
  </mus:music>

  <mus:music mus:type="rock" mus:review="5" mus:year="1991">
```

```
26:       <mus:title>Travelers and Thieves</mus:title>
27:       <mus:artist>Blues Traveler</mus:artist>
28:       <mus:label>A&amp;M Records</mus:label>
29:       <mus:comments>The best Blues Traveler recording, period.</mus:comments>
30:     </mus:music>
31: </mediacollection>
```

In this code, the mov and mus namespaces (lines 3 and 4) are explicitly declared in order to correctly identify the elements and attributes for each type of media. Notice that without these explicit namespaces it would be difficult for an XML processor to tell the difference between the title and comments elements because they are used in both movie and music entries.

Just to help hammer home the distinction between default and explicit namespace declarations, let's take a look at one more example. This time, the media collection declares the movie namespace as the default namespace and then explicitly declares the music namespace using the mus prefix. The end result is that the movie elements and attributes don't require a prefix when referenced, whereas the music elements and attributes do.

Listing 4.2: A Different Version of the Media Collection Example Document That Declares the Movie Namespace as a Default Namespace

```
<?xml version="1.0"?>

<mediacollection xmlns="http://www.michaelmorrison.com/ns/movies"
  xmlns:mus="http://www.michaelmorrison.com/ns/music">
  <movie type="comedy" rating="PG-13" review="5" year="1987">
    <title>Raising Arizona</title>
    <comments>A classic one-of-a-kind screwball love story.</comments>
  </movie>

  <movie type="comedy" rating="R" review="5" year="1988">
    <title>Midnight Run</title>
    <comments>The quintessential road comedy.</comments>
  </movie>

  <mus:music mus:type="indy" mus:review="5" mus:year="1990">
    <mus:title>Cake</mus:title>
    <mus:artist>The Trash Can Sinatras</mus:artist>
    <mus:label>Polygram Records</mus:label>
```

```
19:      <mus:comments>Excellent acoustical instruments and extremely witty
20:        lyrics.</mus:comments>
21:    </mus:music>
22:
23:    <mus:music mus:type="rock" mus:review="5" mus:year="1991">
24:      <mus:title>Travelers and Thieves</mus:title>
25:      <mus:artist>Blues Traveler</mus:artist>
26:      <mus:label>A&amp;M Records</mus:label>
27:     <mus:comments>The best Blues Traveler recording, period.</mus:comments>
28:    </mus:music>
29: </mediacollection>
```

The key to this code is the default namespace declaration, which is identified by the lone xmlns attribute (line 3); the xmlns:mus attribute explicitly declares the music namespace (line 4). When the xmlns attribute is used by itself with no associated prefix, it is declaring a default namespace, which in this case is the music namespace.

XML NAMESPACES

XML namespaces provide a method to avoid element name conflicts.

NAME CONFLICTS

In XML, element names are defined by the developer. This often results in a conflict when trying to mix XML documents from different XML applications. This XML carries HTML table information:

```
<table>
  <tr>
   <td>Apples</td>
   <td>Bananas</td>
  </tr>
</table>
```

This XML carries information about a table (a piece of furniture):

```
<table>
  <name>African Coffee Table</name>
```

```
  <width>80</width>
  <length>120</length>
</table>
```

If these XML fragments were added together, there would be a name conflict. Both contain a <table> element, but the elements have different content and meaning.

An XML parser will not know how to handle these differences.

SOLVING THE NAME CONFLICT USING A PREFIX

Name conflicts in XML can easily be avoided using a name prefix.

This XML carries information about an HTML table and a piece of furniture:

```
<h:table>
 <h:tr>
   <h:td>Apples</h:td>
   <h:td>Bananas</h:td>
 </h:tr>
</h:table>
<f:table>
  <f:name>African Coffee Table</f:name>
  <f:width>80</f:width>
  <f:length>120</f:length>
</f:table>
```

In the example above, there will be no conflict because the two <table> elements have different names.

Code Sample: Namespaces/Demos/Artist.xsd

```
<?xml version="1.0"?>
 <xs:schema targetNamespace="http://www.webucator.com/Artist"
 xmlns:xs="http://www.w3.org/2001/XMLSchema"
 xmlns="http://www.webucator.com/Artist">
 <xs:element name="Title" type="xs:string"/>
 <xs:element name="FirstName" type="xs:string"/>
 <xs:element name="LastName" type="xs:string"/>
 <xs:element name="Name">
   <xs:complexType>
```

```
      <xs:sequence>
       <xs:element ref="Title"/>
       <xs:element ref="FirstName"/>
       <xs:element ref="LastName"/>
      </xs:sequence>
     </xs:complexType>
   </xs:element>
   <xs:element name="Artist">
    <xs:complexType>
     <xs:sequence>
      <xs:element ref="Name"/>
     </xs:sequence>
     <xs:attribute name="BirthYear" type="xs:gYear" use="required"/>
    </xs:complexType>
   </xs:element>
  </xs:schema>
```

This schema would be invalid if the xmlns="http://www.webucator.com/Artist" attribute were removed. That's because the Name and Artist element declarations have child elements that reference elements declared in this schema. We can only reference elements that are declared globally in namespaces used in the document (as indicated by the xmlns attributes).

Instance documents of this XML schema would take the xmlns and xsi:schemaLocation attributes. Again, the xmlns attribute allows global elements declared in the specified namespace to be used in this instance. The xsi:schemaLocation attribute is used to point to the schema associated with a namespace. Its value is the namespace name and the path to the schema separated by a space.

Code Sample: Namespaces/Demos/MichaelJackson.xml

```
<?xml version="1.0"?>
<Artist BirthYear="1958"
 xmlns:xsi="http://www.w3.org/2001/XMLSchema-instance"
 xmlns="http://www.webucator.com/Artist"
 xsi:schemaLocation="http://www.webucator.com/Artist Artist.xsd">
 <Name>
  <Title>Mr.</Title>
  <FirstName>Michael</FirstName>
  <LastName>Jackson</LastName>
 </Name>
</Artist>
```

LOCALLY DECLARED ELEMENTS AND ATTRIBUTES

By default, locally declared elements and attributes in an instance document do not need to be qualified. This can be changed in the schema by including the elementFormDefault and attributeFormDefault attributes of the xs:schema element with the value of "qualified."

Code Sample: Namespaces/Demos/ArtistLocal.xsd

```
<?xml version="1.0"?>
<xs:schema targetNamespace="http://www.webucator.com/Artist"
 xmlns:xs="http://www.w3.org/2001/XMLSchema"
 xmlns="http://www.webucator.com/Artist"
 elementFormDefault="unqualified"
 attributeFormDefault="unqualified">
 <xs:element name="Artist">
  <xs:complexType>
   <xs:sequence>
    <xs:element name="Name">
     <xs:complexType>
      <xs:sequence>
       <xs:element name="Title" type="xs:string"/>
       <xs:element name="FirstName" type="xs:string"/>
       <xs:element name="LastName" type="xs:string"/>
      </xs:sequence>
     </xs:complexType>
    </xs:element>
   </xs:sequence>
   <xs:attribute name="BirthYear" type="xs:gYear" use="required"/>
  </xs:complexType>
 </xs:element>
</xs:schema>
```

Notice that the elementFormDefault and attributeFormDefault attributes are set to "unqualified." This is the default value, so the attributes could just have well been left out.

Code Sample: Namespaces/Demos/MichaelJacksonLocal.xml

```
<?xml version="1.0"?>
<art:Artist BirthYear="1958"
 xmlns:xsi="http://www.w3.org/2001/XMLSchema-instance"
```

```
xmlns:art="http://www.webucator.com/Artist"
xsi:schemaLocation="http://www.webucator.com/Artist ArtistLocal.xsd">
 <Name>
  <Title>Mr.</Title>
  <FirstName>Michael</FirstName>
  <LastName>Jackson</LastName>
 </Name>
</art:Artist>
```

When using unqualified locals, it is not valid to use a default namespace. The schema processor must know that these elements are locally declared within a specific namespace. If a default namespace were used, the schema processor would not be able to differentiate between locally declared and globally declared elements. Therefore, we use the art: prefix to qualify the Artist namespace.

If the elementFormDefault and attributeFormDefault attributes in the xs:schema element are set to “qualified” all locals must be qualified with a prefix.

Code Sample: Namespaces/Demos/ArtistLocalQualified.xsd

```
<?xml version="1.0"?>
<xs:schema xmlns:xs="http://www.w3.org/2001/XMLSchema"
     xmlns="http://www.webucator.com/Artist"
     targetNamespace="http://www.webucator.com/Artist"
     elementFormDefault="qualified"
     attributeFormDefault="qualified">
<xs:element name="Artist">
 <xs:complexType>
  <xs:sequence>
   <xs:element name="Name">
    <xs:complexType>
     <xs:sequence>
      <xs:element name="Title" type="xs:string"/>
      <xs:element name="FirstName" type="xs:string"/>
      <xs:element name="LastName" type="xs:string"/>
     </xs:sequence>
    </xs:complexType>
   </xs:element>
  </xs:sequence>
  <xs:attribute name="BirthYear" type="xs:gYear" use="required"/>
```

```
  </xs:complexType>
 </xs:element>
</xs:schema>
```

Code Sample: Namespaces/Demos/MichaelJacksonLocalQualified.xml

```
<?xml version="1.0"?>
<art:Artist art:BirthYear="1958"
 xmlns:xsi="http://www.w3.org/2001/XMLSchema-instance"
 xmlns:art="http://www.webucator.com/Artist"
 xsi:schemaLocation=
  "http://www.webucator.com/Artist ArtistLocalQualified.xsd">
 <art:Name>
  <art:Title>Mr.</art:Title>
  <art:FirstName>Michael</art:FirstName>
  <art:LastName>Jackson</art:LastName>
 </art:Name>
</art:Artist>
```

The result of qualifying all locals is that instance authors do not have to differentiate between local and global declarations. They simply prefix all elements and attributes with a qualifier. This has two major advantages over using unqualified locals.

Clarity - it is easy to tell which namespace each element belongs to.

Flexibility - the schema author can mix global and local declarations without worrying that the instance author will get confused. As both local and global declarations require prefixes, the instance author doesn't need to know how an element or attribute is declared.

Code Sample: Namespaces/Demos/XMLSchema-instance.xsd

```
<?xml version='1.0'?>
<xs:schema targetNamespace="http://www.w3.org/2001/XMLSchema-instance"
         xmlns:xs="http://www.w3.org/2001/XMLSchema">
   <xs:attribute name="nil"/>
 <xs:attribute name="type"/>
 <xs:attribute name="schemaLocation"/>
 <xs:attribute name="noNamespaceSchemaLocation"/>
</xs:schema>
```

By specifying that an XML document uses the XMLSchema-instance namespace, the instance author gets access to the four attributes declared above. We have already seen three of these attributes used.

- xsi:nil is used to specify that an element has no value.
- xsi:schemaLocation is used to specify the location of a schema for a particular namespace.
- xsi:noNamespaceSchemaLocation is used to specify the location of a schema when no namespace is used.
- xsi:type is infrequently used to specify that the element in the instance is of a different type than the one declared in the schema for that element.

USING MULTIPLE NAMESPACES

Often, it makes sense to use multiple namespaces for a single instance document. As an example, take a look at the following document.

Code Sample: Namespaces/Demos/TheGirlIsMine.xml

```
<?xml version="1.0"?>
<Song xmlns:xsi="http://www.w3.org/2001/XMLSchema-instance"
   xmlns="http://www.webucator.com/Song"
   xmlns:art="http://www.webucator.com/Artist"
   xsi:schemaLocation="http://www.webucator.com/SongSong.xsd
            http://www.webucator.com/Artist Artist.xsd">
 <Title>The Girl Is Mine</Title>
 <Year>1983</Year>
 <Artists>
  <art:Artist BirthYear="1958">
   <art:Name>
    <art:Title>Mr.</art:Title>
    <art:FirstName>Michael</art:FirstName>
    <art:LastName>Jackson</art:LastName>
   </art:Name>
  </art:Artist>
  <art:Artist BirthYear="1942">
   <art:Name>
    <art:Title>Mr.</art:Title>
    <art:FirstName>Paul</art:FirstName>
    <art:LastName>McCartney</art:LastName>
   </art:Name>
```

```
  </art:Artist>
 </Artists>
</Song>
```

The default namespace is the Song namespace. The Artist namespace is qualified with the art: prefix. Locally declared elements (there are none) and attributes (e.g., BirthYear) are unqualified.

Code Sample: Namespaces/Demos/Song.xsd

```
<?xml version="1.0"?>
<xs:schema xmlns:xs="http://www.w3.org/2001/XMLSchema"
     xmlns:art="http://www.webucator.com/Artist"
     xmlns="http://www.webucator.com/Song"
     targetNamespace="http://www.webucator.com/Song">
 <xs:import namespace="http://www.webucator.com/Artist"
  schemaLocation="Artist.xsd"/>
 <xs:element name="Title" type="xs:string"/>
 <xs:element name="Year" type="xs:gYear"/>
 <xs:element name="Artists">
  <xs:complexType>
   <xs:sequence>
    <xs:element ref="art:Artist" maxOccurs="unbounded"/>
   </xs:sequence>
  </xs:complexType>
 </xs:element>
 <xs:element name="Song">
  <xs:complexType>
   <xs:sequence>
    <xs:element ref="Title"/>
    <xs:element ref="Year"/>
    <xs:element ref="Artists"/>
   </xs:sequence>
  </xs:complexType>
 </xs:element>
</xs:schema>
```

By importing the Artist namespace with xs:import and specifying that elements in that namespace can be referenced with the xmlns:art attribute of xs:schema, elements and attributes in the Artist namespace are accessible to this schema.

If you are likely to be working with data-centric content (e.g., more structured data that maps to a database), you should build a schema for the transaction log described below.

A networking Website has a feature that allows people to make connections through other connections they have made in the past. A member can search the member list and on finding someone with whom (s)he would like to connect, (s)he can ask a mutual connection to pass on a message to that person.

UNIFORM RESOURCE IDENTIFIER (URI)

A Uniform Resource Identifier (URI) is a string of characters that identifies an Internet resource.

The most common URI is the Uniform Resource Locator (URL) which identifies an Internet domain address. Another, not so common type of URI, is the Universal Resource Name (URN).

DEFAULT NAMESPACES

Defining a default namespace for an element saves us from using prefixes in all the child elements. It has the following syntax:

```
xmlns="namespaceURI"
```

This XML carries HTML table information:

```
<table xmlns="http://www.w3.org/TR/html4/">
 <tr>
   <td>Apples</td>
   <td>Bananas</td>
 </tr>
</table>
```

This XML carries information about a piece of furniture:

```
<table xmlns="http://www.w3schools.com/furniture">
  <name>African Coffee Table</name>
  <width>80</width>
  <length>120</length>
</table>
```

NAMESPACES IN REAL USE

XSLT is an XML language that can be used to transform XML documents into other formats, like HTML.

In the XSLT document below, you can see that most of the tags are HTML tags.

The tags that are not HTML tags have the prefix xsl, identified by the namespace xmlns:xsl="http://www.w3.org/1999/XSL/Transform":

```
<?xml version="1.0" encoding="ISO-8859-1"?>
<xsl:stylesheet version="1.0"
xmlns:xsl="http://www.w3.org/1999/XSL/Transform">
<xsl:template match="/">
<html>
<body>
  <h2>My CD Collection</h2>
  <table border="1">
    <tr>
     <th align="left">Title</th>
       <th align="left">Artist</th>
</tr>
<xsl:for-each select="catalog/cd">
<tr>
<td><xsl:value-of select="title"/></td>
  <td><xsl:value-of select="artist"/></td>
  </tr>
</xsl:for-each>
</table>
  </body>
  </html>
</xsl:template>
</xsl:stylesheet>
```

QUESTIONS FOR DISCUSSION

1. What are namespaces? Why are they important?
2. What is an XML namespace name?

3. What software is needed to process XML Namespaces?
4. What are the ways to use namespaces?
5. Can you give an executive summary of what XML namespaces are?
6. Can you give an executive summary of what XML namespaces are not?
7. What is a traditional namespace?
8. What is the relationship between different traditional namespaces?
9. What are traditional namespaces used for?
10. What is the purpose of XML namespaces?
11. What are some examples of how XML namespaces are used?
12. Do XML namespaces recommendation define anything except a two-part naming system for element types and attributes?
13. What do XML namespaces actually contain?
14. Are the names of all element types and attributes in some XML namespace?
15. Do XML namespaces apply to entity names, notation names, or processing instruction targets?
16. Who can create an XML namespace?
17. Do you need to use XML namespaces?
18. What is the relationship between XML namespaces and the XML 1.0 recommendation?
19. What are the differences between versions 1.0 and 1.1 of the XML namespaces recommendation?
20. How do you declare an XML namespace in an XML document?
21. Where can you declare an XML namespace?
22. How do you override an XML namespace declaration that uses a prefix?
23. How do you override a default XML namespace declaration?
24. How do you undeclare an XML namespace prefix?
25. How do you undeclare the default XML namespace?

26. Why are special attributes used to declare XML namespaces?
27. How do different XML technologies treat XML namespace declarations?
28. How do you use prefixes to refer to element type and attribute names in an XML namespace?
29. How do you use the default XML namespace to refer to element type names in an XML namespace?
30. How do you use the default XML namespace to refer to attribute names in an XML namespace?
31. When should you use the default XML namespace instead of prefixes?
32. What is the scope of an XML namespace declaration?
33. Does the scope of an XML namespace declaration include the element it is declared on?
34. If an element or attribute is in the scope of an XML namespace declaration, is its name in that namespace?
35. What happens when an XML namespace declaration goes out of scope?
36. What happens if no XML namespace declaration is in scope?
37. Can multiple XML namespace declarations be in scope at the same time?
38. How can you declare XML namespaces so that all elements and attributes are in their scope?
39. Can the content model in an element type declaration contain element types whose names come from other XML namespaces?
40. Can the attribute list of an element type contain attributes whose names come from other XML namespaces?
41. How can you construct an XML document that is valid and conforms to the XML namespaces recommendation?
42. How can you allow the prefixes in my document to be different from the prefixes in my DTD?
43. How can you validate an XML document that uses XML namespaces?

44. If you start using XML namespaces, do you need to change the existing DTDs?
45. How do you use XML namespaces with XML schemas?
46. What are qualified and unqualified local names in XML schemas?
47. Do you have to use XML namespaces with XML schemas?
48. What is a chameleon schema?
49. Is everything defined or declared in an XML schema in an XML namespace?
50. Is there a one-to-one relationship between XML namespaces and XML schemas?
51. How do you validate documents that use XML namespaces against XML schemas?
52. How do you validate documents that use XML namespaces?
53. What is the Namespace-based Validation Dispatching Language (NVDL)?
54. How do you create documents that use XML namespaces?
55. How can you check that a document conforms to the XML namespaces recommendation?
56. Can you use the same document with both namespace-aware and namespace-unaware applications?
57. What software is needed to process XML namespaces?
58. How can you use XML namespaces to combine documents that use different element type and attribute names?
59. How do you use XML namespaces with Internet Explorer 5.0 and/or the MSXML parser?
60. How do applications process documents that use XML namespaces?
61. Can an application process documents that use XML namespaces and documents that don't use XML namespaces?
62. Can an application be both namespace-aware and namespace-unaware?

63. What does a namespace-aware application do when it encounters an error?
64. What is a qualified name?
65. What is a QName?
66. What characters are allowed in a qualified name?
67. Where can qualified names appear?
68. Can qualified names be used in attribute values?
69. How are qualified names mapped to names in XML namespaces?
70. What is a prefixed name?
71. What is an unprefixed name?
72. Are unprefixed names in an XML namespace?
73. What is a local name?
74. What is a namespace name?
75. What is an expanded name?
76. What is an expanded QName?
77. What is a universal name?
78. How are expanded names represented?
79. Are expanded names universally unique?
80. What is an XML namespace prefix?
81. What characters are allowed in an XML namespace prefix?
82. Are prefixes significant?
83. Can you use the same prefix for more than one XML namespace?
84. Can you use more than one prefix for the same XML namespace?
85. How are prefixes declared?
86. Can you undeclare a prefix—that is, dissociate a prefix from an XML namespace?
87. What happens if you use a prefix that is not declared?
88. What happens if there is no prefix on an element type name?

89. What happens if there is no prefix on an attribute name?
90. What is an XML namespace name?
91. What is an XML namespace URI?
92. What characters are allowed in XML namespace names?
93. Can you use a relative URI reference as a namespace name?
94. What does the URI reference used as an XML namespace name point to?
95. Can you resolve the URI reference used as an XML namespace name?
96. Are any XML namespace names reserved?
97. Why does the XML namespaces recommendation use both prefixes and namespace names? Why not use one or the other?
98. Why are XML namespaces so hard to understand and use?
99. Are there any alternatives to XML namespaces?
100. How controversial are XML namespaces?
101. What resources are available for learning about XML namespaces?
102. What utilities are available for working with XML namespaces?
103. What do you understand about XML namespaces and linking?

CHAPTER 5

INTRODUCTION TO XHTML

A QUICK HISTORY OF HTML

To understand the need for XML, at least as it applies to the Web, you have to first consider the role of HTML. In the early days of the Internet, some European physicists created HTML by simplifying another markup language known as SGML (Standard Generalized Markup Language). SGML was overly complicated, at least for the purpose of sharing scientific documents on the Internet. So, pioneering physicists created a simplified version of SGML called HTML that could be used to create what we now know as Web pages. The creation of HTML represented the birth of the World Wide Web, a layer of visual documents that resides on the global network known as the Internet.

HTML was great in its early days because it allowed scientists to share information over the Internet in an efficient and relatively structured manner. It wasn't until later that HTML started to become an all-encompassing formatting and display language for Web pages. It didn't take long before Web browsers caught on and HTML started being used to code more than scientific papers. HTML quickly went from a tidy little markup language for researchers to a full-blown online publishing language. And once it was established that HTML could be jazzed up simply by adding new tags, the creators of Web browsers added new features to the language. Although these new features were neat at first, they compromised the simplicity of HTML and introduced of inconsistencies when it came to how browsers rendered Web pages. HTML had started to resemble a bad remodeling job on a house that really should've been left alone.

As with most revolutions, the birth of the Web was chaotic, and the modifications to HTML reflected that chaos. More recently, a significant effort has been made to address the inconsistencies of HTML and to attempt to restore some order to the language. The problem with disorder in HTML is that Web browsers have to guess at how a page is to be displayed. Ideally, a Web page designer should be able to define exactly how a page is to look and have it look the same regardless of what kind of browser or operating system someone is using. This utopia is still off in the future somewhere, but XML is playing a significant role in leading us toward it, and significant progress has been made.

XML OVER HTML

XML is an acronym; it stands for eXtensible Markup Language. XML is a computer language for describing information. You could say HTML also describes information. But that is not true. XML improves on the HTML approach and makes the Web a better place to do business, to learn, and to have fun.

HTML is a great technology, and it has changed the world. However, a great deal of useful information is lost when data is converted into HTML. The information that if preserved can be used to build a whole new world of computer applications on the Web. To clarify this point, look into the following code snippets.

```
<!-- HTML Snippet -->
<h1>Employee</h1>
<p>Name : Rohit
<p>Age : 25
<<! p>Designation : Marketing Executive
<!-- XML Snippet -->
<Employee>
<Name>Rohit</Name>
<Age>25</Age>
<Designation>Marketing Executive</Designation>
</Employee>
```

Now, if you view these code snippets from the computer's point of view, you would find that the XML document would be easier to process. XML captures the most useful information and has potential uses. This distinction is the very essence of XML.

GETTING MULTILINGUAL WITH XML

XML is a meta-language, which is a fancy way of saying that it is a language used to create other markup languages. It means that XML provides a basic structure and set of rules to which any markup language must adhere. Using XML, you can create a unique markup language to model just about any kind of information, including Web page content. Knowing that XML is a language for creating other markup languages, you could create your own version of HTML using XML. You could also create a markup language called VPML (Virtual Pet Markup Language), for example, which you could use to create and manage virtual pets. The point is that XML lays the ground rules for organizing information in a consistent manner, and that information can be anything from Web pages to virtual pets.

You might be thinking that virtual pets don't necessarily have anything to do with the Web, so why mention them? The reason is because XML is not entirely about Web pages. In fact, XML in the purest sense really has nothing to do with the Web, and can be used to represent any kind of information on any kind of computer. If you can visualize all the information whizzing around the globe between computers, mobile phones, televisions, and radios, you can start to understand why XML has much broader ramifications than just cleaning up Web pages.

However, one of the first applications of XML is to restore some order to the Web. One of the main benefits of XML is the ability to develop XML documents once and then have them viewable on a range of devices, such as desktop computers, handheld computers, mobile phones, and Internet appliances.

XML looks very familiar to anyone who has used HTML to create Web pages. Going back to our virtual pet example, look at the following XML code, which reveals what a hypothetical VPML document might look like:

```
<pets>
  <pet name="Maximillian" type="pot bellied pig"age="3">
   <friend name="Augustus"/>
   <friend name="Nigel"/>
  </pet>
  <pet name="Augustus" type="goat" age="2">
   <friend name="Maximillian"/>
  </pet>
  <pet name="Nigel" type="chipmunk" age="2">
   <friend name="Maximillian"/>
  </pet>
</pets>
```

This XML (VPML) code includes three virtual pets: Maximillian the pot-bellied pig, Augustus the goat, and Nigel the chipmunk. If you study the code, you'll notice that tags are used to describe the virtual pets much as tags are used in HTML code to describe Web pages. However, in this example the tags are unique to the VPML language. It's not too hard to understand the meaning of the code, thanks to the descriptive tags. In fact, an important design parameter of XML was for XML content to always be human-readable.

Unlike HTML, which consists of a predefined set of tags such as <head>, <body>, and <p>, XML allows you to create custom markup languages with tags that are unique to a certain type of data, such as virtual pets.

The virtual pet example demonstrates how flexible XML is in solving data structuring problems. Unlike a traditional database, XML data is pure text, which means it can be processed and manipulated very easily, in addition to being readable by people. For example, you can open up any XML document in a text editor such as Windows Notepad (or TextEdit on Macintosh computers) and view or edit the code.

The fact that XML is pure text also makes it very easy for applications to transfer data between one another, across networks, and also across different computing platforms such as Windows, Macintosh, and Linux. XML essentially establishes a platform-neutral means of structuring data, which is ideal for networked applications, including Web-based applications.

THE CONVERGENCE OF HTML AND XML

Just as some Americans are apprehensive about the proliferation of spoken languages other than English, some Web developers initially feared XML's role in the future of the Web. Is it valid to view XML as posing a risk to the future of HTML? And if you're currently an HTML expert and have yet to explore XML, will you have to throw all you know out the window and start anew with XML? The answer to both of these questions is a resounding no! In fact, once you fully come to terms with the relationship between XML and HTML, you'll realize that XML actually complements HTML as a Web technology. Perhaps more interesting is the fact that XML is in many ways a parent to HTML, as opposed to a rival sibling.

To better understand XML and its relationship to HTML, you need to know why HTML has gotten messy. HTML was originally designed as a means of sharing written ideas among scientific researchers. We say "written ideas" because there were no graphics or images in the early versions of HTML.

So, in its inception, HTML was never intended to support fancy graphics, formatting, or page-layout features. Instead, HTML was intended to focus on the meaning of information or the content of information. It wasn't until Web browser vendors got excited that HTML was expanded to address the presentation of information. In fact, HTML was in many ways changed to focus entirely on how information appears, which is what ultimately prompted the creation of XML.

There are a variety of reasons why this is a good idea, and they all have to do with improving the organization and structure of information. Although presentation plays an important role in any Web site, modern Web applications have evolved to become driven by data of very specific types, such as financial transactions. HTML is a very poor markup language for representing such data. With its support for custom markup languages, XML makes it possible to carefully describe data and the relationships between pieces of data. By focusing on content, XML allows you to describe the information in Web documents. More importantly, XML makes it possible to precisely describe information that is shuttled across the Net between applications. For example, Amazon.com uses XML to describe products on its site and allow developers to create applications that intelligently analyze and extract information about those products.

XML is not a replacement for HTML or even a competitor of HTML. XML's impact on HTML has to do more with cleaning up HTML than it does with dramatically altering HTML. The best way to compare XML and HTML is to remember that XML establishes a set of strict rules that any markup language must follow. HTML is a relatively unstructured markup language that could benefit from the rules of XML. The natural merger of the two technologies is to make HTML adhere to the rules and structure of XML. To accomplish this merger, a new version of HTML has been formulated that adheres to the stricter rules of XML. The new XML-compliant version of HTML is known as XHTML.

XML's relationship with HTML doesn't end with XHTML, however. Although XHTML is a great idea that is already making Web pages cleaner and more consistent for Web browsers to display, we're a ways off from seeing a Web that consists of cleanly structured XHTML documents (pages). It's currently still too convenient to take advantage of the freewheeling flexibility of the HTML language. Where XML is making a significant immediate impact on the Web is in Web-based applications that must shuttle data across the Internet. XML is an excellent medium for representing data that is transferred back and forth across the Internet as part of a complete Web-based application. In this way, XML is used as a behind-the-scenes data transport language, whereas HTML is still used to display traditional Web pages to the user.

ADD HTML TO XML DATA

In the following example, we loop through an XML file ("cd_catalog.xml"), and display the content of each CD element as an HTML table row:

Example

```
<html>
<body>
<script type="text/javascript">
if (window.XMLHttpRequest)
{// code for IE7+, Firefox, Chrome, Opera, Safari
xmlhttp=new XMLHttpRequest();
}
else
{// code for IE6, IE5
xmlhttp=new ActiveXObject("Microsoft.XMLHTTP");
}
xmlhttp.open("GET","cd_catalog.xml",false);
xmlhttp.send();
xmlDoc=xmlhttp.responseXML;
document.write("<table border='1'>");
var x=xmlDoc.getElementsByTagName("CD");
for (i=0;i<x.length;i++)
  {
  document.write("<tr><td>");
  document.write(x[i].getElementsByTagName("ARTIST")[0].childNodes[0].nodeValue);
  documlent.write("</td><td>");
  document.write(x[i].getElementsByTagName("TITLE")[0].childNodes[0].nodeValue);
  document.write("</td></tr>");
}
document.write("</table>");
</script>
</body>
</html>
```

DIFFERENCES BETWEEN XHTML AND HTML

1. **Lower case element and attribute names:** The difference between HTML and XHTML is that XHTML must also meet the requirements of XML. The first important requirement is that XML is case sensitive. XHTML meets this requirement by making all element names and attribute names lower case. In HTML, you can use either upper case or lower case.

Example

This is valid HTML, but invalid XHTML. Do NOT use these.

```
<UL>
  <LI> item 1 </LI>
</UL>
```

This is valid HTML, and valid XHTML. Use these.

```
<ul>
  <li> item 1 </li>
</ul>
```

2. **Close all container elements:** All container elements must be closed in XHTML. You can sometimes get away without closing them in HTML.

Example

This is valid HTML, but invalid XHTML. Do NOT use these.

```
<ul>
  <li>
  <li>
</ul>
```

This is valid HTML, and valid XHTML. Use these.

```
<ul>
  <li></li>
  <li></li>
</ul>
```

3. **Close empty elements with space slash:** Some container elements do not have a closing tag. In XHTML, you must close them with a space slash. The space slash is not required in HTML.

Example

This is valid HTML, but invalid XHTML. Do NOT use these.

```
<hr>
<br>
```

This is valid in both HTML and XHTML.

```
<hr/>
<br/>
```

4. **Do not mix up the closing tags:** All elements within a container elements must be closed before the container is closed. You must do this in XHTML. You should do this in HTML, but can sometimes get by with tags in the wrong order.

Example

Bad. Do NOT use this.

```
<b><i> This text may not work correctly. </b></i>
Good. The i element is inside the b container element
<b><i> This text will be bold italic. </i></b>
```

5. **Every attribute must have a value:** Every attribute you code must have a value in XHTML. A few attribute values may be omitted HTML.

Example

This is valid HTML, but invalid XHTML. Do NOT use these.

```
<hr noshade />
Valid in both HTML and XHTML.
<hr noshade="noshade" />
```

6. **Every attribute value must be in quotes:** Every attribute value must be in single quotes or double quotes in XHTML. Sometimes quotes may be omitted HTML.

Example

This is valid HTML, but invalid XHTML. Do NOT use these.

```
<hr width=4>
```

This is valid in both HTML and XHTML.

```
<hr width='4' />
<hr width="4" />
```

7. **One each of the HTML head, title, and body tags are required in XHTML:** Sometimes one may be omitted or there may be two of one in HTML.

Example

This example is valid in both HTML and XHTML.

```
<html>
 <head>
   <title> sample page </title>
 </head>
 <body>
   Hello.
 </body>
</html>
```

8. **A DOCTYPE element is required in XHTML:** A DOCTYPE element is required in XHTML. It is optional in HTML.

XHTML

All Web markup languages are based on SGML, a complicated language that is not designed for humans to write. SGML is what is called a metalanguage; that is, a language that is used to define other languages. To make its power available to Web developers, SGML was used to create XML, a simplified version, and also a metalanguage.

XML is a powerful format—you create your own tags and attributes to suit the type of document you're writing. By using a set group of tags and attributes and following the rules of XML, you've created a new Markup language.

This is what has been done to create XHTML (eXtensible HyperText Markup Language)—which is why you'll see XHTML being called a subset or application of XML. The pre-existing HTML 4.01 tags and attributes were used as the vocabulary of this new Markup language, with XML providing the rules of how they are put together.

So, using XHTML, you are really writing XML code, but restricting yourself to a predetermined set of elements. This gives you all the benefits of XML (see below), while avoiding the complications of true XML; bridging the gap for developers who might not fancy taking on something as tricky as full-on XML. As you're coding under the guise of XHTML, all of the tags available to you should be familiar. Writing XHTML requires that you follow the rules of conformant XML, such as correct syntax and structure. As XHTML looks so much like classic HTML, it faces no compatibility problems as long as some simple coding guidelines are followed.

If all of this sounds a bit challenging, don't worry. Transitioning to XHTML is a simple process, with only a few rules to remember.

BENEFITS OF XHTML

The benefits of adopting XHTML now or migrating your existing site to the new standards are many. First, they ensure excellent forward-compatibility for your creations. XHTML is the new set of standards that the Web will be built on in the years to come, so future-proofing your work early will save you much trouble later on. Future browser versions might stop supporting deprecated elements from old HTML drafts, and so many old basic-HTML sites may start displaying incorrectly and unpredictably.

Once you have used XHTML for a short time, it is no more difficult to use than HTML, and in some ways, is easier since it is built on a more simplified set of standards. Writing code is a more streamlined experience, as the days of browser hacks and display tricks are gone. Editing your existing code is also a nicer experience, as it is infinitely cleaner and more self-explanatory. Browsers can also interpret and display a clean XHTML page quicker than one with errors.

XHTML CODING

The first thing you need to know about changing over to XHTML as the new standard is that there really isn't much new to learn. No new tags or attributes have been added into your repertoire, like HTML 4 (although a few have been deprecated); this is just a move towards good, valid, and efficient coding. XHTML documents stress logical structure and simplicity, and use CSS for nearly all presentational concerns. It just means you have to change the way you write code. Even if you always wrote great code before, there're a few new practices you need to add in.

XML DECLARATION

An XML declaration at the very top of your document defines both the version of XML you're using as well as the character encoding.

```
<?xml version="1.0" encoding="UTF-8"?>
```

Instead, you use a meta tag in the heading of your document. If you're using Unicode, this is as follows:

```
<meta http-equiv="Content-Type" content="text/html; charset=UTF-8" />
```

And if you're using the more common ISO-8859-1 encoding, use

```
<meta http-equiv="Content-Type" content="text/html; charset=ISO-8859-1" />
```

XHTML DTDs

Whether you use the XML declaration or not, every XHTML document must be defined as such by a line of code at the start of the page, and some attributes in the main <html> tag, which tell the browser what language the text is in. The opening line is the DTD (Document Type Declaration). This tells your browser and validators the nature of your page.

A DTD is the file your browser reads with the names and attributes of all of the possible tags that you can use in your markup defined in it. Newer browsers will usually have the latest specs written into their DTDs. Declare it by putting this at the very top of your code:

```
<!DOCTYPE html PUBLIC "-//W3C//DTD XHTML 1.0 Strict//EN"
"http://www.w3.org/TR/xhtml1/DTD/xhtml1-strict.dtd">
```

That DTD is the one you use if you're committed to writing entirely correct XHTML code. Strict XHTML dispenses with many presentational tags and attributes, and it is very strict.

You won't be permitted to use the font tag at all, nor will attributes like width and height be allowed in your tables. You won't be able to use the border attribute on images, and will have to use the alt attribute on all images if you want to validate. You get the idea—almost all presentational attributes are restricted in favour of wider CSS utilization, so unless you know your stuff in this regard, it'd be best to use the XHTML Transitional below.

If you're going to hover between HTML and XHTML, use the next DTD, which is a bit looser, and if you're putting together a frameset page, use the last one.

```
<!DOCTYPE html PUBLIC "-//W3C//DTD XHTML 1.0 Transitional//EN"
"http://www.w3.org/TR/xhtml1/DTD/xhtml1-transitional.dtd">
<!DOCTYPE html PUBLIC "-//W3C//DTD XHTML 1.0 Frameset//EN"
"http://www.w3.org/TR/xhtml1/DTD/xhtml1-frameset.dtd">
```

Most people will opt for the XHTML Transitional, as changing to Strict can be a daunting prospect.

A correct DTD allows the browser to go into standards mode, which will render your page correctly, and similarly across browsers. Without a full DTD, your browser enters "compatibility," or "quirks" mode, behaving like a version 4 browser, including all of their associated quirks and inconsistencies. Also, these declarations are all case-sensitive, so don't change them in any way.

Finally, you need to define the XML namespace your document uses. It is a definition of which set of tags you're going to be using, and it concerns the modular properties of XHTML. It's set by adding an attribute into the <html> tag. While we're at it, we specify the language of our pages too. Modify your tags to this:

```
<html xmlns="http://www.w3.org/1999/xhtml" xml:lang="en"> </html>
```

THE DOCTYPE DECLARATION

There are three DTDs for XHTML: Strict, Transitional, and Frameset. All XHTML documents must conform to the XML syntax rules.

XHTML STRICT

XHTML documents that conform to the Strict DTD may not use any deprecated HTML tags. The DOCTYPE declaration looks like this:

```
<!DOCTYPE html PUBLIC "-//W3C//DTD XHTML 1.0 Strict//EN"
"http://www.w3.org/TR/xhtml1/DTD/xhtml1-strict.dtd">
```

XHTML TRANSITIONAL

XHTML documents that conform to the Transitional DTD may use deprecated HTML tags, but may not use the <frameset> and <frame> tags. The DOCTYPE declaration looks like this:

```
<!DOCTYPE html PUBLIC "-//W3C//DTD XHTML 1.0
Transitional//EN" "http://www.w3.org/TR/xhtml1/DTD/xhtml1
transitional.dtd">
```

XHTML FRAMESET

XHTML documents that conform to the Frameset DTD may use deprecated HTML tags including the <frameset> and <frame> tags. The DOCTYPE declaration looks like this:

```
<!DOCTYPE html PUBLIC "-//W3C//DTD XHTML 1.0 Frameset//EN"
"http://www.w3.org/TR/xhtml1/DTD/xhtml1-frameset.dtd">
```

THE DOCUMENT ELEMENT

In XHTML, the document element (<html>) must contain a namespace declaration as shown below.

```
<html xmlns="http://www.w3.org/1999/xhtml">
```

A SAMPLE XHTML DOCUMENT

Below is an example XHTML document.

```
Code Sample: XHTML/Demos/Xml101.html
<?xml version="1.0"?>
<!DOCTYPE html PUBLIC "-//W3C//DTD XHTML 1.0 Strict//EN"
 "http://www.w3.org/TR/xhtml1/DTD/xhtml1-strict.dtd">
<html xmlns="http://www.w3.org/1999/xhtml">
<head>
<meta http-equiv="Content-Type" content="text/html; charset=UTF-8" />
<title>Introduction to XML</title>
</head>
<body>
<h1>Introduction to XML</h1>
<div id="courseNum">XML101</div>
<div id="courseLength">3 days</div>
<h2>Prerequisites</h2>
```

```
<ul>
 <li>Experience with Word Processing</li>
 <li>Experience with HTML (optional, but recommended)</li>
</ul>
<h2>Course Outline</h2>
<div id="outline">
<ul>
 <li>
  XML Basics
  <ul>
   <li>What is XML?</li>
   <li>
    XML Benefits
    <ul>
     <li>XML Holds Data, Nothing More</li>
     <li>XML Separates Structure from Formatting</li>
     <li>XML Promotes Data Sharing</li>
     <li>XML is Human-Readable</li>
     <li>XML is Free</li>
    </ul>
   </li>
   </ul>
  <ul>
   <li>
    XML Documents
    <ul>
     <li>The Prolog</li>
     <li>Elements</li>
     <li>Attributes</li>
     <li>CDATA</li>
     <li>XML Syntax Rules</li>
     <li>Special Characters</li>
    </ul>
   </li>
  </ul>
  <ul>
   <li>Creating a Simple XML File</li>
  </ul>
 </li>
```

```
</ul>
</div>
</body>
</html>
```

DOCUMENT FORMATION

The actual XHTML content can be placed. After the Doctype line, as with HTML, XHTML has <html>, <head>, <title>, and <body> tags but, unlike with HTML, they must all be included in a valid XHTML document. The correct setup of your file is as follows:

```
<!DOCTYPE html PUBLIC "-//W3C//DTD XHTML 1.0 Transitional//EN"
"http://www.w3.org/TR/xhtml1/DTD/xhtml1-transitional.dtd">
<html>
<head>
<title>Page Title</title>
OTHER HEAD DATA
</head>
<body>
CONTENT
</body>
</html>
```

It is important that your document follows this basic pattern. This example uses the transitional Doctype, but you can use either of the others (although frames pages are not structured in the same way).

XHTML TAGS

One of the major changes to HTML introduced to XHTML is that tags must always be properly formed. With the old HTML specification, you could be very sloppy in your coding, with missing tags and incorrect formation without many problems, but in XHTML this is very important.

Lower Case

Probably the biggest change in XHTML is that the way in which you write tags must be correct. Luckily, this major change can be easily implemented into a normal HTML document without a problem.

In XHTML, tags must always be lowercase. This means that

```
<FONT>
<Font>
<FoNT>
```

are all incorrect tags and must not be used. The font tag must now be used as follows:

```
<font>
```

If you are not writing your code, but instead use a WYSIWYG editor, you can still begin to migrate your documents to XHTML by setting the editor to output all code in lowercase. For example, in Dreamweaver 4 you can do this by going to

```
Edit -> Preferences -> Code Format
```

and making sure that Case For Tags is set to

```
<lowercase>
```

and also that Case For Attributes is set to

```
lowercase="value"
```

Nesting

The second change to the HTML tags in XHTML is that they must all be properly nested. This means that if you have multiple tags applying to something on your page, you must make sure you open and close them in the correct order. For example, if you have some bold red text in a paragraph, the correct nesting would be one of the following:

```
<p><b><font color="#FF0000">Your Text</font></b></p>
<b><p><font color="#FF0000">Your Text</font></p></b>
<p><font color="#FF0000"><b>Your Text<b></font></p>
```

These are only examples, though, and there are other possibilities for these tags. What you must not do, though, is to close tags in the wrong order, for example:

```
<p><b><font color="#FF0000">Your Text</p></font></b>
```

Although code in this form would be shown correctly using HTML, this is incorrect in the XHTML specification and you must be very careful to nest your tags correctly.

Closing Tags

The previous two changes to HTML should not be a particular problem if your HTML code is already well-formed. The final change to HTML tags probably will require quite a lot of changes to your HTML documents to make them XHTML compliant.

All tags in XHTML must be closed. Most tags in HTML are already closed (for example <p></p>, <font></font>, and <b></b>), but there are several standalone tags which do not get closed. The main three are

```
<br>
<img>
<hr>
```

There are two ways you can deal with the change in the specification. The first way is quite obvious if you know HTML. You can just add a closing tag to each one, e.g.,

```
<br></br>
<img></img>
<hr></hr>
```

Although you must be careful that you do not accidentally place anything between the opening and closing tags, as this would be incorrect coding. The second way is slightly different but will be familiar to anyone who has written WML. You can include the closing in the actual tag:

```
<br />
<img />
<hr />
```

This is probably the best way to close your tags, as it is the recommended way by the W3C who set the XHTML standard. You should notice that, in these examples, there is a space before the />. This is not actually necessary in the XHTML specification (you could have <br/>), but the reason it is included here is that, as well as being correct XHTML, it also makes the tag compatible with past browsers. As every other XHTML change is backwards compatible, it would not be very good to have a space causing problems with site compatibility.

In case you are wondering how the <img> tag works if it has all the normal attributes included, here is an example:

```
<img src="myimage.gif" alt="My Image" width="400" height="300" />
```

Again, notice the space before the />

Attributes

HTML attributes are the extra parts you can add onto tags (such as src in the img tag) to change the way in which they are shown. There are four changes to the way in which attributes are changed.

Lowercase

As with XHTML tags, the attributes for them must be in lowercase. This means that, although in the past, code like

```
<table Width="100%">
```

would have worked, this must now be given as

```
<table width="100%">
```

Although this is a minor issue, it is important to check your code for this mistake.

Correct Quotation

Another change in the HTML syntax is that all attributes in XHTML must be quoted. In HTML you could have used the following:

```
<table width=100%>
```

with absolutely no compatibility problems. This all changes in XHTML. If you use code in this format with XHTML it will be incorrect and must be changed. All attributes must be surrounded by quotes (") so the correct format of this code would be

```
<table width="100%">
```

Attribute Shortening

It has become common practice in HTML to shorten a few of the attributes to save on typing and transfer times. As with other common practices in HTML, this has been removed from the XHTML specification as it causes incompatibilities between browsers and other devices.

An example of a commonly shortened tag is

```
<input type="checkbox" value="yes" name="agree" checked>
```

In this, it is the checked part which is incorrect. In XHTML, all shortened attributes must be given in their "long" format. For example

```
checked="checked"
```

so the checkbox code earlier would now need to be written as

```
<input type="checkbox" value="yes" name="agree"
checked="checked">
```

There are other attributes (such as noresize) that also must be given in full.

The ID Attribute

Probably the biggest change from HTML to XHTML is the one tag attribute change. All other differences just make tags more compatible. This is the only full change.

In HTML, the <img> tag has an attribute "name." This is usually used to refer to the image in javascript for doing actions like image rollovers. This attribute has now been changed to the "id" attribute. So, the HTML code

```
<img src="myimage.gif" name="my_image">
```

would need to be written in XHTML as

```
<img src="myimage.gif" id="my_image"/>
```

Of course, this would not be backward compatible with older browsers, so if you still want your site to work fully in all old browsers (as XHTML is intended to do), you will need to include both id and name attributes (this would also be correct XHTML):

```
<img src="myimage.gif" id="my_image" vname="my_image"/>
```

QUESTIONS FOR DISCUSSION

1. What is XHTML?
2. What does an XHTML document Look Like?
3. What is the relationship between XHTML and HTML?
4. What is the relationship between XHTML and XML?
5. What is the relationship between XHTML and the Web?
6. What is the relationship between XHTML and HTTP?
7. What is the relationship between XHTML and URL?
8. What is a URI?
9. What is the relationship between XHTML and SGML?

10. What is the relationship between XHTML and CSS?
11. What is the relationship between XHTML and DTD?
12. Who developed XHTML?
13. What is the latest XHTML specification?
14. How many tags are defined in XHTML 1.0?
15. How can XHTML documents be validated online?
16. What tools can be used to write XHTML documents?
17. What tools can be used to view XHTML documents?
18. What is an XHTML element?
19. How can we enter comments into XHTML documents?
20. How can we write the opening tag of an XHTML element?
21. How can we close an XHTML element?
22. What is wrong with <br> tags?
23. What is wrong with <meta> tags?
24. Are XHTML elements' names case senstive?
25. How can we enter element content?
26. What is an XHTML element attribute?

CHAPTER 6

CSS STYLE SHEETS

CSS DOCUMENTS

CSS documents allow you to define a style for any HTML element. Thus, you can define the style for an h1 element to be red with a font size of 6. This style can then be applied to every h1 element on your Website. CSS documents allow you to create a uniform style throughout your Web documents without having to enter specific information for each h1 element in each page. If you need to change the style for an h1 element, you need to change it only in the CSS document. If you need to override the style defined in the CSS document for one or more of your h1 elements in a specific page, you can do this, too.

One major problem with using CSS documents is that they are not supported in every browser. Microsoft Internet Explorer 5 supports nearly all the features of CSS documents, and Internet Explorer 4 also supports most of the CSS features. Netscape has released version 6 that supports CSS level 1 and the DOM. If you were to create an XHTML document, you could use CSS documents to define the presentation of the XHTML information. While CSS documents can work for XHTML, they will not work for XML documents that do not contain presentation information. For XML documents without presentation information, you must use XSL.

XML AND CSS

Cascading Style Sheets (CSS) is a style sheet mechanism specifically developed to meet the needs of Web designers and users. CSS provides HTML with far greater control over document presentation in a way that is independent of document content. CSS style sheets can be used to set fonts, colors, white space, positioning, backgrounds, and many other presentational aspects of a document. It is also possible for several documents to share the same style sheet, which allows users to maintain consistent presentation within a collection of related documents without having to modify each document separately.

XML uses markup to describe the structure and data content of a document, making it easy both for authors to write it and for computer programs to process it. CSS, on the other hand, makes it possible to present that document to the user in a browser. CSS or some type of style sheet mechanism is, in fact, a requisite for browsing XML on the Web.

LIMITATIONS OF CSS FOR COMPLEX APPLICATIONS

Although CSS style sheets can be very effective for improving the presentation of HTML documents, the CSS1 standard has a number of important omissions which can limit the effectiveness of CSS style sheets for more complex applications. The following list describes just a few of the major limitations of the CSS standard:

- CSS cannot grab an item (such as a chapter title) from one place and use it again in another place (such as a page header).
- CSS has no concept of sibling relationships. For example, it is impossible to write a CSS stylesheet that will render every other paragraph in bold.
- CSS is not a programming language; it does not support decision structures and cannot be extended by the stylesheet designer.
- CSS cannot calculate quantities or store variables. This means, at the very least, that it cannot store commonly used parameters in one location that is easy to update.
- CSS cannot generate text (page numbers, etc).
- CSS uses a simple box-oriented formatting model that works for current Web browsers, but will not extend to more advanced applications of the markup, such as multiple column sets.

ADVANTAGES OF AUTHORING XML DOCUMENTS WITH CSS

- **Presentability:** This is the most obvious benefit; the style sheets are used to style or "decorate" the document.

- **Servability:** CSS is, as the above quote points out, a requisite for browsing XML documents on the Web. However, XML is a meta-language and authors can construct their own elements (and/or DTDs). The freedom in XML of authors creating their own tags comes with a price: XML tag names have no predefined semantics. This results in all sorts of ambiguities: an <img> could mean an image, or an imaginary number; even the seemingly obvious <manual> could mean a technical book or a form of human labor. (In an informal language (such as English), we (humans) know the difference due to the "context." However, such semantical distinctions are not possible in formal languages being processed by machines.) In such a case, a user agent would not know how to "display" elements of these "home-brewed" languages. This is where the use of a stylesheet language such as CSS becomes necessary, which provides the display semantics to an XML document.
- **Accessibility:** Use of CSS in the document makes it accessible, particularly to people with visual or aural disability. There are various accessibility features of CSS.

AUTHORING APPROACHES

The use of CSS in XML involves the following steps:

- Authoring the XML document
- Authoring the CSS style sheet
- Associating the CSS style sheet with the XML document
- Rendering the XML document associated with the CSS style sheet

AUTHORING XML DOCUMENTS WITH CSS

Authoring software

XML Spy is a professional validating XML editor that provides three integrated views of XML documents: an enhanced grid view for structured display and editing, a low-level source view with syntax coloring, and an integrated browser view that supports CSS stylesheets. Among other features, it includes Unicode and character-set encoding as well as support for XHTML and XML namespaces. Another useful feature of XML Spy is that a DTD may be edited simultaneously with the XML document that references it.

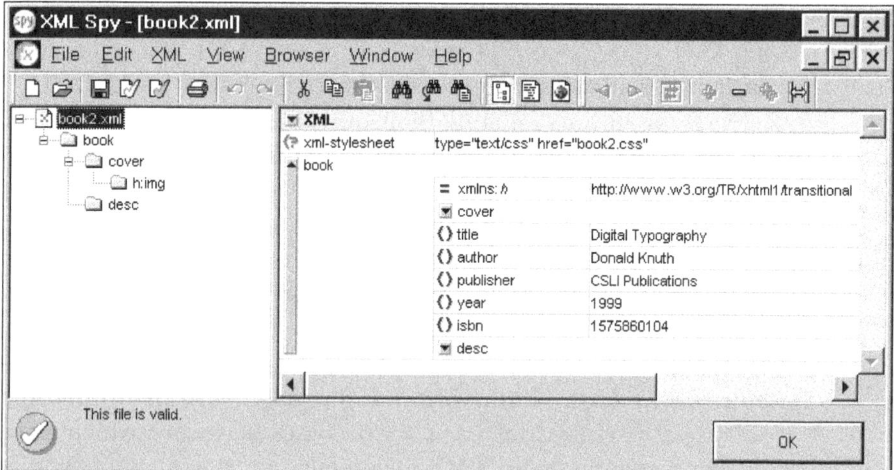

FIGURE 6.1 XML Spy

XMetaL is another notable environment for authoring XML documents with CSS. These visual environments simplify the editing process (and thus reducing the burden on the author) by including required directives or tags. For simple documents, any text-editor (such as Emacs) can be used (assuming that the author is well-versed in XML as well as CSS).

ASSOCIATING CSS STYLESHEETS WITH XML

The association consists of inserting the XML processing instruction at the top of the document, before the root element of the XML document and after the XML prolog. The processing instruction has two required attributes type and href which respectively specify the type of stylesheet (Internet Media Type text/css) and its address (path). An example is

```
<?xml-stylesheet type="text/css" href="fox.css"?>
```

RENDERING XML DOCUMENTS WITH CSS

Browsers that support the combination of XML and CSS are

Microsoft Internet Explorer 5: The CSS2 support is incomplete, but the rendering of XML documents with CSS2 is fairly stable. The caveats are it uses an obsolete version to associate stylesheets, the document is required to use “html” as the namespace name prefix if HTML elements/attributes are being used, XML entity expansion has problems, and printing can lead to unpredictable results.

Mozilla: This Netscape Communicator 5 in the beta releases (called "milestones"). The CSS2 support in Mozilla is incomplete and the rendering of XML documents with CSS2 is unstable. NGLayout, a native document format for Mozilla's graphics-rendering engine, is able to format XML documents using external CSS stylesheets.

Amaya: This is a W3C test-bed browser. It also natively supports XHTML, an XML application that reformulates (or "XMLizes") HTML and CSS2.

CSS SYNTAX

A CSS rule has two main parts: a selector, and one or more declarations:

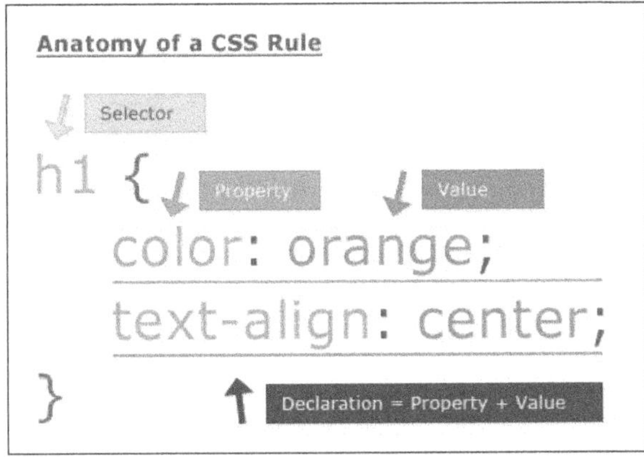

FIGURE 6.2 A CSS rule representation

- **Selector:** This is the hook used to choose what part(s) of your HTML to apply the CSS to. Following the selector is the…
- **Declaration Block:** Everything within the curly brackets, "{" and "}"; this is called the declaration block.
- **Declaration:** Inside a declaration block, you can have as many declarations as you want and each declaration is a combination of a CSS Property and a value.
- **Property:** This is one of the CSS Properties used to tell what part of the selector will be changed (or styled).
- **Value:** This assigns a value to the property.

CSS EXAMPLE

CSS declarations always ends with a semicolon and declaration groups are surrounded by curly brackets:

```
p {color:red;text-align:center;}
```

To make the CSS more readable, you can put one declaration on each line

```
<html>
<head>
<style type="text/css">
p
{
color:red;
text-align:center;
}
</style>
</head>
<body>
<p>Welcome!</p>
<p>This line is styled with CSS.</p>
</body>
</html>
```

Result:

Welcome!

This line is styled with CSS.

CSS COMMENTS

Comments are used to explain your code, and may help you when you edit the source code at a later date. Comments are ignored by browsers.

A CSS comment begins with "/*", and ends with "*/":

```
/*This is a comment*/
p
{
text-align:center;
/*This is another comment*/
color:black;
font-family:arial;
}
```

CSS SELECTORS

CSS Selectors allow us to target specific HTML elements with our style sheets. While there are many different types of CSS Selectors, here we focus on the four essential selectors: type, id, class, and descendant selectors.

1. Type selectors correspond with HTML elements
2. ID selectors are used by adding # in front of an elements ID
3. Class selectors are used by adding a period in front of an element's class
4. Descendant selectors are similar to family trees; you start with the parent element you wish to select, add a space, and continue naming any interior elements until you're arrived at the specific element you wish to select

1. Type Selector: Type selectors are very simple. They correspond with any HTML element type. For example, add the following code to your blank CSS file; these are three simple type selectors:

```
body {
font-family: Arial, sans-serif;
font-size: small;
}
h1{
color: green;
}
em { color:red;
}
```

This code selects and styles our <body> element, as well as all <h1> and <em> elements on our page.

2. Id Selector: The id selector is used to specify a style for a single, unique element. The id selector uses the id attribute of the HTML element, and is defined with a "#". The style rule below will be applied to the element with id="para1":

```
<html>
<head>
<style type="text/css">
#para1
{
text-align:center;
color:red;
}
```

```
</style>
</head>
<body>
<p id="para1">Welcome!</p>
<p>This paragraph is not affected by the style.</p>
</body>
</html>
```

Result:

Welcome!

This paragraph is not affected by the style.

3. Class Selector: The class selector is used to specify a style for a group of elements. Unlike the id selector, the class selector is most often used on several elements. This allows you to set a particular style for any HTML elements with the same class.

The class selector uses the HTML class attribute, and is defined with a "."

In the example below, all HTML elements with class="center" will be center-aligned:

```
<html>
<head>
<style type="text/css">
.center
{
text-align:center;
}
</style>
</head>
<body>
<h1 class="center">Center-aligned heading</h1>
<p class="center">Center-aligned paragraph.</p>
</body>
</html>
```

Result:

Center-aligned heading

Center-aligned paragraph.

You can also specify that only specific HTML elements should be affected by a class. In the example below, all p elements with class="center" will be center-aligned:

```
<html>
<head>
<style type="text/css">
p.center
{
text-align:center;
}
</style>
</head>
<body>
<h1 class="center">This heading will not be affected</h1>
<p class="center">This paragraph will be center-aligned.</p>
</body>
</html>
```

Result:

This heading will not be affected

This paragraph will be center-aligned.

Class attributes: The class attribute that allows you to create subclasses of elements in HTML is also not likely to be available in the majority of XML-based document formats. Of course, CSS lets you select elements based on any attribute, not just class, but the syntax is less convenient.

```
<?xml-stylesheet href="#s1"type="text/css"?>
<doc>
<s id="s1">
s { display: none }
p { display: block }
p .note { color: red }
</s>
<p>Some text... </p>
<p class="note">A note... </p>
</doc>
```

If the document format doesn't specify that class creates a subclass, then you'll have to use the longer selectors with "[ ]:"

```
<?xml-stylesheet href="#s1"type="text/css"?>
<doc>
<s id="s1">
s { display: none }
p { display: block }
```

```
p[class~=note] { color: red }
</s>
<p>Some text... </p>
<p class="note">A note... </p>
</doc>
```

If there is no class attribute, but there is something else we can use, the attribute selectors "[ ]" still apply:

```
<?xml-stylesheet href="#s1" type="text/css"?>
<doc>
<s id="s1">
s { display: none }
p { display: block }
p[warning="yes"] { color: red }
</s>
<p>Some text... </p>
<p warning="yes">A note... </p>
</doc>
```

4. Descendant Selectors: Imagine we wanted the important paragraph in the "intro" Div to look different than the important paragraph at the bottom of the page. We can use a descendant selector to achieve this. Add the following CSS rule at the bottom of our CSS file:

```
#intro .important {
background-color: orange;
}
```

It begins with "#intro" which selects our Intro Div. This is followed by a space, and then ".important." So essentially our selector is telling the Web browser to (1) find the element with the id of intro, (2) go inside that element and find any elements with the class of important.

Within the orange paragraph, the word "important" is red. Let's imagine we want to change the color, since red text on an orange background is difficult to read. The word "important" is inside an <em> element, so we'll use the following code to select and style it:

```
#intro .important em {
color: white;
}
```

This code is telling the browser to (1) find the element with an id of intro, (2) go inside that element and find any elements with a class of important, and (3) go inside that element and select any <em> elements.

EMBEDDING CSS IN WEB PAGE

When a browser reads a style sheet, it will format the document according to it. There are three ways of inserting a style sheet:

1. External style sheet
2. Internal style sheet
3. Inline style

- **External Style Sheet:** An external style sheet is ideal when the style is applied to many pages. With an external style sheet, you can change the look of an entire Website by changing one file. Each page must link to the style sheet using the <link> tag. The <link> tag goes inside the head section:

```
<head>
<link rel="stylesheet" type="text/css" href="mystyle.css" />
</head>
```

  An external style sheet can be written in any text editor. The file should not contain any html tags. Your style sheet should be saved with a .css extension. An example of a style sheet file is shown below:

```
hr {color:sienna;}
p {margin-left:20px;}
body {background-image:url("images/back40.gif");}
```

  Do not leave spaces between the property value and the units! "margin-left:20 px" (instead of "margin-left:20px") will work in IE, but not in Firefox or Opera.

- **Internal Style Sheet:** An internal style sheet should be used when a single document has a unique style. You define internal styles in the head section of an HTML page, by using the <style> tag

```
<head>
<style type="text/css">
hr {color:sienna;}
p {margin-left:20px;}
body {background-image:url("images/back40.gif");}
</style>
</head>
```

- **Inline Styles:** An inline style loses many of the advantages of style sheets by mixing content with presentation. To use inline styles you use the style attribute in the relevant tag. The style attribute can contain any CSS property. The example shows how to change the color and the left margin of a paragraph:

  ```
  <p style="color:sienna;margin-left:20px">This is a paragraph.</p>
  ```

  If some properties have been set for the same selector in different style sheets, the values will be inherited from the more specific style sheet. For example, an external style sheet has these properties for the h3 selector:

  ```
  h3
  {
  color:red;
  text-align:left;
  font-size:8pt;
  }
  ```

  And an internal style sheet has these properties for the h3 selector:

  ```
  h3
  {
  text-align:right;
  font-size:20pt;
  }
  ```

  If the page with the internal style sheet also links to the external style sheet, the properties for h3 are

  ```
  color:red;
  text-align:right;
  font-size:20pt;
  ```

  The color is inherited from the external style sheet and the text-alignment and the font-size is replaced by the internal style sheet.

CSS STYLES

There are different types of style such as backgrounds, text, fonts, links, lists, and tables.

DISPLAYING XML WITH CSS

To demonstrate how XML files can be formatted with CSS, we have compiled the following XML files:

Take a look at this pure XML file: The BOOKSTORE

Then look at this style sheet: The CSS file

Finally, view The BOOKSTORE formatted with the CSS file

Even if it looks right to use CSS this way, we strongly believe that formatting with XSL will be the standard way to format XML in future. This XML file does not appear to have any style information associated with it. The document tree is shown in next page.

```
-
<BOOKSTORE>
-
<BOOK>
<BOOKTITLE> Internet and its applications </BOOKTITLE>
<AUTHOR> K. Ram </ AUTHOR >
<PUBLISHER> RK Publications </ PUBLISHER >
<PRICE> 400.00 </PRICE>
<EDITION>2006 </ EDITION >
</BOOK>
-
<BOOK>
<BOOKTITLE> Java Programming </BOOKTITLE>
<AUTHOR> AK Sharma </ AUTHOR >
<PUBLISHER> Jam Publications </ PUBLISHER >
<PRICE>550.00 </PRICE>
<EDITION>2008 </ EDITION >
</BOOK>
-
<BOOK>
<BOOKTITLE> VB .NET </BOOKTITLE>
<AUTHOR> S. Banzal </ AUTHOR >
<PUBLISHER> Popular Publications </ PUBLISHER >
<PRICE>320.00 </PRICE>
<EDITION>2007</ EDITION >
</BOOK>
.
.
```

```
.
.
</BOOKSTORE>
BOOKSTORE
{
background-color: #ffffff;
width: 100%;
}
BOOK
 {
display: block;
margin-bottom: 30pt;
margin-left: 0;
}
BOOKTITLE
{
color: #FF0000;
font-size: 20pt;
}
AUTHOR
{
color: #0000FF;
font-size: 20pt;
}
PUBLISHER, PRICE, EDITION
{
Display: block;
color: #000000;
margin-left: 20pt;
}
```

Result:

```
Internet and its applications
K. Ram
RK Publications
400.00
2006
 Java Programming
AK Sharma
Jam Publications
550.00
2008
```

XSL TRANSFORMATION

Applying an XSL stylesheet to the XML feed has the advantage of being able to fully customize the display, like being able to add links or change the order of the nodes. The transformation needs to happen on the client so that the XML remains intact.

First we add the reference to the XSL file inside the feed:

```
<?xml version="1.0" encoding="ISO-8859-1" ?>
<?xml-stylesheet type="text/xsl" href="latest.xsl" ?>
<?xml-stylesheet type="text/css" href="latest.css" ?>
<rss version="2.0">
```

We can add the XSLT specification, as well as leave the CSS link there. Having both added is perfectly fine, as only one of them is going to be used in the end. If the browser understands XSL, then it will use that and ignore the CSS. See the complete XSL file:

```
<?xml version="1.0" encoding="ISO-8859-1"?>
<xsl:stylesheet version="1.0" xmlns:xsl="http://www.w3.org/1999/XSL/Transform">
<xsl:template match="/rss">
<html>
<head>
  <link href="xsl.css" rel="stylesheet" type="text/css"/>
  <style type="text/css">
 body {
   font-size:0.83em;
 }
 </style>
</head>
<body>
  <div id="logo">
    <xsl:element name="a">
      <xsl:attribute name="href">
        <xsl:value-of select="channel/link" />
     </xsl:attribute>
    <xsl:value-of select="channel/title" />
  </xsl:element>
</div>
<div class="Snippet" style="border-width:0; background-color:#FFF; margin:1em">
  <div class="titleWithLine">
    <xsl:value-of select="channel/description" />
```

```
        </div>
        <dl style="padding-right:1em">
         <xsl:for-each select="channel/item">
          <dd>
            <xsl:element name="a">
              <xsl:attribute name="href">
                <xsl:value-of select="link"/>
              </xsl:attribute>
            <xsl:value-of select="title"/>
           </xsl:element>
          </dd>
          <dt>
           <xsl:value-of select="description" /><br />
           <span class="comments"><xsl:value-of select="pubDate" /></span>
          </dt>
         </xsl:for-each>
        </dl>
       </div>
      <div id="footer">
         <xsl:value-of select="channel/copyright" />
       </div>
      </body>
      </html>
      </xsl:template>
      </xsl:stylesheet>
```

The important thing to notice here is that you can output complete HTML, together with links to external CSS files, for an improved customization of the display. If you already have a stylesheet that you use on your site, you can make a reference to it, and use it in the XSL file to create a similar look and feel. This is what is shown above, with the link to the CSS file "xsl. css." There are also many ways to define an XSLT file, like using templates.

USING XSL TO PRESENT XML DOCUMENTS

XSL documents are similar to CSS documents in that they both define styles that apply to certain elements, but there are a few differences. CSS defines the typographical style of only XHTML elements, whereas the styles defined in XSL documents apply to entire XML documents. Moreover, XSL might use the styles specified in CSS to produce the output code from XML data. The XSL document must be placed on the same Web server as the file that references it.

As mentioned, most XML data does not contain elements that define how the data should be presented; therefore, you must use XSL documents to transform this XML data into a form that can be presented to the user. In this way, XSL provides a powerful tool to transform XML documents in virtually any way that is necessary.

XSL PATTERNS

XML documents represent a tree of nodes. XSL patterns provide a query language for locating nodes in XML documents. After the nodes in the XML document are identified using a pattern, the nodes will be transformed using a template. The XSL patterns we will be using have the same format as the patterns we used with XPath, such as / (child), // (ancestor), .(current node), @ (attribute), and * (wildcard). In addition to the patterns we already mentioned, XSL also has filter operators to manipulate, sort, and filter XML data.

XML STYLES (REVISITED)

Remember earlier when you referenced an XML processor and sent the browser looking for a file called cats.css? The "css" part of the file that it was looking for indicated that it was a Cascading Style Sheet, which is a special type of file used in XML and some other markup languages to tell the browser how it should position and lay out the information that it has. In other words, it's a sheet the browser uses to figure out the style of the layout.

A Cascading Style Sheet (henceforth known as CSS) can be used to define a number of important items on the page: they can tell the browser what color a portion of text should be, where the section should be located, and any special instructions that the browser should follow when displaying any particular piece of data.While it's true that all of that information could be coded onto the page itself, the use of a style sheet means that multiple pages with the same elements or layout can all reference the same file. This means that you don't have to have all the same information on each and every page something that saves on both loading time and coding time.

One of the best things about CSSs is the fact that they can be used by a multitude of languages, not just XML. You can create a CSS file that's used to define how certain elements are formatted in an XML document, and then turn around and use it in a DHTML document.

CSSs uses data as it encounters it in the document, and isn't as adaptable as some other languages when dealing with XML. It is fairly common and has support in multiple browsers, however and as long as you code with care, many of the drawbacks of using CSS can be easily avoided.

QUESTIONS FOR DISCUSSION

1. What are cascading style sheets?
2. Explain some of the features of CSS.
3. Explain the rules in style sheets.
4. Explain the hover element.
5. State some of the uses of CSS.
6. State the different type of author styles.
7. What are the main goals of applying style sheets?
8. Explain CSS1.
9. Compare CSS2 to CSS1.
10. Explain the CSS filter.
11. Explain the Internet Explorer box model bug.
12. Explain vertical control limitation.
13. Explain the absence of expressions.
14. Explain the lack of orthogonally.
15. Explain the ease of maintenance with CSS.
16. Explain float containment.
17. State some limitations of style sheets.
18. How can we use CSS with XML?

CHAPTER 7

XML SCHEMA BASICS

XML SCHEMA

Generically, we can refer to schema as metadata, or data about data. Some of the schema efforts are not just concerned with defining a vocabulary; they go beyond attempting to explain the relationships between certain types of data.

Schemas refine DTDs by permitting more precision in expressing some concepts in the vocabulary. Schemas use a wholly different syntax than DTDs. They permit us to borrow vocabulary from other schemas, thereby solving the validation problem. Overall, schemas are better answers to the problem of specifying vocabularies.

ROLE OF A SCHEMA

The concept of a schema has been present for many years in both the database and the document world.

The formal role of the schema is to define the set of all possible valid documents.

We need to be careful in using the words "validity schema." In the XML standard, being "valid" means something specific. Informally, it means that a document conforms to the rules in its DTD. A document is said to be valid if it satisfies all the constraints defined by the information model.

W3C supports an XML-based alternative to DTD, called the XML schema.

```
<xs:element name="note">

<xs:complexType>
  <xs:sequence>
```

```
      <xs:element name="to" type="xs:string"/>
      <xs:element name="from" type="xs:string"/>
      <xs:element name="heading" type="xs:string"/>
      <xs:element name="body" type="xs:string"/>
    </xs:sequence>
  </xs:complexType>
  </xs:element>
```

DTD AS A SCHEMA

As a constraint language, DTDs are very limited. They provide some control over which elements can be nested within each other, but say nothing about the text contained within the elements. They offer slightly more control over attributes, but even this is very limited. For example, there is no way of saying that an attribute must be numeric. It is the document itself that decides whether it is going to reference a DTD or not, which DTD it is going to reference, and whether it is going to override any of the declarations in the DTD in its private internal subset.

SCHEMA LANGUAGES AND NOTATIONS

The formal role of a schema is to define the set of all possible valid documents, or in other words, to define what constraints, beyond XML itself, the documents must meet for them to be more meaningful.

One purpose of a schema is to define the difference between a valid document and an invalid one.

The second purpose of a schema is to explain to the document the interpretation and usage of the constructs provided so that the sender and the recipient share a common understanding of the meaning of the message.

As a constraint language, DTDs are very limited. They provide some control over which of the elements can be nested within each other but say nothing about the text contained within the elements.

THE PURPOSE OF XML SCHEMA

XML schema is an XML-based language used to create XML-based languages and data models. An XML schema defines element and attribute names for a class of XML documents. The schema also specifies the structure that those documents must adhere to and the type of content that each element can hold.

XML documents that attempt to adhere to an XML schema are said to be instances of that schema. If they correctly adhere to the schema, then they are valid instances. This is not the same as being well-formed. A well-formed XML document follows all the syntax rules of XML, but it does necessarily adhere to any particular schema. So, an XML document can be well-formed without being valid, but it cannot be valid unless it is well-formed.

THE POWER OF XML SCHEMA

DTDs are similar to XML schemas in that they are used to create classes of XML documents. DTDs were around long before the advent of XML. They were originally created to define languages based on SGML, the parent of XML. Although DTDs are still common, XML Schema is a much more powerful language.

As a means of understanding the power of XML schema, let's look at the limitations of DTD.

- DTDs do not have built-in datatypes.
- DTDs do not support user-derived datatypes.
- DTDs allow only limited control over cardinality (the number of occurrences of an element within its parent).
- DTDs do not support namespaces or any simple way of reusing or importing other schemas.

XML Schema Example

```
<?xml version="1.0"?>
<xs:schema xmlns:xs="http://www.w3.org/2001/XMLSchema">
<xs:element name="note">
  <xs:complexType>
    <xs:sequence>
      <xs:element name="to" type="xs:string"/>
      <xs:element name="from" type="xs:string"/>
      <xs:element name="heading" type="xs:string"/>
      <xs:element name="body" type="xs:string"/>
    </xs:sequence>
```

```
    </xs:complexType>
  </xs:element>
  </xs:schema>
```

A FIRST LOOK

An XML schema describes the structure of an XML instance document by defining what each element must or may contain. An element is limited by its type. For example, an element of complex type can contain child elements and attributes, whereas a simple-type element can only contain text. The diagram below gives a first look at the types of XML schema elements.

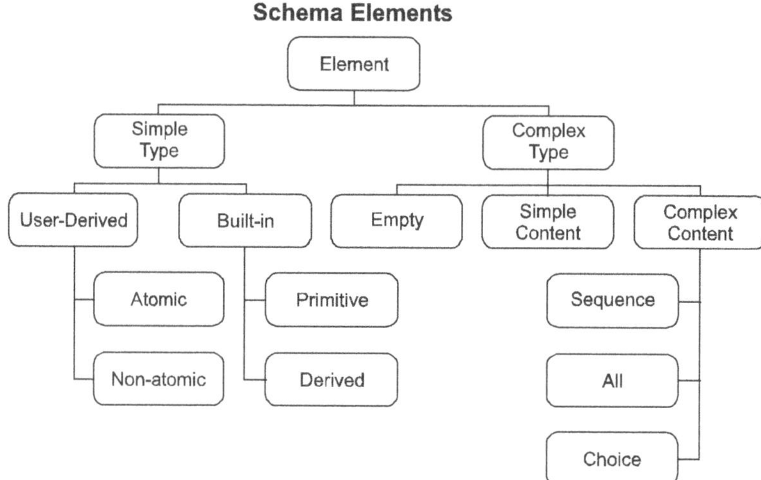

FIGURE 7.1 XML schema elements diagram

Schema authors can define their own types or use the built-in types.

The following is a high-level overview of schema types.

- Elements can be of a simple type or complex type.
- Simple type elements can only contain text. They cannot have child elements or attributes.
- All the built-in types are simple types (e.g, xs:string).
- Schema authors can derive simple types by restricting another simple type. For example, an email type could be derived by limiting a string to a specific pattern.

- Simple types can be atomic (e.g, strings and integers) or non-atomic (e.g, lists).
- Complex-type elements can contain child elements and attributes as well as text.
- By default, complex-type elements have complex content, meaning that they have child elements.
- Complex-type elements can be limited to having simple content, meaning they only contain text. They are different from simple type elements in that they have attributes.
- Complex types can be limited to having no content, meaning they are empty, but they have may have attributes.
- Complex types may have mixed content-a combination of text and child elements.

A Simple XML Document

Look at this simple XML document called "note.xml:"

```
<?xml version="1.0"?>
<note>
  <to>Shashi</to>
  <from>Yashasvi</from>
  <heading>Reminder</heading>
  <body>Don't forget me this weekend!</body>
</note>
```

A DTD File

The following example is a DTD file called "note.dtd" that defines the elements of the XML document above ("note.xml"):

```
<!ELEMENT note (to, from, heading, body)>
<!ELEMENT to (#PCDATA)>
<!ELEMENT from (#PCDATA)>
<!ELEMENT heading (#PCDATA)>
<!ELEMENT body (#PCDATA)>
```

The first line defines the note element to have four child elements: to, from, heading, and body.

Lines 2–5 defines the to, from, heading, and body elements to be of type "#PCDATA."

An XML Schema

The following example is an XML schema file called "note.xsd" that defines the elements of the XML document above ("note.xml"):

```
<?xml version="1.0"?>
<xs:schema xmlns:xs="http://www.w3.org/2001/XMLSchema"
targetNamespace="http://www.abc.com"
xmlns="http://www.abc.com"
elementFormDefault="qualified">
<xs:element name="note">
  <xs:complexType>
    <xs:sequence>
      <xs:element name="to" type="xs:string"/>
      <xs:element name="from" type="xs:string"/>
      <xs:element name="heading" type="xs:string"/>
      <xs:element name="body" type="xs:string"/>
    </xs:sequence>
  </xs:complexType>
</xs:element>
</xs:schema>
```

The note element is a complex type because it contains other elements. The other elements (to, from, heading, and body) are simple types because they do not contain other elements. You will learn more about simple and complex types in the following chapters.

A Reference to a DTD

This XML document has a reference to a DTD:

```
<?xml version="1.0"?>
<!DOCTYPE note SYSTEM
"http://www.abc.com/dtd/note.dtd">
<note>
  <to>Shashi</to>
  <from>Yashasvi</from>
  <heading>Reminder</heading>
  <body>Don't forget me this weekend!</body>
</note>
```

A Reference to an XML Schema

This XML document has a reference to an XML schema:

```
<?xml version="1.0"?>
<note
xmlns="http://www.abc.com"
xmlns:xsi="http://www.w3.org/2001/XMLSchema-instance"
xsi:schemaLocation="http://www.abc.com note.xsd">
  <to>Shashi</to>
  <from>Yashasvi</from>
  <heading>Reminder</heading>
  <body>Don't forget me this weekend!</body>
</note>
XSD - The <schema> Element
```

The <schema> element is the root element of every XML schema.
The <schema> element
The <schema> element is the root element of every XML schema:

```
<?xml version="1.0"?>
<xs:schema>
...
...
</xs:schema>
```

The <schema> element may contain some attributes. A schema declaration often looks something like this:

```
<?xml version="1.0"?>
<xs:schema xmlns:xs="http://www.w3.org/2001/XMLSchema"
targetNamespace="http://www.abc.com"
xmlns="http://www.abc.com"
elementFormDefault="qualified">
...
...
</xs:schema>
```

The following fragment

```
xmlns:xs="http://www.w3.org/2001/XMLSchema"
```

indicates that the elements and data types used in the schema come from the "*http://www.w3.org/2001/XMLSchema*" namespace. It also specifies that the elements and data types that come from the "*http://www.w3.org/2001/XMLSchema*" namespace should be prefixed with xs:

This fragment

```
targetNamespace="http://www.abc.com"
```

indicates that the elements defined by this schema (note, to, from, heading, and body) come from the "http://www.abc.com" namespace.

This fragment

```
xmlns="http://www.abc.com"
```

indicates that the default namespace is "http://www.abc.com".

This fragment

```
elementFormDefault="qualified"
```

indicates that any elements used by the XML instance document which were declared in this schema must be namespace qualified. Referencing a schema in an XML document.

This XML document has a reference to an XML schema:

```
<?xml version="1.0"?>
<note xmlns="http://www.abc.com"
xmlns:xsi="http://www.w3.org/2001/XMLSchema-instance"
xsi:schemaLocation="http://www.abc.com note.xsd">
<to>Shashi</to>
<from>Yashasvi</from>
<heading>Reminder</heading>
<body>Don't forget me this weekend!</body>
</note>
```

The following fragment

```
xmlns="http://www.abc.com"
```

specifies the default namespace declaration. This declaration tells the schema-validator that all the elements used in this XML document are declared in the "http://www.abc.com" namespace.

Once you have the XML schema instance namespace available:

```
xmlns:xsi="http://www.w3.org/2001/XMLSchema-instance"
```

you can use the schema location attribute. This attribute has two values. The first value is the namespace to use. The second value is the location of the XML schema to use for that namespace:

```
xsi:schemaLocation="http://www.abc.com note.xsd"
```

XSD Simple Elements

XML schemas define the elements of your XML files. A simple element is an XML element that contains only text. It cannot contain any other elements or attributes.

However, the "only text" restriction is quite misleading. The text can be of many different types. It can be one of the types included in the XML schema definition (boolean, string, and date) or it can be a custom type that you define yourself.

You can also add restrictions (facets) to a data type in order to limit its content or you can require the data to match a specific pattern.

The syntax for defining a simple element is:

```
<xs:element name="xxx" type="yyy"/>
```

where xxx is the name of the element and yyy is the data type of the element.

The XML schema has a lot of built-in data types. The most common types are

```
xs:string
xs:decimal
xs:integer
xs:boolean
xs:date
xs:time
```

Example: Here are some XML elements:

```
<lastname>Refsnes</lastname>
<age>36</age>
<dateborn>1970-03-27</dateborn>
```

And here are the corresponding simple element definitions:

```
<xs:element name="lastname" type="xs:string"/>
<xs:element name="age" type="xs:integer"/>
<xs:element name="dateborn" type="xs:date"/>
```

Default and Fixed Values for Simple Elements

Simple elements may have a default value OR a fixed value specified.

A default value is automatically assigned to the element when no other value is specified.

In the following example, the default value is "red:"

```
<xs:element name="color" type="xs:string" default="red"/>
```

A fixed value is also automatically assigned to the element, and you cannot specify another value.

In the following example the fixed value is "red:"

```
<xs:element name="color" type="xs:string" fixed="red"/>
```

A SIMPLE XML SCHEMA

Let's take a look at a simple XML schema, which is made up of one complex type element with two child simple type elements.

Code Sample: SchemaBasics/Demos/Author.xsd

```
<?xml version="1.0" encoding="UTF-8"?>
<xs:schema xmlns:xs="http://www.w3.org/2001/XMLSchema">
  <xs:element name="Author">
    <xs:complexType>
      <xs:sequence>
        <xs:element name="FirstName" type="xs:string" />
        <xs:element name="LastName" type="xs:string" />
      </xs:sequence>
    </xs:complexType>
  </xs:element>
</xs:schema>
```

An XML schema is an XML document and must follow all the syntax rules of any other XML document; that is, it must be well formed. XML schemas also have to follow the rules defined in the "schema of schemas," which defines, among other things, the structure of and element and attribute names in an XML schema.

Although it is not required, it is a common practice to use the xs qualifier to identify schema elements and types.

The document element of XML schemas is xs:schema. It takes the attribute xmlns:xs with the value of *http://www.w3.org/2001/XMLSchema*, indicating that the document should follow the rules of XML schema. This will be clearer after you learn about namespaces.

In this XML schema, we see a xs:element element within the xs:schema element. xs:element is used to define an element. In this case, it defines the element Author as a complex type element, which contains a sequence of two elements: FirstName and LastName, both of which are of the simple type, string.

SCHEMA AS A SET OF CONSTRAINTS

One purpose of a schema is to define the difference between a valid document and an invalid one. As far as possible, the rules should be expressed in such a way that software can decide whether a document is valid or not. For example, a rule for scientific journal that authors address should include the city and country only, or that the abstract must be in French.

There is a need for constraints for two reasons: stylistic reasons and processing reasons. The processing reasons define the information requirements of the next stage in the process, i.e., handling the document.

There is a great temptation to use the ability to impose rules thoughtlessly to make the system unnecessarily rigid. Information systems have a bad reputation for inflexibility, and the aim should be to use constraints sensibly to allow the humans in the process the maximum scope for using their intelligence.

SCHEMA AS AN EXPLANATION

The purpose of schema is to explain the document, the interpretation, and usage of the constructs provided. This purpose facilitates a common understanding of the message between the sender and the recipient.

In both the document and database traditions, this role of a schema is only secondary, though it is the more important role.

The schema is often not properly understood by the person who enters the data on the screen. As a result, the user interprets the schema in different ways, and hence attaches various meanings to the data fields, though the structure remains unchanged. Consequently, the system suffers from what is called *semantic drift*.

XSD Attributes

Simple elements cannot have attributes. If an element has attributes, it is considered to be of a complex type. But the attribute itself is always declared as a simple type.

The syntax for defining an attribute is

```
<xs:attribute name="xxx" type="yyy"/>
```

where xxx is the name of the attribute and yyy specifies the data type of the attribute.

The XML schema has a lot of built-in data types. The most common types are

```
xs:string
xs:decimal
xs:integer
xs:Boolean
xs:date
xs:time
```

Example: Here is an XML element with an attribute:

```
<lastname lang="EN">Banzal</lastname>
```

And here is the corresponding attribute definition:

```
<xs:attribute name="lang" type="xs:string"/>
```

Default and Fixed Values for Attributes

Attributes may have a default value OR a fixed value specified.

A default value is automatically assigned to the attribute when no other value is specified.

In the following example, the default value is “EN:”

```
<xs:attribute name="lang" type="xs:string" default="EN"/>
```

A fixed value is also automatically assigned to the attribute, and you cannot specify another value. In the following example, the fixed value is “EN:”

```
<xs:attribute name="lang" type="xs:string" fixed="EN"/>
```

Optional and Required Attributes

Attributes are optional by default. To specify that the attribute is required, use the “use” attribute:

```
<xs:attribute name="lang" type="xs:string" use="required"/>
```

Restrictions on Content

When an XML element or attribute has a data type defined, it puts restrictions on the element's or attribute's content. If an XML element is of type “xs:date” and contains a string like “Hello World,” the element will not validate. With XML schemas, you can also add your own restrictions to your XML elements and attributes.

XSD Restrictions/Facets

Restrictions are used to define acceptable values for XML elements or attributes. Restrictions on XML elements are called *facets*.

Restrictions on Values

The following example defines an element called “age” with a restriction. The value of age cannot be lower than 0 or greater than 120:

```
<xs:element name="age">
  <xs:simpleType>
    <xs:restriction base="xs:integer">
      <xs:minInclusive value="0"/>
      <xs:maxInclusive value="120"/>
    </xs:restriction>
  </xs:simpleType>
</xs:element>
```

Restrictions on a Set of Values

To limit the content of an XML element to a set of acceptable values, we use the enumeration constraint. The example below defines an element called "car" with a restriction. The only acceptable values are Audi, Golf, and BMW:

```
<xs:element name="car">
  <xs:simpleType>
    <xs:restriction base="xs:string">
      <xs:enumeration value="Audi"/>
      <xs:enumeration value="Golf"/>
      <xs:enumeration value="BMW"/>
    </xs:restriction>
  </xs:simpleType>
</xs:element>
```

The example above could also have been written like this:

```
<xs:element name="car" type="carType"/>

<xs:simpleType name="carType">
  <xs:restriction base="xs:string">
    <xs:enumeration value="Audi"/>
    <xs:enumeration value="Golf"/>
    <xs:enumeration value="BMW"/>
  </xs:restriction>
</xs:simpleType>
```

In this case, the type "carType" can be used by other elements because it is not a part of the "car" element.

Restrictions on a Series of Values

To limit the content of an XML element to define a series of numbers or letters that can be used, we would use the pattern constraint. The example below defines an element called "letter" with a restriction. The only acceptable value is ONE of the LOWERCASE letters from a to z:

```
<xs:element name="letter">
  <xs:simpleType>
    <xs:restriction base="xs:string">
      <xs:pattern value="[a-z]"/>
    </xs:restriction>
  </xs:simpleType>
</xs:element>
```

The next example defines an element called "initials" with a restriction. The only acceptable value is THREE of the UPPERCASE letters from a to z:

```
<xs:element name="initials">
  <xs:simpleType>
    <xs:restriction base="xs:string">
      <xs:pattern value="[A-Z][A-Z][A-Z]"/>
    </xs:restriction>
  </xs:simpleType>
</xs:element>
```

The next example also defines an element called "initials" with a restriction. The only acceptable value is THREE of the LOWERCASE OR UPPERCASE letters from a to z:

```
<xs:element name="initials">
  <xs:simpleType>
    <xs:restriction base="xs:string">
      <xs:pattern value="[a-zA-Z][a-zA-Z][a-zA-Z]"/>
    </xs:restriction>
  </xs:simpleType>
</xs:element>
```

The next example defines an element called "choice" with a restriction. The only acceptable value is ONE of the following letters: x, y, OR z:

```
<xs:element name="choice">
  <xs:simpleType>
    <xs:restriction base="xs:string">
      <xs:pattern value="[xyz]"/>
    </xs:restriction>
  </xs:simpleType>
</xs:element>
```

The next example defines an element called "prodid" with a restriction. The only acceptable value is FIVE digits in a sequence, and each digit must be in a range from 0 to 9:

```
<xs:element name="prodid">
  <xs:simpleType>
    <xs:restriction base="xs:integer">
      <xs:pattern value="[0-9][0-9][0-9][0-9][0-9]"/>
    </xs:restriction>
  </xs:simpleType>
</xs:element>
```

Other Restrictions on a Series of Values

The example below defines an element called "letter" with a restriction. The acceptable value is zero or more occurrences of lowercase letters from a to z:

```
<xs:element name="letter">
  <xs:simpleType>
    <xs:restriction base="xs:string">
      <xs:pattern value="([a-z])*"/>
    </xs:restriction>
  </xs:simpleType>
</xs:element>
```

The next example also defines an element called "letter" with a restriction. The acceptable value is one or more pairs of letters, each pair consisting of a lower case letter followed by an upper case letter. For example, "sToP" will be validated by this pattern, but not "Stop" or "STOP" or "stop:"

```
<xs:element name="letter">
  <xs:simpleType>
    <xs:restriction base="xs:string">
      <xs:pattern value="([a-z][A-Z])+"/>
    </xs:restriction>
  </xs:simpleType>
</xs:element>
```

The next example defines an element called "gender" with a restriction. The only acceptable value is male OR female:

```
<xs:element name="gender">
  <xs:simpleType>
    <xs:restriction base="xs:string">
```

```
      <xs:pattern value="male|female"/>
    </xs:restriction>
  </xs:simpleType>
</xs:element>
```

The next example defines an element called "password" with a restriction. There must be exactly eight characters in a row and those characters must be lowercase or uppercase letters from a to z or a number from 0 to 9:

```
<xs:element name="password">
  <xs:simpleType>
    <xs:restriction base="xs:string">
      <xs:pattern value="[a-zA-Z0-9]{8}"/>
    </xs:restriction>
  </xs:simpleType>
</xs:element>
```

Restrictions on Whitespace Characters

To specify how whitespace characters should be handled, we would use the whiteSpace constraint. This example defines an element called "address" with a restriction. The whiteSpace constraint is set to "preserve," which means that the XML processor WILL NOT remove any white space characters:

```
<xs:element name="address">
  <xs:simpleType>
    <xs:restriction base="xs:string">
      <xs:whiteSpace value="preserve"/>
    </xs:restriction>
  </xs:simpleType>
</xs:element>
```

This example also defines an element called "address" with a restriction. The whiteSpace constraint is set to "replace," which means that the XML processor WILL REPLACE all white space characters (line feeds, tabs, spaces, and carriage returns) with spaces:

```
<xs:element name="address">
  <xs:simpleType>
    <xs:restriction base="xs:string">
      <xs:whiteSpace value="replace"/>
    </xs:restriction>
  </xs:simpleType>
</xs:element>
```

This example also defines an element called "address" with a restriction. The whiteSpace constraint is set to "collapse," which means that the XML processor WILL REMOVE all white space characters (line feeds, tabs, spaces, and carriage returns are replaced with spaces, leading and trailing spaces are removed, and multiple spaces are reduced to a single space):

```
<xs:element name="address">
  <xs:simpleType>
    <xs:restriction base="xs:string">
      <xs:whiteSpace value="collapse"/>
    </xs:restriction>
  </xs:simpleType>
</xs:element>
```

Restrictions on Length

To limit the length of a value in an element, we would use the length, maxLength, and minLength constraints. This example defines an element called "password" with a restriction. The value must be exactly eight characters:

```
<xs:element name="password">
  <xs:simpleType>
    <xs:restriction base="xs:string">
      <xs:length value="8"/>
    </xs:restriction>
  </xs:simpleType>
</xs:element>
```

This example defines another element called "password" with a restriction. The value must be a minimum of five characters and a maximum of eight characters:

```
<xs:element name="password">
  <xs:simpleType>
    <xs:restriction base="xs:string">
      <xs:minLength value="5"/>
      <xs:maxLength value="8"/>
    </xs:restriction>
  </xs:simpleType>
</xs:element>
```

Restrictions for Datatypes

Table 7.1 Restrictions for Datatypes

Constraint	Description
enumeration	Defines a list of acceptable values
fractionDigits	Specifies the maximum number of decimal places allowed. Must be equal to or greater than zero
length	Specifies the exact number of characters or list items allowed. Must be equal to or greater than zero
maxExclusive	Specifies the upper bounds for numeric values (the value must be less than this value)
maxInclusive	Specifies the upper bounds for numeric values (the value must be less than or equal to this value)
maxLength	Specifies the maximum number of characters or list items allowed. Must be equal to or greater than zero
minExclusive	Specifies the lower bounds for numeric values (the value must be greater than this value)
minInclusive	Specifies the lower bounds for numeric values (the value must be greater than or equal to this value)
minLength	Specifies the minimum number of characters or list items allowed. Must be equal to or greater than zero
pattern	Defines the exact sequence of characters that are acceptable
totalDigits	Specifies the exact number of digits allowed. Must be greater than zero
whiteSpace	Specifies how white space (line feeds, tabs, spaces, and carriage returns) is handled

DTD VS XML SCHEMA

Schemas show you how dramatically things will change between current practice of DTDs and future practice. Consider the following DTD for naming a person.

```
<!ELEMENT Name (Honorific?, First, MI?, Last, Suffix?)>
<!ELEMENT Honorific (#PCDATA)>
<!ELEMENT First (#PCDATA)>
```

```
<!ELEMENT MI (#PCDATA)>
<!ELEMENT Last (#PCDATA)>
<!ELEMENT Suffix (#PCDATA)>
```

We must minimally have first and last names, but we may optionally have a middle initial, honorific (such as Mr., Ms., and Dr.), and a suffix (such as Jr. and III). When we use the DTD for doing this, we are constrained by the fact that the DTD needs to be changed each time we want to have an element. We cannot possibly have an element, which can be optional. For performing such operations, we can use what can be called as schema-enabled DTD, wherein we can have schema within a DTD.

To start with, we can have a <Schema> element as the root of the schema. Then we have an element called Name, the name of which is set in the name attribute of the <element> tag.

```
<Schema ...>
      <element name="Name">
        <type>
        <element name="Honorific" type="string" minOccurs="0" maxOccurs="1"/>
           <element name="First" type="string"/>
            <element name="MI" type="string" minOccurs="0" maxOccurs="1"/>
             <element name="last" type="string"/>
        <element name="suffix" type="string" minOccurs="0" maxOccurs="1"/>
        </type>
      </element>
</Schema>
<element name="Name">
```

So <element name="Name"> declares a <name> element. We have used it in its simplest form here, but we should know it can be given a name and enclose element declarations. In such a form, it is suitable for reuse elsewhere, and specifies the content model of the <Name> element. Note how the element contained within <Name> is declared. Since they are simple types, we can declare them within the body of the <Name> declaration without further elaboration.

STRUCTURES

Everything we can define with a DTD is accounted for in the structures portion of XML schemas. As XML schemas are written in XML syntax, and structures refer to the XML constructs that we can use to define our markup. This means that XML schemas are really just another application of XML.

The structures section of the XML specification is the part where the elements and attributes for defining schemas are set out. More importantly, the content model for elements is described in this part. The content model clearly specifies the allowable internal structure of an element.

PREAMBLE

A schema consists of a preamble and zero or more definitions and declaration.

The preamble is found within the root element, schema. This must include at least three pieces of information attributes. The following are some of the most commonly used information attributes.

Table 7.2 Information Attributes

TargetNS	contains the namespace and URI of the schema that is being used
version attribute	is used to specify the version of the schema
xmlns attribute	provides the namespace for the XML schemas specification
finalDefault and exactDefault	provide defaults for two types of extensions

SAMPLE PREAMBLE

```
<?xml version="1.0"?>
<schema targetNS="http://myserver/myschema.xsd"
                  version="1.0"
                  xmlns="http://www.w3.org/2003/XMLSchema">
</schema>
```

The code snippet here shows how schema is used in XML with a few attributes. Here, the schema is residing on myserver, and is called myschema.xsd, .xsd being the file extension for XML schemas. The version attribute specifies that the XML used in this schema is of version 1. The default namespace declaration is the schema reference to XML schemas. This is a closed model schema, which means that all documents conforming to this schema will be completely defined by the schema and must not have any outside content.

ATTRIBUTES AND ATTRIBUTE GROUPS

Attribute declarations consist of an <attribute> element, which must minimally include a name attribute.

The <attribute> element also has optional cardinality attributes, minOccurs and maxOccurs, which are used to indicate whether the attribute must appear, and if so, how often.

Attribute declaration may have DEFAULT and FIXED attributes. These function much like the IMPLIED and FIXED keywords in DTDs. The value of the fixed attribute is the value the attribute must always have. The value of the default attribute is the value, which is assumed if the attribute does not explicitly appear in an element within an XML document.

Here are a couple of sample attribute declarations.

```
<attribute name="simpleAttr"/>
<attribute name="seqenceNo" type="integer" default="0"/>
```

CONTENT MODELS

XML schemas provide us with mechanisms for describing content model with a lot more accuracy than DTDs. These use complex type definitions and a new structure, the <group> element, to build the internal contents of an element declaration.

The content attribute tells us what elements describe, although it says nothing about the permitted attributes.

Table 7.3 shows the content attribute value and meaning.

Table 7.3 Content Attribute Value and its Meanings

Content Attribute Value	Meaning
Unconstrained	Content of any kind
Empty	Empty element
Mixed	Elements and character data

Compositors in the schema draft show how the content may be composed. These compositors are values of the order attribute of a <group> element. This new element gives us a way to provide ordered bodies of elements in a declaration. The compositors are shown in Table 7.4.

Table 7.4 Compositor Keyword with its Meaning and DTD Equivalent

Compositor Keyword	Meaning	DTD Equivalent
Seq	Elements must follow in exact order	, (comma)
Choice	Exactly one of the model elements appears	| (pipe)

ELEMENT DECLARATION

Syntax of schemas must be in such a way so as to make it usable in XML. The schemas are hence written using the syntax of XML, so as to make them applicable to XML documents.

```
<element name="Book" />
```

Supposing we had used <!ELEMENT> syntax to declare a <Book> element in a DTD, we now use element declarations inside an XML element. This is declared as shown in the code snippet. Here, the <element /> element is used to declare an element. The name attribute simply takes a value of the element we are creating.

Simple elements are composed of a reference to a data type and a series of attribute declarations or a reference to an attribute group. This is similar to a DTD declaration, where the element contains only PCDATA, except that the content is strongly typed.

DERIVATION

A new type extends another when it adds additional content to its source type. In this case, all the content declared in the source type appears in the derived type.

The code here gives an example of how types are derived. Here, the type FormalPersonName extends from PersonName and adds an additional property of adding an honorific element to the derived type.

```
<type name="PersonName">
            <element name="FirstName" type="string" />
            <element name="MI" type="string" />
            <element name="LastName" type="string" />
</type>
```

```
<type name="FormalPersonName" source="PersonName" derivedBy="extension">
            <element name="honorefic" type="string" />
</type>
<type name="ShortName" source="PersonName" derivedBy="restriction">
             <restrictions>
                     <element name="MI" maxOccurs="0" />
             </restrictions>
</type>
```

We can also impose restrictions on a derived type by giving a restriction value in the derived By attribute and adding the restriction's element, as shown in the piece of code given here.

DATA TYPES

The real world relies on the concepts of numbers, strings, and sets. Hence, the programs written in modern programming languages support elaborate systems of built-in types and procedures for defining new types. Therefore, the addition of data types to XML schemas are a great asset to programmers using XML for data in their applications.

The support for data types includes the ability to check the validity of a value in a document. This also includes aiding an appropriate conversion from text to the native type when processing an XML document.

Schema data types are said to have a set of distinct values called their *value space*.

PRIMITIVE TYPES

Primitive data types are those that are not defined in terms of other types. They are axiomatic. It is natural for the XML schema proposal to include the classic XML 1.0 types, but it also adds some types of its own.

Table 7.5 gives a list of primitive types introduced by XML schema.

Table 7.5 List of Primitive Types

Schema Primitive Type	Definition
String	Finite Sequence of ISO 10646 or Unicode characters, such as "thisisastring".
Boolean	The set (true, false).

(continued)

(continued)

Schema Primitive Type	Definition
Float	Standard mathematical concept of real numbers, corresponding to a single precision 32-bit floating point type.
Double	Standard mathematical concept of real numbers, corresponding to a double precision 64-bit floating point type; doubles consist of a decimal mantissa, followed optionally by the letter E and an integer exponent, (for example 1.06E19).
Decimal	Standard mathematical concept of a real numeric type; it covers a smaller range than doubles, and consists of a sequence of digits separated by a period, such as 0.58.
Timeinstant	The combination of the date and time to define a specific instant in time, encoded as a string. 2003-02-28T10:10:45:00 represents 10:10on 28 Feb 2003, expressed with seconds and fractional seconds. This type is always expressed YYYY-MM DDThh:mm:ss:sss, but can be immediately followed by a Z, to specify that the time is a coordinated universal time. Alternatively, the time zone can be specified by supplying a difference from CUT, using a+ or a- followed by hh:mm.
timeDuration	A combination of data and time to define a period, interval, or duration of time. For example, one month is represented by P0Y1M0T0H0M0S, where the lexical pattern is PnYnMnDTnHnMnS, and can be preceded by a +(or)-. The representation may be truncated on the right when the finer time intervals are not needed, for example P2Y3M for 2 years and 3 months. Note that the number pre-codes the character representing the intervals. Seconds may be expressed by a number including a decimal to represent fractional second. A minus sign preceding the lexical representation indicates a negative duration.

(continued)

Schema Primitive Type	Definition
recurringInstant	An instant of time that recurs with some regular frequency, such as every day; represented by substituting a dash for any period not provided in the lexical pattern for timeInstant. For example, an instant that occurs at 08:00 every day would be expressed - T08:00:00:000.
Binary	Arbitrarily long bodies of binary data
URI	URI reference

GENERATED AND USER DEFINED TYPES

As the name suggests, a generated data type is built from an existing type. The existing type, on which the generated type is built, is called the *base type*. XML schemas specify some generated types that are broadly useful. Generated and user defined types are shown in the table.

Table 7.6 Generated and User Defined Types

Generated Type	Base Type	Meaning
Language	String	Natural Language identifier; a token that meets the Language ID production in XML, for example "en"
NM TOKEN	NMTOKENS	XML 1.0 NMTOKEN
NMTOKENS	String	XML 1.0 NMTOKENS
Name	NMTOKEN	XML 1.0 name
Qname	Name	XML 1.0 Qualified Name
NCNAME	Name	XML 1.0 "non-colonized" name
ID	NCNAME	XML 1.0 attribute type ID
IDREF	IDREFS	XML 1.0 attribute type IDREF
IDREFS	String	XML 1.0 attribute type IDREFS
ENTITY	ENTITIES	XML 1.0 ENTITY
ENTITIES	String	XML 1.0 ENTITIES

(continued)

(continued)

Generated Type	Base Type	Meaning
NOTATION	NCNAME	XML 1.0 NOTATION
integer	decimal	Standard mathematical concept of discrete numeric types
non-negative-integer	integer	Standard mathematical concept of non-negative integers
positive-integer	integer	Standard mathematical concept of positive integers
non-positive-integer	integer	Standard mathematical concept of a negative integer or zero
negative-integer integer	integer	Standard mathematical concept of a strictly negative integer
Date	recurringInstant	Standard concept of a day, that is, an interval beginning at midnight and lasting 24 hours
Time	recurringInstant	Same as the left-truncated representation for timeInstant hh:mm:ss:sss

HYPERLINKS

Hypertext differs from the normal text in that it has hyperlinks. The hyperlinks are identified by the characteristic blue color underlined text that identifies hotspots. These hotspots, when clicked, will take us to the Web pages that are specified as links. Linking or cross-referencing can be done when

- There is a need to provide context-sensitive help, for instance, when we navigate tutorials, it will be easy to understand if elaborations for some technical terms or external references are provided.
- A file has to be referred or displayed on clicking the mouse at a particular point of the document.

LINKS

Link is a functionality that is associated with a text or an object in a document using markup language.

Providing links enables us to refer to an object or a file within the same document or a document in some other location. The object referred to can be an image file or any other file, or text within the same document, or a different document. Within a HTML or an XML document, there may be several links. The active document, which contains these links, is called the *source file*.

The linked file or file that has been referred to is called the *destination file* or the *target*. The target file may be directly opened on clicking a hotspot or it may in turn lead to some other link. In simple terms, a link is the association between a source and the target.

The target may be completely a new HTML page, in which case, the description of the target (locator) would be a Universal Resource Identifier (URI). The target may be a named element within an HTML page. It can be identified using the # symbol, called a *fragment identifier*. Then, the fragment identifier has to be followed by the NAME attribute of the target element.

Both the source and the target file can be viewed simultaneously. One of the best examples of viewing both the source and the target simultaneously is the search index provided in the HELP menu of any application, wherein selecting a particular index opens the corresponding document.

The differences between HTML links and XML links are depicted in Table 7.7.

Table 7.7 Differences between HTML Links and XML Links

HTML Links	XML Links
The linking mechanism is simple.	The linking mechanism is complex.
HTML links are about sources and targets.	XML's Xlink is about linking elements instead of sources.
Links are unidirectional, that is, one link lead the other end of a link in a straight.	Links can be bidirectional, so the other end of link could be a source as well as a target.
The source link leads to the target link.	The source link could refer to the resource, which could be a piece of data obtained as a result of a database query or an external link that acts as an intermediary en route to the final destination. XML's X links allows us to specify multiple or group linked locators.

LINKING AND QUERYING

There are six different areas that need to be addressed while dealing with linking and querying. They are as follows.

- **XML information set:** The World Wide Web Consortium (W3C)'s document defines what an XML information set is. It says that an XML information set comprises various pieces of information, which together make up the XML document.
- Xlink is W3C's mechanism for linking to other resources within an XML document. Xlink also allows no-XML document to be linked together. XPath is the general language specification for addressing parts of an XML document framed by W3C's.
- XPointer is W3C's mechanism for pointing to a particular location within an XML document.
- XML fragment Interchange for transmitting a part of XML document as per the W3C specifications.
- **Querying XML document:** The XML document can be queried using the XSLT technology recommended by W3C.

XML INFORMATION SET

The XML information set, or info set, is a working draft created by the W3C to describe various pieces of information that together form an XML document. There are fifteen distinct types of information that forms the XML document. They are represented in the table.

- Exactly one document information item
- One or more element information items
- Attribute information items
- Processing instruction information items
- Character information items
- Reference to skipped entity information items
- Comment information items
- Document type declaration information items
- Entity information items

- Notation information items
- Entity start marker information items
- Entity end marker information items
- CDATA start marker information items
- CDATA end marker information items
- Namespace declaration items

LINK ELEMENTS

HTML has two link elements namely, A and IMG, whereas in XML links, the link elements are identified by the element attributes.

Any XML element can act as a link element provided it has the right kind of attributes.

<|ELEMENT CORRELATION ANY> <!ATTLIST CORRELATION xlink:form CDATA #FIXED value>

The primary attribute that identifies the XML element as a link is the xlink:form attribute, whose declaration in an XML DTD would be as shown. Here, the value should be a locator and not the linking elements. The value can be simple or extended.

LOCATORS

XML links work with link elements. The link elements contain locators.

Locators are in the form of attributes or other elements that point to specific locations.

In general, a locator is a URI, a fragment identifier, or a URI combined with a fragment identifier. Locators for XML documents are extended pointers.

The syntax of locators allows us to use the two variations as shown here.

URI#fragment: This fetches the whole of the resource identified by the URI and then extracts the part identified by the fragment identifier.

URI|fragment: The application can decide how it will process the URI in order to extract the resource. This could be used to retrieve a particular part of the document.

If the fragment identifier is a character string, the string is treated as the value of the id attribute of an XML element. For instance, the locator sample.html#sa2 points to the element with attribute value of sa2 in the file sample.html.

XLINKS

XML's Xlinks are used to establish hyperlinks in XML documents.

The W3C Xlink working draft defines two categories of links. They are simple links and extended links.

The xml:link attribute is used for specifying a link or location term as shown here. xml:link="simple"| "extended" | "locator" | "group" | "document"

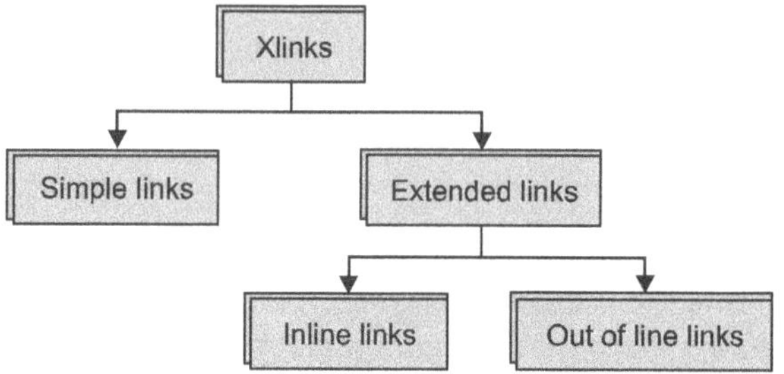

FIGURE 7.2 The outline classification of XML links

SIMPLE LINKS

Simple links are similar to HTML links, which are formed using the element A in HTML.

Simple links are used to jump from one source document to a specified destination either within the same document or another document. Simple links have only one locator and hence move in one direction from source to target location. A simple link contains a piece of text that acts as a resource and one end of the link.

An example for a simple link in a XML document is given here.

```
<sample.link xlink:form="sample" href="http:// m.com/title.XML" >see also
<sample.link>
```

EXTENDED LINKS

Extended links allow us to link together any number of resources, resulting in multiple targets instead of a simple one-to-one link in HTML.

Extended links allow XML documents to link to and from resources that cannot contain the links themselves. This includes graphic files, sound files, read-only documents, and so on, which does not allow us to modify the contents or embed links.

They enable manipulations like filtering, addition, and modification of links. For instance, imagine that we are able to modify the links at a certain point, so experienced readers of a technical manual can traverse a different path from that of novice readers.

Extended links also enable application software to process the links in different ways depending upon the requirements. An extended link does not directly point to anything or link anything together.

An extended link element identifies itself through its xlink:form attribute value and contains a set of locator elements that together form the extended link as shown. Here, the comment element declares itself to be an extended link and an opinion element declares itself to be a locator element.

```
<comment xlink:form="extended">
         <opinion xlink:form="locator" href="link1"/>
         <reference href="#division1"/>
         <reference href="http://one.com/ first.html ">
         <reference href="references.htm"/>
</comment>
```

EXTENDED LINK GROUPS

Links can be located in external documents. This is accomplished through the use of extended link groups. Similar to that of an extended link, an extended link group does not point or link to anything. Instead, it contains a set of document elements, in which each document contains the link resources as shown.

```
<xternal.refs >
<ref.doc href="http:// first.com/one.html"/>
<ref.doc href="list.htm"/>
</xternal.refs>
```

When using extended link groups, there is a possibility of a link element pointing to an extended link group. If an extended link group points back to the original document, or to a document containing another extended link group, then it would lead to infinite loops and links. To prevent infinite linking, we declare a value for the steps attribute of the group element. This specifies the limit of the number of layers that can be nested.

VALIDATING AN XML INSTANCE DOCUMENT

In the last section, you saw an example of a simple XML schema, which defined the structure of an Author element. The code sample below shows a valid XML instance of this XML schema.

Code Sample: SchemaBasics/Demos/MarkTwain.xml

```
<?xml version="1.0"?>
<Author xmlns:xsi="http://www.w3.org/2001/XMLSchema-instance"
 xsi:noNamespaceSchemaLocation="Author.xsd">
   <FirstName>Mark</FirstName>
   <LastName>Twain</LastName>
</Author>
```

This is a simple XML document. Its document element is Author, which contains two child elements, FirstName and LastName, just as the associated XML schema requires.

The xmlns:xsi attribute of the document element indicates that this XML document is an instance of an XML schema. The document is tied to a specific XML schema with the xsi:noNamespaceSchemaLocation attribute.

There are many ways to validate the XML instance. If you are using an XML authoring tool, it very likely is able to perform the validation for you. Alternatively, a couple of simple online XML schema validator tools are available.

SIMPLE-TYPE ELEMENTS

Simple-type elements have no children or attributes. For example, the Name element below is a simple-type element; whereas the Person and HomePage elements are not.

Code Sample: SimpleTypes/Demos/SimpleType.xml

```
<?xml version="1.0"?>
<Person>
 <Name>Mark Twain</Name>
 <HomePage URL="http://www.marktwain.com"/>
</Person>
```

A simple type can either be built-in or user-derived.

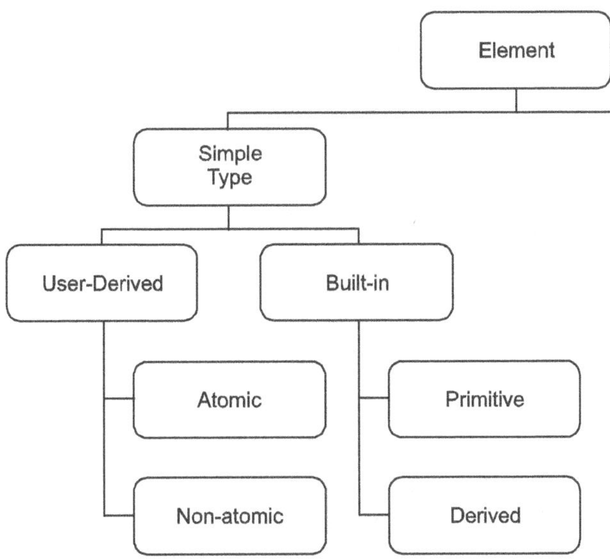

FIGURE 7.3 Classification of the simple-type element

BUILT-IN SIMPLE TYPES

XML schema specifies 44 built-in types, 19 of which are primitive.

19 PRIMITIVE DATA TYPES

The 19 built-in primitive types are as follows:

- string
- boolean
- decimal
- float
- double
- duration
- dateTime
- time
- date

- gYearMonth
- gYear
- gMonthDay
- gDay
- gMonth
- hexBinary
- base64Binary
- anyURI
- QName
- NOTATION

BUILT-IN DERIVED DATA TYPES

The other 25 built-in data types are derived from one of the primitive types listed below.

- normalizedString
- token
- language
- NMTOKEN
- NMTOKENS
- Name
- NCName
- ID
- IDREF
- IDREFS
- ENTITY
- ENTITIES
- integer
- nonPositiveInteger
- negativeInteger
- long
- int

- short
- byte
- nonNegativeInteger
- unsignedLong
- unsignedInt
- unsignedShort
- unsignedByte
- positiveInteger

DEFINING A SIMPLE-TYPE ELEMENT

A simple-type element is defined using the type attribute.

Code Sample: SimpleTypes/Demos/Author.xsd

```
<?xml version="1.0" ?>
<xs:schema xmlns:xs="http://www.w3.org/2001/XMLSchema">
 <xs:element name="Author">
  <xs:complexType>
   <xs:sequence>
    <xs:element name="FirstName" type="xs:string"/>
    <xs:element name="LastName" type="xs:string"/>
   </xs:sequence>
  </xs:complexType>
 </xs:element>
</xs:schema>
```

Notice the FirstName and LastName elements in the code sample below. They are not explicitly defined as simple-type elements. Instead, the type is defined with the type attribute. Because the value (string in both cases) is a simple type, the elements themselves are simple-type elements.

Code Sample: SimpleTypes/Exercises/Song.xsd

```
<?xml version="1.0"?>
<xs:schema xmlns:xs="http://www.w3.org/2001/XMLSchema">
 <xs:element name="Song">
  <xs:complexType>
   <xs:sequence>
    <!--
```

Add three simple-type elements:

1. Title
2. Year
3. Artist

```
    -->
   </xs:sequence>
  </xs:complexType>
 </xs:element>
</xs:schema>
```

USER-DERIVED SIMPLE TYPES

A schema author can derive a new simple type using the <xs:simpleType> element. This simple type can then be used in the same way that built-in simple types are.

Simple types are derived by restricting built-in simple types or other user-derived simple types. For example, you might want to create a simple type called password that is an eight-character string. To do so, you would start with the xs:string type and restrict its length to eight characters. This is done nesting the <xs:restriction> element inside of the <xs:simpleType> element.

Code Sample: SimpleTypes/Demos/Password.xsd

```
<?xml version="1.0"?>
<xs:schema xmlns:xs="http://www.w3.org/2001/XMLSchema">
 <xs:simpleType name="Password">
  <xs:restriction base="xs:string">
   <xs:length value="8"/>
  </xs:restriction>
 </xs:simpleType>
 <xs:element name="User">
  <xs:complexType>
   <xs:sequence>
    <xs:element name="PW" type="Password"/>
   </xs:sequence>
  </xs:complexType>
 </xs:element>
</xs:schema>
```

Code Sample: SimpleTypes/Demos/Password.xml

```
<?xml version="1.0"?>
<User xmlns:xsi="http://www.w3.org/2001/XMLSchema-instance"
 xsi:noNamespaceSchemaLocation="Password.xsd">
 <PW>MyPasWrd</PW>
</User>
```

Simple types can be derived by applying one or more of the following facets.

- length
- minLength
- maxLength
- pattern
- enumeration
- whiteSpace
- minInclusive
- minExclusive
- maxInclusive
- maxExclusive
- totalDigits
- fractionDigits

CONTROLLING LENGTH

The length of a string can be controlled with the length, minLength, and maxLength facets. We used the length facet in the example above to create a Password simple type as an eight-character string. We could use minLength and maxLength to allow passwords that were between six and twelve characters in length.

The schema below shows how this is done. The two XML instances shown below it are both valid, because the length of the password is between six and twelve characters.

Code Sample: SimpleTypes/Demos/Password2.xsd

```
<?xml version="1.0"?>
<xs:schema xmlns:xs="http://www.w3.org/2001/XMLSchema">
 <xs:simpleType name="Password">
```

```
  <xs:restriction base="xs:string">
   <xs:minLength value="6"/>
   <xs:maxLength value="12"/>
  </xs:restriction>
 </xs:simpleType>
 <xs:element name="User">
  <xs:complexType>
   <xs:sequence>
    <xs:element name="PW" type="Password"/>
   </xs:sequence>
  </xs:complexType>
 </xs:element>
</xs:schema>
```

Code Sample: SimpleTypes/Demos/Password2.xml

```
<?xml version="1.0"?>
<User xmlns:xsi="http://www.w3.org/2001/XMLSchema-instance"
 xsi:noNamespaceSchemaLocation="Password2.xsd">
 <PW>MyPass</PW>
</User>
```

Code Sample: SimpleTypes/Demos/Password2b.xml

```
<?xml version="1.0"?>
<User xmlns:xsi="http://www.w3.org/2001/XMLSchema-instance"
 xsi:noNamespaceSchemaLocation="Password2.xsd">
 <PW>MyPassWord</PW>
</User>
```

SPECIFYING PATTERNS

Patterns are specified using the xs:pattern element and regular expressions. For example, you could use the xs:pattern element to restrict the Password simple type to consist of between six and twelve characters, which can only be lowercase and uppercase letters and underscores.

Code Sample: SimpleTypes/Demos/Password3.xsd

```
<?xml version="1.0"?>
<xs:schema xmlns:xs="http://www.w3.org/2001/XMLSchema">
 <xs:simpleType name="Password">
  <xs:restriction base="xs:string">
```

```
    <xs:pattern value="[A-Za-z_]{6,12}"/>
   </xs:restriction>
  </xs:simpleType>
  <xs:element name="User">
   <xs:complexType>
    <xs:sequence>
     <xs:element name="PW" type="Password"/>
    </xs:sequence>
   </xs:complexType>
  </xs:element>
</xs:schema>
```

Code Sample: SimpleTypes/Demos/Password3.xml

```
<?xml version="1.0"?>
<User xmlns:xsi="http://www.w3.org/2001/XMLSchema-instance"
 xsi:noNamespaceSchemaLocation="Password3.xsd">
 <PW>MyPassword</PW>
</User>
```

WORKING WITH NUMBERS

Numeric simple types can be derived by limiting the value to a certain range using minExclusive, minInclusive, maxExclusive, and maxInclusive. You can also limit the total number of digits and the number of digits after the decimal point using totalDigits and fractionDigits, respectively.

MINS AND MAXS

The following example shows how to derive a simple type called Salary, which is a decimal between 10,000 and 90,000.

Code Sample: SimpleTypes/Demos/Employee.xsd

```
<?xml version="1.0"?>
<xs:schema xmlns:xs="http://www.w3.org/2001/XMLSchema">
 <xs:simpleType name="Salary">
  <xs:restriction base="xs:decimal">
   <xs:minInclusive value="10000"/>
   <xs:maxInclusive value="90000"/>
  </xs:restriction>
```

```
  </xs:simpleType>
  <xs:element name="Employee">
   <xs:complexType>
    <xs:sequence>
     <xs:element name="Salary" type="Salary"/>
    </xs:sequence>
   </xs:complexType>
  </xs:element>
</xs:schema>
```

Code Sample: SimpleTypes/Demos/ShashiBanzal.xml

```
<?xml version="1.0"?>
<Employee xmlns:xsi="http://www.w3.org/2001/XMLSchema-instance"
 xsi:noNamespaceSchemaLocation="Employee.xsd">
 <Salary>55000</Salary>
</Employee>
```

NUMBER OF DIGITS

Using totalDigits and fractionDigits, we can further specify that the Salary type should consist of seven digits, two of which come after the decimal point. Both totalDigits and fractionDigits are maximums. That is, if totalDigits is specified as 5 and fractionDigits is specified as 2, a valid number could have no more than five digits total and no more than two digits after the decimal point.

Code Sample: SimpleTypes/Demos/Employee2.xsd

```
<?xml version="1.0"?>
<xs:schema xmlns:xs="http://www.w3.org/2001/XMLSchema">
 <xs:simpleType name="Salary">
  <xs:restriction base="xs:decimal">
   <xs:minInclusive value="10000"/>
   <xs:maxInclusive value="90000"/>
   <xs:fractionDigits value="2"/>
   <xs:totalDigits value="7"/>
  </xs:restriction>
 </xs:simpleType>
 <xs:element name="Employee">
  <xs:complexType>
   <xs:sequence>
```

```
    <xs:element name="Salary" type="Salary"/>
   </xs:sequence>
  </xs:complexType>
 </xs:element>
</xs:schema>
```

Code Sample: SimpleTypes/Demos/MaryBanzal.xml

```
<?xml version="1.0"?>
<Employee xmlns:xsi="http://www.w3.org/2001/XMLSchema-instance"
 xsi:noNamespaceSchemaLocation="Employee2.xsd">
 <Salary>55000.00</Salary>
</Employee>
```

ENUMERATIONS

A derived type can be a list of possible values. For example, the JobTitle element could be a list of pre-defined job titles.

Code Sample: SimpleTypes/Demos/Employee3.xsd

```
<?xml version="1.0"?>
<xs:schema xmlns:xs="http://www.w3.org/2001/XMLSchema">
 <xs:simpleType name="Salary">
  <xs:restriction base="xs:decimal">
   <xs:minInclusive value="10000"/>
   <xs:maxInclusive value="90000"/>
   <xs:fractionDigits value="2"/>
   <xs:totalDigits value="7"/>
  </xs:restriction>
 </xs:simpleType>
 <xs:simpleType name="JobTitle">
  <xs:restriction base="xs:string">
   <xs:enumeration value="Sales Manager"/>
   <xs:enumeration value="Salesperson"/>
   <xs:enumeration value="Receptionist"/>
   <xs:enumeration value="Developer"/>
  </xs:restriction>
 </xs:simpleType>
 <xs:element name="Employee">
  <xs:complexType>
```

```
      <xs:sequence>
       <xs:element name="Salary" type="Salary"/>
       <xs:element name="Title" type="JobTitle"/>
      </xs:sequence>
    </xs:complexType>
  </xs:element>
</xs:schema>
```

Code Sample: SimpleTypes/Demos/SteveBanzal.xml

```
<?xml version="1.0"?>
<Employee xmlns:xsi="http://www.w3.org/2001/XMLSchema-instance"
 xsi:noNamespaceSchemaLocation="Employee3.xsd">
 <Salary>90000.00</Salary>
 <Title>Sales Manager</Title>
</Employee>
```

WHITESPACE HANDLING

By default, whitespace in elements of the datatype xs:string is preserved in XML documents; however, this can be changed for datatypes derived from xs:string. This is done with the xs:whiteSpace element, the value of which must be one of the following:

- preserve—Whitespace is not normalized. That is to say, it is kept as-is.
- replace—All tabs, line feeds, and carriage returns are replaced by single spaces.
- collapse—All tabs, line feeds, and carriage returns are replaced by single spaces and then all groups of single spaces are replaced with one single space. All leading and trailing spaces are then removed (i.e., trimmed).

In SimpleTypes/Demos/Password.xsd, we looked at restricting the length of a Password datatype to eight characters using the xs:length element. If whitespace is preserved, then leading and trailing spaces are considered part of the password. In the following example, we set xs:whiteSpace to collapse, thereby discounting any leading or trailing whitespace. As you can see, this allows the XML instance author to format the document without the consideration of the whitespace.

Code Sample: SimpleTypes/Demos/Password4.xsd

```
<?xml version="1.0"?>
<xs:schema xmlns:xs="http://www.w3.org/2001/XMLSchema">
```

```
 <xs:simpleType name="Password">
  <xs:restriction base="xs:string">
   <xs:length value="8"/>
   <xs:whiteSpace value="collapse"/>
  </xs:restriction>
 </xs:simpleType>
 <xs:element name="User">
  <xs:complexType>
   <xs:sequence>
    <xs:element name="PW" type="Password"/>
   </xs:sequence>
  </xs:complexType>
 </xs:element>
</xs:schema>
```

Code Sample: SimpleTypes/Demos/Password4.xml

```
<?xml version="1.0"?>
<User xmlns:xsi="http://www.w3.org/2001/XMLSchema-instance"
 xsi:noNamespaceSchemaLocation="Password4.xsd">
 <PW>
  12345678
 </PW>
</User>
```

SPECIFYING ELEMENT TYPE LOCALLY

We defined simple types globally and then set the type attribute of element declarations to be of our derived simple types. This makes it easy to reuse a simple type across multiple elements, as we saw with the ProperName type in the last exercise.

It is also possible to define the type of an element locally. The type is then unnamed and applicable only to that element. The only reason to do this is to clearly show that the type is specific to that element and not meant for reuse.

Code Sample: SimpleTypes/Demos/PasswordLocal.xsd

```
<?xml version="1.0"?>
<xs:schema xmlns:xs="http://www.w3.org/2001/XMLSchema">
 <xs:element name="User">
  <xs:complexType>
   <xs:sequence>
```

```
      <xs:element name="PW">
       <xs:simpleType>
        <xs:restriction base="xs:string">
         <xs:length value="8"/>
         <xs:whiteSpace value="collapse"/>
        </xs:restriction>
       </xs:simpleType>
      </xs:element>
     </xs:sequence>
    </xs:complexType>
   </xs:element>
  </xs:schema>
```

NONATOMIC TYPES

All of XML schema's built-in types are atomic, meaning that they cannot be broken down into meaningful bits. The XML schema provides for two nonatomic types: lists and unions.

LISTS

List types are sequences of atomic types separated by whitespace; you can have a list of integers or a list of dates. Lists should not be confused with enumerations. Enumerations provide optional values for an element. Lists represent a single value within an element.

Code Sample: SimpleTypes/Demos/EmployeeList.xsd

```
<?xml version="1.0"?>
<xs:schema xmlns:xs="http://www.w3.org/2001/XMLSchema">
 <xs:simpleType name="Salary">
  <xs:restriction base="xs:decimal">
   <xs:minInclusive value="10000"/>
   <xs:maxInclusive value="90000"/>
   <xs:fractionDigits value="2"/>
   <xs:totalDigits value="7"/>
  </xs:restriction>
 </xs:simpleType>
 <xs:simpleType name="JobTitle">
  <xs:restriction base="xs:string">
```

```
    <xs:enumeration value="Sales Manager"/>
    <xs:enumeration value="Salesperson"/>
    <xs:enumeration value="Receptionist"/>
    <xs:enumeration value="Developer"/>
   </xs:restriction>
  </xs:simpleType>
  <xs:simpleType name="DateList">
   <xs:list itemType="xs:date"/>
  </xs:simpleType>
  <xs:element name="Employee">
   <xs:complexType>
    <xs:sequence>
     <xs:element name="Salary" type="Salary"/>
     <xs:element name="Title" type="JobTitle"/>
     <xs:element name="VacationDays" type="DateList"/>
    </xs:sequence>
   </xs:complexType>
  </xs:element>
</xs:schema>
```

Code Sample: SimpleTypes/Demos/SandyBanzal.xml

```
<?xml version="1.0"?>
<Employee xmlns:xsi="http://www.w3.org/2001/XMLSchema-instance"
 xsi:noNamespaceSchemaLocation="EmployeeList.xsd">
 <Salary>44000</Salary>
 <Title>Salesperson</Title>
 <VacationDays>2006-8-13 2006-08-14 2006-08-15</VacationDays>
</Employee>
```

UNIONS

Union types are groupings of types, essentially allowing for the value of an element to be of more than one type. In the example below, two atomic simple types are derived: RunningRace and Gymnastics. A third simple type, Event, is then derived as a union of the previous two. The Event element is of the Event type, which means that it can either be of the RunningRace or the Gymnastics type.

Code Sample: SimpleTypes/Demos/Program.xsd

```
<?xml version="1.0"?>
<xs:schema xmlns:xs="http://www.w3.org/2001/XMLSchema">
 <xs:simpleType name="RunningRace">
  <xs:restriction base="xs:string">
   <xs:enumeration value="100 meters"/>
   <xs:enumeration value="10 kilometers"/>
   <xs:enumeration value="440 yards"/>
   <xs:enumeration value="10miles"/>
   <xs:enumeration value="Marathon"/>
  </xs:restriction>
 </xs:simpleType>
 <xs:simpleType name="Gymnastics">
  <xs:restriction base="xs:string">
   <xs:enumeration value="Vault"/>
   <xs:enumeration value="Floor"/>
   <xs:enumeration value="Rings"/>
   <xs:enumeration value="Beam"/>
   <xs:enumeration value="Uneven Bars"/>
  </xs:restriction>
 </xs:simpleType>
 <xs:simpleType name="Event">
  <xs:union memberTypes="RunningRace Gymnastics"/>
 </xs:simpleType>
 <xs:element name="Program">
  <xs:complexType>
   <xs:sequence>
    <xs:element name="Event" type="Event"/>
   </xs:sequence>
  </xs:complexType>
 </xs:element>
</xs:schema>
```

Code Sample: SimpleTypes/Demos/100Meters.xml

```
<?xml version="1.0"?>
<Program xmlns:xsi="http://www.w3.org/2001/XMLSchema-instance"
 xsi:noNamespaceSchemaLocation="Program.xsd">
 <Event>100 meters</Event>
</Program>
```

DECLARING GLOBAL SIMPLE-TYPE ELEMENTS

When an element declaration is a child of the xs:schema element, the declared element is global. Global elements can be referenced by other element declarations, allowing for element reuse. Take a look at the following example.

Code Sample: SimpleTypes/Demos/AuthorGlobal.xsd

```
<?xml version="1.0" encoding="UTF-8"?>
<xs:schema xmlns:xs="http://www.w3.org/2001/XMLSchema">
 <xs:element name="FirstName" type="xs:string"/>
 <xs:element name="LastName" type="xs:string"/>
 <xs:element name="Author">
  <xs:complexType>
   <xs:sequence>
    <xs:element ref="FirstName"/>
    <xs:element ref="LastName"/>
   </xs:sequence>
  </xs:complexType>
 </xs:element>
</xs:schema>
```

In this example, the FirstName and LastName elements are both declared globally. The global elements are then referenced as children of the Author sequence.

GLOBAL VS. LOCAL SIMPLE-TYPE ELEMENTS

The major advantage of declaring an element globally is that the element can then be referenced throughout the schema. This makes the code more modular and easier to maintain. For example, suppose that the song schema contained MusicWriter, LyricsWriter, and Singer elements. Each of these elements might have the child element Name. If the Name element is declared globally, any changes to that element can be made in one location.

The major disadvantage of declaring elements globally is that all global elements must have unique names.

Code Sample: SimpleTypes/Demos/BookLocal.xsd

```
<?xml version="1.0"?>
<xs:schema xmlns:xs="http://www.w3.org/2001/XMLSchema">
 <xs:simpleType name="PersonTitle">
```

```
      <xs:restriction base="xs:string">
       <xs:enumeration value="Mr."/>
       <xs:enumeration value="Ms."/>
       <xs:enumeration value="Dr."/>
      </xs:restriction>
     </xs:simpleType>
     <xs:element name="Book">
      <xs:complexType>
       <xs:sequence>
        <xs:element name="Title" type="xs:string"/>
        <xs:element name="Author">
         <xs:complexType>
          <xs:sequence>
           <xs:element name="Title" type="PersonTitle"/>
           <xs:element name="Name" type="xs:string"/>
          </xs:sequence>
         </xs:complexType>
        </xs:element>
       </xs:sequence>
      </xs:complexType>
     </xs:element>
    </xs:schema>
```

Notice that there are two elements named Title, which can appear in different locations in the XML instance and are of different types. When the Title element appears at the root of the XML instance, its value can be any string; when it appears as a child of Author, its value is limited to "Mr.," "Ms.," or "Dr."

The example below defines a similar content model; however, because the elements are declared globally, the name Title cannot be used twice.

Code Sample: SimpleTypes/Demos/BookGlobal.xsd

```
<?xml version="1.0"?>
<xs:schema xmlns:xs="http://www.w3.org/2001/XMLSchema">
 <xs:simpleType name="PersonTitle">
  <xs:restriction base="xs:string">
   <xs:enumeration value="Mr."/>
   <xs:enumeration value="Ms."/>
   <xs:enumeration value="Dr."/>
  </xs:restriction>
```

```
 </xs:simpleType>
 <xs:element name="BookTitle" type="xs:string"/>
 <xs:element name="Title" type="PersonTitle"/>
 <xs:element name="Name" type="xs:string"/>
 <xs:element name="Book">
  <xs:complexType>
   <xs:sequence>
    <xs:element ref="BookTitle"/>
    <xs:element name="Author">
     <xs:complexType>
      <xs:sequence>
       <xs:element ref="Title"/>
       <xs:element ref="Name"/>
      </xs:sequence>
     </xs:complexType>
    </xs:element>
   </xs:sequence>
  </xs:complexType>
 </xs:element>
</xs:schema>
```

DEFAULT VALUES

Elements that do not have any children can have default values. To specify a default value, use the default attribute of the xs:element element.

Code Sample: SimpleTypes/Demos/EmployeeDefault.xsd

```
<?xml version="1.0"?>
<xs:schema xmlns:xs="http://www.w3.org/2001/XMLSchema">
 ---- Code Omitted ----
 <xs:element name="Employee">
  <xs:complexType>
   <xs:sequence>
    <xs:element name="Salary" type="Salary"/>
    <xs:element name="Title" type="JobTitle" default="Salesperson"/>
   </xs:sequence>
  </xs:complexType>
 </xs:element>
</xs:schema>
```

When defaults are set in the XML schema, the following rules apply for the instance document.

- If the element appears in the document with content, the default value is ignored.
- If the element appears without content, the default value is applied.
- If the element does not appear, the element is left out. In other words, providing a default value does not imply that the element should be inserted if the XML instance author leaves it out.

Examine the following XML instance. The Title element cannot be empty; it requires one of the values from the enumeration defined in the JobTitle simple type. However, in accordance with the second item from the list, the schema processor applies the default value of Salesperson to the Title element, so the instance validates successfully.

Code Sample: SimpleTypes/Demos/MikeBanzal.xml

```
<?xml version="1.0"?>
<Employee xmlns:xsi="http://www.w3.org/2001/XMLSchema-instance"
 xsi:noNamespaceSchemaLocation="EmployeeDefault.xsd">
 <Salary>90000</Salary>
 <Title/>
</Employee>
```

FIXED VALUES

Element values can be fixed, meaning that if they appear in the instance document, they must contain a specified value. Fixed elements are often used for boolean switches.

Code Sample: SimpleTypes/Demos/EmployeeFixed.xsd

```
<?xml version="1.0"?>
<xs:schema xmlns:xs="http://www.w3.org/2001/XMLSchema">
 <xs:simpleType name="Salary">
  <xs:restriction base="xs:decimal">
   <xs:minInclusive value="10000"/>
   <xs:maxInclusive value="90000"/>
   <xs:fractionDigits value="2"/>
   <xs:totalDigits value="7"/>
  </xs:restriction>
 </xs:simpleType>
```

```
<xs:simpleType name="JobTitle">
 <xs:restriction base="xs:string">
  <xs:enumeration value="Sales Manager"/>
  <xs:enumeration value="Salesperson"/>
  <xs:enumeration value="Receptionist"/>
  <xs:enumeration value="Developer"/>
 </xs:restriction>
</xs:simpleType>
<xs:element name="Employee">
 <xs:complexType>
  <xs:sequence>
   <xs:element name="Salary" type="Salary"/>
   <xs:element name="Title" type="JobTitle"/>
   <xs:element name="Status" type="xs:string" fixed="current"
    minOccurs="0"/>
  </xs:sequence>
 </xs:complexType>
</xs:element>
</xs:schema>
```

The MinOccurs attribute is used to make the Status element optional. However, if it is used, it must contain the value current or be left empty, in which case, the value "current" is implied. The file SimpleTypes/Demos/LauraBanzal.xml in the Demos folder validates against this schema.

NIL VALUES

When an optional element is left out of an XML instance, it has no clear meaning. For example, suppose a schema declares a Name element as having required FirstName and LastName elements and an optional MiddleName element. And suppose a particular instance of this schema does not include the MiddleName element. Does this mean that the instance author did not know the middle name of the person in question or does it mean the person in question has no middle name?

Setting the nillable attribute of xs:element to true indicates that such elements can be set to nil by setting the xsi:nil attribute to true.

Code Sample: SimpleTypes/Demos/AuthorNillable.xsd

```
<?xml version="1.0"?>
<xs:schema xmlns:xs="http://www.w3.org/2001/XMLSchema">
 <xs:element name="Author">
```

```
    <xs:complexType>
     <xs:sequence>
      <xs:element name="FirstName" type="xs:string"/>
      <xs:element name="MiddleName" type="xs:string" nillable="true"/>
      <xs:element name="LastName" type="xs:string"/>
     </xs:sequence>
    </xs:complexType>
   </xs:element>
  </xs:schema>
```

Code Sample: SimpleTypes/Demos/MarkTwain.xml

```
<?xml version="1.0"?>
<Author xmlns:xsi="http://www.w3.org/2001/XMLSchema-instance"
 xsi:noNamespaceSchemaLocation="AuthorNillable.xsd">
 <FirstName>Mark</FirstName>
 <MiddleName xsi:nil="true"/>
 <LastName>Twain</LastName>
</Author>
```

By including the MiddleName element and setting xsi:nil to true, we are explicitly stating that Mark Twain has no middle name.

COMPLEX-TYPE ELEMENTS

Complex-type elements have attributes, child elements, or some combination of the two. For example, the Name and HomePage elements below are both complex-type elements.

Code Sample: ComplexTypes/Demos/ComplexType.xml

```
<?xml version="1.0"?>
<Person>
 <Name>
  <FirstName>Mark</FirstName>
  <LastName>Twain</LastName>
 </Name>
 <HomePage URL="http://www.marktwain.com"/>
</Person>
```

As the diagram below shows, a complex-type element can be empty, contain simple content such as a string, or can contain complex content such as a sequence of elements.

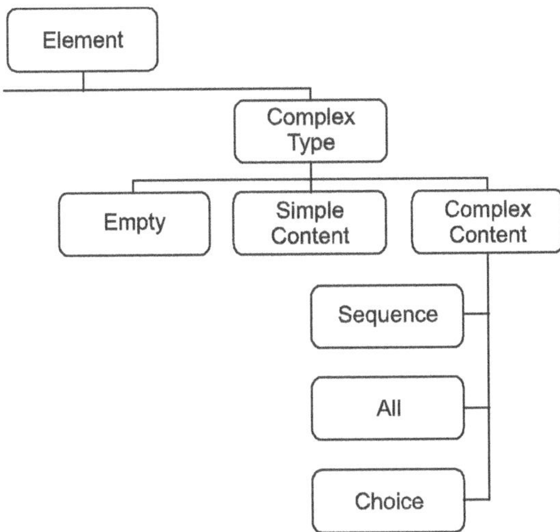

FIGURE 7.4 Classification of complex-type element

Whereas it is not necessary to explicitly declare that a simple-type element is a simple type, it is necessary to specify that a complex-type element is a complex type. This is done with the xs:complexType element as shown below.

Syntax

```
<xs:element name="ElementName">
 <xs:complexType>
  <!--Content Model Goes Here-->
 </xs:complexType>
</xs:element>
```

CONTENT MODELS

Content models are used to indicate the structure and order in which child elements can appear within their parent element. Content models are made up of model groups. The three types of model groups are listed below.

- xs:sequence—the elements must appear in the order specified
- xs:all—the elements must appear, but order is not important
- xs:choice—only one of the elements can appear.
- xs:sequence

The following sample shows the syntax for declaring a complex-type element as a sequence, meaning that the elements must show up in the order they are declared.

Syntax

```
<xs:element name="ElementName">
 <xs:complexType>
  <xs:sequence>
   <xs:element name="Child1" type="xs:string"/>
   <xs:element name="Child2" type="xs:string"/>
   <xs:element name="Child3" type="xs:string"/>
  </xs:sequence>
 </xs:complexType>
</xs:element>
xs:all
```

The following sample shows the syntax for declaring a complex-type element as a conjunction, meaning that the elements can show up in any order.

Syntax

```
<xs:element name="ElementName">
 <xs:complexType>
  <xs:all>
   <xs:element name="Child1" type="xs:string"/>
   <xs:element name="Child2" type="xs:string"/>
   <xs:element name="Child3" type="xs:string"/>
  </xs:all>
 </xs:complexType>
</xs:element>
xs:choice
```

The following sample shows the syntax for declaring a complex-type element as a choice, meaning that only one of the child elements may show up.

Syntax

```
<xs:element name="ElementName">
 <xs:complexType>
  <xs:choice>
   <xs:element name="Child1" type="xs:string"/>
   <xs:element name="Child2" type="xs:string"/>
   <xs:element name="Child3" type="xs:string"/>
  </xs:choice>
```

```
  </xs:complexType>
 </xs:element>
```

COMPLEX MODEL GROUPS

In the examples above, the model groups are all made up of simple-type elements. However, complex-type elements can contain other complex-type elements.

Syntax

```
<xs:element name="ElementName">
 <xs:complexType>
  <xs:choice>
   <xs:element name="Child1" type="xs:string"/>
   <xs:element name="Child2">
    <xs:complexType>
     <xs:sequence>
      <xs:element name="GC1" type="xs:string"/>
      <xs:element name="GC2" type="xs:string"/>
     </xs:sequence>
    </xs:complexType>
   </xs:element>
   <xs:element name="Child3" type="xs:string"/>
  </xs:choice>
 </xs:complexType>
</xs:element>
```

Furthermore, model groups can be nested within each other. The following example illustrates this. Notice that the choice model group, which allows for either a Salary element or a Wage element, is nested within a sequence model group. Both of the subsequent instances are valid according to this schema.

Code Sample: ComplexTypes/Demos/Employee.xsd

```
<?xml version="1.0"?>
<xs:schema xmlns:xs="http://www.w3.org/2001/XMLSchema">
 <xs:simpleType name="Salary">
  <xs:restriction base="xs:decimal">
   <xs:minInclusive value="10000"/>
   <xs:maxInclusive value="90000"/>
  </xs:restriction>
 </xs:simpleType>
```

```
 <xs:element name="Employee">
  <xs:complexType>
   <xs:sequence>
    <xs:element name="Name">
     <xs:complexType>
      <xs:sequence>
       <xs:element name="FirstName"/>
       <xs:element name="LastName"/>
      </xs:sequence>
     </xs:complexType>
    </xs:element>
    <xs:choice>
     <xs:element name="Salary" type="Salary"/>
     <xs:element name="Wage" type="xs:decimal"/>
    </xs:choice>
   </xs:sequence>
  </xs:complexType>
 </xs:element>
</xs:schema>
```

Code Sample: ComplexTypes/Demos/DaveBanzal.xml

```
<?xml version="1.0"?>
<Employee xmlns:xsi="http://www.w3.org/2001/XMLSchema-instance"
 xsi:noNamespaceSchemaLocation="Employee.xsd">
 <Name>
  <FirstName>Dave</FirstName>
  <LastName>Banzal</LastName>
 </Name>
 <Salary>90000</Salary>
</Employee>
```

Code Sample: ComplexTypes/Demos/JillBanzal.xml

```
<?xml version="1.0"?>
<Employee xmlns:xsi="http://www.w3.org/2001/XMLSchema-instance"
 xsi:noNamespaceSchemaLocation="Employee.xsd">
 <Name>
  <FirstName>Jill</FirstName>
  <LastName>Banzal</LastName>
 </Name>
 <Wage>20.50</Wage>
</Employee>
```

OCCURRENCE CONSTRAINTS

By default, elements that are declared locally must show up once, and only once, within their parent. This constraint can be changed using the minOccurs and maxOccurs attributes. The default value of each of these attributes is 1. The value of minOccurs can be any non-negative integer. The value of maxOccurs can be any positive integer or unbounded, meaning that the element can appear an infinite number of times.

The example below shows how minOccurs can be used to make an element optional and how maxOccurs can be used to allow an element to be repeated indefinitely.

Code Sample: ComplexTypes/Demos/Employee2.xsd

```
<?xml version="1.0"?>
<xs:schema xmlns:xs="http://www.w3.org/2001/XMLSchema">
 <xs:simpleType name="Salary">
  <xs:restriction base="xs:decimal">
   <xs:minInclusive value="10000"/>
   <xs:maxInclusive value="90000"/>
  </xs:restriction>
 </xs:simpleType>
 <xs:element name="Employee">
  <xs:complexType>
   <xs:sequence>
    <xs:element name="Name">
     <xs:complexType>
      <xs:sequence>
       <xs:element name="FirstName"/>
       <xs:element name="MiddleName" minOccurs="0"/>
       <xs:element name="LastName"/>
      </xs:sequence>
     </xs:complexType>
    </xs:element>
    <xs:choice>
     <xs:element name="Salary" type="Salary"/>
     <xs:element name="Wage" type="xs:decimal"/>
    </xs:choice>
    <xs:element name="Responsibilities">
     <xs:complexType>
      <xs:sequence>
```

```
        <xs:element name="Responsibility" type="xs:string"
         maxOccurs="unbounded"/>
       </xs:sequence>
      </xs:complexType>
     </xs:element>
    </xs:sequence>
   </xs:complexType>
  </xs:element>
 </xs:schema>
```

Note that minOccurs and maxOccurs can also be applied to model groups (e.g., xs:sequence) to control the number of times a model group can be repeated.

DECLARING GLOBAL COMPLEX-TYPE ELEMENTS

As with simple-type elements, complex-type elements can be declared globally by making the element declaration a child of the xs:schema element.

Globally declared elements cannot take occurrence constraints. However, the minOccurs and maxOccurs constraints can be applied to references to globally declared elements. To illustrate, look at the following example. Notice that all elements, both simple-type and complex-type, are declared globally and then referenced within the model groups. Some of the references (e.g., Responsibilities) have occurrence constraints assigned to them.

Code Sample: ComplexTypes/Demos/Employee3.xsd

```
<?xml version="1.0"?>
<xs:schema xmlns:xs="http://www.w3.org/2001/XMLSchema">
 <xs:simpleType name="Salary">
  <xs:restriction base="xs:decimal">
   <xs:minInclusive value="10000"/>
   <xs:maxInclusive value="90000"/>
  </xs:restriction>
 </xs:simpleType>
 <xs:element name="Name">
  <xs:complexType>
   <xs:sequence>
    <xs:element ref="FirstName"/>
    <xs:element ref="MiddleName" minOccurs="0"/>
```

```
    <xs:element ref="LastName"/>
   </xs:sequence>
  </xs:complexType>
 </xs:element>
 <xs:element name="FirstName"/>
 <xs:element name="MiddleName"/>
 <xs:element name="LastName"/>
 <xs:element name="Wage" type="xs:decimal"/>
 <xs:element name="Salary" type="Salary"/>
 <xs:element name="Responsibilities">
  <xs:complexType>
   <xs:sequence>
    <xs:element ref="Responsibility" maxOccurs="unbounded"/>
   </xs:sequence>
  </xs:complexType>
 </xs:element>
 <xs:element name="Responsibility" type="xs:string"/>
 <xs:element name="Employee">
  <xs:complexType>
   <xs:sequence>
    <xs:element ref="Name"/>
    <xs:choice>
     <xs:element ref="Salary"/>
     <xs:element ref="Wage"/>
    </xs:choice>
    <xs:element ref="Responsibilities" minOccurs="0"/>
   </xs:sequence>
  </xs:complexType>
 </xs:element>
</xs:schema>
```

MIXED CONTENT

Sometimes an element will contain both child elements and character text. For example, a para element might contain mostly plain character text, but it could also have other elements (e.g., emphasis) littered throughout the character text. As an example, let's examine the following XML instance document.

Code Sample: ComplexTypes/Demos/PaulMcCartney.xml

```
<?xml version="1.0"?>
<Employee xmlns:xsi="http://www.w3.org/2001/XMLSchema-instance"
 xsi:noNamespaceSchemaLocation="Employee4.xsd">
 <Name>
  <FirstName>Paul</FirstName>
  <LastName>McCartney</LastName>
 </Name>
 <Salary>90000</Salary>
 <Bio>
  Worked for <Company>the Beatles</Company> as a
   <JobTitle>Singer</JobTitle>.
  Worked for <Company>the Beatles</Company> as a
   <JobTitle>Bass Guitarist</JobTitle>.
  Worked for <Company>the Wings</Company> as a
   <JobTitle>Singer</JobTitle>.
 </Bio>
</Employee>
```

Notice that the Bio element contains child elements Company and JobTitle as well as character text. Such elements are said to contain *mixed content*. The syntax for declaring elements with mixed content is shown below.

Syntax

```
<xs:element name="ElementName">
 <xs:complexType mixed="true">
  <xs:sequence>
   <xs:element name="Child1" type="xs:string"/>
   <xs:element name="Child2" type="xs:string"/>
  </xs:sequence>
 </xs:complexType>
</xs:element>
```

The following example illustrates how to define this in our employee schema.

Code Sample: ComplexTypes/Demos/Employee4.xsd

```
<?xml version="1.0"?>
<xs:schema xmlns:xs="http://www.w3.org/2001/XMLSchema">
 ---- Code Omitted ----
```

```
    <xs:element name="Bio">
     <xs:complexType mixed="true">
      <xs:sequence maxOccurs="unbounded">
       <xs:element name="Company" type="xs:string"/>
       <xs:element name="JobTitle" type="xs:string"/>
      </xs:sequence>
     </xs:complexType>
    </xs:element>
 ---- Code Omitted ----
</xs:schema>
```

DEFINING COMPLEX TYPES GLOBALLY

As with simple types, complex types can be defined globally. The example below shows how this is done.

Code Sample: ComplexTypes/Demos/Author.xsd

```
<?xml version="1.0"?>
<xs:schema xmlns:xs="http://www.w3.org/2001/XMLSchema">
 <xs:complexType name="Person">
  <xs:sequence>
   <xs:element name="FirstName" type="xs:string"/>
   <xs:element name="LastName" type="xs:string"/>
  </xs:sequence>
 </xs:complexType>
 <xs:element name="Author" type="Person"/>
</xs:schema>
```

As you can see, complex types are defined with the xs:complexType element. The major advantage of defining a complex type globally is that it can be reused. For example, a schema might allow for an Illustrator element as well as an Author element. Both elements could be of type Person. This way, if the Person type is changed later, the change will apply to both elements.

The instance document below will validate properly against the schema above.

Code Sample: ComplexTypes/Demos/MarkTwain.xml

```
<?xml version="1.0"?>
<Author xmlns:xsi="http://www.w3.org/2001/XMLSchema-instance"
 xsi:noNamespaceSchemaLocation="Author.xsd">
```

```
  <FirstName>Mark</FirstName>
  <LastName>Twain</LastName>
 </Author>
```

Attributes

While attributes themselves must be of the simple type, only complex-type elements can contain attributes.

EMPTY ELEMENTS

An empty element is an element that contains no content, but it may have attributes. The HomePage element in the instance document below is an empty element. Below the instance is the snippet from the Author.xsd schema that declares the HomePage element.

Code Sample: Attributes/Demos/MarkTwain.xml

```
<?xml version="1.0"?>
<Author xmlns:xsi="http://www.w3.org/2001/XMLSchema-instance"
xsi:noNamespaceSchemaLocation="Author.xsd">
 <Name>
  <FirstName>Mark</FirstName>
  <LastName>Twain</LastName>
 </Name>
 <HomePage URL="http://www.marktwain.com"/>
</Author>
```

Code Sample: Attributes/Demos/Author.xsd

```
<?xml version="1.0"?>
<xs:schema xmlns:xs="http://www.w3.org/2001/XMLSchema">
 ---- Code Omitted ----
   <xs:element name="HomePage">
     <xs:complexType>
      <xs:attribute name="URL" type="xs:anyURI"/>
     </xs:complexType>
    </xs:element>
 ---- Code Omitted ----
</xs:schema>
```

ADDING ATTRIBUTES TO ELEMENTS WITH COMPLEX CONTENT

Elements that have child elements are said to contain complex content. Attributes for such elements are declared after the element's model group. For example, the Name element in the XML instance below has two child elements and two attributes. Below the instance is the snippet from the Author2.xsd schema that declares the Name element.

Code Sample: Attributes/Demos/MarkTwain2.xml

```
<?xml version="1.0"?>
<Author xmlns:xsi="http://www.w3.org/2001/XMLSchema-instance"
 xsi:noNamespaceSchemaLocation="Author2.xsd">
 <Name Pseudonym="true" HomePage="http://www.marktwain.com">
  <FirstName>Mark</FirstName>
  <LastName>Twain</LastName>
 </Name>
</Author>
```

Code Sample: Attributes/Demos/Author2.xsd

```
<?xml version="1.0"?>
<xs:schema xmlns:xs="http://www.w3.org/2001/XMLSchema">
 ---- Code Omitted ----
   <xs:element name="Name">
     <xs:complexType>
      <xs:sequence>
       <xs:element name="FirstName" type="xs:string"/>
       <xs:element name="LastName" type="xs:string"/>
      </xs:sequence>
      <xs:attribute name="Pseudonym" type="xs:boolean"/>
      <xs:attribute name="HomePage" type="xs:anyURI"/>
     </xs:complexType>
    </xs:element>
 ---- Code Omitted ----
</xs:schema>
```

ADDING ATTRIBUTES TO ELEMENTS WITH SIMPLE CONTENT

An element with simple content is one that only contains character data. If such an element contains one or more attributes, then it is a complex-type element. Elements with simple content and attributes are declared using the xs:simpleContent element and then extending the element with the xs:extension element, which must specify the type of simple content contained with the base attribute. The syntax is shown below.

Syntax

```
<xs:element name="ElementName">
 <xs:complexType>
  <xs:simpleContent>
   <xs:extension base="xs:string">
    <xs:attribute name="AttName" type="xs:string"/>
   </xs:extension>
  </xs:simpleContent>
 </xs:complexType>
</xs:element>
```

For example, the FirstName element in the next XML instance contains only simple content and has a single attribute. Below the instance is the snippet from the Author3.xsd schema that declares the FirstName element.

Code Sample: Attributes/Demos/NatHawthorne.xml

```
<?xml version="1.0"?>
<Author xmlns:xsi="http://www.w3.org/2001/XMLSchema-instance"
 xsi:noNamespaceSchemaLocation="Author3.xsd">
 <Name Pseudonym="true" HomePage="http://www.nathanielhawthorne.com">
  <FirstName Full="false">Nat</FirstName>
  <LastName>Hawthorne</LastName>
 </Name>
</Author>
```

Code Sample: Attributes/Demos/Author3.xsd

```
<?xml version="1.0"?>
<xs:schema xmlns:xs="http://www.w3.org/2001/XMLSchema">
 ---- Code Omitted ----
       <xs:element name="FirstName">
        <xs:complexType>
         <xs:simpleContent>
          <xs:extension base="xs:string">
           <xs:attribute name="Full" type="xs:boolean"/>
          </xs:extension>
         </xs:simpleContent>
        </xs:complexType>
```

```
      </xs:element>
 ---- Code Omitted ----
</xs:schema>
```

RESTRICTING ATTRIBUTE VALUES

Attribute values are restricted in the same way that the values of simple-type elements are restricted. Below are three examples.

This first example shows how to restrict an attribute value by defining its type locally. Test Attributes/Demos/HuckFinn.xml against this schema.

Code Sample: Attributes/Demos/Book.xsd

```
<?xml version="1.0"?>
<xs:schema xmlns:xs="http://www.w3.org/2001/XMLSchema">
 <xs:element name="Book">
  <xs:complexType>
   <xs:sequence>
    <xs:element name="Title" type="xs:string"/>
     <xs:element name="Author">
      <xs:complexType>
       <xs:sequence>
        <xs:element name="Name" type="xs:string"/>
       </xs:sequence>
       <xs:attribute name="Title">
        <xs:simpleType>
         <xs:restriction base="xs:string">
          <xs:enumeration value="Mr."/>
          <xs:enumeration value="Ms."/>
          <xs:enumeration value="Dr."/>
        </xs:restriction>
       </xs:simpleType>
      </xs:attribute>
     </xs:complexType>
    </xs:element>
   </xs:sequence>
  </xs:complexType>
 </xs:element>
</xs:schema>
```

This second example shows how to restrict an attribute value by applying a globally defined simple type. You may test Attributes/Demos/TomSawyer.xml against this schema.

Code Sample: Attributes/Demos/Book2.xsd

```
<?xml version="1.0"?>
<xs:schema xmlns:xs="http://www.w3.org/2001/XMLSchema">
 <xs:simpleType name="PersonTitle">
  <xs:restriction base="xs:string">
   <xs:enumeration value="Mr."/>
   <xs:enumeration value="Ms."/>
   <xs:enumeration value="Dr."/>
  </xs:restriction>
 </xs:simpleType>
 <xs:element name="Book">
  <xs:complexType>
   <xs:sequence>
    <xs:element name="Title" type="xs:string"/>
    <xs:element name="Author">
     <xs:complexType>
      <xs:sequence>
       <xs:element name="Name" type="xs:string"/>
      </xs:sequence>
      <xs:attribute name="Title" type="PersonTitle"/>
     </xs:complexType>
    </xs:element>
   </xs:sequence>
  </xs:complexType>
 </xs:element>
</xs:schema>
```

This third example shows how to declare an attribute with a derived type globally. You may test Attributes/Demos/LifeOnTheMississippi.xml against this schema.

Code Sample: Attributes/Demos/Book3.xsd

```
<?xml version="1.0"?>
<xs:schema xmlns:xs="http://www.w3.org/2001/XMLSchema">
 <xs:attribute name="Title">
  <xs:simpleType>
   <xs:restriction base="xs:string">
    <xs:enumeration value="Mr."/>
```

```
    <xs:enumeration value="Ms."/>
    <xs:enumeration value="Dr."/>
   </xs:restriction>
  </xs:simpleType>
 </xs:attribute>
 <xs:element name="Book">
  <xs:complexType>
   <xs:sequence>
    <xs:element name="Title" type="xs:string"/>
    <xs:element name="Author">
     <xs:complexType>
      <xs:sequence>
       <xs:element name="Name" type="xs:string"/>
      </xs:sequence>
      <xs:attribute ref="Title"/>
     </xs:complexType>
    </xs:element>
   </xs:sequence>
  </xs:complexType>
 </xs:element>
</xs:schema>
```

DEFAULT AND FIXED VALUES

Default Values

Attributes can have default values. To specify a default value, use the default attribute of the xs:attribute element. Default values for attributes work slightly differently than they do for elements. If the attribute is not included in the instance document, the schema processor inserts it with the default value. You may test Attributes/Demos/NatHawthorne2.xml against this schema.

Code Sample: Attributes/Demos/Author4.xsd

```
<?xml version="1.0"?>
<xs:schema xmlns:xs="http://www.w3.org/2001/XMLSchema">
 ---- Code Omitted ----
      <xs:element name="FirstName">
        <xs:complexType>
         <xs:simpleContent>
          <xs:extension base="xs:string">
```

```
            <xs:attribute name="Full" type="xs:boolean" default="true"/>
           </xs:extension>
          </xs:simpleContent>
         </xs:complexType>
        </xs:element>
 ---- Code Omitted ----
</xs:schema>
```

FIXED VALUES

Attribute values can be fixed, meaning that, if they appear in the instance document, they must contain a specified value. Like with simple-type elements, this is done with the fixed attribute. You may test Attributes/Demos/NatHawthorne3.xml against this schema.

Code Sample: Attributes/Demos/Author5.xsd

```
<?xml version="1.0"?>
<xs:schema xmlns:xs="http://www.w3.org/2001/XMLSchema">
---- Code Omitted ----
   <xs:element name="Name">
    <xs:complexType>
     <xs:sequence>
      <xs:element name="FirstName">
       <xs:complexType>
        <xs:simpleContent>
         <xs:extension base="xs:string">
          <xs:attribute name="Full" type="xs:boolean" default="true"/>
         </xs:extension>
        </xs:simpleContent>
       </xs:complexType>
      </xs:element>
      <xs:element name="LastName" type="xs:string"/>
     </xs:sequence>
     <xs:attribute name="Pseudonym" type="xs:boolean" fixed="true"/>
     <xs:attribute name="HomePage" type="xs:anyURI"/>
    </xs:complexType>
   </xs:element>
  </xs:sequence>
---- Code ----
</xs:schema>
```

REQUIRING ATTRIBUTES

By default, attributes are optional, but they can be required by setting the use attribute of xs:attribute to required as shown in the next code snippet.

Code Sample: Attributes/Demos/Author6.xsd

```
<?xml version="1.0"?>
<xs:schema xmlns:xs="http://www.w3.org/2001/XMLSchema">
---- Code Omitted ----
   <xs:element name="Name">
    <xs:complexType>
     <xs:sequence>
      <xs:element name="FirstName">
       <xs:complexType>
        <xs:simpleContent>
         <xs:extension base="xs:string">
          <xs:attribute name="Full" type="xs:boolean" default="true"/>
         </xs:extension>
        </xs:simpleContent>
       </xs:complexType>
      </xs:element>
      <xs:element name="LastName" type="xs:string"/>
     </xs:sequence>
     <xs:attribute name="Pseudonym" type="xs:boolean" fixed="true"/>
     <xs:attribute name="HomePage" type="xs:anyURI" use="required"/>
    </xs:complexType>
   </xs:element>
 ---- Code Omitted ----
</xs:schema>
```

Reusing Schema Components

We have already seen several methods of reusing schema parts.

- Declaring elements globally
- Declaring attributes globally
- Defining global simple types
- Defining global complex types

We will now look at some other methods of reuse.

GROUPS

Element and attribute groups can be used to create a set structure for reuse. To illustrate the benefit of groups, let's first look at a simple XML instance and its (rather long) schema that does not use groups.

Code Sample: ReusingComponents/Demos/WinnieThePooh.xml

```
<?xml version="1.0"?>
<Book xmlns:xsi="http://www.w3.org/2001/XMLSchema-instance"
 xsi:noNamespaceSchemaLocation="Book.xsd">
  <Title>Winnie the Pooh</Title>
   <Author Title="Mr." BirthYear="1882">
    <FirstName>A.</FirstName>
    <MiddleName>A.</MiddleName>
    <LastName>Milne</LastName>
    <Specialty>Childrens</Specialty>
   </Author>
   <Illustrator Title="Mr." BirthYear="1879">
    <FirstName>Ernest</FirstName>
    <MiddleName>H.</MiddleName>
    <LastName>Shepard</LastName>
   </Illustrator>
</Book>
```

Code Sample: ReusingComponents/Demos/Book.xsd

```
<?xml version="1.0"?>
<xs:schema xmlns:xs="http://www.w3.org/2001/XMLSchema">
 <xs:element name="Book">
  <xs:complexType>
   <xs:sequence>
    <xs:element name="Title" type="xs:string"/>
    <xs:element name="Author">
     <xs:complexType>
      <xs:sequence>
       <xs:element name="FirstName" type="xs:string"/>
       <xs:element name="MiddleName" type="xs:string" minOccurs="0"/>
       <xs:element name="LastName" type="xs:string"/>
       <xs:element name="Specialty">
        <xs:simpleType>
          <xs:restriction base="xs:string">
           <xs:enumeration value="Mystery"/>
```

```
        <xs:enumeration value="Humor"/>
        <xs:enumeration value="Horror"/>
        <xs:enumeration value="Childrens"/>
       </xs:restriction>
      </xs:simpleType>
     </xs:element>
    </xs:sequence>
    <xs:attribute name="Title">
      <xs:simpleType>
       <xs:restriction base="xs:string">
        <xs:enumeration value="Mr."/>
        <xs:enumeration value="Ms."/>
        <xs:enumeration value="Dr."/>
       </xs:restriction>
      </xs:simpleType>
     </xs:attribute>
     <xs:attribute name="BirthYear" type="xs:gYear"/>
    </xs:complexType>
   </xs:element>
   <xs:element name="Illustrator" minOccurs="0">
    <xs:complexType>
     <xs:sequence>
      <xs:element name="FirstName" type="xs:string"/>
      <xs:element name="MiddleName" type="xs:string" minOccurs="0"/>
      <xs:element name="LastName" type="xs:string"/>
     </xs:sequence>
     <xs:attribute name="Title">
       <xs:simpleType>
        <xs:restriction base="xs:string">
         <xs:enumeration value="Mr."/>
         <xs:enumeration value="Ms."/>
         <xs:enumeration value="Dr."/>
        </xs:restriction>
       </xs:simpleType>
      </xs:attribute>
      <xs:attribute name="BirthYear" type="xs:gYear"/>
    </xs:complexType>
   </xs:element>
  </xs:sequence>
 </xs:complexType>
</xs:element>
</xs:schema>
```

The Author element and the Illustrator element have some elements and attributes in common. Let's see how we can make this code more modular.

Element Groups

First, we'll look at how we can group the FirstName, MiddleName, and LastName elements with xs:group to avoid rewriting the elements.

Code Sample: ReusingComponents/Demos/Book2.xsd

```
<?xml version="1.0"?>
<xs:schema xmlns:xs="http://www.w3.org/2001/XMLSchema">
 <xs:group name="GroupName">
  <xs:sequence>
   <xs:element name="FirstName" type="xs:string"/>
   <xs:element name="MiddleName" type="xs:string" minOccurs="0"/>
   <xs:element name="LastName" type="xs:string"/>
  </xs:sequence>
 </xs:group>
<xs:element name="Book">
 <xs:complexType>
  <xs:sequence>
   <xs:element name="Title" type="xs:string"/>
   <xs:element name="Author">
    <xs:complexType>
     <xs:sequence>
      <xs:group ref="GroupName"/>
---- Code ----
    </xs:complexType>
   </xs:element>
   <xs:element name="Illustrator" minOccurs="0">
    <xs:complexType>
     <xs:sequence>
      <xs:group ref="GroupName"/>
     </xs:sequence>
---- Code ----
     </xs:complexType>
    </xs:element>
   </xs:sequence>
  </xs:complexType>
 </xs:element>
</xs:schema>
```

Attribute Groups

Now let's look at how we can use the xs:attributeGroup element to avoiding rewriting those attributes.

Code Sample: ReusingComponents/Demos/Book3.xsd

```
<?xml version="1.0"?>
<xs:schema xmlns:xs="http://www.w3.org/2001/XMLSchema">
 <xs:group name="GroupName">
  <xs:sequence>
   <xs:element name="FirstName" type="xs:string"/>
   <xs:element name="MiddleName" type="xs:string" minOccurs="0"/>
   <xs:element name="LastName" type="xs:string"/>
  </xs:sequence>
 </xs:group>
 <xs:attributeGroup name="AttGroupPerson">
  <xs:attribute name="Title">
   <xs:simpleType>
    <xs:restriction base="xs:string">
     <xs:enumeration value="Mr."/>
     <xs:enumeration value="Ms."/>
     <xs:enumeration value="Dr."/>
    </xs:restriction>
   </xs:simpleType>
  </xs:attribute>
 <xs:attribute name="BirthYear" type="xs:gYear"/>
</xs:attributeGroup>
<xs:element name="Book">
 <xs:complexType>
  <xs:sequence>
   <xs:element name="Title" type="xs:string"/>
   <xs:element name="Author">
    <xs:complexType>
     <xs:sequence>
      <xs:group ref="GroupName"/>
      <xs:element name="Specialty">
       <xs:simpleType>
        <xs:restriction base="xs:string">
         <xs:enumeration value="Mystery"/>
         <xs:enumeration value="Humor"/>
```

```
          <xs:enumeration value="Horror"/>
          <xs:enumeration value="Childrens"/>
         </xs:restriction>
        </xs:simpleType>
       </xs:element>
      </xs:sequence>
      <xs:attributeGroup ref="AttGroupPerson"/>
     </xs:complexType>
    </xs:element>
    <xs:element name="Illustrator" minOccurs="0">
     <xs:complexType>
      <xs:sequence>
       <xs:group ref="GroupName"/>
      </xs:sequence>
      <xs:attributeGroup ref="AttGroupPerson"/>
     </xs:complexType>
    </xs:element>
   </xs:sequence>
  </xs:complexType>
 </xs:element>
</xs:schema>
```

EXTENDING COMPLEX TYPES

New complex types can be derived by extending existing complex types. Both elements and attributes can be added in the new type, but nothing in the existing type can be overridden. New elements are appended to the content model, such that the original elements and new elements act as two groups that must appear in sequence.

The next example shows how the Person element can be extended.

Code Sample: ReusingComponents/Demos/Book4.xsd

```
<?xml version="1.0"?>
<xs:schema xmlns:xs="http://www.w3.org/2001/XMLSchema">
 <xs:complexType name="Person">
  <xs:sequence>
   <xs:element name="FirstName" type="xs:string"/>
```

```
    <xs:element name="MiddleName" type="xs:string" minOccurs="0"/>
    <xs:element name="LastName" type="xs:string"/>
   </xs:sequence>
   <xs:attributeGroup ref="AttGroupPerson"/>
  </xs:complexType>
  <xs:complexType name="PersonExtended">
   <xs:complexContent>
    <xs:extension base="Person">
     <xs:sequence>
      <xs:element name="Specialty">
       <xs:simpleType>
        <xs:restriction base="xs:string">
         <xs:enumeration value="Mystery"/>
         <xs:enumeration value="Humor"/>
         <xs:enumeration value="Horror"/>
         <xs:enumeration value="Childrens"/>
       </xs:restriction>
      </xs:simpleType>
     </xs:element>
    </xs:sequence>
   </xs:extension>
  </xs:complexContent>
 </xs:complexType>
 ---- Code ----
 <xs:element name="Book">
  <xs:complexType>
   <xs:sequence>
    <xs:element name="Title" type="xs:string"/>
    <xs:element name="Author" type="PersonExtended"/>
    <xs:element name="Illustrator" type="Person" minOccurs="0"/>
   </xs:sequence>
  </xs:complexType>
 </xs:element>
 </xs:schema>
```

No material changes have been made from Book.xsd to Book4.xsd.

ABSTRACT TYPES

When a type is made abstract, it cannot be used directly in an XML instance. One of its derived types must be used instead. The derived type is identified in the instance document using the xsi:type attribute. The schema below includes an abstract type with two derivations.

Code Sample: ReusingComponents/Demos/Animals.xsd

```
<?xml version="1.0"?>
<xs:schema xmlns:xs="http://www.w3.org/2001/XMLSchema">
 <xs:complexType name="Measurement">
  <xs:simpleContent>
   <xs:extension base="xs:integer">
    <xs:attribute name="units" type="xs:string"/>
   </xs:extension>
  </xs:simpleContent>
 </xs:complexType>
 <xs:element name="Weight" type="Measurement"/>
 <xs:element name="Name" type="xs:string"/>
 <!--Abstract Type-->
 <xs:complexType name="Animal" abstract="true">
  <xs:sequence>
   <xs:element ref="Name"/>
   <xs:element ref="Weight"/>
  </xs:sequence>
 </xs:complexType>
 <xs:complexType name="Dog">
  <xs:complexContent>
   <xs:extension base="Animal"/>
  </xs:complexContent>
 </xs:complexType>
 <xs:complexType name="Bird">
  <xs:complexContent>
   <xs:extension base="Animal">
    <xs:sequence>
     <xs:element name="WingSpan" type="Measurement"/>
    </xs:sequence>
   </xs:extension>
```

```
   </xs:complexContent>
  </xs:complexType>
  <xs:element name="Animals">
   <xs:complexType>
    <xs:sequence>
     <xs:element name="Animal" type="Animal" maxOccurs="unbounded"/>
    </xs:sequence>
   </xs:complexType>
  </xs:element>
 </xs:schema>
```

Code Explanation

The Animal type is declared as abstract by setting the abstract attribute to true. It is extended by the Dog and Bird types. The Dog type doesn't actually modify the original type at all, but the Bird type addes a WingSpan element.

Note that the Animal element declared within the Animals element is of the abstract type Animal.

Let's now look at an instance document of this schema:

Code Sample: ReusingComponents/Demos/Animals.xml

```
<?xml version="1.0" encoding="UTF-8"?>
<Animals xmlns:xsi="http://www.w3.org/2001/XMLSchema-instance"
xsi:noNamespaceSchemaLocation="Animals.xsd">
 <Animal xsi:type="Dog">
  <Name>Rover</Name>
  <Weight units="pounds">80</Weight>
 </Animal>
 <Animal xsi:type="Bird">
  <Name>Tweetie</Name>
  <Weight units="grams">15</Weight>
  <WingSpan units="cm">20</WingSpan>
 </Animal>
</Animals>
```

Notice that each of the Animal elements includes an xsi:type attribute. If we were to remove that attribute, the instance would be become invalid because the Animal element is of an abstract type.

XML SCHEMA KEYS

Uniqueness

XML schema provides a mechanism for requiring that each element be unique among like elements. This is best illustrated with an example.

Code Sample: SchemaKeys/Demos/Unique.xsd

```
---- Code ----
   <xs:element name="Artists">
    <xs:complexType>
     <xs:sequence>
      <xs:element name="Artist" maxOccurs="unbounded">
       <xs:complexType>
        <xs:simpleContent>
         <xs:extension base="xs:string">
          <xs:attribute name="aID" type="xs:string" use="required"/>
         </xs:extension>
        </xs:simpleContent>
       </xs:complexType>
      </xs:element>
     </xs:sequence>
    </xs:complexType>
   </xs:element>
   <xs:element name="Lyrics">
    <xs:complexType>
     <xs:sequence>
      <xs:element name="Stanza" maxOccurs="unbounded">
       <xs:complexType>
        <xs:sequence>
         <xs:element name="Line" type="xs:string" maxOccurs="unbounded"/>
        </xs:sequence>
        <xs:attribute name="Artist" type="xs:string"/>
       </xs:complexType>
      </xs:element>
     </xs:sequence>
    </xs:complexType>
   </xs:element>
  </xs:sequence>
 </xs:complexType>
```

```
  <xs:unique name="ArtistKey">
   <xs:selector xpath="Artists/Artist"/>
   <xs:field xpath="@aID"/>
  </xs:unique>
 </xs:element>
</xs:schema>
```

The Artist element has an aID attribute, which we would like to be able to use to uniquely identify the artist. The XML schema xs:unique element is used to enforce this. It takes two children:

- xs:selector—takes an xpath attribute, which holds an XPath 1.0 expression referencing the elements affected by this constraint.
- xs:field—takes an xpath attribute, which holds an XPath 1.0 expression specifying the part of the selected elements that must be unique.

In the example above, the selector XPath identifies all Artist elements that are children of an Artists element. The field XPath identifies the aID attribute as the part of the Artist element that must be unique.

In the XML instance below, each Artist must have a unique aID attribute. Try making them the same and validating.

Code Sample: SchemaKeys/Demos/Unique.xml

```
<?xml version="1.0"?>
<Song xmlns:xsi="http://www.w3.org/2001/XMLSchema-instance"
xsi:noNamespaceSchemaLocation="Unique.xsd">
 <Title Type="duet">The Girl Is Mine</Title>
 <Year>1983</Year>
 <Length>Medium</Length>
 <Artists>
  <Artist aID="MJ">Michael Jackson</Artist>
  <Artist aID="PM">Paul McCartney</Artist>
 </Artists>
 ---- Code Omitted ----
</Song>
```

KEYS

The XML schema also provides a mechanism for keys and key references—that is, for creating a relationship between elements through the value of an attribute or contained element. The xs:key and xs:keyref elements are used to create such a relationship.

Code Sample: SchemaKeys/Demos/Keys.xsd

```
---- Code ----
   <xs:element name="Artists">
    <xs:complexType>
     <xs:sequence>
      <xs:element name="Artist" maxOccurs="unbounded">
       <xs:complexType>
        <xs:simpleContent>
         <xs:extension base="xs:string">
          <xs:attribute name="aID" type="xs:string" use="required"/>
         </xs:extension>
        </xs:simpleContent>
       </xs:complexType>
      </xs:element>
     </xs:sequence>
    </xs:complexType>
   </xs:element>
   <xs:element name="Lyrics">
    <xs:complexType>
     <xs:sequence>
      <xs:element name="Stanza" maxOccurs="unbounded">
       <xs:complexType>
        <xs:sequence>
         <xs:element name="Line" type="xs:string" maxOccurs="unbounded"/>
         </xs:sequence>
         <xs:attribute name="Artist" type="xs:string" use="required"/>
       </xs:complexType>
      </xs:element>
     </xs:sequence>
    </xs:complexType>
   </xs:element>
  </xs:sequence>
 </xs:complexType>
 <xs:key name="ArtistKey">
  <xs:selector xpath="Artists/Artist"/>
  <xs:field xpath="@aID"/>
 </xs:key>
 <xs:keyref name="ArtistKeyRef" refer="ArtistKey">
  <xs:selector xpath="Lyrics/Stanza"/>
```

```
    <xs:field xpath="@Artist"/>
   </xs:keyref>
  </xs:element>
</xs:schema>
```

Like the xs:unique element, the xs:key and xs:keyref elements each contain xs:selector and xs:field child elements.

The xs:key element is used to identify the elements being referenced by the elements specified by the xs:keyref element.

In the example above, the Artist attribute of the Stanza element must point to an Artist element's aID attribute, which must be unique.

In the following XML instance, each Artist must have a unique aID attribute and each Stanza element must have an Artist attribute with the same value as one of the Artist's aID attributes. Try changing the value of a Stanza's Artist attribute to something arbitrary and validating.

Code Sample: SchemaKeys/Demos/Keys.xml

```
<?xml version="1.0"?>
<Song xmlns:xsi="http://www.w3.org/2001/XMLSchema-instance"
xsi:noNamespaceSchemaLocation="Keys.xsd">
 <Title Type="duet">The Girl Is Mine</Title>
 <Year>1983</Year>
 <Length>Medium</Length>
 <Artists>
  <Artist aID="MJ">Michael Jackson</Artist>
  <Artist aID="PM">Paul McCartney</Artist>
 </Artists>
 <Lyrics>
  <Stanza Artist="MJ">
   <Line>Every night she walks right in my dreams</Line>
   <Line>Every night she walks right in my dreams</Line>
 ---- Code Omitted ----
  </Stanza>
  <Stanza Artist="PM">
   <Line>I don't understand the way you think</Line>
   <Line>Saying that she's yours not mine</Line>
 ---- Code Omitted ----
  </Stanza>
  <Stanza Artist="MJ">
   <Line>I know she'll tell you I'm the one for her</Line>
```

```
    <Line>'Cause she said I blow her mind</Line>
  ---- Code Omitted ----
   </Stanza>
  </Lyrics>
 </Song>
```

ANNOTATING XML SCHEMAS

One of the nice features of XML schema is that comments about the schema itself can be made within built-in XML elements. This makes it possible to run a transformation against a schema to build documentation in HTML or some other human-readable format.

ANNOTATING A SCHEMA

The xs:annotation element is used to document a schema. It can take two elements, xs:documentation and xs:appInfo, which are used to provide human-readable and machine-readable notes, respectively.

The xs:annotation element can go at the beginning of most schema constructions, including xs:schema, xs:element, xs:attribute, xs:simpleType, xs:complexType, xs:group, and xs:attributeGroup.

Both the xs:documentation and xs:appInfo elements can contain any content, including undeclared elements and attributes. This allows the schema author to insert elements (e.g., HTML elements) to structure or format the documentation.

Code Sample: AnnotatingXMLSchemas/Demos/Book.xsd

```
<xs:attributeGroup name="AttGroupPerson">
  <xs:annotation>
   <xs:documentation>
```

This attribute group can be used with any element that represents a person. It provides for Title (?) and BirthYear (?).

```
  </xs:documentation>
 </xs:annotation>
 <xs:attribute name="Title">
  <xs:annotation>
   <xs:documentation>
```

This optional attribute provides the title of the person in question. There is no default value.

```
      </xs:documentation>
     </xs:annotation>
     <xs:simpleType>
      <xs:restriction base="xs:string">
       <xs:enumeration value="Mr."/>
       <xs:enumeration value="Ms."/>
       <xs:enumeration value="Dr."/>
      </xs:restriction>
     </xs:simpleType>
    </xs:attribute>
    <xs:attribute name="BirthYear" type="xs:gYear"/>
   </xs:attributeGroup>
   <xs:element name="Book">
    <xs:annotation>
     <xs:documentation>
```

Root Element: Contains the Title, Author, and Illustrator elements.

```
     </xs:documentation>
   </xs:annotation>
   <xs:complexType>
    <xs:sequence>
     <xs:element name="Title" type="xs:string"/>
     <xs:element name="Author">
      <xs:annotation>
       <xs:documentation>
```

The Author element contains the elements defined in the GroupName element group followed by the Specialty element and the attributes defined in the AttGroupPerson attribute group.

```
      </xs:documentation>
     </xs:annotation>
     <xs:complexType>
      <xs:sequence>
       <xs:group ref="GroupName"/>
       <xs:element name="Specialty">
        <xs:simpleType>
         <xs:restriction base="xs:string">
```

```
          <xs:enumeration value="Mystery"/>
          <xs:enumeration value="Humor"/>
          <xs:enumeration value="Horror"/>
          <xs:enumeration value="Childrens"/>
         </xs:restriction>
        </xs:simpleType>
       </xs:element>
      </xs:sequence>
      <xs:attributeGroup ref="AttGroupPerson"/>
     </xs:complexType>
    </xs:element>
    <xs:element name="Illustrator" minOccurs="0">
     <xs:annotation>
      <xs:documentation>
```

The Illustrator element contains the elements defined in the GroupName element group and the attributes defined in the AttGroupPerson attribute group.

```
         </xs:documentation>
        </xs:annotation>
        <xs:complexType>
         <xs:sequence>
          <xs:group ref="GroupName"/>
         </xs:sequence>
         <xs:attributeGroup ref="AttGroupPerson"/>
        </xs:complexType>
       </xs:element>
      </xs:sequence>
     </xs:complexType>
    </xs:element>
   </xs:schema>
```

XSD Complex Elements

A complex element contains other elements and/or attributes. A complex element is an XML element that contains other elements and/or attributes. There are four kinds of complex elements:

- empty elements
- elements that contain only other elements

- elements that contain only text
- elements that contain both other elements and text

Examples of Complex Elements

A complex XML element, "product," which is empty, is as follows:

```
<product pid="1345"/>
```

A complex XML element, "employee," which contains only other elements, is as follows:

```
<employee>
  <firstname>Shashi</firstname>
  <lastname>Banzal</lastname>
</employee>
```

A complex XML element, "food," which contains only text is as follows:

```
<food type="dessert">Ice cream</food>
```

A complex XML element, "description", which contains both elements and text, is as follows:

```
<description>
```

It happened on <date lang="norwegian">03.03.99</date> ....

```
</description>
```

How to Define a Complex Element

Look at this complex XML element, "employee," which contains only other elements:

```
<employee>
  <firstname>Shashi</firstname>
  <lastname>Banzal</lastname>
</employee>
```

We can define a complex element in an XML schema two different ways:

1. The "employee" element can be declared directly by naming the element:

```
<xs:element name="employee">
  <xs:complexType>
    <xs:sequence>
      <xs:element name="firstname" type="xs:string"/>
      <xs:element name="lastname" type="xs:string"/>
```

```
    </xs:sequence>
  </xs:complexType>
</xs:element>
```

If you use the method described above, only the “employee” element can use the specified complex type. Note that the child elements, “firstname” and “lastname,” are surrounded by the <sequence> indicator. This means that the child elements must appear in the same order as they are declared. You will learn more about indicators in the XSD Indicators chapter.

2. The “employee” element can have a type attribute that refers to the name of the complex type to use:

```
<xs:element name="employee" type="personinfo"/>

<xs:complexType name="personinfo">
  <xs:sequence>
    <xs:element name="firstname" type="xs:string"/>
    <xs:element name="lastname" type="xs:string"/>
  </xs:sequence>
</xs:complexType>
```

If you use the method described above, several elements can refer to the same complex type, like this:

```
<xs:element name="employee" type="personinfo"/>
<xs:element name="student" type="personinfo"/>
<xs:element name="member" type="personinfo"/>

<xs:complexType name="personinfo">
  <xs:sequence>
    <xs:element name="firstname" type="xs:string"/>
    <xs:element name="lastname" type="xs:string"/>
  </xs:sequence>
</xs:complexType>
```

You can also base a complex element on an existing complex element and add some elements, like this:

```
<xs:element name="employee" type="fullpersoninfo"/>

<xs:complexType name="personinfo">
  <xs:sequence>
    <xs:element name="firstname" type="xs:string"/>
    <xs:element name="lastname" type="xs:string"/>
  </xs:sequence>
</xs:complexType>
```

```
<xs:complexType name="fullpersoninfo">
  <xs:complexContent>
    <xs:extension base="personinfo">
      <xs:sequence>
        <xs:element name="address" type="xs:string"/>
        <xs:element name="city" type="xs:string"/>
        <xs:element name="country" type="xs:string"/>
      </xs:sequence>
    </xs:extension>
  </xs:complexContent>
</xs:complexType>
```

XSD Empty Elements

An empty complex element cannot have contents, only attributes. An empty XML element is as follows:

```
<product prodid="1345" />
```

The "product" element above has no content at all. To define a type with no content, we must define a type that allows elements in its content, but we do not actually declare any elements, like this:

```
<xs:element name="product">
  <xs:complexType>
    <xs:complexContent>
      <xs:restriction base="xs:integer">
        <xs:attribute name="prodid" type="xs:positiveInteger"/>
      </xs:restriction>
    </xs:complexContent>
  </xs:complexType>
</xs:element>
```

In the example above, we define a complex type with a complex content. The complexContent element signals that we intend to restrict or extend the content model of a complex type, and the restriction of integer declares one attribute but does not introduce any element content.

However, it is possible to declare the "product" element more compactly, like this:

```
<xs:element name="product">
  <xs:complexType>
    <xs:attribute name="prodid" type="xs:positiveInteger"/>
  </xs:complexType>
</xs:element>
```

Or you can give the complexType element a name, and let the "product" element have a type attribute that refers to the name of the complexType (if you use this method, several elements can refer to the same complex type):

```
<xs:element name="product" type="prodtype"/>
<xs:complexType name="prodtype">
  <xs:attribute name="prodid" type="xs:positiveInteger"/>
</xs:complexType>
```

XSD Elements Only

An "elements-only" complex type contains an element that contains only other elements. An XML element, "person," that contains only other elements:

```
<person>
  <firstname>Shashi</firstname>
  <lastname>Banzal</lastname>
</person>
```

You can define the "person" element in a schema, like this:

```
<xs:element name="person">
  <xs:complexType>
    <xs:sequence>
      <xs:element name="firstname" type="xs:string"/>
      <xs:element name="lastname" type="xs:string"/>
    </xs:sequence>
  </xs:complexType>
</xs:element>
```

Notice the <xs:sequence> tag. It means that the elements defined ("firstname" and "lastname") must appear in that order inside a "person" element.

Or you can give the complexType element a name, and let the "person" element have a type attribute that refers to the name of the complexType (if you use this method, several elements can refer to the same complex type):

```
<xs:element name="person" type="persontype"/>

<xs:complexType name="persontype">
  <xs:sequence>
    <xs:element name="firstname" type="xs:string"/>
    <xs:element name="lastname" type="xs:string"/>
  </xs:sequence>
</xs:complexType>
```

XSD Text-Only Elements

A complex text-only element can contain text and attributes. This type contains only simple content (text and attributes), therefore we add a simpleContent element around the content. When using simple content, you must define an extension OR a restriction within the simpleContent element, like this:

```
<xs:element name="somename">
  <xs:complexType>
    <xs:simpleContent>
      <xs:extension base="basetype">
        ....
        ....
      </xs:extension>
    </xs:simpleContent>
  </xs:complexType>
</xs:element>
```

OR

```
<xs:element name="somename">
  <xs:complexType>
    <xs:simpleContent>
      <xs:restriction base="basetype">
        ....
        ....
      </xs:restriction>
    </xs:simpleContent>
  </xs:complexType>
</xs:element>
```

Use the extension/restriction element to expand or to limit the base simple type for the element. Here is an example of an XML element, "shoesize," that contains text only:

```
<shoesize country="france">35</shoesize>
```

The following example declares a complexType, "shoesize." The content is defined as an integer value, and the "shoesize" element also contains an attribute named "country:"

```
<xs:element name="shoesize">
  <xs:complexType>
    <xs:simpleContent>
      <xs:extension base="xs:integer">
```

```
          <xs:attribute name="country" type="xs:string" />
        </xs:extension>
      </xs:simpleContent>
    </xs:complexType>
</xs:element>
```

We could also give the complexType element a name, and let the "shoesize" element have a type attribute that refers to the name of the complexType (if you use this method, several elements can refer to the same complex type):

```
<xs:element name="shoesize" type="shoetype"/>

<xs:complexType name="shoetype">
  <xs:simpleContent>
    <xs:extension base="xs:integer">
      <xs:attribute name="country" type="xs:string" />
    </xs:extension>
  </xs:simpleContent>
</xs:complexType>
```

XSD Mixed Content

A mixed complex type element can contain attributes, elements, and text. An XML element, "letter," that contains both text and other elements:

```
<letter>
  Dear Mr.<name>Ram Mandal</name>.
  Your order <orderid>1032</orderid>
  will be shipped on <shipdate>2001-07-13</shipdate>.
</letter>
```

The following schema declares the "letter" element:

```
<xs:element name="letter">
  <xs:complexType mixed="true">
    <xs:sequence>
      <xs:element name="name" type="xs:string"/>
      <xs:element name="orderid" type="xs:positiveInteger"/>
      <xs:element name="shipdate" type="xs:date"/>
    </xs:sequence>
  </xs:complexType>
</xs:element>
```

To enable character data to appear between the child-elements of "letter," the mixed attribute must be set to "true." The <xs:sequence> tag means that the elements defined (name, ordered, and shipdate) must appear in that order inside a "letter" element.

We could also give the complexType element a name, and let the "letter" element have a type attribute that refers to the name of the complexType (if you use this method, several elements can refer to the same complex type):

```
<xs:element name="letter" type="lettertype"/>
<xs:complexType name="lettertype" mixed="true">
  <xs:sequence>
    <xs:element name="name" type="xs:string"/>
    <xs:element name="orderid" type="xs:positiveInteger"/>
    <xs:element name="shipdate" type="xs:date"/>
  </xs:sequence>
</xs:complexType>
```

XSD INDICATORS

We can control HOW elements are to be used in documents with indicators. There are seven indicators.

Order indicators:

- All
- Choice
- Sequence

Occurrence indicators:

- maxOccurs
- minOccurs

Group indicators:

- Group name
- attributeGroup name

Order indicators

- Order indicators are used to define the order of the elements.

All Indicator

- The <all> indicator specifies that the child elements can appear in any order, and that each child element must occur only once:

```
<xs:element name="person">
  <xs:complexType>
    <xs:all>
      <xs:element name="firstname" type="xs:string"/>
      <xs:element name="lastname" type="xs:string"/>
    </xs:all>
   </xs:complexType>
</xs:element>
```

When using the <all> indicator you can set the <minOccurs> indicator to 0 or 1 and the <maxOccurs> indicator can only be set to 1 (the <minOccurs> and <maxOccurs> are described later).

Choice Indicator

The <choice> indicator specifies that either one child element or another can occur:

```
<xs:element name="person">
  <xs:complexType>
    <xs:choice>
      <xs:element name="employee" type="employee"/>
      <xs:element name="member" type="member"/>
    </xs:choice>
  </xs:complexType>
</xs:element>
```

Sequence Indicator

The <sequence> indicator specifies that the child elements must appear in a specific order:

```
<xs:element name="person">
  <xs:complexType>
   <xs:sequence>
     <xs:element name="firstname" type="xs:string"/>
     <xs:element name="lastname" type="xs:string"/>
   </xs:sequence>
  </xs:complexType>
</xs:element>
```

Occurrence Indicators

Occurrence indicators are used to define how often an element can occur.

For all "Order" and "Group" indicators (any, all, choice, sequence, group name, and group reference) the default value for maxOccurs and minOccurs is 1.

maxOccurs Indicator

The <maxOccurs> indicator specifies the maximum number of times an element can occur:

```
<xs:element name="person">
  <xs:complexType>
    <xs:sequence>
      <xs:element name="full_name" type="xs:string"/>
      <xs:element name="child_name" type="xs:string" maxOccurs="10"/>
    </xs:sequence>
  </xs:complexType>
</xs:element>
```

The example above indicates that the "child_name" element can occur a minimum of one time (the default value for minOccurs is 1) and a maximum of ten times in the "person" element.

minOccurs Indicator

The <minOccurs> indicator specifies the minimum number of times an element can occur:

```
<xs:element name="person">
  <xs:complexType>
    <xs:sequence>
      <xs:element name="full_name" type="xs:string"/>
      <xs:element name="child_name" type="xs:string"
      maxOccurs="10" minOccurs="0"/>
    </xs:sequence>
  </xs:complexType>
</xs:element>
```

The example above indicates that the "child_name" element can occur a minimum of zero times and a maximum of ten times in the "person" element.

To allow an element to appear an unlimited number of times, use the maxOccurs="unbounded" statement:

A working example:

An XML file called "Myfamily.xml" is as follows:

```
<?xml version="1.0" encoding="ISO-8859-1"?>
<persons xmlns:xsi="http://www.w3.org/2001/XMLSchema-instance"
xsi:noNamespaceSchemaLocation="family.xsd">
<person>
  <full_name>Hege Refsnes</full_name>
  <child_name>Cecilie</child_name>
</person>
<person>
  <full_name>Shashi Refsnes</full_name>
  <child_name>Hege</child_name>
  <child_name>Stale</child_name>
  <child_name>Jim</child_name>
  <child_name>Borge</child_name>
</person>
<person>
  <full_name>Stale Refsnes</full_name>
</person>
</persons>
```

The XML file above contains a root element named "persons." Inside this root element, we have defined three "person" elements. Each "person" element must contain a "full_name" element and it can contain up to five "child_name" elements.

Here is the schema file "family.xsd."

```
<?xml version="1.0" encoding="ISO-8859-1"?>
<xs:schema xmlns:xs="http://www.w3.org/2001/XMLSchema"
elementFormDefault="qualified">
<xs:element name="persons">
  <xs:complexType>
    <xs:sequence>
      <xs:element name="person" maxOccurs="unbounded">
        <xs:complexType>
          <xs:sequence>
            <xs:element name="full_name" type="xs:string"/>
            <xs:element name="child_name" type="xs:string"
            minOccurs="0" maxOccurs="5"/>
          </xs:sequence>
        </xs:complexType>
```

```
      </xs:element>
    </xs:sequence>
  </xs:complexType>
</xs:element>

</xs:schema>
```

Group Indicators

Group indicators are used to define related sets of elements.

Element Groups

Element groups are defined with the group declaration, like this:

```
<xs:group name="groupname">
...
</xs:group>
```

You must define an all, choice, or sequence element inside the group declaration. The following example defines a group named "persongroup," that defines a group of elements that must occur in an exact sequence:

```
<xs:group name="persongroup">
  <xs:sequence>
    <xs:element name="firstname" type="xs:string"/>
    <xs:element name="lastname" type="xs:string"/>
    <xs:element name="birthday" type="xs:date"/>
  </xs:sequence>
</xs:group>
```

After you have defined a group, you can reference it in another definition, like this:

```
<xs:group name="persongroup">
  <xs:sequence>
    <xs:element name="firstname" type="xs:string"/>
    <xs:element name="lastname" type="xs:string"/>
    <xs:element name="birthday" type="xs:date"/>
  </xs:sequence>
</xs:group>

<xs:element name="person type="personinfo"/>

<xs:complexType name="personinfo">
  <xs:sequence>
```

```
    <xs:group ref="persongroup"/>
    <xs:element name="country" type="xs:string"/>
  </xs:sequence>
</xs:complexType>
```

Attribute Groups

Attribute groups are defined with the attributeGroup declaration, like this:

```
<xs:attributeGroup name="groupname">
...
</xs:attributeGroup>
```

The following example defines an attribute group named "personattrgroup:"

```
<xs:attributeGroup name="personattrgroup">
  <xs:attribute name="firstname" type="xs:string"/>
  <xs:attribute name="lastname" type="xs:string"/>
  <xs:attribute name="birthday" type="xs:date"/>
</xs:attributeGroup>
```

After you have defined an attribute group, you can reference it in another definition, like this:

```
<xs:attributeGroup name="personattrgroup">
  <xs:attribute name="firstname" type="xs:string"/>
  <xs:attribute name="lastname" type="xs:string"/>
  <xs:attribute name="birthday" type="xs:date"/>
</xs:attributeGroup>

<xs:element name="person">
  <xs:complexType>
    <xs:attributeGroup ref="personattrgroup"/>
  </xs:complexType>
</xs:element>
XSD The <any> Element
```

The <any> element enables us to extend the XML document with elements not specified by the schema.

```
The <any> Element
```

The following example is a fragment from an XML schema called "family.xsd." It shows a declaration for the "person" element. By using the <any> element we can extend (after <lastname>) the content of "person" with any element:

```
<xs:element name="person">
  <xs:complexType>
    <xs:sequence>
      <xs:element name="firstname" type="xs:string"/>
      <xs:element name="lastname" type="xs:string"/>
      <xs:any minOccurs="0"/>
    </xs:sequence>
  </xs:complexType>
</xs:element>
```

Now we want to extend the "person" element with a "children" element. In this case we can do so, even if the author of the schema above never declared any "children" element. Look at this schema file, called "children.xsd:"

```
<?xml version="1.0" encoding="ISO-8859-1"?>
<xs:schema xmlns:xs="http://www.w3.org/2001/XMLSchema"
targetNamespace="http://www.abc.com"
xmlns="http://www.abc.com"
elementFormDefault="qualified">

<xs:element name="children">
  <xs:complexType>
    <xs:sequence>
      <xs:element name="childname" type="xs:string"
      maxOccurs="unbounded"/>
    </xs:sequence>
  </xs:complexType>
</xs:element>

</xs:schema>
```

The XML file below (called "Myfamily.xml") uses components from two different schemas, "family.xsd" and "children.xsd:"

```
<?xml version="1.0" encoding="ISO-8859-1"?>
<persons xmlns="http://www.microsoft.com"
xmlns:xsi="http://www.w3.org/2001/XMLSchema-instance"
xsi:SchemaLocation="http://www.microsoft.com family.xsd
http://www.abc.com children.xsd">

<person>
  <firstname>Hege</firstname>
  <lastname>Refsnes</lastname>
  <children>
```

```
    <childname>Cecilie</childname>
  </children>
</person>
<person>
  <firstname>Stale</firstname>
  <lastname>Refsnes</lastname>
</person>
</persons>
```

The XML file above is valid because the schema "family.xsd" allows us to extend the "person" element with an optional element after the "lastname"element.

The <any> and <anyAttribute> elements are used to make EXTENSIBLE documents. They allow documents to contain additional elements that are not declared in the main XML schema.

```
XSD The <anyAttribute> Element
```

The <anyAttribute> element enables us to extend the XML document with attributes not specified by the schema.

```
The <anyAttribute> Element
```

The following example is a fragment from an XML schema called "family.xsd." It shows a declaration for the "person" element. By using the <anyAttribute> element, we can add any number of attributes to the "person" element:

```
<xs:element name="person">
  <xs:complexType>
    <xs:sequence>
      <xs:element name="firstname" type="xs:string"/>
      <xs:element name="lastname" type="xs:string"/>
    </xs:sequence>
    <xs:anyAttribute/>
  </xs:complexType>
</xs:element>
```

Now, we want to extend the "person" element with a "gender" attribute. In this case, we can do so, even if the author of the schema above never declared any "gender" attribute. Look at this schema file, called "attribute.xsd:"

```
<?xml version="1.0" encoding="ISO-8859-1"?>
<xs:schema xmlns:xs="http://www.w3.org/2001/XMLSchema"
targetNamespace="http://www.abc.com"
xmlns="http://www.abc.com"
```

```
elementFormDefault="qualified">
<xs:attribute name="gender">
  <xs:simpleType>
    <xs:restriction base="xs:string">
      <xs:pattern value="male|female"/>
    </xs:restriction>
  </xs:simpleType>
</xs:attribute>
</xs:schema>
```

The XML file below (called "Myfamily.xml") uses components from two different schemas, "family.xsd" and "attribute.xsd:"

```
<?xml version="1.0" encoding="ISO-8859-1"?>
<persons xmlns="http://www.microsoft.com"
xmlns:xsi="http://www.w3.org/2001/XMLSchema-instance"
xsi:SchemaLocation="http://www.microsoft.com family.xsd
http://www.abc.com attribute.xsd">
<person gender="female">
  <firstname>Hege</firstname>
  <lastname>Refsnes</lastname>
</person>
<person gender="male">
  <firstname>Stale</firstname>
  <lastname>Refsnes</lastname>
</person>
</persons>
```

The XML file above is valid because the schema "family.xsd" allows us to add an attribute to the "person" element.

XSD Element Substitution

With XML schemas, one element can be substituted for another element.

Element Substitution

Let's say that we have users from two different countries: England and Norway. We would like the ability to let the user choose whether he or she would like to use the Norwegian element names or the English element names in the XML document.

To solve this problem, we could define a substitutionGroup in the XML schema. First, we declare a head element and then we declare the other elements that state that they are substitutable for the head element.

```
<xs:element name="name" type="xs:string"/>
<xs:element name="navn" substitutionGroup="name"/>
```

In the example above, the "name" element is the head element and the "navn" element is substitutable for "name." Look at this fragment of an XML schema:

```
<xs:element name="name" type="xs:string"/>
<xs:element name="navn" substitutionGroup="name"/>

<xs:complexType name="custinfo">
  <xs:sequence>
    <xs:element ref="name"/>
  </xs:sequence>
</xs:complexType>

<xs:element name="customer" type="custinfo"/>
<xs:element name="kunde" substitutionGroup="customer"/>
```

A valid XML document (according to the schema above) could look like this:

```
<customer>
  <name>Ram Mandal</name>
</customer>
```

or like this:

```
<kunde>
  <navn>Ram Mandal</navn>
</kunde>
```

Blocking Element Substitution

To prevent other elements from substituting another specified element, use the block attribute:

```
<xs:element name="name" type="xs:string" block="substitution"/>
```

Look at this fragment of an XML schema:

```
<xs:element name="name" type="xs:string" block="substitution"/>
<xs:element name="navn" substitutionGroup="name"/>

<xs:complexType name="custinfo">
```

```
  <xs:sequence>
    <xs:element ref="name"/>
  </xs:sequence>
</xs:complexType>
<xs:element name="customer" type="custinfo" block="substitution"/>
<xs:element name="kunde" substitutionGroup="customer"/>
```

A valid XML document (according to the schema above) looks like this:

```
<customer>
  <name>Ram Mandal</name>
</customer>
```

BUT THIS IS NO LONGER VALID

```
<kunde>
  <navn>Ram Mandal</navn>
</kunde>
```

Using SubstitutionGroup

The type of the substitutable elements must be the same as, or derived from, the type of the head element. If the type of the substitutable element is the same as the type of the head element, you will not have to specify the type of the substitutable element.

Note that all elements in the substitutionGroup (the head element and the substitutable elements) must be declared as global elements, otherwise it will not work.

Global Elements

Global elements are elements that are immediate children of the "schema" element. Local elements are elements nested within other elements.

An XML Document

Let's have a look at this XML document called "shiporder.xml:"

```
<?xml version="1.0" encoding="ISO-8859-1"?>
<shiporder orderid="889923"
xmlns:xsi="http://www.w3.org/2001/XMLSchema-instance"
```

```
xsi:noNamespaceSchemaLocation="shiporder.xsd">
  <orderperson>Ram Mandal</orderperson>
  <shipto>
    <name>Kshitij Banzal</name>
    <address>20, I.G. Nagar</address>
    <city>Indore</city>
    <country>India</country>
  </shipto>
  <item>
    <title>World wide web</title>
    <note>Special Edition</note>
    <quantity>1</quantity>
    <price>120.00</price>
  </item>
  <item>
    <title>Summer special</title>
    <quantity>1</quantity>
    <price>239.00</price>
  </item>
</shiporder>
```

The XML document above consists of a root element, "shiporder," that contains a required attribute called "ordered." The "shiporder" element contains three different child elements: "orderperson," "shipto" and "item." The "item" element appears twice, and it contains a "title," an optional "note" element, a "quantity", and a "price" element.

The line above: xmlns:xsi=*"http://www.w3.org/2001/XMLSchema-instance"* tells the XML parser that this document should be validated against a schema. The line xsi:noNamespaceSchemaLocation="shiporder.xsd" specifies WHERE the schema resides (here it is in the same folder as "shiporder.xml").

CREATE AN XML SCHEMA

Now we want to create a schema for the XML document above.

We start by opening a new file that we will call "shiporder.xsd." To create the schema, we could simply follow the structure in the XML document and define each element as we find it. We will start with the standard XML declaration followed by the xs:schema element that defines a schema:

```
<?xml version="1.0" encoding="ISO-8859-1" ?>
<xs:schema xmlns:xs="http://www.w3.org/2001/XMLSchema">
...
</xs:schema>
```

In the schema above, we use the standard namespace (xs), and the URI associated with this namespace is the schema language definition, which has the standard value of *http://www.w3.org/2001/XMLSchema.*

Next, we have to define the "shiporder" element. This element has an attribute and it contains other elements, therefore we consider it as a complex type. The child elements of the "shiporder" element are surrounded by a xs:sequence element that defines an ordered sequence of sub elements:

```
<xs:element name="shiporder">
  <xs:complexType>
    <xs:sequence>
      ...
    </xs:sequence>
  </xs:complexType>
</xs:element>
```

Then, we have to define the "orderperson" element as a simple type (because it does not contain any attributes or other elements). The type (xs:string) is prefixed with the namespace prefix associated with XML schema that indicates a predefined schema data type:

```
<xs:element name="orderperson" type="xs:string"/>
```

Next, we have to define two elements that are of the complex type: "shipto" and "item." We start by defining the "shipto" element:

```
<xs:element name="shipto">
  <xs:complexType>
    <xs:sequence>
      <xs:element name="name" type="xs:string"/>
      <xs:element name="address" type="xs:string"/>
      <xs:element name="city" type="xs:string"/>
      <xs:element name="country" type="xs:string"/>
    </xs:sequence>
  </xs:complexType>
</xs:element>
```

With schemas, we can define the number of possible occurrences for an element with the maxOccurs and minOccurs attributes. maxOccurs specifies the maximum number of occurrences for an element and minOccurs specifies the minimum number of occurrences for an element. The default value for both maxOccurs and minOccurs is 1.

Now we can define the "item" element. This element can appear multiple times inside a "shiporder" element. This is specified by setting the maxOccurs attribute of the "item" element to "unbounded," which means that there can be as many occurrences of the "item" element as the author wishes. Notice that the "note" element is optional. We have specified this by setting the minOccurs attribute to zero:

```
<xs:element name="item" maxOccurs="unbounded">
  <xs:complexType>
    <xs:sequence>
      <xs:element name="title" type="xs:string"/>
      <xs:element name="note" type="xs:string" minOccurs="0"/>
      <xs:element name="quantity" type="xs:positiveInteger"/>
      <xs:element name="price" type="xs:decimal"/>
    </xs:sequence>
  </xs:complexType>
</xs:element>
```

We can now declare the attribute of the "shiporder" element. Since this is a required attribute, we specify use="required." The attribute declarations must always come last:

```
<xs:attribute name="orderid" type="xs:string" use="required"/>
```

Here is the complete listing of the schema file called "shiporder.xsd:"

```
<?xml version="1.0" encoding="ISO-8859-1" ?>
<xs:schema xmlns:xs="http://www.w3.org/2001/XMLSchema">
<xs:element name="shiporder">
  <xs:complexType>
    <xs:sequence>
      <xs:element name="orderperson" type="xs:string"/>
      <xs:element name="shipto">
        <xs:complexType>
          <xs:sequence>
            <xs:element name="name" type="xs:string"/>
            <xs:element name="address" type="xs:string"/>
            <xs:element name="city" type="xs:string"/>
```

```
            <xs:element name="country" type="xs:string"/>
          </xs:sequence>
        </xs:complexType>
      </xs:element>
      <xs:element name="item" maxOccurs="unbounded">
        <xs:complexType>
          <xs:sequence>
            <xs:element name="title" type="xs:string"/>
            <xs:element name="note" type="xs:string" minOccurs="0"/>
            <xs:element name="quantity" type="xs:positiveInteger"/>
            <xs:element name="price" type="xs:decimal"/>
          </xs:sequence>
        </xs:complexType>
      </xs:element>
    </xs:sequence>
    <xs:attribute name="orderid" type="xs:string" use="required"/>
  </xs:complexType>
</xs:element>

</xs:schema>
```

Divide the Schema

The previous design method is very simple, but can be difficult to read and maintain when documents are complex.

The next design method is based on defining all elements and attributes first, and then referring to them using the ref attribute. Here is the new design of the schema file ("shiporder.xsd"):

```
<?xml version="1.0" encoding="ISO-8859-1" ?>

<xs:schema xmlns:xs="http://www.w3.org/2001/XMLSchema">
<!-- definition of simple elements -->
<xs:element name="orderperson" type="xs:string"/>
<xs:element name="name" type="xs:string"/>
<xs:element name="address" type="xs:string"/>
<xs:element name="city" type="xs:string"/>
<xs:element name="country" type="xs:string"/>
<xs:element name="title" type="xs:string"/>
<xs:element name="note" type="xs:string"/>
<xs:element name="quantity" type="xs:positiveInteger"/>
<xs:element name="price" type="xs:decimal"/>
```

```
<!-- definition of attributes -->
<xs:attribute name="orderid" type="xs:string"/>

<!-- definition of complex elements -->
<xs:element name="shipto">
  <xs:complexType>
    <xs:sequence>
      <xs:element ref="name"/>
      <xs:element ref="address"/>
      <xs:element ref="city"/>
      <xs:element ref="country"/>
    </xs:sequence>
  </xs:complexType>
</xs:element>

<xs:element name="item">
  <xs:complexType>
    <xs:sequence>
      <xs:element ref="title"/>
      <xs:element ref="note" minOccurs="0"/>
      <xs:element ref="quantity"/>
      <xs:element ref="price"/>
    </xs:sequence>
  </xs:complexType>
</xs:element>

<xs:element name="shiporder">
  <xs:complexType>
    <xs:sequence>
      <xs:element ref="orderperson"/>
      <xs:element ref="shipto"/>
      <xs:element ref="item" maxOccurs="unbounded"/>
    </xs:sequence>
    <xs:attribute ref="orderid" use="required"/>
  </xs:complexType>
</xs:element>

</xs:schema>
```

Using Named Types

The third design method defines classes or types that enable us to reuse element definitions. This is done by naming the simpleTypes and complexTypes elements, and then point to them through the type attribute of the element. Here is the third design of the schema file ("shiporder.xsd"):

```
<?xml version="1.0" encoding="ISO-8859-1" ?>
<xs:schema xmlns:xs="http://www.w3.org/2001/XMLSchema">
<xs:simpleType name="stringtype">
  <xs:restriction base="xs:string"/>
</xs:simpleType>
<xs:simpleType name="inttype">
  <xs:restriction base="xs:positiveInteger"/>
</xs:simpleType>
<xs:simpleType name="dectype">
  <xs:restriction base="xs:decimal"/>
</xs:simpleType>
<xs:simpleType name="orderidtype">
  <xs:restriction base="xs:string">
    <xs:pattern value="[0-9]{6}"/>
  </xs:restriction>
</xs:simpleType>
<xs:complexType name="shiptotype">
  <xs:sequence>
    <xs:element name="name" type="stringtype"/>
    <xs:element name="address" type="stringtype"/>
    <xs:element name="city" type="stringtype"/>
    <xs:element name="country" type="stringtype"/>
  </xs:sequence>
</xs:complexType>
<xs:complexType name="itemtype">
  <xs:sequence>
    <xs:element name="title" type="stringtype"/>
    <xs:element name="note" type="stringtype" minOccurs="0"/>
    <xs:element name="quantity" type="inttype"/>
    <xs:element name="price" type="dectype"/>
  </xs:sequence>
</xs:complexType>
<xs:complexType name="shipordertype">
  <xs:sequence>
    <xs:element name="orderperson" type="stringtype"/>
    <xs:element name="shipto" type="shiptotype"/>
```

```
        <xs:element name="item" maxOccurs="unbounded" type="itemtype"/>
      </xs:sequence>
      <xs:attribute name="orderid" type="orderidtype" use="required"/>
    </xs:complexType>
    <xs:element name="shiporder" type="shipordertype"/>
    </xs:schema>
```

The restriction element indicates that the datatype is derived from a W3C XML schema namespace datatype. So, the following fragment means that the value of the element or attribute must be a string value:

```
<xs:restriction base="xs:string">
```

The restriction element is more often used to apply restrictions to elements. Look at the following lines from the schema above:

```
<xs:simpleType name="orderidtype">
  <xs:restriction base="xs:string">
    <xs:pattern value="[0-9]{6}"/>
  </xs:restriction>
</xs:simpleType>
```

This indicates that the value of the element or attribute must be a string, it must be exactly six characters in a row, and those characters must be a number from 0 to 9.

XSD String Data Types

String data types are used for values that contains character strings.

String Data Type

The string data type can contain characters, line feeds, carriage returns, and tab characters. The following is an example of a string declaration in a schema:

```
<xs:element name="customer" type="xs:string"/>
```

An element in your document might look like this:

```
<customer>Ram Mandal</customer>
```

Or it might look like this:

```
<customer>Ram Mandal</customer>
```

The XML processor will not modify the value if you use the string data type.

Normalized String Data Type

The normalizedString data type is derived from the String data type.

The normalizedString data type also contains characters, but the XML processor will remove line feeds, carriage returns, and tab characters. The following is an example of a normalizedString declaration in a schema:

```
<xs:element name="customer" type="xs:normalizedString"/>
```

An element in your document might look like this:

```
<customer>Ram Mandal</customer>
```

Or it might look like this:

```
<customer>    RamMandal    </customer>
```

In the example above, the XML processor will replace the tabs with spaces.

Token Data Type

The token data type is also derived from the String data type.

The token data type also contains characters, but the XML processor will remove line feeds, carriage returns, tabs, leading and trailing spaces, and multiple spaces.

The following is an example of a token declaration in a schema:

```
<xs:element name="customer" type="xs:token"/>
```

An element in your document might look like this:

```
<customer>Ram Mandal</customer>
```

Or it might look like this:

```
<customer>    RamMandal    </customer>
```

In the example above, the XML processor will remove the tabs.

String Data Types

Note that all of the data types below derive from the String data type (except for string itself).

Name	Description
ENTITIES	
ENTITY	

(continued)

(continued)

Name	Description
ID	A string that represents the ID attribute in XML (only used with schema attributes)
IDREF	A string that represents the IDREF attribute in XML (only used with schema attributes)
IDREFS	
language	A string that contains a valid language id
Name	A string that contains a valid XML name
NCName	
NMTOKEN	A string that represents the NMTOKEN attribute in XML (only used with schema attributes)
NMTOKENS	
normalizedString	A string that does not contain line feeds, carriage returns, or tabs
QName	
string	A string
token	A string that does not contain line feeds, carriage returns, tabs, leading or trailing spaces, or multiple spaces

Restrictions on String Data Types

Restrictions that can be used with String data types:

- enumeration
- length
- maxLength
- minLength
- pattern (NMTOKENS, IDREFS, and ENTITIES cannot use this constraint)
- whiteSpace

XSD DATE AND TIME DATA TYPES

Date and time data types are used for values that contain the date and time.

Date Data Type

The date data type is used to specify a date.

The date is specified in the following form "YYYY-MM-DD" where

- YYYY indicates the year
- MM indicates the month
- DD indicates the day

The following is an example of a date declaration in a schema:

```
<xs:element name="start" type="xs:date"/>
```

An element in your document might look like this:

```
<start>2002-09-24</start>
```

Time Zones

To specify a time zone, you can either enter a date in UTC time by adding a "Z" behind the date—like this:

```
<start>2002-09-24Z</start>
```

or you can specify an offset from the UTC time by adding a positive or negative time behind the date—like this:

```
<start>2002-09-24-06:00</start>
```

or

```
<start>2002-09-24+06:00</start>
```

Time Data Type

The time data type is used to specify a time. The time is specified in the following form "hh:mm:ss" where

- hh indicates the hour
- mm indicates the minute
- ss indicates the second

The following is an example of a time declaration in a schema:

```
<xs:element name="start" type="xs:time"/>
```

An element in your document might look like this:

```
<start>09:00:00</start>
```

Or it might look like this:

```
<start>09:30:10.5</start>
```

Time Zones

To specify a time zone, you can either enter a time in UTC time by adding a "Z" behind the time—like this:

```
<start>09:30:10Z</start>
```

or you can specify an offset from the UTC time by adding a positive or negative time behind the time—like this:

```
<start>09:30:10-06:00</start>
```

or

```
<start>09:30:10+06:00</start>
```

DateTime Data Type

The dateTime data type is used to specify a date and a time. The dateTime is specified in the following form "YYYY-MM-DDThh:mm:ss" where

- YYYY indicates the year
- MM indicates the month
- DD indicates the day
- T indicates the start of the required time section
- hh indicates the hour
- mm indicates the minute
- ss indicates the second

The following is an example of a dateTime declaration in a schema:

```
<xs:element name="startdate" type="xs:dateTime"/>
```

An element in your document might look like this:

```
<startdate>2002-05-30T09:00:00</startdate>
```

Or it might look like this:

```
<startdate>2002-05-30T09:30:10.5</startdate>
```

Time Zones

To specify a time zone, you can either enter a dateTime in UTC time by adding a "Z" behind the time—like this:

```
<startdate>2002-05-30T09:30:10Z</startdate>
```

or you can specify an offset from the UTC time by adding a positive or negative time behind the time—like this:

```
<startdate>2002-05-30T09:30:10-06:00</startdate>
```

or

```
<startdate>2002-05-30T09:30:10+06:00</startdate>
```

Duration Data Type

The duration data type is used to specify a time interval.

The time interval is specified in the following form "PnYnMnDTnHnMnS" where

- P indicates the period (required)
- nY indicates the number of years
- nM indicates the number of months
- nD indicates the number of days
- T indicates the start of a time section (required if you are going to specify hours, minutes, or seconds)
- nH indicates the number of hours
- nM indicates the number of minutes
- nS indicates the number of seconds

The following is an example of a duration declaration in a schema:

```
<xs:element name="period" type="xs:duration"/>
```

An element in your document might look like this:

```
<period>P5Y</period>
```

The example above indicates a period of five years.

Or it might look like this:

```
<period>P5Y2M10D</period>
```

The example above indicates a period of five years, two months, and 10 days.

Or it might look like this:

```
<period>P5Y2M10DT15H</period>
```

The example above indicates a period of five years, two months, 10 days, and 15 hours.

Or it might look like this:

```
<period>PT15H</period>
```

The example above indicates a period of 15 hours.

Negative Duration

To specify a negative duration, enter a minus sign before the P:

```
<period>-P10D</period>
```

The example above indicates a period of minus 10 days.

Date and Time Data Types

Name	Description
date	Defines a date value
dateTime	Defines a date and time value
duration	Defines a time interval
gDay	Defines a part of a date - the day (DD)
gMonth	Defines a part of a date - the month (MM)
gMonthDay	Defines a part of a date - the month and day (MM-DD)
gYear	Defines a part of a date - the year (YYYY)
gYearMonth	Defines a part of a date - the year and month (YYYY-MM)
time	Defines a time value

Restrictions on Date Data Types

Restrictions that can be used with Date data types are as follows:

- enumeration
- maxExclusive
- maxInclusive
- minExclusive
- minInclusive
- pattern
- whiteSpace

XSD Numeric Data Types

Decimal data types are used for numeric values.

Decimal Data Type

The decimal data type is used to specify a numeric value. The following is an example of a decimal declaration in a schema:

```
<xs:element name="prize" type="xs:decimal"/>
```

An element in your document might look like this:

```
<prize>999.50</prize>
```

Or it might look like this:

```
<prize>+999.5450</prize>
```

Or it might look like this:

```
<prize>-999.5230</prize>
```

Or it might look like this:

```
<prize>0</prize>
```

Or it might look like this:

```
<prize>14</prize>
```

The maximum number of decimal digits you can specify is 18.

Integer Data Type

The integer data type is used to specify a numeric value without a fractional component. The following is an example of an integer declaration in a schema:

```
<xs:element name="prize" type="xs:integer"/>
```

An element in your document might look like this:

```
<prize>999</prize>
```

Or it might look like this:

```
<prize>+999</prize>
```

Or it might look like this:

```
<prize>-999</prize>
```

Or it might look like this:

```
<prize>0</prize>
```

Numeric Data Types

Note that all of the data types below derive from the Decimal data type (except for decimal itself).

Name	Description
byte	A signed 8-bit integer
decimal	A decimal value
int	A signed 32-bit integer
integer	An integer value
long	A signed 64-bit integer
negativeInteger	An integer containing only negative values (..,-2,-1)
nonNegativeInteger	An integer containing only non-negative values (0,1,2,..)
nonPositiveInteger	An integer containing only non-positive values (..,-2,-1,0)
positiveInteger	An integer containing only positive values (1,2,..)
short	A signed 16-bit integer
unsignedLong	An unsigned 64-bit integer
unsignedInt	An unsigned 32-bit integer
unsignedShort	An unsigned 16-bit integer
unsignedByte	An unsigned 8-bit integer

Restrictions on Numeric Data Types

Restrictions that can be used with Numeric data types are as follows:

- enumeration
- fractionDigits
- maxExclusive
- maxInclusive
- minExclusive
- minInclusive
- pattern
- totalDigits
- whiteSpace

XSD Miscellaneous Data Types

Other miscellaneous data types are boolean, base64Binary, hexBinary, float, double, anyURI, QName, and NOTATION.

Boolean Data Type

The boolean data type is used to specify a true or false value. The following is an example of a boolean declaration in a schema:

```
<xs:attribute name="disabled" type="xs:boolean"/>
```

An element in your document might look like this:

```
<prize disabled="true">999</prize>
```

Legal values for boolean are true, false, 1 (which indicates true), and 0 (which indicates false).

Binary Data Types

Binary data types are used to express binary-formatted data. We have two binary data types:

- base64Binary (Base64-encoded binary data)
- hexBinary (hexadecimal-encoded binary data)

The following is an example of a hexBinary declaration in a schema:

```
<xs:element name="blobsrc" type="xs:hexBinary"/>
```

AnyURI Data Type

The anyURI data type is used to specify a URI. The following is an example of an anyURI declaration in a schema:

```
<xs:attribute name="src" type="xs:anyURI"/>
```

An element in your document might look like this:

```
<pic src="http://www.abc.com/images/smiley.gif" />
```

If a URI has spaces, replace them with %20.

Miscellaneous Data Types

Name	Description
anyURI	
base64Binary	
Boolean	
double	

(continued)

(continued)

Name	Description
float	
hexBinary	
NOTATION	
QName	

Restrictions on Miscellaneous Data Types

Restrictions that can be used with the other data types are as follows:

- enumeration (a Boolean data type cannot use this constraint)
- length (a Boolean data type cannot use this constraint)
- maxLength (a Boolean data type cannot use this constraint)
- minLength (a Boolean data type cannot use this constraint)
- pattern
- whiteSpace

XML EDITORS

If you are serious about XML, you will benefit from using a professional XML editor.

XML is Text-based

XML is a text-based markup language. One great thing about XML is that XML files can be created and edited using a simple text-editor like Notepad. However, when you start working with XML, you will soon find that it is better to edit XML documents using a professional XML editor.

Many Web developers use Notepad to edit both HTML and XML documents because Notepad is included with the most common OS and it is simple to use.

But, if you use Notepad for XML editing, you will soon run into problems. Notepad does not know that you are writing XML, so it will not be able to assist you.

XML is an important technology, and development projects use XML-based technologies like

- XML schema to define XML structures and data types
- XSLT to transform XML data
- SOAP to exchange XML data between applications
- WSDL to describe Web services
- RDF to describe Web resources
- XPath and XQuery to access XML data
- SMIL to define graphics
- To be able to write error-free XML documents, you will need an intelligent XML editor.

Professional XML editors will help you to write error-free XML documents, validate your XML against a DTD or a schema, and force you to stick to a valid XML structure.

An XML editor should be able to

- Add closing tags to your opening tags automatically
- Force you to write valid XML
- Verify your XML against a DTD
- Verify your XML against a schema
- Color code your XML syntax

We have been using XMLSpy for many years. XMLSpy, our favorite XML editor, includes a built-in graphical XML schema editor. These are some of the features we especially like:

- Easy to use, graphical schema editing
- Context-sensitive entry helpers
- Display of all globally defined particles in a list view
- Detailed visual views of content models with drag & drop editing
- Built in DTD and/or XML schema-based validation
- Enhanced support for editing identity constraints
- Find and replace in single or multi-file schemas
- Schema-based code generation in Java, C#, and C++
- XML schema documentation generation in HTML or Word

QUESTIONS FOR DISCUSSION

1. What do you understand about schema?
2. What is an XML schema?
3. Why use an XML schema?
4. How do you write an XML schema?
5. Define simple types in an XML schema.
6. Define complex types in an XML schema.
7. Why we can say XML schemas are the successors of DTDs?
8. Explain why XML schemas are extensible.
9. How you define elements of XML document in an XML schema?
10. How you define complex and simple types of elements?
11. Give an example that shows an XML document has a reference to an XML schema.
12. How you use the schema element in an XML Document?
13. What do you mean by a simple element?
14. Which data types do we use in XML schema?
15. How you set default and fixed values for simple elements?
16. How you define attributes in the XML schema?
17. How you set default and fixed values for attributes?
18. How you define optional and required attributes?

CHAPTER 8

XSL BASICS

INTRODUCTION TO XSL

XSL stands for EXtensible Stylesheet Language. It started with XSL and ended up with XSLT, XPath, and XSL-FO. The World Wide Web Consortium (W3C) started to develop XSL because there was a need for an XML-based Stylesheet Language. XML does not use predefined tags (we can use any tag names we like), and therefore the meaning of each tag is not well understood.

A <table> tag could mean an HTML table, a piece of furniture, or something else—and a browser does not know how to display it. XSL describes how the XML document should be displayed. XSL consists of three parts:

- XSLT—a language for transforming XML documents
- XPath—a language for navigating in XML documents
- XSL-FO—a language for formatting XML documents

With the XSL, you can freely do modify any of the source text. Stylesheet 1 and the Stylesheet 2 produce different output from the same source file.

XSL Stylesheet 1

```
<xsl:stylesheet xmlns:xsl='http://www.w3.org/1999/XSL/Transform' >
<xsl:template match="/">
<H1><xsl:value-of select="//title"/></H1>
<H2><xsl:value-of select="//author"/></H2>
</xsl:template>
</xsl:stylesheet>
```

XSL Stylesheet 2

```
<xsl:stylesheet xmlns:xsl='http://www.w3.org/1999/XSL/Transform' >
<xsl:template match="/">
<H2><xsl:value-of select="//author"/></H2>
<H1><xsl:value-of select="//title"/></H1>
</xsl:template>
</xsl:stylesheet>
```

AN XML SYNTAX

An every XSL stylesheet should start with the xsl:stylesheet element. Attribute xmlns:xsl specifies the version of the XSL(T) specification. This example shows the simplest possible stylesheet. The default is used here because this does not contain any information.

```
<xsl:stylesheet xmlns:xsl='http://www.w3.org/1999/XSL/Transform' >
</xsl:stylesheet>
```

AN XSL PROCESSOR

The XSL processors parses the XML source and tries to find the matching template rule. If it can find it, then the instructions inside the matching template are evaluated.

The contents of the original elements can be recovered from a original sources in two basic ways. Stylesheet 1 uses the xsl:value-of a construct. In this case, the contents of the element are used without any further processing. The xsl:apply-templates in Stylesheet 2 are different. The parser further processes the selected elements.

XSL Stylesheet 1

```
<xsl:stylesheet xmlns:xsl='http://www.w3.org/1999/XSL/Transform'>
<xsl:template match="employee">
<B><xsl:value-of select="."/></B>
</xsl:template>
<xsl:template match="surname">
<i><xsl:value-of select="."/></i>
</xsl:template>
</xsl:stylesheet>
```

XSL Stylesheet 2

```
<xsl:stylesheet xmlns:xsl='http://www.w3.org/1999/XSL/Transform' >
<xsl:template match="employee">
<B><xsl:apply-templates select="firstName"/></B>
<B><xsl:apply-templates select="surname"/></B>
</xsl:template>
<xsl:template match="surname">
<i> <xsl:value-of select="."/></i>
</xsl:template>
</xsl:stylesheet>
```

THE XSL TEMPLATES

The XSL processor parses the XML source and tries to find the matching template rule. If it finds it, then the instructions inside the matching template are evaluated.

XML Source

```
<?xml version="1.0"?>
<xslTutorial >
<bold>Hello, world.</bold>
<red>I am </red>
<italic>fine.</italic>
</xslTutorial>
```

HTML Output 1

```
<P>
<B>Hello, world.</B></P>
<P style="color:red">I am </P>
<P>
<i>fine.</i></P>
```

XSL Stylesheet 1

```
<xsl:stylesheet xmlns:xsl='http://www.w3.org/1999/XSL/Transform'>
<xsl:template match="bold">
<P><B><xsl:value-of select="."/></B></P>
```

```
</xsl:template>
<xsl:template match="red">
<P style="color:red"><xsl:value-of select="."/></P>
</xsl:template>
<xsl:template match="italic">
<P><i><xsl:value-of select="."/></i></P>
</xsl:template>
</xsl:stylesheet>
```

LOCATION PATHS

The parts of the XML document to which the template should be applied are determined by the location paths. A required syntax is specified in the XPath specification. Simple cases look similar to file system addressing.

XML Source

```
<?xml version="1.0"?>
<xslTutorial >
<AAA id='a1' pos='start'>
<BBB id='b1'/>
<BBB id='b2'/>
</AAA>
<AAA id='a2'>
<BBB id='b3'/>
<BBB id='b4'/>
<CCC id='c1'>
<DDD id='d1'/>
</CCC>
<BBB id='b5'>
<CCC id='c2'/>
</BBB>
</AAA>
</xslTutorial>
```

HTML Output 1

```
<DIV style="color:purple">BBB id=b1</DIV>
<DIV style="color:purple">BBB id=b2</DIV>
```

```
<DIV style="color:purple">BBB id=b3</DIV>
<DIV style="color:purple">BBB id=b4</DIV>
<DIV style="color:red">DDD id=d1</DIV>
<DIV style="color:purple">BBB id=b5</DIV>
```

XSL Stylesheet 1

```
<xsl:stylesheet xmlns:xsl='http://www.w3.org/1999/XSL/Transform'>
<xsl:template match="BBB">
<DIV style="color:purple">
<xsl:value-of select="name()"/>
<xsl:text> id=</xsl:text>
<xsl:value-of select="@id"/>
</DIV>
</xsl:template>
<xsl:template match="/xslTutorial/AAA/CCC/DDD">
<DIV style="color:red">
<xsl:value-of select="name()"/>
<xsl:text> id=</xsl:text>
<xsl:value-of select="@id"/>
</DIV>
</xsl:template>
</xsl:stylesheet>
```

The processing always starts with the template match="/". This is a root element and its only child is the document element, in our case, it is XSl tutorial. Many of the stylesheets do not contain this element explicitly. When the explicit template does not exist, the implicit template, which contains the instructions, is called. It processes the children of the current node, including the text nodes.

Wildcard

A template can match the selection of a location path, and the individual paths are separated with the"|" (see Stylesheet 1). The wildcard * selects all the possibilities. Compare Stylesheet 1 with Stylesheet 2.

XML Source

```
<?xml version="1.0"?>
<xslTutorial >
<employee>
```

```
<firstName>Joe</firstName>
<surname>Smith</surname>
</employee>
</xslTutorial>
```

HTML Output 1

```
<DIV>[template: firstName outputs Joe ]</DIV>
<DIV>[template: surname outputs Smith ]</DIV>
```

XSL Stylesheet 1

```
<xsl:stylesheet xmlns:xsl='http://www.w3.org/1999/XSL/Transform'>
<xsl:template match="firstName|surname">
<DIV><xsl:text> [template: </xsl:text>
<xsl:value-of select="name()"/>
<xsl:text> outputs </xsl:text>
<xsl:apply-templates/ >
<xsl:text> ]</xsl:text> </DIV>
</xsl:template>
</xsl:stylesheet>
```

XSL Stylesheet 2

```
<xsl:stylesheet xmlns:xsl='http://www.w3.org/1999/XSL/Transform'>
<xsl:template match="*">
<DIV><xsl:text> [template: </xsl:text>
<xsl:value-of select="name()"/>
<xsl:text> outputs </xsl:text>
<xsl:apply-templates/ >
<xsl:text> ]</xsl:text> </DIV>
</xsl:template>
</xsl:stylesheet>
```

Modes in XSL allow the element to be processed multiple times, each time producing a different result. In Stylesheet 2, one of the modes does not exist.

XML Source

```
<?xml version="1.0"?>
<xslTutorial >
<AAA id='a1' pos='start'>
```

```
<BBB id='b1'/>
<BBB id='b2'/>
</AAA>
<AAA id='a2'>
<BBB id='b3'/>
<BBB id='b4'/>
<CCC id='c1'>
<CCC id='c2'/>
</CCC>
<BBB id='b5'>
<CCC id='c3'/>
</BBB>
</AAA>
</xslTutorial>
```

HTML Output 1

```
<DIV style="color:red">CCC id=c1</DIV>
<DIV style="color:red">CCC id=c2</DIV>
<DIV style="color:red">CCC id=c3</DIV>
<DIV style="color:blue">CCC id=c1</DIV>
<DIV style="color:blue">CCC id=c2</DIV>
<DIV style="color:blue">CCC id=c3</DIV>
<DIV style="color:purple">CCC id=c1</DIV>
<DIV style="color:purple">CCC id=c2</DIV>
<DIV style="color:purple">CCC id=c3</DIV>
```

XSL Stylesheet 1

```
<xsl:stylesheet xmlns:xsl='http://www.w3.org/1999/XSL/Transform'>
<xsl:template match="/">
<xsl:apply-templates select="//CCC" mode="red"/>
<xsl:apply-templates select="//CCC" mode="blue"/>
<xsl:apply-templates select="//CCC"/>
</xsl:template>
<xsl:template match="CCC" mode="red">
<DIV style="color:red">
<xsl:value-of select="name()"/>
<xsl:text> id=</xsl:text>
<xsl:value-of select="@id"/>
</DIV>
```

```
</xsl:template>
<xsl:template match="CCC" mode="blue">
<DIV style="color:blue">
<xsl:value-of select="name()"/>
<xsl:text> id=</xsl:text>
<xsl:value-of select="@id"/>
</DIV>
</xsl:template>
<xsl:template match="CCC">
<DIV style="color:purple">
<xsl:value-of select="name()"/>
<xsl:text> id=</xsl:text>
<xsl:value-of select="@id"/>
</DIV>
</xsl:template>
</xsl:stylesheet>
```

XSL Stylesheet 2

```
<xsl:stylesheet xmlns:xsl='http://www.w3.org/1999/XSL/Transform'>
<xsl:template match="/">
<xsl:apply-templates select="//CCC" mode="red"/>
<xsl:apply-templates select="//CCC" mode="yellow"/>
</xsl:template>
<xsl:template match="CCC" mode="red">
<DIV style="color:red">
<xsl:value-of select="name()"/>
<xsl:text> id=</xsl:text>
<xsl:value-of select="@id"/>
</DIV>
</xsl:template>
<xsl:template match="CCC">
<DIV style="color:purple">
<xsl:value-of select="name()"/>
<xsl:text> id=</xsl:text>
<xsl:value-of select="@id"/>
</DIV>
</xsl:template>
</xsl:stylesheet>
```

TEMPLATE ORDERING

Very often, several of the templates match the selected element in the XML source. It should be therefore decided which one to use. Templates are ordered according to their priority, which can be specified with the priority attribute. If a template does not contain this attribute, its priority is calculated according to several rules.

XSL Attributes

An attribute can be accessed in the way similar to the elements. Notice @ in front of the attribute name.

XML Source

```
<?xml version="1.0"?>
<xslTutorial >
<dog name='Joe'>
<data weight='18 kg' color="black"/>
</dog>
</xslTutorial>
```

HTML Output 1

```
<HTML>
<HEAD> </HEAD>
<BODY>
<P>
<B>Dog: </B>Joe</P>
<P>
<B>Color: </B>black</P>
</BODY>
</HTML>
```

XSL Stylesheet 1

```
<xsl:stylesheet xmlns:xsl='http://www.w3.org/1999/XSL/Transform' >
<xsl:template match="dog">
<P><B><xsl:text> Dog: </xsl:text> </B>
<xsl:value-of select="@name"/></P>
<P><B><xsl:text> Color: </xsl:text> </B>
```

```
<xsl:value-of select="data/@color"/></P>
</xsl:template>
</xsl:stylesheet>
```

You can process the attribute in the same way as the element. You can also select the elements which that contain or do not contain a given attribute.

HTML Output 2

```
<HTML>
<HEAD> </HEAD>
<BODY>
<P>Car: a005</P>
</BODY>
</HTML>
```

XSL Stylesheet 1

```
<xsl:stylesheet xmlns:xsl='http://www.w3.org/1999/XSL/Transform' >
<xsl:template match="car[@checked]">
<P><xsl:text> Car: </xsl:text>
<xsl:value-of select="@id"/></P>
</xsl:template>
</xsl:stylesheet>
```

XSL Stylesheet 2

```
<xsl:stylesheet xmlns:xsl='http://www.w3.org/1999/XSL/Transform' >
<xsl:template match="car[not(@checked)]">
<P><xsl:text> Car: </xsl:text>
<xsl:value-of select="@id"/></P>
</xsl:template>
</xsl:stylesheet>
```

AXES

Axes play very a important role in XSL. All the axes are used in the example given below.

XML Source

```
<?xml version="1.0"?>
<xslTutorial >
<doc>
<ancprec>
<p>Preceeding Ancestor. <br/></p>
</ancprec>
<gf>
<p>Ancestor. <br/></p>
<pprec choice="a">
<p>Preceeding Parent.<br/> </p>
</pprec>
<par>
<p>Parent. <br/></p>
<sibprec>
<p>Preceeding sibling.<br/> </p>
</sibprec>
<me id="id001">
<p>Me.<br/> </p>
<!-- Comment after Me -->
<chprec >
<p>Preceeding child.<br/> </p >
</chprec>
<child idref="id001">
<p>Child. <br/></p>
<?pi Processing Instruction ?>
<dprec>
<p>preceeding Descendant.<br/> </p>
</dprec>
<desc>
<p>Descendant.<br/> </p>
</desc>
<dfoll>
<p>Following Descendant.<br/> </p>
</dfoll>
</child>
<chfoll>
<p>following child.<br/> </p>
```

```
</chfoll>
</me>
<sibfoll>
<p>Following Sibling.<br/> </p>
</sibfoll>
</par>
<pfoll>
<p>Following Parent.<br/> </p>
</pfoll>
</gf>
<ancfoll>
<p>following Ancestor.<br/></p>
</ancfoll>
</doc>
</xslTutorial>
```

HTML Output 1

```
<HTML>
<HEAD></HEAD>
<BODY>
<!DOCTYPE html PUBLIC "-//W3C//DTD HTML 4.0 Transitional//EN">
<html>
<head>
<title>Document</title> </head>
<body>
<H2>Following Axis</H2>
<b>Following Sibling.
<br> Following Parent.
<br> following Ancestor.
<br> </b>
<H2>Descendant or Self Axis</H2>
<b>Me.
<br> Preceeding child.
<br> Child.
<br>preceeding Descendant.
<br> Descendant.
<br> Following Descendant.
<br> following child.
<br> </b>
```

```
<H2>Descendant Axis</H2>
<b>Preceeding child.
<br> Child.
<br>preceeding Descendant.
<br> Descendant.
<br> Following Descendant.
<br> following child.
<br> </b>
<H2>Self Axis</H2>
<b>Me.
<br> </b>
<H2>Child Axis</H2>
<b>Preceeding child.
<br> Child.
<br>following child.
<br> </b>
<H2>Following Axis</H2>
<p>
<b>Following Sibling.
<br> Following Parent.
<br> following Ancestor.
<br> </b>
<br>
<i>Note the lack of ancestors here?
<br>Learned anything about document order yet?</i> </p>
<H2>Following Sibling Axis</H2>
<b> Following Sibling.
<br> </b>
<H2>Attribute Axis</H2>
<b>id001</b>
<H2>Parent Axis</H2>
<b>Parent.
<br> </b>
<H2>Ancestor or Self Axis</H2>
<b>Ancestor.
<br>Parent.
<br>Me.
<br> </b>
<H2>Ancestor Axis</H2>
```

```
<b>Ancestor.
<br>Parent.
<br> </b>
<H2>Preceding Sibling Axis</H2>
<b>Preceeding sibling.
<br> </b>
<H2>Preceeding Axis</H2>
<b>
<i>Not Implemented in XT 22 09 99</i></b>
<H2>Namespace Axis</H2>
<b>
<i>Not Implemented in XT 22 09 99</i></b>
</body>
</html>
</BODY>
</HTML>
```

XSL Stylesheet 1

```
<xsl:stylesheet xmlns:xsl='http://www.w3.org/1999/XSL/Transform' >
<xsl:template match="/">
```

Note how the initial context node is reduced by the apply templates; this stops the "leaking" of content when all we want is a subset of the whole in the result tree.

```
<xsl:apply-templates select="//me"/>
</xsl:template>
<xsl:template match="br">
<br />
</xsl:template>
<xsl:template match="me" priority="10">
<html>
<head>
<title> <xsl:text> Document</xsl:text> </title>
</head>
<body>
<H2>Following Axis</H2>
<b><xsl:apply-templates select="following::*/p"/></b>
<H2>Descendant or Self Axis</H2>
<b><xsl:apply-templates select="descendant-or-self::*/p"/></b>
<H2>Descendant Axis</H2>
```

```
<b><xsl:apply-templates select="descendant::*/p"/></b>
<H2>Self Axis</H2>
<b><xsl:apply-templates select="self::*/p"/></b>
<H2>Child Axis</H2>
<b><xsl:apply-templates select="child::*/p"/></b>
<H2>Following Axis</H2>
<p><b><xsl:apply-templates select="following::*/p"/></b>
<br /><i>Note the lack of ancestors here? <br />Learned anything
about document order yet?</i></p>
<H2>Following Sibling Axis</H2>
<b><xsl:apply-templates select="following-sibling::*"/></b>
<H2>Attribute Axis</H2>
<b>
<H2>Parent Axis</H2>
<b><xsl:apply-templates select="parent::*/p"/></b>
<H2>Ancestor or Self Axis</H2>
<b><xsl:apply-templates select="ancestor-or-self::*/p"/></b>
<H2>Ancestor Axis</H2>
<b><xsl:apply-templates select="ancestor::*/p"/></b>
<H2>Preceding Sibling Axis</H2>
<b><xsl:apply-templates select="preceding-sibling::*/p"/></b>
<H2>Preceeding Axis</H2>
<b><i>Not Implemented in XT 22 09 99</i></b>
<H2>Namespace Axis</H2>
<b><i>Not Implemented in XT 22 09 99</i></b>
</body>
</html>
</xsl:template>
</xsl:stylesheet>
```

The child axis:: can be omitted from the location step as it is a default axis. The Axis attribute:: can be abbreviated to an @. // is short for the /descendant-or-self::, is short for self:: and .. is the short for parent::.

REPETITIONS AND SORTINGS IN XSL

XSL for-each Instruction

An xsl:for-each instruction contains the template, which is been applied to each node selected with the select attribute.

XML Source

```
<?xml version="1.0"?>
<xslTutorial >
<AAA id='a1' pos='start'>
<BBB id='b1'/>
<BBB id='b2'/>
</AAA>
<AAA id='a2'>
<BBB id='b3'/>
<BBB id='b4'/>
<CCC id='c1'>
<DDD id='d1'/>
</CCC>
<BBB id='b5'>
<CCC id='c2'/>
</BBB>
</AAA>
</xslTutorial>
```

HTML Output 1

```
<DIV style="color:red">BBB id=b1</DIV>
<DIV style="color:red">BBB id=b2</DIV>
<DIV style="color:red">BBB id=b3</DIV>
<DIV style="color:red">BBB id=b4</DIV>
<DIV style="color:red">BBB id=b5</DIV>
<DIV style="color:navy">CCC id=c1</DIV>
```

XSL Stylesheet 1

```
<xsl:stylesheet xmlns:xsl='http://www.w3.org/1999/XSL/Transform'>
<xsl:template match="/">
<xsl:for-each select="//BBB">
<DIV style="color:red">
<xsl:value-of select="name()"/>
<xsl:text> id=</xsl:text>
<xsl:value-of select="@id"/>
</DIV>
</xsl:for-each>
```

```
<xsl:for-each select="xslTutorial/AAA/CCC">
<DIV style="color:navy">
<xsl:value-of select="name()"/>
<xsl:text> id=</xsl:text>
<xsl:value-of select="@id"/>
</DIV>
</xsl:for-each>
</xsl:template>
</xsl:stylesheet>
```

XSL SORTING

The nodes selected with an xsl:for-each (see Stylesheet 1 and Stylesheet 2) or the xsl:apply-templates (see Stylesheet 3) can be sorted. Order of the sorting determines the order of an attribute. Stylesheet 1 sorts in ascending order and Stylesheet 2 sorts in descending mode.

XML Source

```
<?xml version="1.0"?>
<xslTutorial >
<name>John</name>
<name>Josua</name>
<name>Charles</name>
<name>Alice</name>
<name>Martha</name>
<name>George</name>
</xslTutorial>
```

HTML Output 1

```
<HTML>
<HEAD> </HEAD>
<BODY>
<TABLE>
<TR>
<TH>Alice</TH></TR>
<TR>
<TH>George</TH></TR>
```

```
<TR>
<TH>Charles</TH></TR>
<TR>
<TH>John</TH></TR>
<TR>
<TH>Josua</TH></TR>
<TR>
<TH>Martha</TH></TR>
</TABLE>
</BODY>
</HTML>
```

XSL Stylesheet 1

```
<xsl:stylesheet xmlns:xsl='http://www.w3.org/1999/XSL/Transform' >
<xsl:template match="/">
<TABLE>
<xsl:for-each select="//name">
<xsl:sort order="ascending" select="."/>
<TR><TH><xsl:value-of select="."/></TH></TR>
</xsl:for-each>
</TABLE>
</xsl:template>
</xsl:stylesheet>
```

Stylesheet 1 sorts the text and the Stylesheet 2 sorts the numeric mode. Notice the most important difference. "Two" comes after "one" alphabetically, so 2 goes after 10 in text mode.

XML Source

```
<?xml version="1.0"?>
<xslTutorial >
<car id="11"/>
<car id="6"/>
<car id="105"/>
<car id="28"/>
<car id="9"/>
</xslTutorial>
```

HTML Output 1

```
<HTML>
<HEAD> </HEAD>
<BODY>
<TABLE>
<TR>
<TH>Car-105</TH></TR>
<TR>
<TH>Car-11</TH></TR>
<TR>
<TH>Car-28</TH></TR>
<TR>
<TH>Car-6</TH></TR>
<TR>
<TH>Car-9</TH></TR>
</TABLE>
</BODY>
</HTML>
```

HTML Output 2

```
<HTML>
<HEAD> </HEAD>
<BODY>
<TABLE>
<TR>
<TH>Car-6</TH></TR>
<TR>
<TH>Car-9</TH></TR>
<TR>
<TH>Car-11</TH></TR>
<TR>
<TH>Car-28</TH></TR>
<TR>
<TH>Car-105</TH></TR>
</TABLE>
</BODY>
</HTML>
```

XSL Stylesheet 1

```
<xsl:stylesheet xmlns:xsl='http://www.w3.org/1999/XSL/Transform' >
<xsl:template match="/">
<TABLE>
<xsl:for-each select="//car">
<xsl:sort data-type="text" select="@id"/>
<TR><TH><xsl:text> Car-</xsl:text> <xsl:value-of
select="@id"/></TH></TR>
</xsl:for-each>
</TABLE>
</xsl:template>
</xsl:stylesheet>
```

XSL Stylesheet 2

```
<xsl:stylesheet xmlns:xsl='http://www.w3.org/1999/XSL/Transform' >
<xsl:template match="/">
<TABLE>
<xsl:for-each select="//car">
<xsl:sort data-type="number" select="@id"/>
<TR><TH><xsl:text> Car-</xsl:text> <xsl:value-of
select="@id"/></TH></TR>
</xsl:for-each>
</TABLE>
</xsl:template>
</xsl:stylesheet>
```

UPPERCASE AND LOWERCASE SORTING

Stylesheet 1 sorts the uppercase letters first, and Stylesheet 2 sorts the lowercase letters first.

XML Source

```
<?xml version="1.0"?>
<xslTutorial >
<word id="czech"/>
<word id="Czech"/>
<word id="cook"/>
```

```
<word id="TooK"/>
<word id="took"/>
<word id="Took"/>
</xslTutorial>
```

HTML Output 1

```
<HTML>
<HEAD> </HEAD>
<BODY>
<TABLE>
<TR>
<TH>cook</TH></TR>
<TR>
<TH>Czech</TH></TR>
<TR>
<TH>czech</TH></TR>
<TR>
<TH>TooK</TH></TR>
<TR>
<TH>Took</TH></TR>
<TR>
<TH>took</TH></TR>
</TABLE>
</BODY>
</HTML>
```

HTML Output 2

```
<HTML>
<HEAD> </HEAD>
<BODY>
<TABLE>
<TR>
<TH>cook</TH></TR>
<TR>
<TH>czech</TH></TR>
<TR>
<TH>Czech</TH></TR>
<TR>
<TH>took</TH></TR>
```

```
<TR>
<TH>Took</TH></TR>
<TR>
<TH>TooK</TH></TR>
</TABLE>
</BODY>
</HTML>
```

XSL Stylesheet 1

```
<xsl:stylesheet xmlns:xsl='http://www.w3.org/1999/XSL/Transform' >
<xsl:template match="/">
<TABLE>
<xsl:for-each select="//word">
<xsl:sort case-order="upper-first" select="@id"/>
<TR><TH><xsl:value-of
select="@id"/></TH></TR>
</xsl:for-each>
</TABLE>
</xsl:template>
</xsl:stylesheet>
```

XSL Stylesheet 2

```
<xsl:stylesheet xmlns:xsl='http://www.w3.org/1999/XSL/Transform' >
<xsl:template match="/">
<TABLE>
<xsl:for-each select="//word">
<xsl:sort case-order="lower-first" select="@id"/>
<TR><TH><xsl:value-of
select="@id"/></TH></TR>
</xsl:for-each>
</TABLE>
</xsl:template>
</xsl:stylesheet>
\XSl Element
```

The xsl:element generates the elements at the time of processing.

XML Source

```
<?xml version="1.0"?>
<xslTutorial >
```

```
<text size="H1">Header1</text>
<text size="H3">Header3</text>
<text size="b">Bold text</text>
<text size="sub">Subscript</text>
<text size="sup">Superscript</text>
</xslTutorial>
```

HTML Output 1

```
<HTML>
<HEAD> </HEAD>
<BODY>
<H1>Header1</H1>
<H3>Header3</H3>
<b>Bold text</b>
<sub>Subscript</sub>
<sup>Superscript</sup>
</BODY>
</HTML>
```

XSL Stylesheet 1

```
<xsl:stylesheet xmlns:xsl='http://www.w3.org/1999/XSL/Transform' >
<xsl:template match="/">
<xsl:for-each select="//text">
<xsl:element name="{@size}"><xsl:value-of select="."/></xsl:element>
</xsl:for-each>
</xsl:template>
</xsl:stylesheet>
```

The XSL Attribute

The xsl:attribute generates the elements at the time of processing. It creates the attribute in the element in which it is enclosed.

XML Source

```
<?xml version="1.0"?>
<xslTutorial >
<color>blue</color>
<color>navy</color>
```

```
<color>green</color>
<color>lime</color>
<color>red</color>
```

HTML Output 1

```
<HTML>
<HEAD> </HEAD>
<BODY>
<TABLE>
<TR>
<TD style=" color:blue">blue</TD></TR></TABLE>
<TABLE>
<TR>
<TD style=" color:navy">navy</TD></TR></TABLE>
<TABLE>
<TR>
<TD style=" color:green">green</TD></TR></TABLE>
<TABLE>
<TR>
<TD style=" color:lime">lime</TD></TR></TABLE>
<TABLE>
<TR>
<TD style=" color:red">red</TD></TR>
</TABLE>
</BODY>
</HTML>
```

XSL Stylesheet 1

```
<xsl:stylesheet xmlns:xsl='http://www.w3.org/1999/XSL/Transform' >
<xsl:template match="color">
<TABLE>
<TR><TD>
<xsl:attribute name="style">
color:<xsl:value-of select="."/>
</xsl:attribute>
<xsl:value-of select="."/>
</TD></TR>
```

```
</TABLE>
</xsl:template>
</xsl:stylesheet>
```

The Copy and Copy-of Constructs

The copy and copy-of constructs are used for the node copying. The copy element copies down only the current node without the children and the attributes, while the copy-of copies everything.

XML Source

```
<?xml version="1.0"?>
<xslTutorial >
<p id="a12">
Compare <B>these constructs</B>
</p>
</xslTutorial>
```

HTML Output 1

```
<HTML>
<HEAD> </HEAD>
<BODY>
<DIV>
<B>copy-of : </B>
<p id="a12"> Compare
<B>these constructs</B>. </p></DIV>
<DIV>
<B>copy : </B>
<p/></DIV>
<DIV>
<B>value-of : </B> Compare these constructs.
</DIV>
</BODY>
</HTML>
```

XSL Stylesheet 1

```
<xsl:stylesheet xmlns:xsl='http://www.w3.org/1999/XSL/Transform' >
<xsl:template match="p">
```

```
<DIV><B><xsl:text> copy-of : </xsl:text> </B>
; <xsl:copy-of select="."/>
</DIV>
<DIV><B><xsl:text> copy : </xsl:text> </B>
<xsl:copy/ >
</DIV>
<DIV><B><xsl:text> value-of : </xsl:text> </B>
<xsl:value-of select="."/>
</DIV>
</xsl:template>
</xsl:stylesheet>
```

XSL CONDITIONAL PROCESSING

The xsl:if instruction enables the conditional processing. Stylesheet 1 demonstrates the typical case of a xsl:for-each usage, adding up the text between the individual entries. Often, you do not want to add up the text after the last element. The xsl-if construct comes in handy here (see Stylesheet 2).

XML Source

```
<?xml version="1.0"?>
<xslTutorial >
<list>
<entry name="A"/>
<entry name="B"/>
<entry name="C"/>
<entry name="D"/>
</list>
</xslTutorial>
```

HTML Output 1

```
<HTML>
<HEAD> </HEAD>
<BODY> A, B, C, D,
</BODY>
</HTML>
```

HTML Output 2

```
<HTML>
<HEAD> </HEAD>
<BODY> A, B, C, D
</BODY>
</HTML>
```

XSL Stylesheet 1

```
<xsl:stylesheet xmlns:xsl='http://www.w3.org/1999/XSL/Transform' >
<xsl:template match="list">
<xsl:for-each select="entry">
<xsl:value-of select="@name"/>
<xsl:text> , </xsl:text>
</xsl:for-each>
</xsl:template>
</xsl:stylesheet>
```

XSL Stylesheet 2

```
<xsl:stylesheet xmlns:xsl='http://www.w3.org/1999/XSL/Transform'>
<xsl:template match="list">
<xsl:for-each select="entry">
<xsl:value-of select="@name"/>
<xsl:if test="not(position()=last())">
<xsl:text> , </xsl:text>
</xsl:if>
</xsl:for-each>
</xsl:template>
</xsl:stylesheet>
```

The Choose Element

The xsl:choose element is used to make a choice among the several possibilities.

XML Source

```
<?xml version="1.0"?>
<xslTutorial >
<SECTION>
```

```
<DATA>I need a pen.</DATA>
<DATA>I need some paper.</DATA>
<SUMMARY>I need a pen and some paper.</SUMMARY>
</SECTION>
<SECTION>
<DATA>I need bread.</DATA>
<DATA>I need butter.</DATA>
</SECTION>
</xslTutorial>
```

HTML Output 1

```
<HTML>
<HEAD> </HEAD>
<BODY>
<P>SUMMARY: I need a pen and some paper.</P>
<P>DATA: I need bread.</P>
<P>DATA: I need butter.</P>
</BODY>
</HTML>
```

XSL Stylesheet 1

```
<xsl:stylesheet xmlns:xsl='http://www.w3.org/1999/XSL/Transform' > <xsl:template
match="//SECTION">
<xsl:choose>
<xsl:when test='SUMMARY'>
<P><xsl:text> SUMMARY: </xsl:text>
<xsl:value-of select="SUMMARY"/></P>
</xsl:when>
<xsl:otherwise>
<xsl:for-each select="DATA">
<P><xsl:text> DATA: </xsl:text>
<xsl:value-of select="."/></P>
</xsl:for-each>
</xsl:otherwise>
</xsl:choose>
</xsl:template>
</xsl:stylesheet>
```

NUMBER GENERATION AND FORMATTING IN XSL

Stylesheet 1 demonstrates a default behavior of the xsl:number element. Numbering of the individual chapter elements depends on the position of a chapter element. Each level of the chapter is numbered independently. Setting an attribute level to multiple in Stylesheet 2 enables more natural numbering.

XML Source

```
<?xml version="1.0"?>
<xslTutorial >
<chapter>First Chapter</chapter>
<chapter>Second Chapter
<chapter>Subchapter 1</chapter>
<chapter>Subchapter 2</chapter>
</chapter>
<chapter>Third Chapter
<chapter>Subchapter A</chapter>
<chapter>Subchapter B
<chapter>sub a</chapter>
<chapter>sub b</chapter>
</chapter>
<chapter>Subchapter C</chapter>
</chapter>
</xslTutorial>
```

HTML Output 1

```
<HTML>
<HEAD> </HEAD>
<BODY>
<TABLE BORDER="1">
TR>
<TH>Number</TH>
; <TH>text</TH></TR>
<TR>
<TD>1</TD>
<TD>First Chapter</TD></TR>
<TR>
<TD>2</TD>
```

```
<TD>Second Chapter </TD></TR>
<TR>
<TD>1</TD>
<TD>Subchapter 1</TD></TR>
<TR>
<TD>2</TD>
<TD>Subchapter 2</TD></TR>
<TR>
<TD>3</TD>
<TD>Third Chapter </TD></TR>
<TR>
<TD>1</TD>
<TD>Subchapter A</TD></TR>
<TR>
<TD>2</TD>
<TD>Subchapter B </TD></TR>
<TR>
<TD>1</TD>
<TD>sub a</TD></TR>
<TR>
<TD>2</TD>
<TD>sub b</TD></TR>
<TR>
<TD>3</TD>
<TD>Subchapter C</TD></TR>
</TABLE>
</BODY>
</HTML>
```

HTML Output 2

```
<HTML>
<HEAD> </HEAD>
<BODY>
<TABLE BORDER="1">
<TR>
<TH>Number</TH>
<TH>text</TH></TR>
<TR>
```

```
<TD>1</TD>
<TD>First Chapter</TD></TR>
<TR>
<TD>2</TD>
<TD>Second Chapter </TD></TR>
<TR>
<TD>2.1</TD>
<TD>Subchapter 1</TD></TR>
<TR>
<TD>2.2</TD>
<TD>Subchapter 2</TD></TR>
<TR>
<TD>3</TD>
<TD>Third Chapter </TD></TR>
<TR>
<TD>3.1</TD>
<TD>Subchapter A</TD></TR>
<TR>
<TD>3.2</TD>
<TD>Subchapter B </TD></TR>
<TR>
<TD>3.2.1</TD>
<TD>sub a</TD></TR>
<TR>
<TD>3.2.2</TD>
<TD>sub b</TD></TR>
<TR>
<TD>3.3</TD>
<TD>Subchapter C</TD></TR>
</TABLE>
</BODY>
</HTML>
```

XSL Stylesheet 1

```
<xsl:stylesheet xmlns:xsl='http://www.w3.org/1999/XSL/Transform' >
<xsl:template match="/">
<TABLE BORDER="1">
<TR><TH>Number</TH><TH>text</TH></TR>
```

```
<xsl:for-each select="//chapter">
<TR><TD>
<xsl:number/ >
</TD><TD>
<xsl:value-of select="./text()"/>
</TD></TR>
</xsl:for-each>
</TABLE>
</xsl:template>
</xsl:stylesheet>
```

The Format Attribute

An xsl:numbers inserts formatted numbers into the output. The format is given with the format attribute. An attribute starts with a format identificator followed by separator characters.

XML Source

```
<?xml version="1.0"?>
<xslTutorial >
<n>one</n>
<n>two</n>
<n>three</n>
<n>four</n>
</xslTutorial>
```

HTML Output 1

```
<HTML>
<HEAD> </HEAD>
<BODY>
<TABLE>
<TR>
<TD>1. one</TD></TR>
<TR>
<TD>2. two</TD></TR>
<TR>
<TD>3. three</TD></TR>
<TR>
<TD>4. four</TD></TR>
```

```
</TABLE>
</BODY>
</HTML>
<xsl:stylesheet xmlns:xsl='http://www.w3.org/1999/XSL/Transform' >
<xsl:template match="/">
<TABLE>
<xsl:for-each select="//n">
<TR><TD>
<xsl:number value="position()" format="1. "/>
<xsl:value-of select="."/>
</TD></TR>
</xsl:for-each>
</TABLE>
</xsl:template>
</xsl:stylesheet>
```

XSL Stylesheet 1

FORMATTING MULTILEVEL NUMBERS

Stylesheet 1 and Stylesheet 2 are examples of formatting multilevel numbers.

XML Source

```
<?xml version="1.0"?>
<xslTutorial >
<chapter>First Chapter</chapter>
<chapter>Second Chapter
<chapter>Subchapter 1</chapter>
<chapter>Subchapter 2</chapter>
</chapter>
<chapter>Third Chapter
<chapter>Subchapter A</chapter>
<chapter>Subchapter B
<chapter>sub a</chapter>
<chapter>sub b</chapter>
</chapter>
<chapter>Subchapter C</chapter>
</chapter>
</xslTutorial>
```

HTML Output 1

```
<HTML>
<HEAD> </HEAD>
<BODY>
<TABLE BORDER="1">
<TR>
<TH>Number</TH>
<TH>text</TH></TR>
<TR>
<TD>1 </TD>
<TD>First Chapter</TD></TR>
<TR>
<TD>2 </TD>
<TD>Second Chapter </TD></TR>
<TR>
<TD>2.A </TD>
<TD>Subchapter 1</TD></TR>
<TR>
<TD>2.B </TD>
<TD>Subchapter 2</TD></TR>
<TR>
<TD>3 </TD>
<TD>Third Chapter </TD></TR>
<TR>
<TD>3.A </TD>
<TD>Subchapter A</TD></TR>
<TR>
<TD>3.B </TD>
<TD>Subchapter B </TD></TR>
<TR>
<TD>3.B.a </TD>
<TD>sub a</TD></TR>
<TR>
<TD>3.B.b </TD>
<TD>sub b</TD></TR>
<TR>
<TD>3.C </TD>
<TD>Subchapter C</TD></TR>
```

```
</TABLE>
</BODY>
</HTML>
```

HTML Output 2

```
<HTML>
<HEAD> </HEAD>
<BODY>
<TABLE BORDER="1">
<TR>
<TH>Number</TH>
<TH>text</TH></TR>
<TR>
<TD>I:</TD>
<TD>First Chapter</TD></TR>
<TR>
<TD>II:</TD>
<TD>Second Chapter </TD></TR>
<TR>
<TD>II-1:</TD>
<TD>Subchapter 1</TD></TR>
<TR>
<TD>II-2:</TD>
<TD>Subchapter 2</TD></TR>
<TR>
<TD>III:</TD>
<TD>Third Chapter </TD></TR>
<TR>
<TD>III-1:</TD>
<TD>Subchapter A</TD></TR>
<TR>
<TD>III-2:</TD>
<TD>Subchapter B
<TR>
<TD>III-2-a:</TD>
<TD>sub a</TD></TR>
<TR>
<TD>III-2-b:</TD>
```

```
<TD>sub b</TD></TR>
<TR>
<TD>III-3:</TD>
<TD>Subchapter C</TD></TR>
</TABLE>
</BODY>
</HTML>
```

XSL Stylesheet 1

```
<xsl:stylesheet xmlns:xsl='http://www.w3.org/1999/XSL/Transform' >
<xsl:template match="/">
<TABLE BORDER="1">
<TR><TH>Number</TH><TH>text</TH></TR>
<xsl:for-each select="//chapter">
<TR><TD>
<xsl:number level="multiple" format="1.A.a "/>
</TD><TD>
<xsl:value-of select="./text()"/>
</TD></TR>
</xsl:for-each>
</TABLE>
</xsl:template>
</xsl:stylesheet>
```

XSL Stylesheet 2

```
<xsl:stylesheet xmlns:xsl='http://www.w3.org/1999/XSL/Transform' >
<xsl:template match="/">
<TABLE BORDER="1">
<TR><TH>Number</TH><TH>text</TH></TR>
<xsl:for-each select="//chapter">
<TR><TD>
<xsl:number level="multiple" format="I-1-a:"/>
</TD><TD>
<xsl:value-of select="./text()"/>
</TD></TR>
</xsl:for-each>
</TABLE>
</xsl:template>
</xsl:stylesheet>
```

NUMERIC CALCULATION IN XSL

A function transform its argument into number. XSL stylesheet 1 demonstrates the string conversion, and XSL stylesheet 2 converts the boolean values to either true or false.

XSL Stylesheet 1

```
<xsl:stylesheet version = '1.0'
xmlns:xsl='http://www.w3.org/1999/XSL/Transform'>
<xsl:template match="/">
<TABLE border="1">
<TR>
<TH>text</TH>
<TH>number</TH>
</TR>
<xsl:for-each select="//text">
<TR>
<TD>
<xsl:value-of select="."/>
</TD>
<TD>
<xsl:value-of select="number()"/>
</TD>
</TR>
</xsl:for-each>
</TABLE>
</xsl:template>
</xsl:stylesheet>
```

XSL Stylesheet 2

```
<xsl:stylesheet version = '1.0'
xmlns:xsl='http://www.w3.org/1999/XSL/Transform'>
<xsl:template match="/">
<TABLE border="1">
<TR>
<TH>text</TH>
<TH>number</TH>
</TR>
```

```
<xsl:for-each select="//text[text() = 'true' or text() = 'false()']">
<TR>
<TD>
<xsl:value-of select="."/>
</TD>
<TD>
<xsl:value-of select="number()"/>
</TD>
</TR>
</xsl:for-each>
</TABLE>
<P>
<xsl:text>but:</xsl:text>
</P>
<TABLE border="1">
<TR>
<TH>function</TH>
<TH>number</TH>
</TR>
<TR>
<TD>true()</TD>
<TD>
<xsl:value-of select="number(true())"/>
</TD>
</TR>
<TR>
<TD>false()</TD>
<TD>
<xsl:value-of select="number(false())"/>
</TD>
</TR>
<TR>
<TD>5>7</TD>
<TD>
<xsl:value-of select="number(5 > 7)"/>
</TD>
</TR>
<TR>
<TD>5<7</TD>
```

```
<TD>
<xsl:value-of select="number(5<7)"/>
</TD>
</TR>
</TABLE>
</xsl:template>
</xsl:stylesheet>
```

Add, subtract a and multiply use, common syntax, (see the XSL Stylesheet 1). The division syntax is less familiar. A slash " / " symbol is used in the patterns, and so the keyword div is used instead (see XSL Stylesheet 2). The operator mod returns a remainder from truncating the division.

XML Source

```
<source>
<number>1</number>
<number>3</number>
<number>4</number>
<number>17</number>
<number>8</number>
<number>11</number>
</source>
```

Output

```
<P>1 + 3 = 4</P>
<P>4 - 17 = -13</P>
<P>8 * 11 = 88</P>
```

XSL Stylesheet 1

```
<xsl:stylesheet version = '1.0'
xmlns:xsl='http://www.w3.org/1999/XSL/Transform'>
<xsl:template match="/">
<P>
<xsl:value-of select="//number[1]"/>
<xsl:text> + </xsl:text>
<xsl:value-of select="//number[2]"/>
<xsl:text> = </xsl:text>
<xsl:value-of select="//number[1] + //number[2]"/>
```

```
</P>
<P>
<xsl:value-of select="//number[3]"/>
<xsl:text> - </xsl:text>
<xsl:value-of select="//number[4]"/>
<xsl:text> = </xsl:text>
<xsl:value-of select="//number[3] - //number[4]"/>
</P>
<P>
<xsl:value-of select="//number[5]"/>
<xsl:text> * </xsl:text>
<xsl:value-of select="//number[6]"/>
<xsl:text> = </xsl:text>
<xsl:value-of select="//number[5] * //number[6]"/>
</P>
</xsl:template>
</xsl:stylesheet>
```

XML Source

```
<source>
<number>1</number>
<number>3</number>
<number>4</number>
<number>17</number>
<number>8</number>
<number>11</number>
</source>
```

Output

```
<P>8 / 11 = 0.7272727272727273</P>
<P>8 mod 11 = 8</P>
```

XSL Stylesheet 2

```
<xsl:stylesheet version = '1.0'
xmlns:xsl='http://www.w3.org/1999/XSL/Transform'>
<xsl:template match="/">
<P>
```

```
<xsl:value-of select="//number[5]"/>
<xsl:text> / </xsl:text>
<xsl:value-of select="//number[6]"/>
<xsl:text> = </xsl:text>
<xsl:value-of select="//number[5] div //number[6]"/>
</P>
<P>
<xsl:value-of select="//number[5]"/>
<xsl:text> mod </xsl:text>
<xsl:value-of select="//number[6]"/>
<xsl:text> = </xsl:text>
<xsl:value-of select="//number[5] mod //number[6]"/>
</P>
</xsl:template>
</xsl:stylesheet>
```

CEILING, FLOOR, AND ROUND

The functions ceiling(), floor(), and the round() transform a floating point number into an integer in a specified way.

XML Source

```
<source>
<number>6</number>
<number>3.8</number>
<number>1.234</number>
<number>-6</number>
<number>-3.8</number>
<number>-1.234</number>
</source>
```

Output

```
<TABLE border="1">
<TR>
<TH>number</TH>
<TH>floor</TH>
<TH>ceiling</TH>
```

```
<TH>round</TH>
</TR>
<TR>
<TD>6</TD>
<TD>6</TD>
<TD>6</TD>
<TD>6</TD>
</TR>
<TR>
<TD>3.8</TD>
<TD>3</TD>
<TD>4</TD>
<TD>4</TD>
</TR>
<TR>
<TD>1.234</TD>
<TD>1</TD>
<TD>2</TD>
<TD>1</TD>
</TR>
<TR>
<TD>-6</TD>
<TD>-6</TD>
<TD>-6</TD>
<TD>-6</TD>
</TR>
<TR>
<TD>-3.8</TD>
<TD>-4</TD>
<TD>-3
<td>-4></td>-4>
</TR>
<TR>
<TD>-1.234</TD>
<TD>-2</TD>
<TD>-1</TD>
<TD>-1</TD>
</TR>
</TABLE>
```

XSL Stylesheet

```
<xsl:stylesheet version = '1.0'
xmlns:xsl='http://www.w3.org/1999/XSL/Transform'>
<xsl:template match="/">
<TABLE border="1">
<TR>
<TH>number</TH>
<TH>floor</TH>
<TH>ceiling</TH>
<TH>round</TH>
</TR>
<xsl:for-each select="//number">
<TR>
<TD>
<xsl:value-of select="."/>
</TD>
<TD>
<xsl:value-of select="floor(.)"/>
</TD>
<TD>
<xsl:value-of select="ceiling(.)"/>
</TD>
<TD>
<xsl:value-of select="round(.)"/>
</TD>
</TR>
</xsl:for-each>
</TABLE>
</xsl:template>
</xsl:stylesheet>
```

STRING FUNCTION

The function string() transforms all its argument into a string. This function is not used directly in the stylesheets since it is called by default. XSL stylesheet 1 shows examples of the number-to-string conversions. Notice the results of a zero division.

XML Source

```
<source>
<number>9</number>
<number>0</number>
<number>-9</number>
<number/>
</source>
```

Output

```
<P>9</P>
<P>NaN</P>
<P>9/0 = Infinity</P>
<P>-9/0 = -Infinity</P>
<P>0/0 = NaN</P>
```

XSL Stylesheet

```
<xsl:stylesheet version = '1.0'
xmlns:xsl='http://www.w3.org/1999/XSL/Transform'>
<xsl:variable name="A" select="number(//number[1])"/>
<xsl:variable name="B" select="number(//number[2])"/>
<xsl:variable name="C" select="number(//number[3])"/>
<xsl:variable name="D" select="number(//number[4])"/>
<xsl:template match="/">
<P>
<xsl:value-of select="string(number($A))"/>
</P>
<P>
<xsl:value-of select="string(number($D))"/>
</P>
<P>
<xsl:value-of select="$A"/>
<xsl:text>/</xsl:text>
<xsl:value-of select="$B"/>
<xsl:text> = </xsl:text>
<xsl:value-of select="string($A div $B)"/>
</P>
<P>
```

```
<xsl:value-of select="$C"/>
<xsl:text>/</xsl:text>
<xsl:value-of select="$B"/>
<xsl:text> = </xsl:text>
<xsl:value-of select="string($C div $B)"/>
</P>
<P>
<xsl:value-of select="$B"/>
<xsl:text>/</xsl:text>
<xsl:value-of select="$B"/>
<xsl:text> = </xsl:text>
<xsl:value-of select="$B div $B"/>
</P>
</xsl:template>
</xsl:stylesheet>
```

In XSL Stylesheet 1, strings are the arguments of the boolean() function. The string is true if, and only if, the length of it is a non-zero integer.

XML Source

```
<source>
<text>124</text>
<text>AB234</text>
<text>-16</text>
<text>0</text>
<text/>
<text>false</text>
</source>
```

Output

```
<TABLE border="1">
<TR>
<TH>text</TH>
<TH>boolean</TH>
</TR>
<TR>
<TD>124</TD>
<TD>true</TD>
```

```
</TR>
<TR>
<TD>AB234</TD>
<TD>true</TD>
</TR>
<TR>
<TD>-16</TD>
<TD>true</TD>
</TR>
<TR>
<TD>0</TD>
<TD>true</TD>
</TR>
<TR>
<TD/>
<TD>false</TD>
</TR>
<TR>
<TD>false</TD>
<TD>true</TD>
</TR>
</TABLE>
```

XSL Stylesheet

```
<xsl:stylesheet version = '1.0'
xmlns:xsl='http://www.w3.org/1999/XSL/Transform'>
<xsl:template match="/">
<TABLE border="1">
<TR>
<TH>text</TH>
<TH>boolean</TH>
</TR>
<xsl:for-each select="//text">
<TR>
<TD>
<xsl:value-of select="."/>
<xsl:text/>
</TD>
```

```
<TD>
<xsl:value-of select="boolean(text())"/>
</TD>
</TR>
</xsl:for-each>
</TABLE>
</xsl:template>
</xsl:stylesheet>
```

Not Function

The not function returns true if the argument passed to it is false, and returns false otherwise.

XML Source

```
<source>
<car id="a234" checked="yes"/>
<car id="a111" checked="yes"/>
<car id="a005"/>
</source>
```

Output

```
<P>
<B style="color:blue">a234</B>
</P>
<P>
<B style="color:blue">a111</B>
</P>
<P>
<B style="color:red">a005</B>
</P>
```

XSL Stylesheet

```
<xsl:stylesheet version = '1.0'
xmlns:xsl='http://www.w3.org/1999/XSL/Transform'>
<xsl:template match="car[not(@checked)]">
<P>
<B style="color:red">
```

```
<xsl:value-of select="@id"/>
</B>
</P>
</xsl:template>
<xsl:template match="car[@checked]">
<P>
<B style="color:blue">
<xsl:value-of select="@id"/>
</B>
</P>
</xsl:template>
</xsl:stylesheet>
```

The functions true() and false() are useful for testing conditions.

XML Source

```
<source>
<number>0</number>
<number>1</number>
</source>
```

Output

```
<P>true not false</P>
<P>true not false</P>
```

XSL Stylesheet

```
<xsl:stylesheet version = '1.0'
xmlns:xsl='http://www.w3.org/1999/XSL/Transform'>
<xsl:template match="number">
<P>
<xsl:if test="true()">
<xsl:text>true </xsl:text>
</xsl:if>
<xsl:if test="not(false())">
<xsl:text>not false</xsl:text>
</xsl:if>
</P>
</xsl:template>
</xsl:stylesheet>
```

The lang function returns true or false depending on the language of the context node as specified by the xml:lang attributes. It is the same as or is the sublanguage of the language that is specified by an argument string. The language of the context node is determined by a value of the xml:lang attribute on the context node, or, if the context node has no xml:lang attribute, by a value of the xml:lang attribute on the nearest ancestor of a context node that has an xml:lang attribute. If there exists no such attribute, then the lang returns false. If such an attribute exists, then the lang returns true if the attribute value is equal to an argument ignoring the case, or if there is some suffix starting with it, such that an attribute value is equal to an argument ignoring the suffix of an attribute value and ignoring the case.

XML Source

```
<source>
<P xml:lang="de">
<text xml:lang="cs">a</text>
<text xml:lang="en">and</text>
<text>und</text>
</P>
</source>
```

Output

```
<P>Czech: a</P>
<P>English: and</P>
<P>German: und</P>
```

XSL Stylesheet

```
<xsl:stylesheet version = '1.0'
xmlns:xsl='http://www.w3.org/1999/XSL/Transform'>
<xsl:template match="text">
<P>
<xsl:choose>
<xsl:when test='lang("cs")'>
<xsl:text>Czech: </xsl:text>
</xsl:when>
<xsl:when test='lang("en")'>
<xsl:text>English: </xsl:text>
```

```
</xsl:when>
<xsl:when test='lang("de")'>
<xsl:text>German: </xsl:text>
</xsl:when>
</xsl:choose>
<xsl:value-of select="."/>
</P>
</xsl:template>
</xsl:stylesheet>
```

XSL STRING FUNCTIONS

```
string()
```

The function string() transforms the argument into a string. This function is not usually directly used in the stylesheets, as in most cases called by a default. XSL stylesheet 1 shows the examples of the number-to-string conversion. Notice the results of the zero divisions.

XML Source

```
<source>
<number>9</number>
<number>0</number>
<number>-9</number>
<number/>
</source>
```

Output

```
<P>9</P>
<P>NaN</P>
<P>9/0 = Infinity</P>
<P>-9/0 = -Infinity</P>
<P>0/0 = NaN</P>
```

XSL Stylesheet

```
<xsl:stylesheet version = '1.0'
xmlns:xsl='http://www.w3.org/1999/XSL/Transform'>
```

```
<xsl:variable name="A" select="number(//number[1])"/>
<xsl:variable name="B" select="number(//number[2])"/>
<xsl:variable name="C" select="number(//number[3])"/>
<xsl:variable name="D" select="number(//number[4])"/>
<xsl:template match="/">
<P>
<xsl:value-of select="string(number($A))"/>
</P>
<P>
<xsl:value-of select="string(number($D))"/>
</P>
<P>
<xsl:value-of select="$A"/>
<xsl:text>/</xsl:text>
<xsl:value-of select="$B"/>
<xsl:text> = </xsl:text>
<xsl:value-of select="string($A div $B)"/>
</P>
<P>
<xsl:value-of select="$C"/>
<xsl:text>/</xsl:text>
<xsl:value-of select="$B"/>
<xsl:text> = </xsl:text>
<xsl:value-of select="string($C div $B)"/>
</P>
<P>
<xsl:value-of select="$B"/>
<xsl:text>/</xsl:text>
<xsl:value-of select="$B"/>
<xsl:text> = </xsl:text>
<xsl:value-of select="$B div $B"/>
</P>
</xsl:template>
</xsl:stylesheet>
```

CONCATINATION

The string concat function returns the concatenation of the arguments passed to it.

XML Source

```
<source>
<text>Start</text>
<text>Body</text>
<text>Finish</text>
</source>
```

Output

```
<P>Start - Body - Finish</P>
```

XSL Stylesheet

```
<xsl:stylesheet version = '1.0'
xmlns:xsl='http://www.w3.org/1999/XSL/Transform'>
<xsl:variable name="T" select="concat(//text[1],' - ',//text[2],' - ',//text[3])"/>
<xsl:template match="/">
<P>
<xsl:value-of select="$T"/>
</P>
</xsl:template>
</xsl:stylesheet>
```

A starts-with function returns true if the first argument string starts with a second argument string, otherwise it will return false. The contains function returns true if the first argument string contains the second argument string, otherwise it will return false.

XML Source

```
<source>
<text>Welcome to XSL world.</text>
<string>Welcome</string>
<string>XSL</string>
<string>XML</string>
</source>
```

Output

```
<TABLE border="1">
<TR>
```

```
<TH colspan="3">Welcome to XSL world.</TH>
</TR>
<TR>
<TH>string</TH>
<TH>starts-with</TH>
<TH>contains</TH>
</TR>
<TR>
<TD>Welcome</TD>
<TD>true</TD>
<TD>true</TD>
</TR>
<TR>
<TD>XSL</TD>
<TD>false</TD>
<TD>true</TD>
</TR>
<TR>
<TD>XML</TD>
<TD>false</TD>
<TD>false</TD>
</TR>
</TABLE>
```

XSL Stylesheet

```
<xsl:stylesheet version = '1.0'
xmlns:xsl='http://www.w3.org/1999/XSL/Transform'>
<xsl:template match="/">
<TABLE border="1">
<TR>
<TH colspan="3">
<xsl:value-of select="//text"/>
</TH>
</TR>
<TR>
<TH>string</TH>
<TH>starts-with</TH>
<TH>contains</TH>
```

```
</TR>
<xsl:for-each select="//string">
<TR>
<TD>
<xsl:value-of select="."/>
</TD>
<TD>
<xsl:value-of select="starts-with(//text,.)"/>
</TD>
<TD>
<xsl:value-of select="contains(//text,.)"/>
</TD>
</TR>
</xsl:for-each>
</TABLE>
</xsl:template>
</xsl:stylesheet>
```

The substring-before function returns a substring of the first argument string that precedes the substring after the function that follows first occurrence of a second argument string in first argument string. The substring function returns a substring of the first argument starting at a position specified in the second argument with the length specified in the third argument. If the third argument is not specified, returns the substring starting at a position specified in a second argument and continues until the end of a string. The counting starts with 1.

Output

```
<DIV>
<B>Text: </B>Welcome to XSL world.</DIV>
<B>Text before XSL: </B>Welcome to <DIV>
<B>Text after XSL: </B> world.</DIV>
<DIV>
<B>Text from position 4: </B>come to XSL world.</DIV>
<DIV> <B>Text from position 4 of length 10: </B>come to XS</DIV>
```

XSL Stylesheet

```
<xsl:stylesheet version = '1.0'
xmlns:xsl='http://www.w3.org/1999/XSL/Transform'>
```

```
<xsl:template match="/">
<DIV>
<B>
<xsl:text>Text: </xsl:text>
</B>
<xsl:value-of select="//text"/>
</DIV>
<B>
<xsl:text>Text before </xsl:text>
<xsl:value-of select="//string"/>
<xsl:text>: </xsl:text>
</B>
<xsl:value-of select="substring-before(//text,//string)"/>
<DIV>
<B>
<xsl:text>Text after </xsl:text>
<xsl:value-of select="//string"/>
<xsl:text>: </xsl:text>
</B>
<xsl:value-of select="substring-after(//text,//string)"/>
</DIV>
<DIV>
<B>
<xsl:text>Text from position </xsl:text>
<xsl:value-of select="//start"/>
<xsl:text>: </xsl:text>
</B>
<xsl:value-of select="substring(//text,//start)"/>
</DIV>
<DIV>
<B>
<xsl:text>Text from position </xsl:text>
<xsl:value-of select="//start"/>
<xsl:text> of length </xsl:text>
<xsl:value-of select="//end"/>
<xsl:text>: </xsl:text>
</B>
<xsl:value-of select="substring(//text,//start,//end)"/>
```

```
</DIV>
</xsl:template>
</xsl:stylesheet>
```

The string-length function returns the number of characters in a string. The normalize-space function returns the argument string with a white space normalized by the stripping leading and trailing a whitespace. It replaces the sequences of whitespace characters a single white space.

Output

```
<TABLE>
<TR>
<TH colspan="4">Normalized text</TH>
</TR>
<TR>
<TD>Starting length:</TD>
<TD>15</TD>
<TD>Normalized length:</TD>
<TD>15</TD>
</TR>
<TR>
<TH colspan="4">Sequences of whitespace characters</TH>
</TR>
<TR>
<TD>Starting length:</TD>
<TD>41</TD>
<TD>Normalized length:</TD>
<TD>34</TD>
</TR>
<TR>
<TH colspan="4"> Leading and trailing whitespace. </TH>
</TR>
<TR>
<TD>Starting length:</TD>
<TD>40</TD>
<TD>Normalized length:</TD>
<TD>32</TD>
</TR>
</TABLE>
```

XSL Stylesheet

```
<xsl:stylesheet version = '1.0'
xmlns:xsl='http://www.w3.org/1999/XSL/Transform'>
<xsl:template match="/">
<TABLE>
<xsl:for-each select="//text">
<TR>
<TH colspan="4">
<xsl:value-of select="."/>
</TH>
</TR>
<TR>
<TD>Starting length:</TD>
<TD>
<xsl:value-of select="string-length(.)"/>
</TD>
<TD>Normalized length:</TD>
<TD>
<xsl:value-of select="string-length(normalize-space(.))"/> </TD>
</TR>
</xsl:for-each>
</TABLE>
</xsl:template>
</xsl:stylesheet>
```

XSL OUTPUT ELEMENT

An xsl:output element allows the stylesheet authors to specify how they wish a result tree to be output. If the XSL processor outputs a result tree, it must do so as specified by a xsl:output element; however, it is not required to do so. An xsl:output element is allowed only as the top-level element.

XML Source

```
<source>
<hr/>
<hr/>
<hr/>
</source>
```

Output

```
<source>
<hr>
<hr>
<hr>
</source>
```

When an xml:output element is not present, the default output method is “xml” (see XSL Stylesheet 1). If the document element of the output has a value “html” that is case insensitive and it does not have the xmlns attribute, then the html method is used.

Output

```
<h1> XML output </h1>
<hr/>
```

XSL Stylesheet

```
<xsl:stylesheet version = '1.0'
xmlns:xsl='http://www.w3.org/1999/XSL/Transform'>
<xsl:template match="/">
<xsl:copy-of select="/source/*"/>
</xsl:template>
</xsl:stylesheet>
```

HTML OUTPUT METHOD

An html output method must not output the end tag for an empty element specified in the HTML specification. An html output method must not perform the escape for a script or the style elements.

XML Source

```
<source>
<h1> HTML output </h1>
<AAA/>
<HR/>
<script>if (a < b) foo(); if (cc < dd) foo() </script>
<hr/>
```

```
<hr/>
<Hr/>
<hR/>
</source>
```

Output

```
<h1> HTML output </h1>
<AAA></AAA>
<HR><script>if (a < b)foo();
if (cc < dd) foo()
</script><hr>
<hr>
<Hr>
<hR>
```

XSL Stylesheet

```
<xsl:stylesheet version = '1.0'
xmlns:xsl='http://www.w3.org/1999/XSL/Transform'>
<xsl:output method="html"/>
<xsl:template match="/">
<xsl:copy-of select="/source/*"/>
</xsl:template>
</xsl:stylesheet>
```

The encoding attribute specifies the preferred encoding to be used. An html output method must add the META element immediately after start tag of the HEAD element specifying the character encoding actually being used. XSL Stylesheet 1 outputs in the UTF-8. An xml source contains the characters which are not present in the specified character set and they are therefore escaped.

XML Source

```
<source>
<html>
<head>
<title>HTML</title>
</head>
<body>
<h1> HTML output </h1> ?í?ala ?nek ko?ka pa?ez be?ka me?ec vyr
```

```
</body>
</html>
</source>
```

Output

```
<html>
<head>
<meta http-equiv="Content-Type" content="text/html; charset=UTF-8">
<title>HTML</title>
</head>
<body>
<h1> HTML output </h1>
?í?ala ?nek
ko?ka pa?ez
be?ka m??ec vyr
</body>
</html>
```

XSL Stylesheet

```
<xsl:stylesheet version = '1.0'
xmlns:xsl='http://www.w3.org/1999/XSL/Transform'>
<xsl:output method="html" encoding="UTF-8"/>
<xsl:template match="/">
<xsl:copy-of select="/source/*"/>
</xsl:template>
</xsl:stylesheet>
```

TEXT OUTPUT METHOD

A text output method outputs the result tree by outputting a string value of every text node in a result tree in the document order without doing any escaping.

XML Source

```
<source>
<AAA id="12"/>
</source>
```

Output

```
<!ELEMENT AAA ANY><!ATTLIST AAAid ID #REQUIRED>Look at my source in your browser
```

XSL Stylesheet

```
<xsl:stylesheet version = '1.0'
xmlns:xsl='http://www.w3.org/1999/XSL/Transform'>
<xsl:output method="text"/>
<xsl:template match="AAA">
<xsl:text><!ELEMENT </xsl:text>
<xsl:value-of select="name()"/>
<xsl:text> ANY></xsl:text>
<xsl:text><!ATTLIST </xsl:text>
<xsl:value-of select="name()"/>
<xsl:text/>
<xsl:value-of select="name(@*)"/>
<xsl:text> ID #REQUIRED></xsl:text>
<xsl:text>Look at my source in your browser</xsl:text>
</xsl:template>
</xsl:stylesheet>
```

COPY AND COPY-OF CONSTRUCTS IN XSL

The copy and copy-of constructs are used for copying the nodes. Copy the element copies only a current node without the children and the attributes, while the copy-of copies everything, including the children and the attributes.

XML Source

```
<source>
<p id="a12"> Compare
<B>these constructs</B>.
</p>
</source>
```

Output

```
<DIV>
<B>copy-of : </B>
```

```
<p id="a12">
Compare <B>these constructs</B>.
</p>
</DIV>
<DIV>
<B>copy : </B>
<p/>
</DIV>
<DIV>
<B>value-of : </B>
Compare these constructs.
</DIV>
```

XSL Stylesheet

```
<xsl:stylesheet version = '1.0'
xmlns:xsl='http://www.w3.org/1999/XSL/Transform'>
<xsl:template match="p">
<DIV>
<B>
<xsl:text>copy-of : </xsl:text>
</B>
<xsl:copy-of select="."/>
</DIV>
<DIV>
<B>
<xsl:text>copy : </xsl:text>
</B>
<xsl:copy/>
</DIV>
<DIV>
<B>
<xsl:text>value-of : </xsl:text>
</B>
<xsl:value-of select="."/>
</DIV>
</xsl:template>
</xsl:stylesheet>
```

USE-ATTRIBUTE-SETS ATTRIBUTE

An xsl:copy element may have the use-attribute-sets attribute. In this way, the attributes for the copied element can be specified. XSL Stylesheet 2 does not work as been expected because the expressions in the attributes that do refer to the named XSL objects are not evaluated.

XML Source

```
<source>
<h1>GREETING</h1>
<p>Hello, world!</p>
</source>
```

Output

```
<h1 align="center" style="color:red">GREETING</h1>
<p align="left" style="color:blue">Hello, world!</p>
```

XSL Stylesheet

```
<xsl:stylesheet version = '1.0'
xmlns:xsl='http://www.w3.org/1999/XSL/Transform'>
<xsl:template match="/">
<xsl:apply-templates select="/source/*"/>
</xsl:template>
<xsl:template match="h1">
<xsl:copy use-attribute-sets="H1">
<xsl:value-of select="."/>
</xsl:copy>
</xsl:template>
<xsl:template match="p">
<xsl:copy use-attribute-sets="P ">
<xsl:value-of select="."/>
</xsl:copy>
</xsl:template>
<xsl:attribute-set name="H1">
<xsl:attribute name="align">center</xsl:attribute>
<xsl:attribute name="style">color:red</xsl:attribute>
</xsl:attribute-set>
```

```
<xsl:attribute-set name="P">
<xsl:attribute name="align">left</xsl:attribute>
<xsl:attribute name="style">color:blue</xsl:attribute>
</xsl:attribute-set>
</xsl:stylesheet>
```

MISCELLANEOUS ADDITIONAL FUNCTIONS

The Current Function

A current function returns the node-set that has the current node as the only member. For the outermost expression that is not occurring within another expression, current node is always same as a context node. However, within the square brackets, the current node is usually different from the context node.

XML Source

```
<?xml version="1.0"?>
<xslTutorial >
<AAA name="first">
<BBB name="first">11111</BBB>
<BBB name="second">22222</BBB>
</AAA>
<AAA name="second">
<BBB name="first">33333</BBB>
; <BBB name="second">44444</BBB>
</AAA>
</xslTutorial>
```

HTML Output 1

```
<TABLE border="1">
<TR>
<TH> . </TH>
<TH>current()</TH></TR>
<TR>
<TD>first</TD>
<TD>first</TD></TR>
```

```
<TR>
<TD>11111</TD>
<TD>1111122222</TD></TR>
<TR>
<TD>second</TD>
<TD>second</TD></TR>
<TR>
<TD>33333</TD>
<TD/></TR></TABLE>
```

XSL Stylesheet 1

```
<xsl:stylesheet xmlns:xsl='http://www.w3.org/1999/XSL/Transform'>
<xsl:template match="/">
<TABLE border="1">
<TR><TH> . </TH><TH>current()</TH></TR>
<xsl:apply-templates select="//AAA"/>
</TABLE>
</xsl:template>
<xsl:template match="AAA">
<TR>
<TD>
<xsl:value-of select="./@name"/>
</TD><TD>
<xsl:value-of select="current()/@name"/>
</TD></TR>
<TR><TD>
<xsl:apply-templates select="BBB[./@name='first']"/>
</TD><TD>
<xsl:apply-templates select="BBB[current()/@name='first']"/>
</TD></TR>
</xsl:template>
</xsl:stylesheet>
```

Generate Id

The function generate-id generates the id conforming to the XML spec. Stylesheet 2 does uses the generate-id function to add the id to all the elements in the source XML.

XML Source

```
<?xml version="1.0"?>
<xslTutorial >
<AAA name='top'>
<BBB pos='1' val='bbb'>11111</BBB>
<BBB>22222</BBB>
</AAA>
<AAA name='bottom'>
<BBB>33333</BBB>
<BBB>44444</BBB>
</AAA>
</xslTutorial>
```

HTML Output 1

```
<DIV>
<B>generate-id(//AAA) : </B>N3</DIV>
<DIV>
<B>generate-id(//BBB) : </B>N6</DIV>
<DIV>
<B>generate-id(//AAA[1]) : </B>N3</DIV>
<DIV>
<B>generate-id(//*[1]) : </B>N1</DIV>
<DIV>
<B>generate-id(//xslTutorial/*[1]) : </B>N3</DIV>
```

XSL Stylesheet 1

```
<xsl:stylesheet xmlns:xsl='http://www.w3.org/1999/XSL/Transform' >
<xsl:template match="/">
<DIV><B><xsl:text> generate-id(//AAA) : </xsl:text> </B>
<xsl:value-of select="generate-id(//AAA) "/></DIV>
<DIV><B><xsl:text> generate-id(//BBB) : </xsl:text> </B>
<xsl:value-of select="generate-id(//BBB) "/></DIV>
<DIV><B><xsl:text> generate-id(//AAA[1]) : </xsl:text> </B>
<xsl:value-of select="generate-id(//AAA[1]) "/></DIV>
<DIV><B><xsl:text> generate-id(//*[1]) : </xsl:text> </B>
<xsl:value-of select="generate-id(//*[1]) "/></DIV>
<DIV><B><xsl:text> generate-id(//xslTutorial/*[1]) : </xsl:text> </B>
```

```
<xsl:value-of select="generate-id(//xslTutorial/*[1]) "/></DIV>
</xsl:template>
</xsl:stylesheet>
```

XML Source

```
<?xml version="1.0"?>
<xslTutorial >
<AAA name='top'>
<BBB pos='1' val='bbb'>11111</BBB>
<BBB>22222</BBB>
</AAA>
<AAA name='bottom'>
<BBB>33333</BBB>
<BBB>44444</BBB>
</AAA>
</xslTutorial>
```

HTML Output 2

```
<xslTutorial id="N1">
<AAA id="N3" name="top">
<BBB id="N6" pos="1" val="bbb">11111</BBB>
<BBB id="N11">22222</BBB> </AAA>
<AAA id="N15" name="bottom">
<BBB id="N18">33333</BBB>
<BBB id="N21">44444</BBB> </AAA> </xslTutorial>
```

XSL Stylesheet 2

```
<xsl:stylesheet xmlns:xsl='http://www.w3.org/1999/XSL/Transform'>
<xsl:template match="*">
<xsl:copy select=".">
<xsl:attribute name="id">
<xsl:value-of select="generate-id()"/>
</xsl:attribute>
<xsl:for-each select="@*">
<xsl:attribute name="{name()}">
<xsl:value-of select="."/>
</xsl:attribute>
```

```
</xsl:for-each>
<xsl:apply-templates/ >
</xsl:copy>
</xsl:template>
</xsl:stylesheet>
```

COMBINING XSL

Many other stylesheets can be imported using xsl:import or xsl:include.

Importing the stylesheet is the same as including, except that the definitions and the template rules for importing the stylesheet takes precedence over the template rules and the definitions in an imported stylesheet. Stylesheet 1 was imported into Stylesheet 2.

XML Source

```
<?xml version="1.0"?>
<xslTutorial >
<H1>IMPORTING STYLESHEETS</H1>
</xslTutorial>
```

HTML Output 1

IMPORTING STYLESHEETS

XSL Stylesheet 1

```
<xsl:stylesheet xmlns:xsl='http://www.w3.org/1999/XSL/Transform'>
<xsl:variable name="id2">Stylesheet 1(id2.xsl)</xsl:variable>
<xsl:variable name="t">Variable t from id2.xsl</xsl:variable>
</xsl:stylesheet>
```

The xsl:import element children should precede all the other element children of the xsl:stylesheet element, including any of the xsl:include element children. When the xsl:include is used to include the stylesheet, any of the xsl:import elements in an included document are moved up in an including document to after any of the existing xsl:import elements in an including document.

HTML Output 3

```
<P>Stylesheet 1(id2.xsl)
```

XSL Stylesheet 2

```
<xsl:stylesheet xmlns:xsl='http://www.w3.org/1999/XSL/Transform'>
<xsl:include href="id2.xsl"/>
<xsl:template match="/">
<P><xsl:value-of select="$id2"/></P>
<P><xsl:value-of select="$id3"/></P>
</xsl:template>
</xsl:stylesheet>
```

The Results of Stylesheet Combining

The results of combining stylesheets depends on the position of a xsl:include or the xsl:import function.

XML Source

```
<?xml version="1.0"?>
<xslTutorial >
<AAA/>
<BBB/>
<CCC/>
</xslTutorial>
```

HTML Output 4

```
<DIV style="color:red">AAA (according to Stylesheet 1 (id2.xsl)</DIV>
<DIV style="color:red">BBB (according to Stylesheet 1 (id2.xsl)</DIV>
<DIV style="color:red">CCC (according to Stylesheet 1 (id2.xsl)</DIV>
```

XSL Stylesheet 4

```
<xsl:stylesheet xmlns:xsl='http://www.w3.org/1999/XSL/Transform'>
<xsl:template match="/">
<xsl:apply-templates/ >
</xsl:template>
<xsl:template match="/*/*">
<DIV style="color:blue">
```

```
<xsl:value-of select="name()"/>
<xsl:text> (according to this stylesheet)</xsl:text>
</DIV>
</xsl:template>
<xsl:include href="id2.xsl"/>
</xsl:stylesheet>
```

APPLY-IMPORT FUNCTION

You can use the xsl:apply-imports element to get the information from the imported template for the elements whose behavior is changing. Stylesheet 2 imports Stylesheet 1 and overrides the template.

XML Source

```
<?xml version="1.0"?>
<xslTutorial >
<AAA/>
<BBB/>
<CCC/>
</xslTutorial>
```

HTML Output 1

```
<DIV style="color:red">AAA</DIV>
<DIV style="color:red">BBB</DIV>
<DIV style="color:red">CCC</DIV>
```

XSL Stylesheet 1

```
<xsl:stylesheet xmlns:xsl='http://www.w3.org/1999/XSL/Transform'>
<xsl:template match="/*/*">
<DIV style="color:red">
<xsl:value-of select="name()"/>
</DIV>
</xsl:template>
</xsl:stylesheet>
```

Overrides

Stylesheet 2 imports Stylesheet 1 and overrides the template.

XML Source

```
<?xml version="1.0"?>
<xslTutorial >
<AAA/>
<BBB/>
<CCC/>
</xslTutorial>
```

HTML Output 2

```
<EM>AAA</EM>
<EM>BBB</EM>
<EM>CCC</EM>
```

XSL Stylesheet 2

```
<xsl:stylesheet xmlns:xsl='http://www.w3.org/1999/XSL/Transform'>
<xsl:import href="id2.xsl"/>
<xsl:template match="/*/*">
<EM>
<xsl:value-of select="name()"/>
</EM>
</xsl:template>
</xsl:stylesheet>
```

Import Precedence

The import precedence is more important than the priority precedence.

XML Source

```
<?xml version="1.0"?>
<xslTutorial >
<AAA id='a1' pos='start'>
<BBB id='b1'/>
<BBB id='b2'/>
</AAA>
```

```
<AAA id='a2'>
<BBB id='b3'/>
<BBB id='b4'/>
<CCC id='c1'>
<CCC id='c2'/>
</CCC>
<BBB id='b5'>
<CCC id='c3'/>
</BBB>
</AAA>
</xslTutorial>
```

HTML Output 1

```
<H3 style="color:blue">CCC (id=c1)</H3>
<H3 style="color:blue">CCC (id=c2)</H3>
<H3 style="color:blue">CCC (id=c3)</H3>
```

HTML Output 2

XSL Stylesheet 1

```
<xsl:stylesheet xmlns:xsl='http://www.w3.org/1999/XSL/Transform'>
<xsl:template match="/">
<xsl:apply-templates select="//CCC"/>
</xsl:template>
<xsl:template match="CCC" priority="10">
<H3 style="color:blue">
<xsl:value-of select="name()"/>
<xsl:text> (id=</xsl:text>
<xsl:value-of select="@id"/>
<xsl:text> )</xsl:text>
</H3>
</xsl:template>
</xsl:stylesheet>
```

XSL Stylesheet 2

```
<xsl:stylesheet xmlns:xsl='http://www.w3.org/1999/XSL/Transform'>
<xsl:import href="id2.xsl"/>
<xsl:template match="/">
```

```
<xsl:apply-templates select="//CCC"/>
</xsl:template>
<xsl:template match="CCC" priority="-100">
<H3 style="color:red">
<xsl:value-of select="name()"/>
<xsl:text> (id=</xsl:text>
<xsl:value-of select="@id"/>
<xsl:text> )</xsl:text>
</H3>
</xsl:template>
</xsl:stylesheet>
```

QUESTIONS FOR DISCUSSION

1. Describe the role that XSL can play when dynamically generating HTML pages from a relational database.
2. What tool is the most in-demand for XSL?
3. How you can enhance your XSL tests?
4. What is an XSL checkpoint?
5. What is XSL?
6. How is XSL different from Cascading Style Sheets? Why is a new Stylesheet language needed?
7. What is the role of an XSL transformer?
8. What is an XSL template?

CHAPTER 9

XSLT BASICS

XSLT (EXTENSIBLE STYLESHEET LANGUAGE)

The eXtensible Stylesheet Language is divided into two sub-languages, eXtensible Stylesheet Language Transformations (XSLT) and eXtensible Stylesheet Language-Formatting Objects (XSL-FO). In this chapter, we look at the basics of XSLT, which is used to transform XML documents.

XSLT documents are well-formed XML documents that describe how another XML document should be transformed. For XSLT to work, it needs an XML document to transform and an engine to make the transformation take place. In addition, parameters can be passed in to XSLTs, providing further instructions on how to do the transformation. Figure 9.1 shows how this all works.

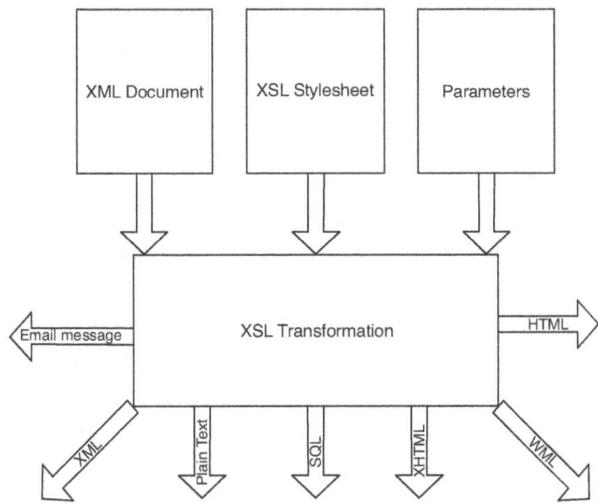

FIGURE 9.1 XSL Transformation representation

XSLT SAMPLE PROGRAM

XSL Transformations is a language for describing how to transform an XML document (explicitly or implicitly represented as a tree) into another. XSLT is a tree-to-tree transformation from a source tree to a result tree. It allows for defining templates (rules) that are applied on elements from the source document and inserting elements in the result tree. The resulting document can be another well-formed XML document (XML or WML), an HTML document, a text document, or any other format provided that the proper output method is available. XSLT uses XPath expressions to query elements from the source tree or to evaluate document fragments to be inserted into the result tree.

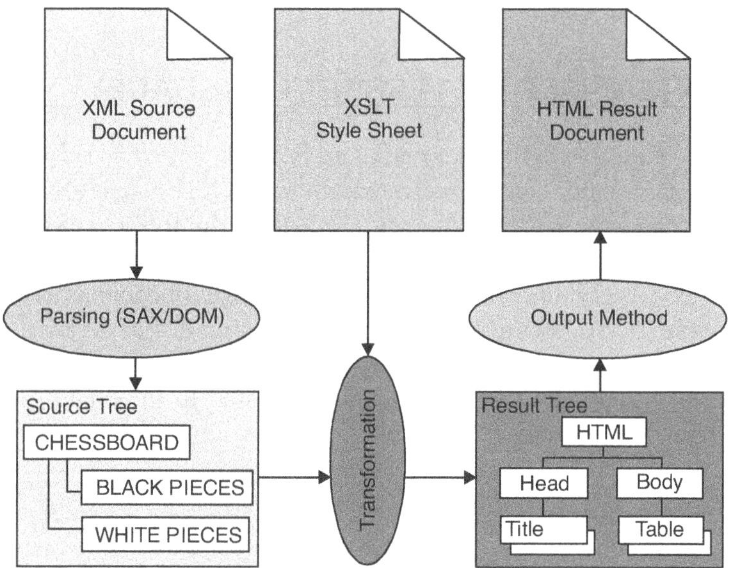

FIGURE 9.2 XSL Transformations transform an XML source document into another document that can be of any format (XML, HTML, text, and so on) by applying a style sheet.

An XSLT processor reads both a source XML document and an XSL style sheet. The XSL style sheet is itself a well-formed XML document. Depending on the implementation, an XSLT engine may be able to read an input source as SAX events or DOM trees and also generates SAX events or DOM trees.

This program uses an XSLT engine and a style sheet to transform an XML document describing a set of chessboard configurations into its corresponding text format. A TransformerFactory is used to create a new Transformer from the style sheet and the Transformer is then used to process the source document generated.

THE TRANSFORMATION PROCESS

An XSLT looks at an XML document as a collection of nodes of the following types:

- Root node
- Element nodes
- Attribute nodes
- Text nodes
- Processing instruction nodes
- Comment nodes

An XSLT document contains one or more templates, which are created with the <xsl:template /> tag. When an XML document is transformed with an XSLT, the XSLT processor reads through the XML document starting at the root, which is one level above the document element, and progresses from top to bottom, just as a person would read the document. Each time the processor encounters a node, it looks for a matching template in the XSLT.

If it finds a matching template, it applies it; otherwise, it uses a default template as defined by the XSLT specification. The default templates are shown in Table 9.1.

Table 9.1 Default Templates

Node Type	Default Template
Root	Apply templates for child nodes.
Element	Apply templates for child nodes.
Attribute	Output attribute value.
Text	Output text value.
Processing Instruction	Do nothing.
Comment	Do nothing.

In this context, attributes are not considered children of the elements that contain them, so attributes get ignored by the XSLT processor unless they are explicitly referenced by the XSLT document.

PROCESSING A TRANSFORMATION

A transformation can take place in one of three locations:

- On the server
- On the client (for example, your Web browser)
- With a standalone program

The examples in this chapter use the client for transforming the XML documents.

You might have noticed that the "After" shot contains more than the raw XML file. It contains a heading ("Good Books") and some text ("Yes, go through these books!"). This is one of the benefits of XSLT.

APPLYING XSLT TO AN XML DOCUMENT

Instead of linking to a CSS file, we link to an XSL file.

Step 1 (XML file): Create an XML file with the following content and save it.

```
<?xml version="1.0" encoding="UTF-8" standalone="yes"?>
<?xml-stylesheet type="text/xsl" href="Books.xsl"?>
<Books>
<Book>
<authorname>Shashi Banzal</authorname>
<booktitle >XML Book</booktitle>
</Book>
<Book>
<authorname>S Sharma</authorname>
<booktitle >HTML Book</booktitle>
</Book>
</Books>
```

Step 2 (XSL file): Create a file with the following content and save it as Books.xsl into the same directory as the XML file.

```
<?xml version="1.0"?>
<xsl:stylesheet version="1.0" xmlns:xsl="http://www.w3.org/1999/XSL/Transform">
<xsl:template match="/">
<html>
<head>
<title>XML XSL Example</title>
<style type="text/css">
```

```
body
{
margin:10px;
background-color:#ccff00;
font-family:verdana,helvetica,sans-serif;
}
.Book-authorname
{
display:block;
font-weight:bold;
}
.Book-booktitle
{
display:block;
color:#636363;
font-size:small;
font-style:italic;
}
</style>
</head>
<body>
<h2>Good Books</h2>
<p> Yes, go through these books!</p>
 <xsl:apply-templates/>
</body>
</html>
</xsl:template>
<xsl:template match="Book">
 <span class="Book-authorname"><xsl:value-of select="authorname"/></span>
 <span class="Book-booktitle "><xsl:value-of select="booktitle "/></span>
</xsl:template>
</xsl:stylesheet>
```

This XSL file contains XSL markup, HTML markup, and CSS.

XSLT SYNTAX

All XSLT documents need to be well-formed and valid XML documents, so you need to follow the same syntax rules that apply to any other XML document. As well as ensuring that your XSLT documents are valid XML, you need to ensure they are valid XSLT documents.

XML VERSION

XSL documents are also XML documents and so we should include the XML version in the document's prolog. We should also set the standalone attribute to "no" as we now rely on an external resource (i.e., the external XSL file).

```
<?xml version="1.0" standalone="no"?>
```

XSL ROOT ELEMENT

Then we open the root element—xsl:stylesheet. The root element needs to include the XSL version as well as the XSL namespace (hence the xsl prefix and the xmlns... part).

```
<xsl:stylesheet version="1.0" xmlns:xsl="http://www.w3.org/1999/XSL/Transform">
```

XSL Namespace Prefix

All XSL elements in your XSLT document must include the XSL prefix.

Syntax

```
<xsl:element_authorname>
```

Example

```
<xsl:template match="/">
....
</xsl:template>
```

XSLT <template> Element

XSLT is all about being able to select one or more nodes from your XML document and transforming or replacing that content with something else. A node could be any of the following: elements, attributes, text, namespaces, processing-instructions, and comments.

The <xsl:template> element is what you use to select a node from your XML document and transform its contents.

To select an element, you use the match attribute. To transform its contents, you simply place the new content between the opening (<xsl:template>) and closing (</xsl:template>) tags.

Example

In this case, we select the root node (i.e., Books). By selecting this node, the template element tells the XSLT processor how to transform the output. We tell the processor to replace the root node (i.e., the whole XML document) with what is written between the <xsl:template> tags.

In this case, the contents of an HTML document are written inside the <xsl:template> tags. When a user views any XML document that uses this XSL document, they will simply see the line "New content..." and the browser's title bar will read "My XSLT Example."

```
<xsl:template match="Books">
  <html>
    <head>
      <title>My XSLT Example</title>
    </head>
    <body>
      <p>New content...</p>
    </body>
  </html>
</xsl:template>
```

SELECTING THE ROOT NODE

In the example above, we selected the "Books" node which happens to be the root node of our XML document. Another way of selecting the root node is to use a forward slash in place of the node's authorname. The following example results in the same output as the above example.

Example

```
<xsl:template match="/">
  <html>
    <head>
      <title>My XSLT Example</title>
    </head>
    <body>
      <p>New content...</p>
    </body>
  </html>
</xsl:template>
```

XSLT <apply-templates> Element

We've already learned that the <xsl:template> element allows us to select any node in our XML document and transform its contents. You'll probably be happy to learn that we can also use this element to work with the children of that node.

The XSLT <xsl:apply-templates/> element allows us to determine where the content of its children appear on our transformed document.

USAGE EXAMPLE

Here, we are using two <xsl:template> elements; one for the root node and one for its children. We have placed the <xsl:apply-templates/> element within the <xsl:template> element for the root node. Doing this applies the results of our other <xsl:template> element.

```
<xsl:template match="/">
 (other content/HTML markup goes here)
 <xsl:apply-templates/>
</xsl:template>
<xsl:template match="child">
 (other content/XSLT/HTML markup goes here)
</xsl:template>
```

So, by doing this, we can use other XSLT elements to retrieve data from the child elements, and pass it to the main template for display. In particular, the XSLT <xsl:value-of/> element is useful for retrieving data from an XML element. We'll look at that element next.

XSLT <value-of> ELEMENT

The <xsl:value-of> element allows you to retrieve the value from a node.

When using the <xsl:value-of> element, you use the select attribute to specify which node you want to retrieve data from.

USAGE EXAMPLE

This example is a continuation of the example from the previous lesson. Here, we have added the <xsl:value-of/> element to extract data from the child nodes called "authorname" and "booktitle."

```
<xsl:template match="/">
(other content/HTML markup goes here)
 <xsl:apply-templates/>
</xsl:template>
<xsl:template match="Book">
 <xsl:value-of select="authorname"/>
 <xsl:value-of select="booktitle "/>
</xsl:template>
```

So, let's have another look at our XML document, and see which values will be selected:

```
<?xml version="1.0" standalone="no"?>
<?xml-stylesheet type="text/xsl" href="Books.xsl"?>
<Books>
<Book>
<authorname>Shashi Banzal</authorname>
<booktitle >XML Book</booktitle>
</Book>
<Book>
<authorname>S Sharma</authorname>
<booktitle>HTML Book</booktitle >
</Book>
</Books>
```

And just to refresh your memory, these values will be displayed where we choose to place the XSLT <xsl:apply-templates> element.

XSLT <for-each> ELEMENT

The XSLT <xsl:for-each> element allows you to loop through multiple nodes that match the selection criteria. This, in turn, enables you to retrieve data from these nodes.

For example, imagine if our XML file had two elements called "authorname," each under the "Book" element.

```
<?xml version="1.0" standalone="no"?>
<?xml-stylesheet type="text/xsl" href="Books.xsl"?>
<Books>
<Book>
<authorname>Shashi Banzal</authorname>
<authorname>R. Gupta</authorname>
```

```
<booktitle>XML Book</booktitle >
</Book>
<Book>
<authorname>S Sharma</authorname>
<authorname>Ram Joshi</authorname>
<booktitle >HTML Book</booktitle >
</Book>
</Books>
```

To extract data from both “authorname” elements, we can use <xsl:for-each> in conjunction with <xsl:value-of>.

<xsl:for-each> EXAMPLE

Here, we use <xsl:for-each> to loop through each “authorname” element and <xsl:value-of> to extract data from each node.

Note the value of the select attribute (“.”). This expression specifies the current node. The <xsl:element authorname=“br”/> element/attribute is there simply for readibility purposes. It provides a line break after each iteration.

```
<?xml version="1.0"?>
<xsl:stylesheet version="1.0" xmlns:xsl="http://www.w3.org/1999/XSL/Transform">
<xsl:template match="/">
 <xsl:apply-templates/>
 </xsl:template>
 <xsl:template match="Book">
 <xsl:for-each select="authorname">
 <xsl:value-of select="."/><xsl:element authorname="br"/>
 </xsl:for-each>
 </xsl:template>
</xsl:stylesheet>
```

XSLT <sort> Element

The XSLT <xsl:sort> element allows you to sort the output of the <xsl:for-each> element.

<xsl:sort> Example

Here, we use <xsl:for-each> to loop through each “Book” element and <xsl:sort> to sort by the “authorname” node. We then use the <xsl:value-of> to extract data from the “authorname” node.

```
<?xml version="1.0" standalone="no"?>
<xsl:stylesheet version="1.0" xmlns:xsl="http://www.w3.org/1999/
XSL/Transform">
<xsl:template match="/">
<xsl:apply-templates/>
</xsl:template>
<xsl:template match="Books">
<xsl:for-each select="Book">
<xsl:sort select="authorname"/>
<xsl:value-of select="authorname"/><xsl:element
authorname="br"/>
</xsl:for-each>
</xsl:template>
</xsl:stylesheet>
```

RESULT

So, let's see what would happen if we applied the above XSLT document to the following XML document:

```
<Books>
 <Book>
 <authorname>Shashi Banzal</authorname>
 <booktitle>XML Book</booktitle>
 </Book>
 <Book>
 <authorname>S Sharma</authorname>
 <booktitle>HTML Book</booktitle>
 </Book>
</Books>
```

BEFORE

This is how the contents would be displayed before applying the <xsl:sort> element:

XML Book

HTML Book

AFTER

This is how the contents would be displayed after applying the <xsl:sort> element:

HTML Book

XML Book

XSLT <if> ELEMENT

The XSLT <xsl:if> element allows you to perform conditional statements against the contents of your XML document. For example, you can present different content only if a given condition is met.

This element can be used in conjunction with the <xsl:for-each> element to present different content depending on the contents of the XML file.

<xsl:if> Example

THE SOURCE FILE

Imagine you have an XML file containing a list of food and its nutritional value.

```
<?xml version="1.0"?>
<food_list>
 <food_item type="vegetable">
 <name>Tomato</name>
 <carbs_per_serving>81</carbs_per_serving>
 <fiber_per_serving>8</fiber_per_serving>
 <fat_per_serving>0.5</fat_per_serving>
 <kj_per_serving>1280</kj_per_serving>
 </food_item>
 <food_item type="vegetable">
 <name>Spinach</name>
 <carbs_per_serving>1</carbs_per_serving>
 <fiber_per_serving>1</fiber_per_serving>
 <fat_per_serving>0</fat_per_serving>
 <kj_per_serving>40</kj_per_serving>
 </food_item>
 <food_item type="vegetable">
 <name>French beans</name>
```

```
<carbs_per_serving>0</carbs_per_serving>
<fiber_per_serving>1</fiber_per_serving>
<fat_per_serving>0</fat_per_serving>
<kj_per_serving>14</kj_per_serving>
</food_item>
<food_item type="vegetable">
<name>Lady finger</name>
<carbs_per_serving>21.5</carbs_per_serving>
<fiber_per_serving>2</fiber_per_serving>
<fat_per_serving>1</fat_per_serving>
<kj_per_serving>460</kj_per_serving>
</food_item>
<food_item type="vegetable">
<name>Broccoli</name>
<carbs_per_serving>6</carbs_per_serving>
<fiber_per_serving>1</fiber_per_serving>
<fat_per_serving>0.5</fat_per_serving>
<kj_per_serving>150</kj_per_serving>
</food_item>
<food_item type="vegetable">
<name>Carrots</name>
<carbs_per_serving>30.5</carbs_per_serving>
<fiber_per_serving>2</fiber_per_serving>
<fat_per_serving>0.5</fat_per_serving>
<kj_per_serving>550</kj_per_serving>
</food_item>
<food_item type="vegetable">
<name>Sweet Potatoes</name>
<carbs_per_serving>1.5</carbs_per_serving>
<fiber_per_serving>1.5</fiber_per_serving>
<fat_per_serving>0.5</fat_per_serving>
<kj_per_serving>55</kj_per_serving>
</food_item>
<food_item type="seafood">
<name>Crab</name>
<carbs_per_serving>0</carbs_per_serving>
<fiber_per_serving>0</fiber_per_serving>
<fat_per_serving>1</fat_per_serving>
<kj_per_serving>400</kj_per_serving>
</food_item>
```

```
    <food_item type="seafood">
    <name>Crawfish</name>
    <carbs_per_serving>0</carbs_per_serving>
    <fiber_per_serving>0</fiber_per_serving>
    <fat_per_serving>2</fat_per_serving>
    <kj_per_serving>390</kj_per_serving>
    </food_item>
    <food_item type="fruit">
    <name>Orange</name>
    <carbs_per_serving>15</carbs_per_serving>
    <fiber_per_serving>2.5</fiber_per_serving>
    <fat_per_serving>0</fat_per_serving>
    <kj_per_serving>250</kj_per_serving>
    </food_item>
    <food_item type="fruit">
    <name>Banana</name>
    <carbs_per_serving>7.5</carbs_per_serving>
    <fiber_per_serving>2.5</fiber_per_serving>
    <fat_per_serving>0</fat_per_serving>
    <kj_per_serving>150</kj_per_serving>
    </food_item>
    <food_item type="grain">
    <name>Rice</name>
    <carbs_per_serving>62</carbs_per_serving>
    <fiber_per_serving>14</fiber_per_serving>
    <fat_per_serving>7</fat_per_serving>
    <kj_per_serving>1400</kj_per_serving>
    </food_item>
    <food_item type="grain">
    <name>Corn</name>
    <carbs_per_serving>1.5</carbs_per_serving>
    <fiber_per_serving>1</fiber_per_serving>
    <fat_per_serving>0.5</fat_per_serving>
    <kj_per_serving>70</kj_per_serving>
    </food_item>
  </food_list>
```

Now, imagine we're only interested in the vegetables—we only want to display the food that have a type attribute of "vegetable." We can display it nicely formatted in an HTML table.

THE SOLUTION

To achieve the above outcome, we use `<xsl:for-each>` to loop through each "food_item" element and `<xsl:if>` to check the value of the "type" attribute (we do this by using the `@` symbol—that's how you specify an attribute). If the attribute value equals "vegetable," we output the details.

```
<?xml version="1.0"?>
<xsl:stylesheet version="1.0" xmlns:xsl="http://www.w3.org/1999/XSL/Transform">
<xsl:template match="/">
<xsl:apply-templates/>
</xsl:template>
<xsl:template match="food_list">
 <table>
 <tr style="background-color:#ccff00">
 <th>Food Item</th>
 <th>Carbs (g)</th>
 <th>Fiber (g)</th>
 <th>Fat (g)</th>
 <th>Energy (kj)</th>
 </tr>
 <xsl:for-each select="food_item">
 <xsl:if test="@type = 'vegetable'">
 <tr style="background-color:#00cc00">
 <td><xsl:value-of select="name"/></td>
 <td><xsl:value-of select="carbs_per_serving"/></td>
 <td><xsl:value-of select="fiber_per_serving"/></td>
 <td><xsl:value-of select="fat_per_serving"/></td>
 <td><xsl:value-of select="kj_per_serving"/></td>
 </tr>
 </xsl:if>
 </xsl:for-each>
 </table>
</xsl:template>
</xsl:stylesheet>
```

XSLT <choose> Element

The XSLT `<xsl:choose>` element allows you to compare a value against a range of possible values in your XML document.

This element is used in conjunction with the <xsl:when> and (optionally) <xsl:otherwise> elements to present different content depending on the outcome of each test.

<xsl:choose> Example

THE SOURCE FILE

Imagine we have an XML file containing different food items and their nutritional value—like this:

```
<?xml version="1.0"?>
<food_list>
 <food_item type="vegetable">
 <name>Tomato</name>
 <carbs_per_serving>81</carbs_per_serving>
 <fiber_per_serving>8</fiber_per_serving>
 <fat_per_serving>0.5</fat_per_serving>
 <kj_per_serving>1280</kj_per_serving>
 </food_item>
 <food_item type="vegetable">
 <name>Spinach</name>
 <carbs_per_serving>1</carbs_per_serving>
 <fiber_per_serving>1</fiber_per_serving>
 <fat_per_serving>0</fat_per_serving>
 <kj_per_serving>40</kj_per_serving>
 </food_item>
 <food_item type="vegetable">
 <name>French beans</name>
 <carbs_per_serving>0</carbs_per_serving>
 <fiber_per_serving>1</fiber_per_serving>
 <fat_per_serving>0</fat_per_serving>
 <kj_per_serving>14</kj_per_serving>
 </food_item>
 <food_item type="vegetable">
 <name>Lady finger</name>
 <carbs_per_serving>21.5</carbs_per_serving>
 <fiber_per_serving>2</fiber_per_serving>
 <fat_per_serving>1</fat_per_serving>
 <kj_per_serving>460</kj_per_serving>
 </food_item>
```

```
<food_item type="vegetable">
<name>Broccoli</name>
<carbs_per_serving>6</carbs_per_serving>
<fiber_per_serving>1</fiber_per_serving>
<fat_per_serving>0.5</fat_per_serving>
<kj_per_serving>150</kj_per_serving>
</food_item>
<food_item type="vegetable">
<name>Carrots</name>
<carbs_per_serving>30.5</carbs_per_serving>
<fiber_per_serving>2</fiber_per_serving>
<fat_per_serving>0.5</fat_per_serving>
<kj_per_serving>550</kj_per_serving>
</food_item>
<food_item type="vegetable">
<name>Sweet Potatoes</name>
<carbs_per_serving>1.5</carbs_per_serving>
<fiber_per_serving>1.5</fiber_per_serving>
<fat_per_serving>0.5</fat_per_serving>
<kj_per_serving>55</kj_per_serving>
</food_item>
<food_item type="seafood">
<name>Crab</name>
<carbs_per_serving>0</carbs_per_serving>
<fiber_per_serving>0</fiber_per_serving>
<fat_per_serving>1</fat_per_serving>
<kj_per_serving>400</kj_per_serving>
</food_item>
<food_item type="seafood">
<name>Crawfish</name>
<carbs_per_serving>0</carbs_per_serving>
<fiber_per_serving>0</fiber_per_serving>
<fat_per_serving>2</fat_per_serving>
<kj_per_serving>390</kj_per_serving>
</food_item>
<food_item type="fruit">
<name>Orange</name>
<carbs_per_serving>15</carbs_per_serving>
<fiber_per_serving>2.5</fiber_per_serving>
<fat_per_serving>0</fat_per_serving>
```

```
<kj_per_serving>250</kj_per_serving>
</food_item>
<food_item type="fruit">
<name>Banana</name>
<carbs_per_serving>7.5</carbs_per_serving>
<fiber_per_serving>2.5</fiber_per_serving>
<fat_per_serving>0</fat_per_serving>
<kj_per_serving>150</kj_per_serving>
</food_item>
<food_item type="grain">
<name>Rice</name>
<carbs_per_serving>62</carbs_per_serving>
<fiber_per_serving>14</fiber_per_serving>
<fat_per_serving>7</fat_per_serving>
<kj_per_serving>1400</kj_per_serving>
</food_item>
<food_item type="grain">
<name>Corn</name>
<carbs_per_serving>1.5</carbs_per_serving>
<fiber_per_serving>1</fiber_per_serving>
<fat_per_serving>0.5</fat_per_serving>
<kj_per_serving>70</kj_per_serving>
</food_item>
</food_list>
```

Now, imagine if we want to present the contents of our XML file in a table and highlight the rows a different color depending on the type of food it is.

THE SOLUTION

We could do this using the following XSL file. In this file, we check the `type` attribute of the `<food_item>` element. We can find the value of the attribute by typing its name with a `@`. If the value is "grain," we specify one color. If it's "vegetable," we specify another. If it's neither of these, we specify a default color using the following code:

```
<xsl:otherwise>.
<?xml version="1.0"?>
<xsl:stylesheet version="1.0" xmlns:xsl="http://www.w3.org/1999/XSL/Transform">
```

```
<xsl:template match="/">
 <xsl:apply-templates/>
</xsl:template>
<xsl:template match="food_list">
<table>
<tr style="background-color:#ccff00">
<th>Food Item</th>
<th>Carbs (g)</th>
<th>Fiber (g)</th>
<th>Fat (g)</th>
<th>Energy (kj)</th>
</tr>
<xsl:for-each select="food_item">
 <xsl:choose>
   <xsl:when test="@type = 'grain'">
     <tr style="background-color:#cccc00">
       <td><xsl:value-of select="name"/></td>
       <td><xsl:value-of select="carbs_per_serving"/></td>
       <td><xsl:value-of select="fiber_per_serving"/></td>
       <td><xsl:value-of select="fat_per_serving"/></td>
       <td><xsl:value-of select="kj_per_serving"/></td>
     </tr>
 </xsl:when>
  <xsl:when test="@type = 'vegetable'">
    <tr style="background-color:#00cc00">
      <td><xsl:value-of select="name"/></td>
      <td><xsl:value-of select="carbs_per_serving"/></td>
      <td><xsl:value-of select="fiber_per_serving"/></td>
      <td><xsl:value-of select="fat_per_serving"/></td>
      <td><xsl:value-of select="kj_per_serving"/></td>
     </tr>
 </xsl:when>
 <xsl:otherwise>
   <tr style="background-color:#cccccc">
     <td><xsl:value-of select="name"/></td>
     <td><xsl:value-of select="carbs_per_serving"/></td>
     <td><xsl:value-of select="fiber_per_serving"/></td>
     <td><xsl:value-of select="fat_per_serving"/></td>
     <td><xsl:value-of select="kj_per_serving"/></td>
```

```
        </tr>
       </xsl:otherwise>
      </xsl:choose>
     </xsl:for-each>
    </table>
   </xsl:template>
  </xsl:stylesheet>
```

QUESTIONS FOR DISCUSSION

1. What is XSLT?
2. Who developed XSLT?
3. What do XSLT processing models involve?
4. Can you use the XSLT to convert HTML into VXML?
5. Do you feel that you are a good XSLT programmer?
6. Which was the first processor related to XSLT?
7. Do you feel that you have chosen the right technology (XSLT)?
8. How do you use filtering in XSLT?
9. How do you use <xsl:sort> element in XSLT?
10. How do you define templates in XSLT?
11. How do you transform an XML document into XHTML document?
12. How do you transform an XML document into another XML document?
13. Compare XSLT and XPath.
14. How do you use filtering function in XSLT?
15. Can we encode mathematics using XML?
16. Explain non-XML resources.
17. Using XSLT, how would you extract a specific attribute from an element in an XML document?
18. What is the structure of XSLT?

19. What is XSLT?
20. Can we use the same XSLT processor and still specify different processing options for different pipelines?
21. Can we use different XSLT processors when processing different pipelines?
22. How does Internet Explorer format XML files in a collapsible view, and how can we modify this behavior?
23. How can we call MSXML from the command line to do batch processing of XSLT?
24. Where does Microsoft provide documentation about compliance with MSXML?
25. Does IE5.5 include a newer XSLT processor?
26. By using XSLT, how do we map an XML file to another XML file? We have data in a particular format. How can we automatically generate the XSL mapping file so that it can become input to XSLT?
27. Is it possible to use XSLT to remove elements with duplicate values from an XML file?
28. What is XML-RPC?

CHAPTER 10

SOAP

SOAP

SOAP is a protocol for accessing a Web service. SOAP is a simple XML-based protocol that lets applications exchange information over HTTP.

SOAP acts as a medium to provide basic messaging framework. Abstract layers are built on these basic messaging frameworks. It transfers messages across the board in different protocols; it also acts as a medium to transmit XML-based messages over the network.

The Simple Object Access Protocol (SOAP) uses XML to define a protocol for the exchange of information in distributed computing environments. SOAP consists of three components: an envelope, a set of encoding rules, and a convention for representing remote procedure calls. Unless experience with SOAP is a direct requirement for the open position, knowing the specifics of the protocol, or how it can be used in conjunction with HTTP, it is not as important as identifying it as a natural application of XML.

Simple Object Access Protocol (SOAP) version 1.1 is an industry standard designed to improve cross-platform interoperability using the Web and XML. The Web has evolved from simply pushing out static pages to creating customized content that performs services for users. A user can be a customer retrieving specialized Web pages for placing orders or a business partner using a customized form for reviewing stock and sales figures. A wide range of components located on various computers are involved in performing these Web-based services. Because these systems consist of many computers, including the client computer, middle-tier servers, and usually a database server, these systems are called *distributed systems*. To understand how SOAP works, let's take a look at the distributed system first.

SOAP version 1.2 provides a simple and lightweight mechanism for exchanging structured and typed information between peers in a decentralized, distributed environment using XML. SOAP does not itself define any application semantics such as a programming model or implementation specific semantics; rather it defines a simple mechanism for expressing application semantics by providing a modular packaging model and encoding mechanisms for encoding application defined data. This allows SOAP to be used in a large variety of systems, ranging from messaging systems to remote procedure calls (RPC).

SOAP is a simple XML-based protocol to let applications exchange information over HTTP. Or more simply: SOAP is a protocol for accessing a Web Service.

- SOAP stands for Simple Object Access Protocol. It is a communication protocol.
- SOAP is platform and language independent. It is based on XML and is simple.

It is important for application development to allow Internet communication between programs.

Today's applications communicate using Remote Procedure Calls (RPC) between objects like DCOM and CORBA, but HTTP was not designed for this. RPC represents a compatibility and security problem; firewalls and proxy servers normally block this kind of traffic.

A better way to communicate between applications is over HTTP, because HTTP is supported by all Internet browsers and servers. SOAP was created to accomplish this.

SOAP provides a way to communicate between applications running on different operating systems, with different technologies and programming languages.

Role of XML in SOAP

XML was chosen as a standard format because it was already in use by many large companies due to its open source nature. A wide variety of tools are available which ease the process of transition to SOAP.

Advantages and Disadvantages of SOAP

There are some advantages and some disadvantages of SOAP.

Advantages

There are some advantages of SOAP, such as:

1. SOAP bypasses all firewalls.
2. It has a huge collection of protocols.
3. It is platform- and language-independent.
4. It is simple and extensible.

Disadvantages

There are some disadvantages of SOAP, such as

1. SOAP is slower than middleware technologies (CORBA or RMI or IIOP) due to the lengthy XML format that it has to follow and the parsing of the envelope that is required.
2. SOAP depends on WSDL and does not have any standardized mechanism for the dynamic discovery of the services.
3. The usage of HTTP for transporting messages, and not the defined ESB or WS-Addressing interaction of parties over a message, is fixed.
4. Information regarding the usability of HTTP for different purposes is not present, which makes the application protocol level problematic.

COMMUNICATION OVER DISTRIBUTED SYSTEMS

Distributed systems commonly use two models for communication: message passing (which can be combined with message queuing) and request/response messaging. A message passing system allows messages to be sent at any time. Once a message has been sent, the application that sent the message usually moves on. This type of system is called asynchronous. An asynchronous system typically uses messages, but it can also be based on other models. With the request/response model, the request and the response are paired together and can be thought of as a synchronous system. The request is sent by an application, and the application usually waits until a response is received before continuing. When one application calls an object on another computer by making a Remote Procedure Call (RPC), we can think of this call as synchronous request/response message passing.

The remote call procedure is a very important function in SOAP. In RCP, a user (node) sends a request to another node (server) where the information is processed and sent to the user. It immediately sends the message across the network.

RPC is useful in implementing the client-to-server interaction model. When the server is interacting and searching for information, the client side messaging is blocked and the server activity goes on. RPC has a huge pool of protocols which can be difficult to work with. Client server interaction is best achieved by RPC.

The request/response model is commonly used to allow components on different computers to communicate with each other using RPCs. Over the last several years, many attempts have been made to develop a standard that would allow this communication between components on different computers. Currently, the two most commonly used standards are Distributed Component Object Model (DCOM) and the Object Management Group's Internet Inter-Orb Protocol (IIOP). Both of these standards work well; their greatest shortcoming is that they do not natively interoperate with each other. Therefore, you cannot arbitrarily make a call to a component on a server from a client without first knowing what standard that server is using. Usually, you will also have to configure the client so that it can communicate with the server, especially when there are security issues. DCOM works best when all the computers in the system are using Microsoft operating systems. An IIOP system works best when all the computers in the system use the same CORBA Object Request Broker (ORB).

When you are working on an internal system, it might be possible to limit the system to one platform or the other. Once you start working with the Internet or expanding an intranet out to extranets (for example, networks that include the corporation and its partners), it is impossible to have a uniform platform across the entire system. At this point, DCOM and IIOP will no longer allow communication between any two components within the system, and neither of these two standards allows users to cross trust domains easily. Thus, for larger systems expanding across computers with multiple platforms, we need a way to enable objects to communicate with each other. The solution to this problem is SOAP.

In SOAP there are several different types of messaging patterns, but by far the most common is the Remote Procedure Call (RPC) pattern, in which one network node (the client) sends a request message to another node (the server) and the server immediately sends a response message to the client.

A major design goal for SOAP is simplicity and extensibility.

REMOTE PROCEDURE CALL (RPC)

RPC is a protocol that allows a computer program running on one computer to cause a subroutine on another computer to be executed without the programmer explicitly coding the details for this interaction.

RPC is a powerful technique for constructing distributed, client-server based applications.

It is a client/server infrastructure that increases the interoperability, portability, and flexibility of an application by allowing the application to be distributed over multiple heterogeneous platforms.

RPC increases the flexibility of an architecture by allowing a client component of an application to employ a function call to access a server on a remote system. It allows the remote component to be accessed without knowledge of the network address or any other lower-level information. Most RPCs use a synchronous, request-reply ("call/wait") protocol, which involves the blocking of the client until the server fulfills its request.

SOAP SYNTAX

SOAP Building Blocks

A SOAP message is an ordinary XML document containing the following elements.

Envelope Element

It identifies the XML document as a SOAP message. A SOAP message always appears within an envelope.

Header Element

The header element is optional and it contains header information.

Body Element

The body element is required and it contains call and response information.

Fault Element

The fault element is optional. It provides information about the errors that occurred while processing the message.

All the elements above are declared in the default namespace for the SOAP envelope:

http://www.w3.org/2001/12/soap-envelope

and the default namespace for SOAP encoding and data types is

http://www.w3.org/2001/12/soap-encoding

Syntax Rules in SOAP

Some of the important syntax rules are as follows:

1. SOAP should be coded in XML.
2. A SOAP envelope should be used for a SOAP message.
3. A SOAP encoding namespace must be used by SOAP.
4. A DTD reference and a XML processing instruction should not be contained.

SOAP MESSAGE STRUCTURE

```
<?xml version="1.0"?>
<soap:Envelope
xmlns:soap="http://www.w3.org/2001/12/soap-envelope"
soap:encodingStyle="http://www.w3.org/2001/12/soap-encoding">
<soap:Header>
...
</soap:Header>
<soap:Body>
...
 <soap:Fault>
 ...
 </soap:Fault>
</soap:Body>
</soap:Envelope>
```

A SOAP message always appears within an envelope. The envelope can have a header, just like an HTML document would, but this is not required. The message must have a body. The message content appears within the body.

```
<?xml version="1.0"?>
<soap:Envelope
xmlns:soap="http://www.w3.org/2001/12/soap-envelope" soap:encodingStyle="http:
//www.w3.org/2001/12/soap-encoding">
```

```
<soap:Head>
<soap:/Head>
<soap:Body>
 <GetName>
 <FirstName>ABC</FirstName>
 <LastName>XYZ</LastName>
 </GetName>
</soap:Body>
</soap:Envelope>
```

THE SOAP ENVELOPE ELEMENT

The SOAP envelope element is the root element of a SOAP message.

The required SOAP envelope element is the root element of a SOAP message. This element defines the XML document as a SOAP message.

Example

```
<?xml version="1.0"?>
<soap:Envelope
xmlns:soap="http://www.w3.org/2001/12/soap-envelope"
soap:encodingStyle="http://www.w3.org/2001/12/soap-encoding">
 ...
 Message information goes here
 ...
</soap:Envelope>
```

The xmlns:soap Namespace

Notice the xmlns:soap namespace in the example above. It should always have the value of *http://www.w3.org/2001/12/soap-envelope*. The namespace defines the envelope as a SOAP envelope. If a different namespace is used, the application generates an error and discards the message.

The encodingStyle Attribute

The encodingStyle attribute is used to define the data types used in the document. This attribute may appear on any SOAP element, and it applies to the element's contents and all child elements. A SOAP message has no default encoding.

Syntax

```
soap:encodingStyle="URI"
```

Example

```
<?xml version="1.0"?>
<soap:Envelope
xmlns:soap="http://www.w3.org/2001/12/soap-envelope"
soap:encodingStyle="http://www.w3.org/2001/12/soap-encoding">
 ...
 Message information goes here
 ...
</soap:Envelope>
```

The SOAP header element contains header information.

THE SOAP HEADER ELEMENT

The optional SOAP header element contains application-specific information (like authentication and payment) about the SOAP message. If the header element is present, it must be the first child element of the envelope element.

Example

```
<?xml version="1.0"?>
<soap:Envelope
xmlns:soap="http://www.w3.org/2001/12/soap-envelope"
soap:encodingStyle="http://www.w3.org/2001/12/soap-encoding">
<soap:Header>
 <m:Trans xmlns:m="http://www.abc.com/transaction/"
 soap:mustUnderstand="1">234
 </m:Trans>
</soap:Header>
...
...
</soap:Envelope>
```

The example above contains a header with a "Trans" element, a "mustUnderstand" attribute with a value of 1 and a value of 234.

SOAP defines three attributes in the default namespace (*"http://www.w3.org/2001/12/soap-envelope"*). These attributes are

1. mustUnderstand
2. actor
3. encodingStyle

The attributes defined in the SOAP header defines how a recipient should process the SOAP message.

The mustUnderstand Attribute

The SOAP mustUnderstand attribute can be used to indicate whether a header entry is mandatory or optional for the recipient to process.

If you add mustUnderstand="1" to a child element of the header element, it indicates that the receiver processing the header must recognize the element. If the receiver does not recognize the element, it will fail when processing the header.

Syntax

```
soap:mustUnderstand="0|1"
```

Example

```
<?xml version="1.0"?>
<soap:Envelope
xmlns:soap="http://www.w3.org/2001/12/soap-envelope"
soap:encodingStyle="http://www.w3.org/2001/12/soap-encoding">
<soap:Header>
 <m:Trans xmlns:m="http://www.abc.com/transaction/"
 soap:mustUnderstand="1">234
 </m:Trans>
</soap:Header>
...
...
</soap:Envelope>
```

The Actor Attribute

A SOAP message may travel from a sender to a receiver by passing different endpoints along the message path. However, not all parts of a SOAP message may be intended for the ultimate endpoint; instead, it may be intended for one or more of the endpoints on the message path.

The SOAP actor attribute is used to address the header element to a specific endpoint.

Syntax

```
soap:actor="URI"
```

Example

```
<?xml version="1.0"?>
<soap:Envelope
xmlns:soap="http://www.w3.org/2001/12/soap-envelope"
soap:encodingStyle="http://www.w3.org/2001/12/soap-encoding">
<soap:Header>
<m:Trans xmlns:m="http://www.abc.com/transaction/"
 soap:actor="http://www.abc.com/appml/">234
 </m:Trans>
</soap:Header>
...
...
</soap:Envelope>
```

The encodingStyle Attribute

The encodingStyle attribute is used to define the data types used in the document. This attribute may appear on any SOAP element, and it will apply to that element's contents and all child elements. A SOAP message has no default encoding.

Syntax

```
soap:encodingStyle="URI"
```

THE SOAP BODY ELEMENT

The SOAP body element contains the actual SOAP message. The required SOAP body element contains the actual SOAP message intended for the ultimate endpoint of the message. Immediate child elements of the SOAP body element may be namespace-qualified.

Example

```
<?xml version="1.0"?>
<soap:Envelope
xmlns:soap="http://www.w3.org/2001/12/soap-envelope"
soap:encodingStyle="http://www.w3.org/2001/12/soap-encoding">
<soap:Body>
 <m:GetPrice xmlns:m="http://www.abc.com/prices">
 <m:Item>Apples</m:Item>
 </m:GetPrice>
</soap:Body>
</soap:Envelope>
```

The example above requests the price of apples. Note that the m:GetPrice and the Item elements above are application-specific elements. They are not a part of the SOAP namespace. A SOAP response could look something like this:

```
<?xml version="1.0"?>
<soap:Envelope
xmlns:soap="http://www.w3.org/2001/12/soap-envelope"
soap:encodingStyle="http://www.w3.org/2001/12/soap-encoding">
<soap:Body>
 <m:GetPriceResponse xmlns:m="http://www.abc.com/prices">
 <m:Price>1.90</m:Price>
 </m:GetPriceResponse>
</soap:Body>
</soap:Envelope>
```

THE SOAP FAULT ELEMENT

The SOAP fault element holds errors and status information for a SOAP message.

The optional SOAP fault element is used to indicate error messages. If a fault element is present, it must appear as a child element of the Body element. A fault element can only appear once in a SOAP message. The SOAP fault element has several sub elements.

Table 10.1 The SOAP Fault Element

Sub Element	Description
<faultcode>	A code for identifying the fault
<faultstring>	A human readable explanation of the fault
<faultactor>	Information about who caused the fault to happen
<detail>	Holds application-specific error information related to the body element

Soap Fault Codes

The faultcode values shown in Table 10.2 must be used in the faultcode element when describing faults.

Table 10.2 The Faultcode Values

Error	Description
VersionMismatch	Found an invalid namespace for the SOAP envelope element
MustUnderstand	An immediate child element of the header element, with the mustUnderstand attribute set to "1", was not understood
Client	The message was incorrectly formed or contained incorrect information
Server	There was a problem with the server so the message could not proceed

Faultstring

```
<faultstring xmlns="> string </faultstring>
```

The faultstring element is of type string. It provides a human-readable description of whatever fault occurred.

Faultactor

```
<faultactor xmlns="> uriReference </faultactor>
```

The faultactor element is of type uriReference. It indicates the source of the fault.

Detail

```
<detail xmlns="> any number of elements in any namespace </detail>
```

The detail element is used to carry application-specific error information. It may be annotated with any number of attributes from any namespace and may have any number of namespace-qualified element children. The detail element must be present if the fault is the result of the recipient being unable to process the body element. This element is not used to provide error information in the case of the recipient being unable to process an element child of the header element. In such cases, error information is placed inside the header element.

THE HTTP PROTOCOL

HTTP communicates over TCP/IP. An HTTP client connects to an HTTP server using TCP. After establishing a connection, the client can send an HTTP request message to the server:

```
POST/item HTTP/1.1
Host: 189.123.345.239
Content-Type: text/plain
Content-Length: 200
```

The server then processes the request and sends an HTTP response back to the client. The response contains a status code that indicates the status of the request:

```
200 OK
Content-Type: text/plain
Content-Length: 200
```

In the example above, the server returned a status code of 200. This is the standard success code for HTTP. If the server could not decode the request, it could have returned something like this:

```
400 Bad Request
Content-Length: 0
```

SOAP HTTP BINDING

A SOAP method is an HTTP request/response that complies with the SOAP encoding rules.

HTTP + XML = SOAP

A SOAP request could be an HTTP POST or an HTTP GET request.

The HTTP POST request specifies at least two HTTP headers:

1. Content-Type
2. Content-Length

CONTENT-TYPE

The Content-Type header for a SOAP request and response defines the MIME type for the message and the character encoding (optional) used for the XML body of the request or response.

Syntax

```
Content-Type: MIMEType; charset=character-encoding
```

Example

```
POST /item HTTP/1.1
Content-Type: application/soap+xml; charset=utf-8
```

CONTENT-LENGTH

The Content-Length header for a SOAP request and response specifies the number of bytes in the body of the request or response.

Syntax

```
Content-Length: bytes
```

Example

```
POST/item HTTP/1.1
Content-Type: application/soap+xml; charset=utf-8
Content-Length: 250
```

A SOAP EXAMPLE

In the example below, a GetStockPrice request is sent to a server. The request has a StockName parameter, and a Price parameter that will be returned in the response. The namespace for the function is defined in *http://www.example.org/stock*.

A SOAP Request

POST/InStock HTTP/1.1
Host: www.example.org
Content-Type: application/soap+xml; charset=utf-8
Content-Length: nnn

```
<?xml version="1.0"?>
<soap:Envelope
xmlns:soap="http://www.w3.org/2001/12/soap-envelope"
soap:encodingStyle="http://www.w3.org/2001/12/soap-encoding">
<soap:Body xmlns:m="http://www.example.org/stock">
 <m:GetStockPrice>
 <m:StockName>IBM</m:StockName>
 </m:GetStockPrice>
</soap:Body>
</soap:Envelope>
```

The SOAP Response

HTTP/1.1 200 OK
Content-Type: application/soap+xml; charset=utf-8
Content-Length: nnn

```
<?xml version="1.0"?>
<soap:Envelope
xmlns:soap="http://www.w3.org/2001/12/soap-envelope"
soap:encodingStyle="http://www.w3.org/2001/12/soap-encoding">
<soap:Body xmlns:m="http://www.example.org/stock">
 <m:GetStockPriceResponse>
 <m:Price>34.5</m:Price>
 </m:GetStockPriceResponse>
</soap:Body>
</soap:Envelope>
```

TRANSPORT METHODS IN SOAP

The Internet application layer is used to transfer messages from one end to another end. Various products have been transported successfully from one end to another end using SOAP. Both SMTP and HTTP are successful transport protocols used in transmitting information.

SOAP AND THE REQUEST/RESPONSE MODEL

The SOAP standard introduces no new concepts—it's built completely from existing technology. It currently uses HTTP as its request/response messaging transport and is completely platform independent. HTTP connects computers across the entire world. HTTP can go through firewalls and is the easiest means to transport messages to any computer in the world. It's likely that SOAP will evolve to use other protocols in the future.

HTTPS is similar to HTTP but it has an additional layer underneath the Internet application layer that encrypts data. This protocol is more widely used than IOP or DCOM because those protocols are filtered by firewalls. The HTTPS protocol advocates the WS-I method to provide security for transmission of secured data.

A SOAP package contains information that can be used to invoke a method. How that method is called is not defined in the SOAP specification. SOAP also does not handle distributed garbage collection, message box carrying, type safety, or bidirectional HTTP. What SOAP does allow you to do is pass parameters and commands between HTTP clients and servers, regardless of the platforms and applications on the client and server. The parameters and commands are encoded using XML. Let's take a look at how SOAP uses the standard HTTP headers.

HTTP HEADERS AND SOAP

Two types of headers are available in HTTP: request headers and response headers. When you are using your Web browser to surf the Internet, each time you navigate to a new URL, the Web browser will create a request and send it to the Web server. These requests are written in plain text; each has headers in a standard format. When creating SOAP messages, you will be adding additional information to these standard formats. HTTP servers generate a response message upon receiving the client request. This message contains a status line and response headers.

REQUEST HEADERS

A typical HTTP message in a SOAP request being passed to a Web server looks like this:

```
POST/Order HTTP/1.1
Host: www.northwindtraders.com
Content-Type: text/xml
Content-Length: nnnn
SOAPAction: "urn:northwindtraders.com:PO#UpdatePO"
```

Information being sent is located here.

The first line of the message contains three separate components: the request method, the request URI, and the protocol version. In this case, the request method is POST; the request URI is /Order; and the version number is HTTP/1.1. The Internet Engineering Task Force (IETF) has standardized the request methods. The GET method is commonly used to retrieve information on the Web. The POST method is used to pass information from the client to the server. The information passed by the POST method is then used by applications on the server. Only certain types of information can be sent using GET; any type of data can be sent using POST. SOAP also supports sending messages using M-POST. When working with the POST method in a SOAP package, the request URI contains the name of the method to be invoked.

The second line is the URL of the server that the request is being sent to. The request URL is implementation-specific—that is, each server defines how it will interpret the request URL. In the case of a SOAP package, the request URL usually represents the name of the object that contains the method being called.

The third line contains the content type, text/xml, which indicates that the payload is XML in the plain text format. The payload refers to the essential data being carried to the destination. The payload information could be used by a server or a firewall to validate the incoming message. A SOAP request must use the text/xml as its content type. The fourth line specifies the size of the payload in bytes. The content type and content length are required with a payload.

The SOAPAction header field must be used in a SOAP request to specify the intent of the SOAP HTTP request. The fifth line of the message, SOAPAction: "urn: northwindtraders.com:PO#UpdatePO," is a namespace followed by the method name. By combining this namespace with the request URL, our example calls the UpdatePO method of the Order object and is scoped by the urn:northwindtraders.com:PO namespace URI. The following are also valid SOAPAction header field values:

SOAPAction: "UpdatePO"
SOAPAction: ""
SOAPAction:

The header field value of the empty string means that the HTTP request URI provides the intent of the SOAP message. A header field without a specified value indicates that the intent of the SOAP message isn't available.

Notice that there is a single blank line between the fifth line and the payload request. When you are working with message headers, the carriage-return/line-feed sequence delimits the headers and an extra carriage-return/line-feed sequence is used to signify that the header information is complete and that what follows is the payload.

RESPONSE HEADERS

A typical response message that contains the response headers is shown here:

200 OK
Content-Type: text/plain
Content-Length: nnnn

The first line of this message contains a status code and a message associated with that status code. In this case, the status code is 200 and the message is OK, meaning that the request was successfully decoded and that an appropriate response was returned. If an error had occurred, the following headers might have been returned:

400 Bad Request
Content-Type: text/plain
Content-Length: 0

In this case, the status code is 400 and the message is Bad Request, meaning that the request cannot be decoded by the server because of incorrect syntax.

SENDING MESSAGES USING M-POST

We can restrict messages coming through a firewall or a proxy server by using the M-POST method instead of POST. M-POST is a new HTTP method defined using the HTTP Extension Framework. This method is used when you are including mandatory information in the HTTP header, just as you used the mustUnderstand attribute in the SOAP header element.

SOAP supports both POST and M-POST requests. A client first makes a SOAP request using M-POST. If the request fails and either a 501 status code or a 510 status code returns, the client should retry the request using the POST method. If the client fails the request again and a 405 status code returns, the client should fail the request. If the returning status code is 200, the message has been received successfully. Firewalls can force a client to use the M-POST method to submit SOAP requests by blocking regular POSTs of the text/xml-SOAP content type.

If you use M-POST, you must use a mandatory extension declaration that refers to a namespace in the envelope element declaration. The namespace prefix must precede the mandatory headers. The following example illustrates how to use M-POST and the mandatory headers:

```
M-POST /Order HTTP/1.1
Host: www.northwindtraders.com
Content-Type: text/xml
Content-Length: nnnn
Man: "http://schemas.xmlsoap.org/soap/envelope; ns=49"
49-SOAPAction: "urn:northwindtraders.com:PO#UpdatePO"
```

A SCHEMA FOR THE BODY CONTENT OF THE SOAP MESSAGE

As you can see, we have not yet defined the NPO schema located at *http://www.northwindtraders.com/schemas/NPOSchema.xsd*. This schema can be defined as follows:

```
<xsd:schema xmlns:xsd="http://www.w3.org/1999/XMLSchema"
   targetNamespace="http://schemas.xmlsoap.org/soap/envelope"
   xmlns:SOAP="http://schemas.xmlsoap.org/soap/envelope">
   <xsd:complexType name="NorthwindHeader">
    <xsd:element name="GUID" type="string"/>
   </xsd:complexType>
     <xsd:complexType name="NorthwindBody">
      <xsd:element name="UpdatePO">
       <xsd:complexType>
        <element name="orderID" type="integer"/>
```

```
          <element name="customerNumber" type="integer"/>
          <element name="item" type="double"/>
          <element name="quantity" type="double"/>
        </xsd:complexType>
      </xsd:element>
    </xsd:complexType>
  </xsd:schema>
```

This schema creates two elements: NorthwindBody and Northwind-Header. Using the xsi:type attribute, we can extend the SOAP body element with the NorthwindBody complex type and extend the header element with the NorthwindHeader complex type. You can then create the following SOAP document:

```
<SOAP-ENV:Envelope
  xmlns:xsi="http://www.w3.org/1999/XMLSchema/instance"
  xmlns:SOAP-ENV="http://schemas.xmlsoap.org/soap/envelope"
  xsi:schemaLocation=
   "http://www.northwindtraders.com/schemas/NPOSchema.xsd">
 <SOAP-ENV:Header xsi:type="NorthwindHeader">
   <COM:GUID xmlns:COM="http://comobject.northwindtraders.com">
    10000000-0000-abcd-0000-000000000001
   </COM:GUID>
 </SOAP-ENV:Header>
 <SOAP-ENV:Body xsi:type="NorthwindBody">
   <UpdatePO>
   <orderID>0</orderID>
   <customerNumber>999</customerNumber>
   <item>89</item>
   <quantity>3000</quantity>
  </UpdatePO>
 </SOAP-ENV:Body>
</SOAP-ENV:Envelope>
```

SOAP ENCODING

The SOAP encoding style provides a means to define data types similar to what is found in most programming languages, including types and arrays. SOAP defines simple and complex data types just as the schema standard does. The simple type elements are the same as those defined in the second schema standard. The complex type elements include those defined in the first SOAP standard and are a special way of defining arrays. Structures follow the definitions of the complex type. For example, we could have the following structure:

```
<e:Customer>
  <CName>Janson Maru</CName>
  <Address>18,I.G. NAGAR</Address>
  <ID>4</ID>
</e:Customer>
```

This structure would be defined as follows:

```
<element name=Customer>
  <element name="CName" type="xsd:string"/>
  <element name="Address" type="xsd:string"/>
  <element name="ID" type="xsd:string"/>
</element>
```

Arrays will have an additional attribute, type="SOAP-ENC:Array", to define an element as an array. An array could be as follows:

```
<CustomerIDs SOAP-ENC:arrayType="xsd:int[3]">
  <number>345</number>
  <number>354</number>
  <number>399</number>
</CustomerIDs>
```

The schema would be as follows:

```
<element name="CustomerIDs" type="SOAP-ENC:Array"/>
```

In this example, the array CustomerIDs contains three members; each member has a value of type xsd:int.

ENCODING STYLE ATTRIBUTE

This is used to define the data types in the document. Any SOAP element may use this format and it gets implemented on the child and contents of the SOAP. The SOAP element never has a default encoding.

QUESTIONS FOR DISCUSSION

1. Explain SOAP.
2. Give an example of how SOAP works.
3. Explain remote call procedure.
4. Explain transport methods in SOAP.
5. Explain HTTPS in SOAP.
6. Explain the role of XML in SOAP.
7. What are the advantages of SOAP?
8. State some disadvantages of SOAP.
9. Explain message passing in RPC.
10. Explain the difference between RPC and local calls.
11. What are the elements in a SOAP message?
12. Explain the syntax rules in SOAP.
13. Explain the encoding style attribute.
14. Explain the SOAP envelope element.
15. Explain the actor element.
16. Explain the mustUnderstand Attribute.
17. Explain the SOAP body element.
18. What is SOAP and how does it relate to XML?

CHAPTER 11

DOM PROGRAMMING INTERFACE

DOM (DOCUMENT OBJECT MODEL)

DOM is an Application Programming Interface (API) that represents an XML file as a document object, which allows application programs to manage the information contained in the document object through the interface.

When accessing XML files, the DOM should always be the access method of choice. Using the DOM has several advantages over other available mechanisms for the generation of XML documents, such as writing directly to a stream.

Since the DOM transforms the text into an abstract representation of a node tree, problems like unclosed tags and improperly nested tags can be completely avoided.

When manipulating an XML document with a DOM, the developer need not worry about the text expression of the document, but only about the parent-child relationships and associated information.

The node tree created by the DOM is a logical representation of the content found in the XML file; it shows what information is present and how is it related without necessarily being bound to the XML grammar.

A developer using the DOM to change the structure of an XML file will have a much simpler task than one who is attempting to do so using traditional file manipulation mechanisms.

The way in which the DOM represents the relationship between data elements is very similar to the way that this information is represented in modern hierarchical and relational databases. This makes it very easy to move information between a database and an XML file using DOM.

We learned the ways to handle the structure of an XML document and the ways to describe the hierarchical information. We now discuss the ways to access the XML document from the programs. One of these ways is through the Document Object Model.

The W3C specifies that the DOM is a language; it is a platform neutral definition, that is, interfaces are defined for the different objects comprising this DOM, but no specifics of implementation are provided, and it could be done in any programming language.

The DOM layout a standard functionality for document navigation and the manipulation of the content and structure of HTML and XML documents.

XML DOM TREE

The XML DOM defines a standard way for accessing and manipulating XML documents. The DOM presents an XML document as a tree structure. XML DOM is a must for anyone working with XML.

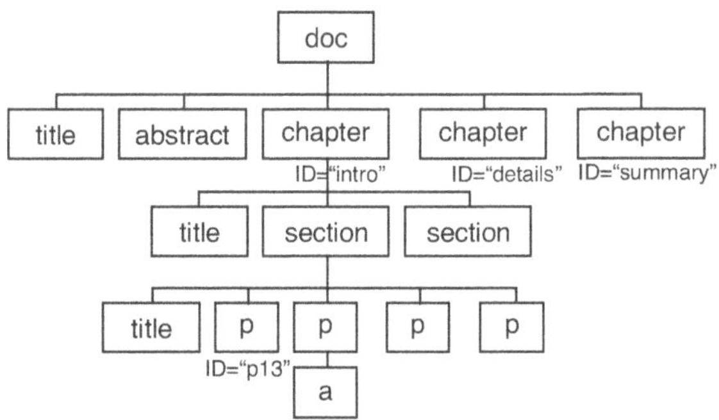

FIGURE 11.1 An XML document as a tree-structure

HIGH LEVEL ARCHITECTURE OF A DOM/XML APPLICATION

An XML application reads an XML file, after which it can modify and rewrite the XML, and/or it can print output based on that XML (commonly called "rendering"). Note that "rendering" can take widely diverse forms, including changing which fields are available on a form, printing a vector graphic, or rendering marked up text. Rendering can even take the form of configuring an application or executing remote procedures.

The DOM model is easy to understand. Figure 11.2 shows the architecture of an XML app using DOM.

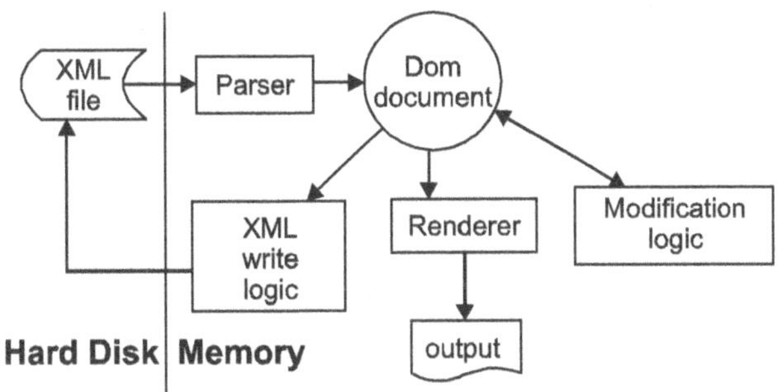

FIGURE 11.2 The architecture of an XML app using DOM

A parser reads the XML file and builds a DOM document to match the XML file. From that point until a save is performed, all interaction between the app and XML hits the DOM document rather than the corresponding XML file. It's interesting to note that almost all XML parsers use SAX. The reason is simple enough. Before you build a DOM document, you must detect events such as the start of an element (start tag encountered), end of element (end tag encountered), new attribute (name followed by equal sign followed by quoted string encountered), and the like. DOM can be thought of as an extra abstraction to lessen the programmer's workload at the expense of memory usage.

Modifications are made directly to the DOM document. Elements can be added, deleted, renamed, and rearranged. Text nodes can be added, deleted, or changed. Elements can be moved either within the same level or promoted or demoted to different levels.

Obviously, the DOM is modified in apps that rewrite the XML file. But DOM modification is also often done in an app that only renders the XML. The classic example is in a "DOMWalker" app, which simply walks the DOM tree and prints what it finds in a hierarchical outline. In fact, the new lines and spaces intended to make the XML file more readable are actually legitimate text nodes in XML, but in an XML app concerned only with a hierarchy, they're extraneous. Therefore, the first thing a DOMWalker program does is delete text nodes made up only of whitespace.

Rendering is the challenging part of most XML apps. It's often graphics intensive. Consider the Dia vector drawing program, which keeps all drawing information in XML but renders it as geometric shapes. Often, there are several rendering processes, one for each kind of output. Thus a book authored in XML could be rendered as a paper book, as a PDF, as a Postscript file, or as an HTML page or series of HTML pages. Indeed, this is one of the primary benefits of stylesheet-based documents. Often the rendering itself is decoupled from the app by use of XSL (eXtensible Style Language), much the same as program logic is decoupled from the app using XML.

Rewriting the XML file is easy—about what you'd expect for your last class project in a college Programming 101 course. In the case of DOM, you've already assembled the output in a DOM document, so you just walk its tree and write the markup.

In the case of SAX-based XML apps it's a little harder because you often don't read the information in the same order you want to write it. In other words, if your app's specification calls for something occurring later in the input modifying something earlier in the output, you can't just use a read-write loop. So you do the typical stuff—keep some things in memory, or may be write an intermediate file and then sort it, or run 2 passes through the XML. This is why for apps interacting with small XML files, DOM are better.

DOM Sample Program

The DOM is a W3C specification presented as "a platform-and language-neutral interface that will allow programs and scripts to dynamically access and update the content, structure and style of documents." It is essentially a tree data structure and a set of methods to access and edit that structure. Since it's an in-memory data structure, the memory usage is much higher than for SAX, but the document model can be accessed randomly and processed multiple times.

The DOM API defines interfaces for each of the entities of an XML document:

- `org.w3c.dom.Node` interface: a single node in the document tree
  - Defines methods to access, insert, remove, and replace the child nodes
  - Defines methods to access the parent node
  - Defines methods to access the document
- `org.w3c.dom.Document` interface is a node that represents the entire XML document
- `org.w3c.dom.Element` interface is a node that represents an XML element

- `org.w3c.dom.Text` interface is a node that represents the textual content of an XML element

The application may apply its business logic directly to the DOM tree or go first through an additional stage of mapping relevant information from the DOM tree to business objects.

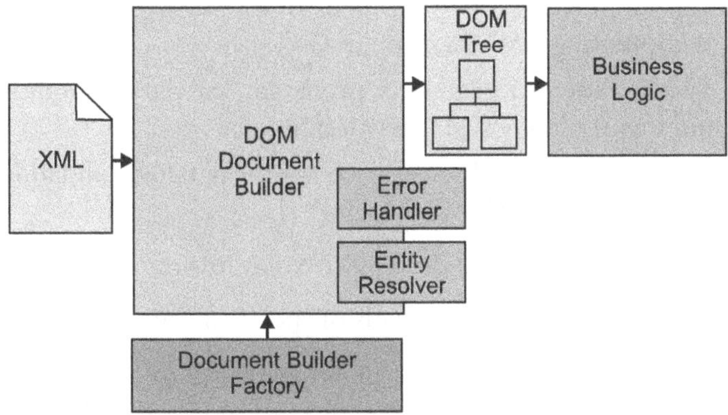

FIGURE 11.3 When using the DOM API, the application has to access or edit an in-memory representation of the source document.

The program presented below uses the DOM API to parse and load in memory an XML document describing a set of chessboard configurations. It then walks through the resulting DOM tree and outputs the same chessboard configurations in text format.

Two different implementations are used to highlight the potential differences in performance when using different methods of the DOM API: either accessing the elements by their names or relative to their parents.

DOM IMPLEMENTATION

DOM has been implemented in many languages:

- DOM has been implemented in Java in J2SDK 1.4.1.
- DOM has been implemented in PHP 4.
- DOM has been implemented in Perl. XML::DOM is a DOM Perl implementation developed by Enno Derkson.
- DOM has been implemented in JavaScript and Web browsers supporting JavaScript.

- DOM has been implemented in VBScript and Web browsers supporting VBScript.

The Apache Xerces is an Apache project that produces implementations of DOM for 3 programming languages. (See *http://xerces.apache.org/* for more information.)

- Apache Xerces C++ — A processor for parsing, validating, serializing, and manipulating XML, written in C++
- Apache Xerces2 Java — A processor for parsing, validating, serializing, and manipulating XML, written in Java
- Apache Xerces Perl — A processor for parsing, validating, serializing, and manipulating XML, written in Perl

DOM Specifications and the DOM Node Interface

Currently, DOM has 4 levels of specifications:

- DOM Level 0 — No formal specifications published: A collection of HTML document functionalities offered by Web browsers in 1996
- DOM Level 1 — Latest version published in 1998: Two modules: the Core module is for XML documents; and the HTML module is for HTML documents
- DOM Level 2 — Published in 2000: 14 modules such as Core, XML, HTML, Views, StyleSheets, and CSS
- DOM Level 3 — Published in 2004: 21 modules such as Core, XML, HTML, XPath, Traversal, Range, and Validation

Based the Core module of the DOM Level 1 specification, an XML file is represented with a tree structure, called a *document*. Each node in the tree is a node object, which represents a unit of information in the XML file.

A node object is actually an instance of classes that implement the node interface, which contains these methods:

- getNodeType(): Returns the node type
- getNodeName(): Returns the node name
- getNodeValue(): Returns the value associated with this node
- getChildNodes(): Returns a list of nodes nested inside this node

- getAttributes(): Returns a list of nodes that represents the attributes of this node

The DOM Level 1 Core module specifies these nodes type, each of which could be implemented as a separate class:

```
 2 ATTRIBUTE_NODE
 4 CDATA_SECTION_NODE
 8 COMMENT_NODE
11 DOCUMENT_FRAGMENT_NODE
 9 DOCUMENT_NODE
10 DOCUMENT_TYPE_NODE
 1 ELEMENT_NODE
 6 ENTITY_NODE
 5 ENTITY_REFERENCE_NODE
12 NOTATION_NODE
 7 PROCESSING_INSTRUCTION_NODE
 3 TEXT_NODE
```

THE DOM SPECIFICATION

As with any other Internet standards, the DOM specification is maintained by the W3C. At present, the W3C has prepared two documents, the Level 1 and Level 2 documents.

The W3C document for DOM Level 1 has a status of Recommendation. This document contains two main sections. The Document Object Model (Core) Level 1 contains the specification for interfaces that can access any structured document, with some specific extensions that allow access to XML documents.

The second section explains the HTML-specific extensions to DOM.

The DOM specification explains how strings are to be manipulated by the DOM by defining the data type DOMString. The DOMString data type is defined as a double-byte character set string, encoded using the UTF-16 encoding scheme.

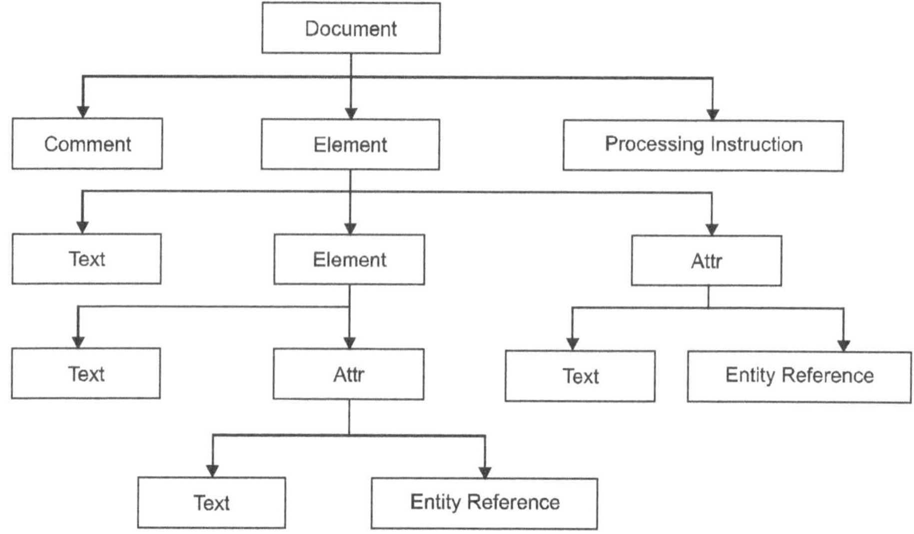

FIGURE 11.4 DOM implementation

We now take a look at the objects, methods, and properties that make up the DOM Level 1 specification. The behavior that is specified applies only to XML documents; the DOM may behave differently when used to access HTML documents.

XML DOM NODES

According to the DOM, everything in an XML document is a node.

The DOM says

- The entire document is a document node.
- Every XML element is an element node.
- The text in the XML elements are text nodes.
- Every attribute is an attribute node.
- Comments are comment nodes.

DOM Example

Look at the following XML file (books.xml):

```
<?xml version="1.0" encoding="ISO-8859-1"?>
<bookstore>
  <book category="Litrature">
    <title lang="en">World war</title>
    <author>Ram sharma</author>
    <year>2009</year>
    <price>300.00</price>
  </book>
  <book category="children">
    <title lang="en">A sweet play</title>
    <author>M. Rashmi</author>
    <year>2010</year>
    <price>424.00</price>
  </book>
  <book category="GK">
    <title lang="en">A good knowledge maker</title>
    <author>s. John</author>
    <author>Preet Moare</author>
    <author>K. Raute</author>
    <author>Raj Ben</author>
    <year>2008</year>
    <price>249.99</price>
  </book>
  <book category="Internet" cover="paperback">
    <title lang="en">Learning HTML</title>
    <author> Ramesh Arya</author>
    <year>2010</year>
    <price>239.00</price>
  </book>
</bookstore>
```

The root node in the XML above is named <bookstore>. All other nodes in the document are contained within <bookstore>. The root node <bookstore> holds four <book> nodes.

The first <book> node holds four nodes: <title>, <author>, <year>, and <price>, which contain one text node each. Text is Always Stored in Text Nodes a, s, t, n.

A common error in DOM processing is to expect an element node to contain text. However, the text of an element node is stored in a text node.

XML DOM NODE TREE

The XML DOM views an XML document as a node tree. All the nodes in the tree have a relationship to each other.

The XML DOM views an XML document as a tree structure. The tree structure is called a node tree. All nodes can be accessed through the tree. Their contents can be modified or deleted, and new elements can be created.

The node tree shows the set of nodes and the connections between them. The tree starts at the root node and branches out at the lowest level of the tree.

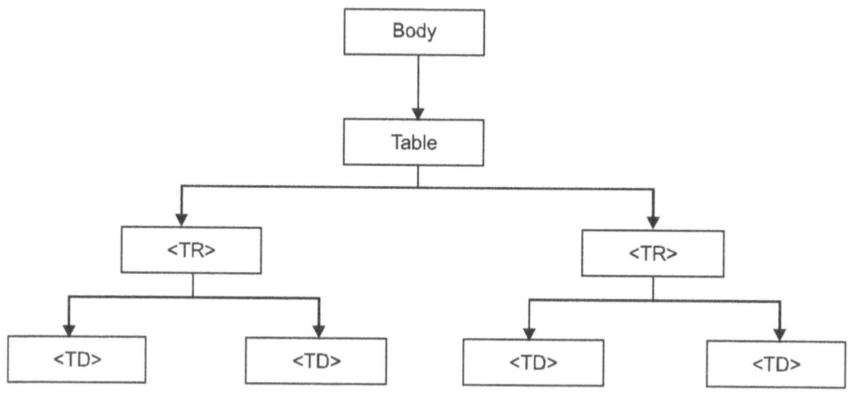

FIGURE 11.5 HTML node tree

Node Parents, Children, and Siblings

The nodes in the node tree have a hierarchical relationship to each other. The terms parent, child, and sibling are used to describe the relationships. Parent nodes have children. Children on the same level are called siblings (brothers or sisters).

- In a node tree, the top node is called the root.
- Every node, except the root, has exactly one parent node.
- A node can have any number of children.
- A leaf is a node with no children.
- Siblings are nodes with the same parent.

Figure 11.6 illustrates a part of the node tree and the relationship between the nodes.

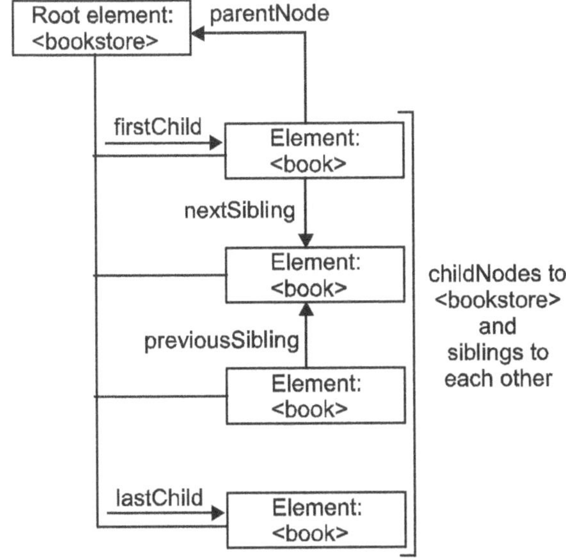

FIGURE 11.6 A part of the node tree and the relationship between the nodes

Because the XML data is structured in a tree form, it can be traversed without knowing the exact structure of the tree and without knowing the type of data contained within.

FIRST CHILD - LAST CHILD

Look at the following XML fragment:

```
<bookstore>
  <book category="Litrature">
    <title lang="en">World war</title>
    <author>Ram sharma</author>
    <year>2009</year>
    <price>300.00</price>
  </book>
</bookstore>
```

In the XML above, the <title> element is the first child of the <book> element, and the <price> element is the last child of the <book> element.

Furthermore, the <book> element is the parent node of the <title>, <author>, <year>, and <price> elements.

DOM LEVEL 2 SPECIFICATION

As of press time, the W3C DOM level 2 specification has the status of Candidate Recommendation. In addition to the objects we just discussed, the DOM 2 specification includes support for namespaces, style sheets, filtering, event model, and ranges.

Namespaces are used to distinguish discrete data elements with the same name in XML. The DOM Level 2 provides mechanisms for interrogating and modifying the namespace for a document.

The DOM Level 2 specification includes an object model for style sheets, as well as methods to query and manipulate the style sheet for a particular object.

The DOM Level 2 specification adds methods for filtering the content in an XML document.

An event model is in the planning stages as far as the DOM Level 2 specification is concerned.

This includes the functions for manipulating large blocks of text that will be useful to those working with traditional documents in XML.

XML DOCUMENT STRUCTURE

```
<INVOICE>
        <CUSTOMER> Sam </CUSTOMER>
        <ADDRESS>57, M.G.Road</ADDRESS>
        <CITY>Bangalore</CITY>
        <STATE>Karnataka</STATE>
        <PRODUCT1>Cheese</PRODUCT1>
        <UNITS>2</UNITS>
        <PRODUCT2>Champagne</PRODUCT2>
        <UNITS2>3</UNITS2>
        <PRODUCT3>Gel</PRODUCT3>
        <UNITS3>5</UNITS3>
        <PRODUCT4>Bread</PRODUCT4>
        <UNITS4>4</UNITS4>
</INVOICE>
```

Developers new to XML assume that the main purpose of XML is to enable pieces of information in a file to be named so that others may easily understand them. As a result, documents prepared by beginners to XML often resemble “tag soup“—an unordered list of data elements with meaningful tag names, but containing the same level of information as a flat file. The ability of XML that many developers overlook is its ability to show relationships between elements-specifically, the ability to imply a parent-child relationship between two elements. The invoice example shows the preparation of an XML document called INVOICE that could be better expressed in XML as shown in the following code.

```
<INVOICE>
          <CUSTOMER NAME = "Sam"
                 ADDRESS = "57, M.G. Road"
                    CITY = "Bangalore"
                   STATE = "Karnataka">
       <LINEITEM PRODUCT = "Cheese"
                   UNITS = "2"/>
       <LINEITEM PRODUCT = "Champagne"
                   UNITS = "3"/>
       <LINEITEM PRODUCT = "Gel"
                   UNITS = "5"/>
       <LINEITEM PRODUCT = "Bread"
                   UNITS = "4"/>
</INVOICE>
```

In this document, it immediately becomes apparent that the INVOICE element has four children, that is, the line item elements. It also makes the search in the document easier. If we are searching for the orders for CHEESE, we can do so by looking for the LINEITEM elements with a PRODUCT attribute value of CHEESE, instead of looking at the PRODUCT1 element, PRODUCT2 element, and so on.

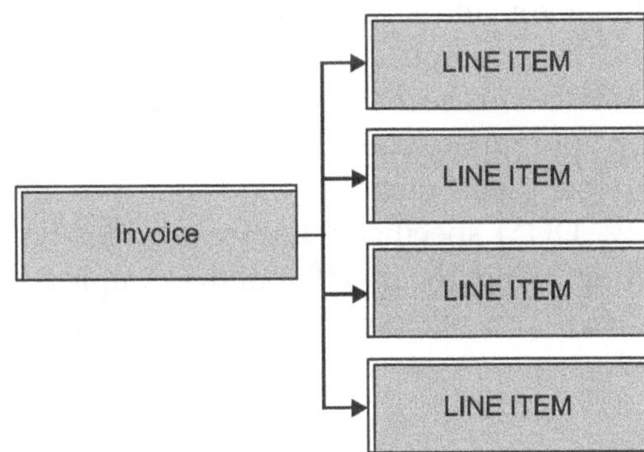

FIGURE 11.7 Flow diagram of INVOICE and its child elements

This document structure can be represented as a node tree that shows all the elements and their relationships to one another.

With the DOM, we would be able to operate on the document in the node form with its tree structure. We would be able to add any information easily and attach it as a child to the node rather than to read through the information and go past the last item to insert new information.

When the DOM is used to manipulate an XML text file, the first thing it does is parse the file, breaking the file out into individual elements, attributes, and comments.

The next thing it does is create, in the memory, a representation of the XML file as a node tree. The developer may access the contents of the document through the node tree and make the necessary modifications.

The DOM goes a step further and treats every item as a node—elements, attributes, comments, processing instructions, and text. The DOM provides a robust set of interfaces to facilitate the manipulation of the DOM node tree.

WORKING WITH DOM

We have discussed the structure of the DOM, taking XML documents and transforming them into node trees that may be accessed programmatically. We have also talked about the specification provided by W3C, and that it is only a description of the access mechanisms. How do we take this information and implement it? This can be done using the DOM API.

When writing a piece of software that accesses XML files using the DOM, a particular implementation of the DOM must be used. The implementation, the DOM API, is a library designed to run on a particular hardware and software platform and to access a particular data store.

API is the acronym for Application Programming Interface. It is a set of libraries used by a component to instruct another component to carry out lower level services. As such, the API must be an implementation of an interface with the appropriate code to connect to other components and instruct them to carry out their functions.

The W3C DOM specification only provides the interface definition for the DOM libraries, not the specifics of their implementation. It therefore falls to third parties to provide implementations of the DOM that may be used by programmers.

CLIENT SIDE AND SERVER SIDE DOM

There are many applications for the DOM and XML, and they can loosely be classified into two types: those deployed on the server and those deployed on the client.

The first applications of DOM were on the server side. The DOM can be used to simplify the data interchange between disparate business systems, as well as provide an ideal mechanism for the archiving and retrieval of data.

XML facilitates inter-process or inter-business communications. This is mainly because XML allows for the use of platform-independent, self-describing and hierarchical information.

XML is an ideal storage medium for archived information, especially if it comes from an object-oriented or hierarchical database.

As of now, only Internet Explore 5.0 comes with DOM functionality built-in. Netscape and other browser developers are in the process of adding DOM support to their systems. Once they are in use, Internet developers will be able to take advantage of the DOM on the client to improve the way information is rendered and decrease roundtrips to the server.

XML DOM PARSER

Most browsers have a built-in XML parser to read and manipulate XML.

The parser converts XML into a JavaScript accessible object (the XML DOM).

XML PARSER

The XML DOM contains methods (functions) to traverse XML trees, and access, insert, and delete nodes. However, before an XML document can be accessed and manipulated, it must be loaded into an XML DOM object. An XML parser reads XML and converts it into an XML DOM object that can be accessed with JavaScript.

Most browsers have a built-in XML parser.

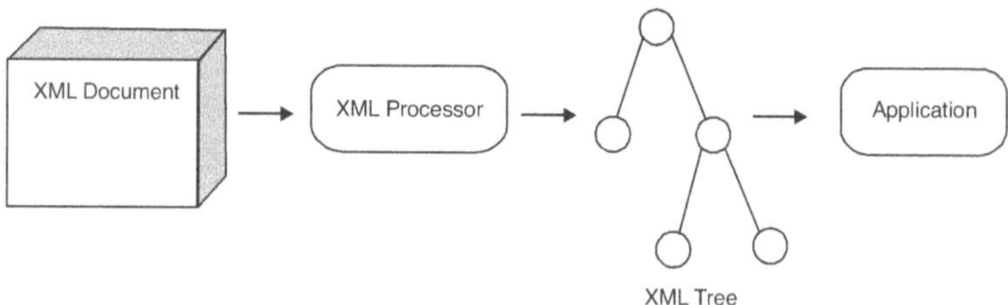

FIGURE 11.8 XML parser mechanism

LOAD AN XML DOCUMENT

The following JavaScript fragment loads an XML document ("books.xml"):

```
<html>
<body>
<script type="text/javascript">
if (window.XMLHttpRequest)
  {
  xhttp=new XMLHttpRequest();
  }
else // for IE 5/6
  {
  xhttp=new ActiveXObject("Microsoft.XMLHTTP");
  }
xhttp.open("GET","books.xml",false);
xhttp.send();
xmlDoc=xhttp.responseXML;
document.write("XML document loaded into an XML DOM Object.");
</script>
</body>
</html>
```

Result:

To load an XML document into an XML DOM Object

- Create an XML HTTP object
- Open the XML HTTP object
- Send an XML HTTP request to the server
- Set the response as an XML DOM object

QUESTIONS FOR DISCUSSION

1. What is DOM?
2. What is DOM and how does it relate to XML?
3. How do you use XML namespaces with DOM Level 1?
4. How do you use XML namespaces with DOM Level 2?
5. How do you use XML namespaces with DOM Level 3?
6. How you define DOM in XML?
7. Explain the architecture of DOM/XML applications.
8. Do SAX and DOM validating parsers take the same amount of memory while validating a document?
9. Can you use a generic SAX/DOM XML parser for Tomcat instead of parser.jar?
10. How do you convert a DOM document object into an XML file using JAXP?
11. You want to parse an XML file stored on a remote server. Can you use the DOM without downloading the file?
12. Is there some API which can modify a very large XML file? DOM runs out of memory and SAX just doesn't fit the bill.
13. You have to build an XML document from pieces of existing ones, and then output it as a string. What libraries should you use?
14. How do you write a DOM document as an XML file?
15. Does DOM include APIs for diffing and merging XML documents?
16. How can you map a DOM tree to javax.swing.tree.TreeNode or some object so that you can view an XML document as JTree?
17. Where can you get an XML parser/DOM implementation that allows you to programmatically query the DTD?

CHAPTER 12

SAX (SIMPLE API FOR XML)

INTRODUCTION TO SAX

XML 1.0 allows you to encode your information in textual form and create tags which allow you to structure the information stored in XML documents. This information must, be read by some program to do something useful, like viewing, modifying or printing it.

In order for your programs to access this information, you can use the SAX (Simple API for XML) or the DOM (Document Object Model) APIs. Both of these APIs must be implemented by the XML parser of your choice (which also must be written in the programming language of your choice).

For Java, these parsers include the Sun TR2 XML Parser, Data channel XJ2, IBM XML Parser for Java, and OpenXML (among many others). All of these parsers implement the SAX API (and also the DOM API). There are fewer differences in the implementation of SAX compared to the implementation of DOM 1.0 (simply because SAX is so much smaller and simpler than DOM).

So, Java programs must use an XML Parser written in Java that implements the SAX API in order to use SAX.

SAX (SIMPLE API FOR XML)

Unlike the DOM, which creates a tree based representation for the information in our XML documents, SAX does not have a default object model. This means that when you create a SAX parser and read in a document (unlike DOM), you will not be given a default object model.

The benefit of SAX is that processing can be conducted while analyzing the XML document—there is no need to load the entire document first as with DOM. On the other hand, not having an API for XML document updating means that any XML document updates have to be handled from within the application.

Also, SAX only loads an XML document in order from top to bottom, so the forward or backward referencing of XML documents must be performed by the application. SAX is especially suited for searching for and extracting data from XML documents.

SAX is a specification created through the XML-DEV mailing list, rather than being a W3C-recommended specification. Processing via SAX is light and quick in contrast to DOM. SAX loads an XML document in order from top to bottom, and is an event-driven API that notifies the application of an event regarding information associated with the detection of an element's start tag or end tag or occurrences of text. On the application side, the event received is processed to acquire the data from within the XML document.

A SAX parser is only required to read in your XML document and fire events based on the things it encounters in your XML document. Events are fired when the following things happen:

- Open element tags are encountered in your document
- Close element tags are encountered in your document
- #PCDATA and CDATA sections are encountered in your document
- Processing instructions, comments, entity declarations, are encountered in your document.

We start by looking at the open and close element tag events and the #PCDATA and CDATA events. One thing to remember about SAX is that the sequence of these events is very important, because the sequence in which events are fired determines how you will have to interpret each event.

SAX is an event-driven API that allows applications to process XML files by handling events fired by the parser while it traverses the XML structure.

If an application wants to use SAX to process XML files, it must provide SAX event handlers and call back methods to perform whatever the application want to do. If no event handler is provided, nothing will be performed on the XML files.

SAX was originally developed for Java language by David Megginson in 1998. Now SAX has been implemented in all major languages:

- SAX Project—The original SAX Java project is an open source project located at *http://www.saxproject.org/*.

- SAX has been implemented in Java in J2SDK 1.4.1.
- SAX has been implemented in PHP. Sax4PHP is a PHP5 class to manage XML with a Java like SAX API. See *http://sax4php.sourceforge.net/* for more information.
- SAX has been implemented in Perl. Perl SAX is a SAX Perl implementation developed as an open source product.

The Apache Xerces is an Apache project that produces implementations of SAX for 3 programming languages.

- Apache Xerces C++—A processor for parsing, validating, serializing, and manipulating XML, written in C++.
- Apache Xerces2 Java—A processor for parsing, validating, serializing, and manipulating XML, written in Java.
- Apache Xerces Perl—A processor for parsing, validating, serializing, and manipulating XML, written in Perl.

DOM AND TREE-BASED PROCESSING

The DOM is the "traditional" way of handling XML data. With DOM, the data is loaded into memory in a tree-like structure. For instance, the same document used as an example in the preceding example would be represented as nodes.

The rectangular boxes represent element nodes and the ovals represent text nodes. DOM uses a root node and parent-child relationships. For instance, in this case, samples would be the root node with five children: three text nodes (the white space), and the two element nodes, server and monitor. One important thing to realize is that the server and monitor actually have values of null.

PROS AND CONS OF TREE-BASED PROCESSING

DOM, and by extension tree-based processing, has several advantages. First, because the tree is persistent in memory, it can be modified so an application can make changes to the data and the structure. It can also work its way up and down the tree at any time, as opposed to the "one-shot deal" of SAX. DOM can also be much simpler to use. On the other hand, there is a lot of overhead involved in building these trees in memory. It's not unusual for large files to completely overrun a system's capacity. In addition, creating a DOM tree can be a very slow process.

HOW TO CHOOSE BETWEEN SAX AND DOM

Whether you choose DOM or SAX is going to depend on several factors:

- **Purpose of the application:** If you are going to have to make changes to the data and output it as XML, then in most cases, DOM is the way to go. This is particularly true if the changes are to the data itself, as opposed to a simple structural change that can be accomplished with XSL transformations.
- **Amount of data:** For large files, SAX is a better bet.
- **The need for speed:** SAX implementations are normally faster than DOM implementations.

It's important to remember that SAX and DOM are not mutually exclusive. You can use DOM to create a SAX stream of events, and you can use SAX to create a DOM tree.

THE SAX API IS DEFINED IN 4 INTERFACES UNDER THE ORG.XML.SAX PACKAGE

org.xml.sax.DocumentHandler: This is the main interface of SAX. It defines event handler methods (callback methods) that an application should implement to handle events fired by the parser while it traverses the input XML files.

org.xml.sax.ErrorHandler: It defines error handler methods (callback methods) that an application should implement to add special handling logics when the parse encounters parsing errors.

org.xml.sax.DTDHandler: If an application needs to work with notations and unparsed (binary) entities, it must implement this interface to receive notification of the NOTATION and ENTITY declarations.

org.xml.sax.EntityResolver: If an application needs to redirect URIs in documents (or other types of custom handling), it must provide an implementation of this interface.

The main interface of SAX, org.xml.sax.ContentHandler, defines the following event handler methods to be implemented by applications:

- startDocument(): Called when parsing reaches the beginning of the XML document
- endDocument(): Called when parsing reaches the end of the XML document
- startElement(): Called when parsing reaches the beginning of an XML element
- endElement(): Called when parsing reaches the end of an XML element
- characters(): Called when parsing reaches the end of an character section
- ignorableWhitespace(): Called when parsing reaches any ignorable white spaces between elements

Of course, some of the event handlers will receive information parsed from the XML file as parameters. For example,

- startElement() passes all the attributes as an org.xml.sax.Attributes object.
- characters() passes all the characters of the parsed text as char[] object.

SAX SAMPLE PROGRAM

The SAX API (Simple API for XML) uses an event-based model and allows the processing of a source document as a stream of events. The events are fired while parsing as a continuous flow of callback method invocations. The events are nested in the same way as the document elements, therefore no intermediate document model is created. While the memory usage is low, the programming model can be complex, especially if the document structure doesn't faithfully match the application data structures. Because it generates a transient flow of events, the SAX API cannot be used when a document model has to be edited or processed several times.

The SAX API defines several interfaces (some of the interfaces from SAX 1.0 were renamed in SAX 2.0):

- `org.xml.sax.Parser` (XMLReader in SAX 2.0) interface for SAX parsers:
  - Parses an XML document
  - Allows an application to register

    - A document event handler
    - An error handler
    - A DTD handler
    - An entity resolver
- `org.xml.sax.DocumentHandler` (ContentHandler in SAX 2.0) interface to receive document events, the notification of
    - The start or end of a document
    - The start or end of an element
    - Character data
    - Ignorable whitespace in element content
    - A processing instruction
- `org.xml.sax.ErrorHandler` interface to receive SAX error events, the notification of
    - A recoverable error
    - A non-recoverable/fatal error
    - A warning
- `org.xml.sax.DTDHandler` interface to receive notification of basic DTD-related events, the notification of
    - A notation declaration event
    - An unparsed entity declaration event
- `org.xml.sax.EntityResolver` interface for resolving external entity references
- `org.xml.sax.HandlerBase` (DefaultHandler in SAX 2.0) default implementation of the four previous interfaces.

An application must provide at least a document (or content) handler in order to catch relevant events and process them.

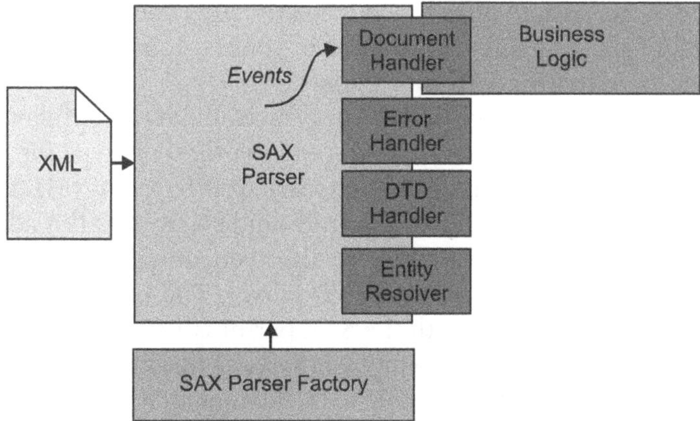

FIGURE 12.1 When using the SAX API, the bare minimum a developer has to do is to implement a DocumentHandler (ContentHandler in SAX 2.0) or subclass BaseHandler (DefaultHandler)

The sample program presented next implements the interface, HandlerBase, and the startElement callback method. A SAXParserFactory is used to create a new SAXParser. The custom implementation of the interface HandlerBase and the path of the XML source document to be processed is then passed to the parser. While parsing, the startElement method is called for every single start tag in the source document.

THREE STEPS TO SAX

Since SAX does not come with a default object model representation for the data in your XML document, the first thing you have to when using SAX is create your own custom Java object model for your data. This could be something as simple as creating an AddressBook class if your XML document is an address book. After your custom object model has been created to "hold" your data (inside your Java program), the next step is creating a SAX document handler to create instances of your custom object models from the information stored in the XML document. This "document handler" is a listener for the various events that are fired by the SAX parser based on the contents of your XML document. This is very similar to the AWT 1.1 Event Delegation Model, where UI components generate events based on user input and event listeners perform some useful function when these events are fired. Most of the work in using SAX is in creating this document handler. Once you have created the custom object model and the SAX document handler you can use the SAX parser to create instances of your custom object model based on the data stored in your XML documents.

This process is illustrated using an example in the following paragraphs. This example shows you how to perform these 3 steps for an AddressBook example. The example problem is that you have an XML document which contains your address book and you would like to view this address book using a Swing program and a Servlet. Also, you would like to use a SAX parser to do this instead of using a DOM parser. The first thing to do is create an object model and deal with the SAX parser issues before even thinking about the presentation layers (Swing and Servlet) for object model (AddressBook). Here is what the address book XML document looks like:

```
<?xml version = "1.0"?>
<addressbook>
<person>
<lastname>Idris</lastname>
<firstname>Nazmul</firstname>
<company>The Bean Factory, LLC.</company>
<email>xml@beanfactory.com</email>
</person>
</addressbook>
```

The three steps to using SAX in our programs are

- Create a custom object model (like Person and AddressBook classes)
- Create a SAX parser
- Create a DocumentHandler (to turn your XML document into instances of your custom object model)

Step 1: Create a custom object model

We have created a simple Java object model to represent the information in the address book XML document. We created 2 classes, an AddressBook class and a Person class. The object model is a simple mapping from the elements into classes. The following is a description of these classes.

The AddressBook class is a container of the Person objects. The AddressBook class is a simple adapter over the java.util.List interface. The AddressBook class has methods to allow you to add Person objects, get Person objects, and find out how many Person objects are in the AddressBook. The addressbook element maps to the AddressBook class.

The Person class simply holds 4 String objects: the last name, first name, email, and company name. This information is embedded within the <person> tag. The person element maps into the Person class. The firstname, lastname, company, and email elements map into the String class.

Here is a listing of the Person class:

```
public class Person{

// Data Members
String fname, lname, company, email;


// accessor methods
public String getCompany(){return company;}
public String getEmail(){return email;}
public String getFirstName(){return fname;}
public String getLastName(){return lname;}


// mutator methods
public void setLastName( String s ){lname = s;}
public void setFirstName( String s ){fname = s;}
public void setCompany( String s ){company = s;}
public void setEmail( String s ){email = s;}


// toXML() method
public String toXML(){
  StringBuffer sb = new StringBuffer();
  sb.append( "<PERSON>\n" );
  sb.append( "\t<LASTNAME>"+lname+"</LASTNAME>\n" );
  sb.append( "\t<FIRSTNAME>"+fname+"</FIRSTNAME>\n" );
  sb.append( "\t<COMPANY>"+company+"</COMPANY>\n" );
  sb.append( "\t<EMAIL>"+email+"</EMAIL>\n" );
  sb.append( "</PERSON>\n" );
```

```
  return sb.toString();
}}
```

Please note the toXML() method. This method returns a string that contains the XML representation of a Person object. This kind of method is not only very useful for debugging, but it can be used to save Person objects to an XML file (or other kind of XML persistence/storage engine). The AddressBook class also has an toXML() method, and that method uses the Person class's toXML() method, too.

Here is a listing of the AddressBook class:

```
public class AddressBook{

// Data Members
List persons = new java.util.ArrayList();


// mutator method
public void addPerson( Person p ){persons.add( p );}


// accessor methods
public int getSize(){ return persons.size();}
public Person getPerson( int i ){
return (Person)persons.get( i );}

// toXML method
public String toXML(){
  StringBuffer sb = new StringBuffer();
  sb.append( "<?xml version=\"1.0\"?>\n" );
  sb.append( "<ADDRESSBOOK>\n\n" );
  for(int i=0; i<persons.size(); i++) {
  sb.append( getPerson(i).toXML() );
  sb.append( "\n" );
}
sb.append( "</ADDRESSBOOK>" );
return sb.toString();
}}
```

As you can see, these are very simple classes. The interesting part (in this case) is Step 3.

Step 2: Creating a SAX parser

You have to create an XML document handler class for the parser (so that something useful gets done as the parser parses the XML document).

Here is code to create a SAX parser:

```
import java.net.*;
import java.io.*;
import org.xml.sax.*;

...

try{
  //create an InputSource from the XML document source
  InputStreamReader isr = new InputStreamReader(
    new URL("http://host/AddressBook.xml").openStream();
    //new FileReader( new File( "AddressBook.xml" ))
);

InputSource is = new InputSource( isr );

//create an documenthandler to create obj model
DocumentHandler handler = //new YourHandler();

//create a SAX parser using SAX interfaces and classes
String parserClassName = "com.sun.xml.parser.Parser";

org.xml.sax.Parser.parser = org.xml.sax.helpers.ParserFactory.
  makeParser( parserClassName );

//create document handler to do something useful
//with the XML document being parsed by the parser.
parser.setDocumentHandler( handler );

parser.parse( is );
}
catch(Throwable t){
    System.out.println( t );
    t.printStackTrace();
}
```

The code example above uses the Sun TR2 parser. The classes used from TR2 include the com.sun.xml.parser.Parser, which is used to create a non-validating SAX parser.

Step 3: Creating a DocumentHandler

The SAX parser that was created in Step 2 reads an XML document and fires events as it encounters open tags, close tags, CDATA, and #PCDATA sections. These events are fired as the SAX parser reads the XML document from top to bottom, a tag at a time. In order for the SAX parser to notify some object that these events are occurring, an interface called DocumentHandler is used (it's in the org.xml.sax package). There are 3 other interfaces that exist called EntityResolver, DTDHandler, and ErrorHandler. These 4 interfaces together include all the methods that correspond to all possible events that the SAX parser can fire (as its reading an XML document). The most frequently used interface is the DocumentHandler interface. You have to provide an implementation of at least the DocumentHandler interface to the SAX parser, which then will invoke the right methods in the right sequence on your DocumentHandler implementation class. As the SAX parser reads an XML document, events are fired, which are then translated into method calls on all the "registered document event listeners" (which is your DocumentHandler implementation class). So as these events are fired as the XML document is read, method calls are made on your Document Handler implementation class. This class must do something useful with these method calls and the sequence of the calls.

CREATING THE SAX PARSER THE SAMPLE FILE

This chapter demonstrates the construction of an application that uses SAX to tally the responses from a group of users asked to take a survey regarding their alien abduction experiences. The XML code for the survey form and resultant form are shown below.

```
<?xml version="1.0"?>
<surveys>
<response username="bob">
<question subject="appearance">A</question>
<question subject="communication">B</question>
<question subject="ship">A</question>
<question subject="inside">D</question>
<question subject="implant">B</question>
```

```
</response>
<response username="sue">
<question subject="appearance">C</question>
<question subject="communication">A</question>
<question subject="ship">A</question>
<question subject="inside">D</question>
<question subject="implant">A</question>
</response>
<response username="carol">
<question subject="appearance">A</question>
<question subject="communication">C</question>
<question subject="ship">A</question>
<question subject="inside">D</question>
<question subject="implant">C</question>
</response>
</surveys>
```

SAX INTERFACE JAVA EXAMPLE

SAXBrowser.java

Let's build a simple SAX based XML browser by implementing those event handler methods defined in the org.xml.sax.DocumentHandler interface:

```
/**
 * SAXBrowser.java
 import java.io.File;
 import java.io.IOException;
 import javax.xml.parsers.SAXParserFactory;
 import javax.xml.parsers.SAXParser;
 import javax.xml.parsers.ParserConfigurationException;
 import org.xml.sax.Attributes;
 import org.xml.sax.SAXException;
 import org.xml.sax.helpers.DefaultHandler;
 class SAXBrowser {
    public static void main(String[] args) {
     try {
       File x = new File(args[0]);
       SAXParserFactory f = SAXParserFactory.newInstance();
       SAXParser p = f.newSAXParser();
       DefaultHandler h = new MyContentHandler();
```

```
        p.parse(x,h);
    } catch (ParserConfigurationException e) {
      System.out.println(e.toString());
    } catch (SAXException e) {
      System.out.println(e.toString());
    } catch (IOException e) {
      System.out.println(e.toString());
    }
  }
  private static class MyContentHandler extends DefaultHandler {
   static String p = "_";
   public void startDocument() throws SAXException {
     System.out.println("Starting document...");
   }
   public void endDocument() throws SAXException {
     System.out.println("Ending document...");
   }
   public void startElement(String ns, String sName, String qName,
     Attributes attrs) throws SAXException {
     String eName = sName;
     if (sName.equals("")) eName = qName;
     System.out.println("e"+p+eName);
     if (attrs!=null) {
        for (int i=0; i<attrs.getLength(); i++) {
            String aName = attrs.getLocalName(i);
            if (aName.equals("")) aName = attrs.getQName(i);
            System.out.println("a"+p+" "+aName+"="
             +attrs.getValue(i));
        }
     }
     p = p + "_";
   }
   public void endElement(String ns, String sName, String qName)
     throws SAXException {
     p = p.replaceFirst("___ ", "_");
   }
   public void characters(char buf[], int offset, int len)
   throws SAXException {
   String s = new String(buf, offset, len);
   System.out.println("c"+p+s);
```

```
  }
  public void ignorableWhitespace(char buf[], int offset, int len)
    throws SAXException {
    String s = new String(buf, offset, len);
    System.out.println("i"+p+s);
   }
 }
}
```

Instead of implementing the ContentHandler interface directly, extended the DefaultHandler class, which implemented handling methods for all events (by doing nothing). In this way, we only need to override the handling methods that we are interested in.

The "_" character is used to indent sub-elements in nested elements.

Let's try this with hello.xml:

```
<?xml version="1.0"?>
<p>Hello world!</p>
Ran java SAXBrowser hello.xml, I got:
Starting document...
e_p
c_Hello world!
Ending document...
```

SAX PARSING PATTERN EXAMPLE

Now let's use another XML file, user.xml, with more elements to show the SAX parsing pattern:

```
<?xml version="1.0"?>
<user status="active">
 <!-- This is not a real user. -->
 <first_name>John</first_name>
 <last_name>Smith</last_name>
</user>
```

RUNNING java SAXBrowser user.xml:

```
Starting document...
e_user
a_ status=active
c__
c__
```

```
c__
c__
c__
c__
e__first_name
c__John
c__
c__
c__
e__last_name
c__Smith
c__
c__
```

Ending document...

The program still works. But why did the parser fire so many "characters()" events? It looks like the parser didn't group the space character, line feed, and cartridge return into a single char[] and fire one "characters()" event. It fired multiple events, one per character.

QUESTIONS FOR DISCUSSION

1. What is SAX?
2. How do you use XML namespaces with SAX 1.0?
3. How do you use XML namespaces with SAX 2.0?
4. What are the interfaces of SAX?
5. What is the difference between the SAX parser and DOM parser?
6. How do you define SAX in XML?
7. How is SAX different than DOM?
8. How do you define XMLA?

CHAPTER 13

XPATH

XPATH INTRODUCTION

XML was created to be a self-describing markup format. As XML matured, new XML-related creations were invented. XPath is a syntax for defining parts of an XML document.

Although you could create a nicely structured document with XML, there didn't seem to be an easy way to find information inside the document.

XML documents can be thought of as a tree structure, made up of parent, child, and sibling relationships. Because of this very logical layout of an XML document, it seems like there should be a standard way to find information.

XPath is a language that enables you to navigate and find data within your XML documents. Using XPath, you can select one or more nodes to retrieve the data they contain. XPath is used quite extensively with XSLT and is a major element in XSLT.

XPath uses path expressions to select nodes or node-sets in an XML document. These path expressions look very much like the expressions you see when you work with a traditional computer file system.

XPath is a technology that enables you to address parts of an XML document, such as a specific element or set of elements. XPath is implemented as a non-XML expression language, which makes it suitable for use in situations where XML markup isn't really applicable, such as within attribute values. Attribute values are simple text and therefore can't contain additional XML markup. So, although XPath expressions are used within XML markup, they don't directly use tags and attributes themselves. This makes XPath considerably different from its XSL counterparts (XSLT and XSL-FO) in that it isn't implemented as an XML language. XPath's departure from XML syntax also makes it both flexible and compact, which are important benefits when you consider that XPath is typically used in constrained situations, such as attribute values.

XPath is a very important XML technology that provides a flexible means of addressing XML document parts. Any time you need to reference a portion of an XML document, such as with XSLT, you ultimately must rely on XPath. The XPath language is not based upon XML, but it is somewhat familiar because it relies on a path notation that is commonly used in computer file systems. In fact, the name XPath stems from the fact that the path notation used to address XML documents is similar to path names used in file systems to describe the locations of files. Not surprisingly, the syntax used by XPath is extremely concise because it is designed for use in URIs and XML attribute values.

XPATH SYNTAX

XPath uses path expressions to select nodes or node sets in an XML document. The node is selected by following a path or steps.

THE XML EXAMPLE DOCUMENT

We use the following XML document in the examples below.

```
<?xml version="1.0" encoding="ISO-8859-1"?>
<bookstore>
<book>
  <title lang="eng">Children </title>
  <price>9.00</price>
</book>
<book>
  <title lang="eng">Learning XML</title>
  <price>39.00</price>
</book>
</bookstore>
```

Similar to other XML technologies, XPath operates under the notion that a document consists of a tree of nodes. XPath defines different types of nodes that are used to describe nodes that appear within a tree of XML content. There is always a single root node that serves as the root of an XPath tree, and that appears as the first node in the tree. Every element in a document has a corresponding element node that appears in the tree under the root node. Within an element node, there are other types of nodes that correspond to the element's content. Element nodes may have a unique identifier associated with them that is used to reference the node with XPath. Figure 13.1 shows the relationship between different kinds of nodes in an XPath tree.

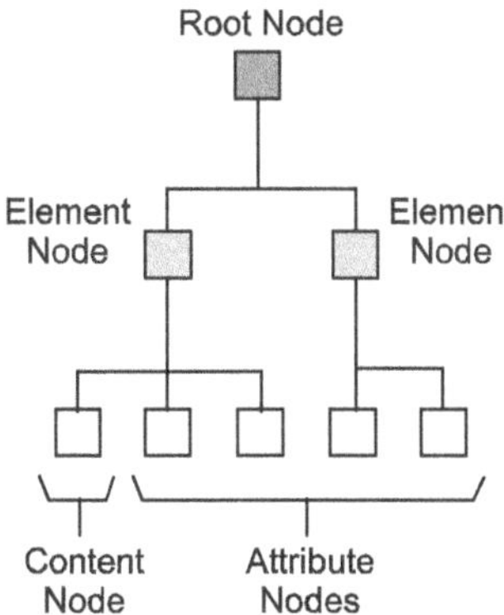

FIGURE 13.1 XPath is based upon the notion of an XML document consisting of a hierarchical tree of nodes

Nodes within an XML document can generally be broken down into element nodes, attribute nodes, and text nodes. Some nodes have names, which can consist of an optional namespace URI and a local name; a name that includes a namespace prefix is known as an *expanded name*. The following is an example of an expanded element name:

```
<xsl:value-of select="."/>
```

In this example, the local name is value-of and the namespace prefix is xsl. If you were to declare the XSL namespace as the default namespace for a document, you could get away with dropping the namespace prefix part of the expanded name, in which case the name becomes this:

```
<value-of select="."/>
```

If you declare more than one namespace in a document, you will have to use expanded names for at least some of the elements and attributes. It's generally a good idea to use them for all elements and attributes in this situation just to make the code clearer and eliminate the risk of name clashes.

Getting back to node types in XPath, following are the different types of nodes that can appear in an XPath tree:

- Root node
- Element nodes
- Text nodes
- Attribute nodes
- Namespace nodes
- Processing instruction nodes
- Comment nodes

You should have a pretty good feel for these node types, considering that you've learned enough about XML and have dealt with each type of node. The root node in XPath serves the same role as it does in the structure of a document: it serves as the root of an XPath tree and appears as the first node in the tree. Every element in a document has a corresponding element node that appears in the tree under the root node. Within an element node appear all of the other types of nodes that correspond to the element's content. Element nodes may have a unique identifier associated with them, which is useful when referencing the node with XPath.

The point of all this naming and referencing of nodes is to provide a means of traversing an XML document to arrive at a given node. You use XPath to build expressions, which are typically used in the context of some other operation, such as a document transformation. Upon being processed and evaluated, XPath expressions result in a data object of one of the following types:

- Node set A collection of nodes
- String A text string
- Boolean A true/false value
- Number A floating-point number

Similar to a database query, the data object resulting from an XPath expression can then be used as the basis for some other process, such as an XSLT transformation. For example, you might create an XPath expression that results in a node set that is transformed by an XSLT template. On the other hand, you can also use XPath with XLink, where a node result of an expression could form the basis of a linked document.

NAVIGATING A DOCUMENT WITH XPATH PATTERNS

XPath expressions are usually built out of patterns, which describe a branch of an XML tree. A pattern therefore is used to reference one or more hierarchical nodes in a document tree. Patterns can be constructed to perform relatively complex pattern matching tasks and ultimately form somewhat of a mini-query language that is used to query documents for specific nodes. Patterns can be used to isolate specific nodes or groups of nodes and can be specified as absolute or relative. An absolute pattern spells out the exact location of a node or node set, whereas a relative pattern identifies a node or node set relative to a certain context.

The next few sections examine the ways in which patterns are used to access nodes within XML documents. To better understand how patterns are used, it's worth seeing them in the context of a real XML document. The following program contains the code for the familiar training log sample document.

```
<?xml version="1.0"?>
<!DOCTYPE trainlog SYSTEM "etml.dtd">

<trainlog>
 <!This session was part of the marathon training group run. >
 <session date="11/19/05" type="running" heartrate="158">
  <duration units="minutes">45</duration>
  <distance units="miles">5.5</distance>
  <location>Warner Park</location>
  <comments>Mid-morning run, a little winded throughout.</comments>
 </session>

<session date="11/21/05" type="cycling" heartrate="153">
<duration units="hours">2.5</duration>
<distance units="miles">37.0</distance>
<location>Natchez Trace Parkway</location>
 <comments>Hilly ride, felt strong as an ox.</comments>
</session>

<session date="11/24/05" type="running" heartrate="156">
<duration units="hours">1.5</duration>
<distance units="miles">8.5</distance>
<location>Warner Park</location>
<comments>Afternoon run, felt reasonably strong.</comments>
</session>
</trainlog>
```

You may want to keep a bookmark around for this page, as several of the XPath examples throughout the next section rely on the training log sample code.

REFERENCING NODES

The most basic of all XPath patterns is the pattern that references the current node, which consists of a simple period:

```
.
```

If you're traversing a document tree, a period obtains the current node. The current node pattern is therefore a relative pattern because it makes sense only in the context of a tree of data. As a contrast to the current pattern, which is relative, consider the pattern that is used to select the root node of a document. This pattern is known as the root pattern and consists of a single forward slash:

```
/
```

If you were to use a single forward slash in an expression for the training log sample document, it would refer to the trainlog element (line 4) because this element is the root element of the document. Because the root pattern directly references a specific location in a document (the root node), it is considered an absolute pattern. The root pattern is extremely important to XPath because it represents the starting point of any document's node tree.

XPath relies on the hierarchical nature of XML documents to reference nodes. The relationship between nodes in this type of hierarchy is best described as a familial relationship, which means that nodes can be described as parent, child, or sibling nodes, depending upon the context of the tree. For example, the root node is the parent of all nodes. Nodes might be parents of some nodes and siblings of others. To reference child nodes using XPath, you use the name of the child node as the pattern. So, in the training log example, you can reference a session element (line 6, for example) as a child of the root node by simply specifying the name of the element: session. Of course, this assumes that the root node (line 4) is the current context for the pattern, in which case a relative child path is okay. If the root node isn't the current context, you should fully specify the child path as /session. Notice in this case that the root pattern is combined with a child pattern to create an absolute path.

If there are child nodes, there must also be parent nodes. To access a parent node, you must use two periods:

```
..
```

As an example, if the current context is one of the distance elements (line 15, for example) in the training log document, the .. parent pattern will reference the parent of the node, which is a session element (line 13). You can put patterns together to get more interesting results. For example, to address a sibling node, you must first go to the parent and then reference the sibling as a child. In other words, you use the parent pattern (..) followed by a forward slash (/) followed by the sibling node name, like this:

../duration

This pattern assumes that the context is one of the child elements of the session element (other than duration). Assuming this context, the ../duration pattern will reference the duration element (line 14) as a sibling node.

Thus far, we've focused on referencing individual nodes. However, it's also possible to select multiple nodes. For example, you can select all of the child nodes (descendants) of a given node using the double slash pattern:

//

As an example, if the context is one of the session elements in the training log document (line 20, for example), you can select all of its child nodes by using double slashes. This results in the duration (line 21), distance (line 22), location (line 23), and comments (line 24) elements being selected. Another way to select multiple nodes is to use the wildcard pattern, which is an asterisk:

*

The wildcard pattern selects all of the nodes in a given context. So, if the context was a session element and you used the pattern */distance, all of the distance elements in the document would be selected. This occurs because the wildcard pattern first results in all of the sibling session elements being selected, after which the selection is limited to the child distance elements.

To summarize, the following are the primary building blocks used to reference nodes in XPath:

- Current node.
- Root node/
- Parent node..
- Child nodeChild
- Sibling node/Sibling
- All child nodes//
- All nodes*

These pattern building blocks form the core of XPath, but they don't tell the whole story.

XPATH (XML PATH) LANGUAGE

XPath is an expression evaluation language to produce a value that represents the sub-structure of an XML document.

You can compare XPath with regular expression, which is an expression language used to produce a value that represents the sub-structure of a text string.

You can compare XPath with the DOS path naming convention, which is a simple expression language to produce a value that represents a sub-structure of a file system.

Writing an XPath expression involves following aspects:

- Data types, literals, and variables
- Evaluation context
- Operations
- Built-in functions

XPath is used currently in both XSLT and XPointer. Here are some examples of XPath expressions:

```
.            Represents the current node
img          Represents child elements named "img"
@color       Represents the attribute named "id"
/html        Represents the root element named "html"
p[1]         Represents the first occurrence of child "p" elements
p[@id=open] Represents child "p" elements with id="open" attribute
```

DATA TYPES, LITERALS, AND VARIABLES

This section provides a quick introduction of data types used in XPath: Boolean, Number, String, and Node Set.

XPath supports 4 data types:

- **Boolean:** A data type with two possible values: true and false
- **Number:** A data type representing floating-point numbers with double-precision defined by IEEE 754
- **String:** A data type representing sequences of characters from the same character used by XML
- **Node set:** A data type representing unordered collections of nodes defined by the Document Object Model (DOM)

Boolean: A data type with two possible values: true and false. Operations that produce boolean type of data objects are as follows:

```
= Equal to
!= Not equal to
< Less than
> Greater than
<= Less than or equal to
>= Greater than or equal to
or Logical or
and Logical and
```

Number: A data type representing floating-point numbers with double-precision defined by IEEE 754. Operations that produce numbers are as follows:

```
+ Addition
- Subtraction
* Multiplication
div Division
mod Remainder
```

String: A data type representing sequences of characters from the same character used by XML

Node set: A data type representing unordered collections of nodes defined by the Document Object Model (DOM)

XPATH OPERATORS

An XPath expression returns either a node-set, a string, a Boolean, or a number.

Table 13.1 shows a list of the operators that can be used in XPath expressions:

Table 13.1 List of the Operators used in XPath Expressions

<table>
<tr><th>Operator</th><th>Description</th><th>Example</th><th>Return value</th></tr>
<tr><td>|</td><td>Computes two node sets</td><td>//book | //cd</td><td>Returns a node set with all book and cd elements</td></tr>
<tr><td>+</td><td>Addition</td><td>6 + 4</td><td>10</td></tr>
<tr><td>-</td><td>Subtraction</td><td>6 – 4</td><td>2</td></tr>
</table>

(continued)

(continued)

Operator	Description	Example	Return value
*	Multiplication	6 * 4	24
div	Division	8 div 4	2
=	Equal	price=9.80	true if price is 9.80 false if price is 9.90
!=	Not equal	price!=9.80	true if price is 9.90 false if price is 9.80
<	Less than	price<9.80	true if price is 9.00 false if price is 9.80
<=	Less than or equal to	price<=9.80	true if price is 9.00 false if price is 9.90
>	Greater than	price>9.80	true if price is 9.90 false if price is 9.80
>=	Greater than or equal to	price>=9.80	true if price is 9.90 false if price is 9.70
or	or	price=9.80 or price=9.70	true if price is 9.80 false if price is 9.50
and	and	price>9.00 and price<9.90	true if price is 9.80 false if price is 8.50
mod	Modulus (division remainder)	5 mod 2	1

EVALUATION CONTEXT

XPath expressions are always evaluated with respect to a context, which consists of the following:

Context node: A node referring to the current node in the source XML structure

Context position: An integer indicating position of the context node in the current node set

Context size: An integer indicating the number of nodes in the current node set

Variable bindings: A collection of pairs of variable names and values

The context node is referring to the current node in the source XML structure, which is represented as a tree of different types of nodes according to the Document Object Model (DOM):

- **Root node:** A top and first node of the XML structure
- **Element node:** A node that has child nodes
- **Text node:** A node representing a unit of text in the content of a parent node
- **Attribute node:** A node representing an attribute
- **Namespace node:** A node representing a name declaration statement
- **Processing instruction node:** A node representing a processing instruction statement
- **Comment node:** A node representing a comment statement

BUILT-IN FUNCTIONS

XPath also supports built-in functions. Commonly used build-in functions are

- **boolean(number):** Returns true, if the number is not a zero
- **boolean(string):** Returns true, if the length of the string is great than zero
- **boolean(node_set):** Returns true, if the set is not empty
- **concat(string, string, ...):** Returns the concatenation of all given string objects
- **contains(string_1, string_2):** Returns true if the first string object contains the second string object
- **count(node_set):** Returns the number of nodes in the given node set object
- **last():** Returns the context size of the evaluation context
- **name():** Returns the qualified name of the context node
- **name(node_set):** Returns the qualified name of the first node in the given node set object
- **not(boolean):** Returns true, if the given boolean object is false
- **position():** Returns the context position of the evaluation context
- **string():** Returns the string value of the context node

- **string(boolean):** Returns true or false based on the given boolean object
- **string(number):** Returns the string presentation of the given number object
- **string(node_set):** Returns the string value of the first node in the given node set object

XPath Nodes

In XPath, there are seven kinds of nodes: element, attribute, text, namespace, processing-instruction, comment, and document nodes. XML documents are treated as trees of nodes. The topmost element of the tree is called the *root element*. Look at the following XML document:

```
<?xml version="1.0" encoding="ISO-8859-1"?>
<bookstore>
 <book>
  <title lang="en">Children</title>
  <author> Param Sen </author>
  <year>2019</year>
  <price>9.00</price>
 </book>
</bookstore>
```

Example of nodes in the XML document above:

```
<bookstore> (root element node)
<author> Param Sen </author> (element node)
lang="en" (attribute node)
```

USING XPATH FUNCTIONS

Before getting into the specifics of the XPath functions at your disposal, it's worth taking a look at their general use. The functions supported by XPath, which are available for use in creating XPath expressions, can be roughly divided along the lines of the data types on which they operate:

- Node functions
- String functions
- Boolean functions
- Number functions

NODE FUNCTIONS

Node functions are XPath functions that relate to the node tree. Although all of XPath technically relates to the node tree, node functions are very direct in that they allow you to ascertain the position of nodes in a node set, as well as how many nodes are in a set. The following are the most common XPath node functions:

- position() determines the numeric position of a node.
- last() determines the last node in a node set.
- count() determines the number of nodes in a node set.

Although these node functions might seem somewhat abstract, keep in mind that they can be used to carry out some interesting tasks when used in the context of a broader expression. For example, the following code shows how to use the count() function to calculate the total distance in the training log document for sessions whose distances are recorded in miles:

```
count(*/distance[@units='miles'])
```

The following is another example that shows how to reference a child node based solely upon its position within a document:

```
child::item[position()=3]
```

Assuming there are several child elements of the type item, this code references the third child item element of the current context. To reference the last child item, you use the last() function instead of an actual number, like this:

```
child::item[position()=last()]
```

STRING FUNCTIONS

XPath string functions are used to manipulate strings of text. With the string functions, you can concatenate strings, slice them up into substrings, and determine the length of them. The following are the most popular string functions in XPath:

- concat() concatenates two strings together.
- starts-with() determines if a string begins with another string.
- contains() determines if a string contains another string.
- substring-before() retrieves a substring that appears before another string.
- substring-after() retrieves a substring that appears after another string.

- substring() retrieves a substring of a specified length starting at an index within another string.
- string-length() determines the length of a string.

These XPath string functions can come in quite handy when building expressions, especially when you consider that XML content is always specified as raw text. In other words, it is possible to manipulate most XML content as a string, regardless of whether the underlying value of the content is numeric or some other data type. The following is an example that demonstrates how to extract the month of a training session from a date attribute in the training log document:

```
substring-after(/session[1]@date, "/")
```

In this example, the substring-after() function is called and passed the date attribute. Because a forward slash (/) is passed as the second argument to the function, it is used as the basis for finding the substring. If you look back at one of the date attributes in the document (line 6, for example), you'll notice that the month appears just after the first forward slash. As a comparison, you could extract the year as a substring by providing the same arguments but instead using the substring-before() function:

```
substring-before(/session[1]@date, '/')
```

Another use of the string functions is finding nodes that contain a particular substring. For example, if you wanted to analyze your training data and look for training sessions where you felt strong, you could use the contains() function to select session elements where the comments child element contains the word "strong:"

```
*/session[contains(comments, 'strong')]
```

In this example, the second and third session elements would be selected because they both contain the word "strong" in their comments child elements (lines 17 and 24).

BOOLEAN FUNCTIONS

Boolean functions are pretty simple in that they operate solely on Boolean (true/false) values. The following are the two primary Boolean functions that you may find useful in XPath expressions:

- not() negates a Boolean value.
- lang() determines if a certain language is being used.

The not() function is straightforward in that it simply reverses a Boolean value: true becomes false and false becomes true. The lang() function is a little more interesting because it actually queries a node to see what language it uses. As an example, many English-language XML documents set the xml:lang attribute to en in the root element. Although this value typically cascades down to all elements within the document, it's possible for a document to use multiple languages. The lang() function allows you to check the language setting for any node. The following is an example of how to use the not() and lang() functions to determine if the English language is not being used in a document:

```
not(lang("en"))
```

NUMBER FUNCTIONS

The XPath number functions should be somewhat familiar to you from when you created XSLT stylesheets that relied on the number functions. The following are the most commonly used number functions in XPath:

- ceiling() rounds up a decimal value to the nearest integer.
- floor() rounds down a decimal value to the nearest integer.
- round() rounds a decimal value to the nearest integer.
- sum() adds a set of numeric values.

The following is an example of how to use the sum() function to add up attribute values:

```
sum(cart/item/@price)
```

Of course, you can make nested calls to the XPath number functions. For example, you can round the result of the sum() function by using the round() function, like this:

```
round(sum(cart/item/@price))
```

THE ROLE OF XPATH

You may have noticed that we used the word "select" often in this chapter when explaining how an XPath expression effectively selects part of a document. However, this selection process doesn't take place within XPath alone. XPath is always used in the context of another technology such as XSLT,

XPointer, or XLink. The examples of XPath that you've seen in this lesson must therefore be used in conjunction with additional code. For example, the following code shows how one of the training log expressions from earlier in the chapter might be used in an XSLT stylesheet:

```
<xsl:value-of select="*/session[@type='running']" />
```

In this code, the XPath expression appears within the select attribute of the xsl: value-of element, which is responsible for inserting content from a source XML document into an output document during the transformation of the source document. The point is that the XSLT xsl:value-of element is what makes the XPath expression useful.

Similar to its role in XSLT, XPath serves as the addressing mechanism in XPointer. XPointer is used to address parts of XML documents and is used heavily in XLink. XPointer uses XPath to provide a means of navigating the tree of nodes that comprise an XML document. Sounds familiar, right? XPointer takes XPath a step further by defining a syntax for fragment identifiers, which are in turn used to specify parts of documents. In doing so, XPointer provides a high degree of control over the addressing of XML documents. When coupled with XLink, the control afforded by XPointer makes it possible to create interesting links between documents that simply aren't possible in HMTL, at least in theory.

USING XPATH IN XSLT TEMPLATES

XPath expressions can be used in XSLT templates to produce a set of nodes of the source XML document that can be matched or selected. For example,

```
<xsl:template match="LocationPathExpression">
<xsl:apply-templates select="LocationPathExpression"/>
<xsl:for-each select="LocationPathExpression"/>
```

XPath expressions can also be used in XSLT "value-of" elements to product a string output. For example,

```
<xsl:value-of select="StringExpression"/>
```

Note that in this case, the resulting value of data types, including node set, will be converted to a string.

Let's review a sample XML file, dictionary_xsl.xml:

```
<?xml version="1.0"?>
<?xml-stylesheet type="text/xsl" href="dictionary.xsl"?>
<dictionary>
<!— dictionary_xsl.xml
-->
  <word acronym="true">
  <name>XML</name>
  <definition referenece="Hero's Notes">eXtensible Markup
Language.</definition>
 <update date="2002-12-23"/>
 </word>
 <word symbol="true">
 <name><</name>
 <definition>Mathematical symbol representing the "less than" logical
operation, like: 1<2.</definition>
 <definition>Reserved symbol in XML representing the beginning of
tags, like: <![CDATA[<p>Hello world!</p>]]>
  </definition>
 </word>
 <word symbol="false" acronym="false">
 <name>extensible</name>
 <definition>Capable of being extended.</definition>
 </word>
</dictionary>
```

And apply the following XSL file:

```
<?xml version="1.0"?>
<xsl:stylesheet version="1.0"
 xmlns:xsl="http://www.w3.org/1999/XSL/Transform">
<!— dictionary.xsl, version 3.0
 -->
 <xsl:template match="/child::*">
 <pre>
d_<xsl:value-of select="name(self::node())"/>
 <xsl:for-each select="child::word">
w__<xsl:value-of select="name(self::node())"/>
 <xsl:apply-templates select="self::node()"/>
 </xsl:for-each>
 </pre>
 </xsl:template>
```

```
<xsl:template match="child::word">
<xsl:for-each select="attribute::*">
a___<xsl:value-of select="name(.)"/>=<xsl:value-of select="."/>
</xsl:for-each>
<xsl:for-each select="child::*">
e___<xsl:value-of select="name(self::node())"/>
<xsl:apply-templates select="self::node()"/>
</xsl:for-each>
</xsl:template>
<xsl:template match="child::name | child::definition | child::update">
<xsl:for-each select="attribute::*">
a____<xsl:value-of select="name(.)"/>=<xsl:value-of select="."/>
</xsl:for-each>
<xsl:for-each select="child::text()">
t____<xsl:value-of select="self::node()"/>
</xsl:for-each>
</xsl:template>
</xsl:stylesheet>
```

The following output:

```
d_dictionary
w__word
a___acronym=true
e___name
t____XML
e___definition
a____referenece=Herong's Notes
t____eXtensible Markup Language.
e___update
a____date=2002-12-23
w___word
a___symbol=true
e___name
t____<
e___definition
t___Mathematical symbol representing the "less than" logical operation, like:
1<2.
e___definition
t____Reserved symbol in XML representing the beginning of tags, like:
```

```
t____<p>Hello world!</p>
w__word
a___symbol=false
a___acronym=false
e___name
t____extensible
e___definition
t____Capable of being extended.
```

XPATH LOCATION PATH

XPath programming consists of writing expressions to select the node/s you need to work with. Often, you're selecting the data within the nodes, but you could also be applying some programming logic in order to modify the output of your XML document.

To select a node (or set of nodes) in XPath, you use a location path. A location path is used to specify the exact path to the node you need to select. It's a bit like using the HTML <img src=""> tag to specify the location of an image only XPath is more powerful.

LOCATION PATH EXAMPLE

For example, here's a simple XPath expression to select the "title" node, which is a child of the "rock" node, which in turn is a child of the "albums" node:

```
albums/rock/title
```

The above expression could be applied against the following XML document:

```
<albums>
  <rock>
   <title>Tool Box</title>
   <artist>Green Velly</artist>
  </rock>
  <blues>
   <title>Summer Occasion</title>
   <artist>Marris Mano</artist>
  </blues>
```

```
  <country>
   <title> Atlas </title>
   <artist>Romi</artist>
  </country>
</albums>
```

If we wanted to select the artist instead, we would use this location path:

```
albums/rock/artist
```

The above expression would select the artist node instead:

```
<albums>
 <rock>
  <title>Tool Box</title>
  <artist>Green Velly</artist>
 </rock>
 <blues>
  <title>Summer Occasion</title>
  <artist>Marris Mano</artist>
 </blues>
 <country>
  <title> Atlas </title>
  <artist>Romi</artist>
 </country>
</albums>
```

XPATH LOCATION STEP

A location path consists of one or more location steps. The location steps are separated by either one forward slash (/) or two forward slashes (//) depending on the node you're trying to select.

1. ***Absolute Location Path***

Your location path can be absolute or relative. If your location path starts with the root node or a forward slash (/), you are using an absolute location path and your location path begins from the root node.

2. ***Relative Location Path***

If your location path begins with the name of a descendant, you're using a relative location path. This node is referred to as the context node.

XPATH LOCATION PATH – ABSOLUTE

A location path specifies the path through the XML document's hierarchy that you'd like to work with.

Your location path can be absolute or relative. If your location path starts with the root node or a forward slash (/), you are using an absolute location path and your location path begins from the root node. If your location path begins with the name of a descendant, you're using a relative location path. This node is referred to as the context node.

EXAMPLE OF AN ABSOLUTE LOCATION PATH

Consider the following XML document:

```
<albums>
 <rock>
  <title>Tool Box</title>
  <artist>Green Velly</artist>
 </rock>
 <blues>
  <title>Summer Occasion</title>
  <artist>Marris Mano</artist>
 </blues>
 <country>
  <title> Atlas </title>
  <artist>Romi</artist>
 </country>
</albums>
```

If we wanted to select the "title" node of all albums, we could use the following (absolute) location paths:

```
albums/rock/title
albums/blues/title
albums/country/title
```

Here are the nodes that are selected using the above location path.

```
<albums>
 <rock>
  <title>Tool Box</title>
  <artist>Green Velly</artist>
```

```
  </rock>
  <blues>
   <title>Summer Occasion</title>
   <artist>Marris Mano</artist>
  </blues>
  <country>
   <title>Atlas</title>
   <artist>Romi</artist>
  </country>
</albums>
```

SELECTING NODES

XPath uses path expressions to select nodes in an XML document. The node is selected by following a path or steps. The most useful path expressions are listed in Table 13.2:

Table 13.2 Most Useful Path Expressions

Expression	Description
nodename	Selects all child nodes of the named node
/	Selects from the root node
//	Selects nodes in the document from the current node that match the selection no matter where they are
.	Selects the current node
..	Selects the parent of the current node
@	Selects attributes

In Table 13.3, we have listed some path expressions and the result of the expressions.

Table 13.3 Path Expression Examples

Path Expression	Result
bookstore	Selects all the child nodes of the bookstore element
/bookstore	Selects the root element bookstore Note: If the path starts with a slash (/), it always represents an absolute path to an element

(continued)

Path Expression	Result
bookstore/book	Selects all book elements that are children of bookstore
//book	Selects all book elements no matter where they are in the document
bookstore//book	Selects all book elements that are descendant of the bookstore element, no matter where they are under the bookstore element
//@lang	Selects all attributes that are named lang

PREDICATES

Predicates are used to find a specific node or a node that contains a specific value.

Predicates are always embedded in square brackets. In Table 13.4, we have listed some path expressions with predicates and the result of the expressions.

Table 13.4 Path Expression Examples with Predicates

Path Expression	Result
/bookstore/book[1]	Selects the first book element that is the child of the bookstore element. Note: IE5 and later implemented that [0] should be the first node, but according to the W3C standard, it should have been [1]
/bookstore/book[last()]	Selects the last book element that is the child of the bookstore element
/bookstore/book[last()-1]	Selects the last but one book element that is the child of the bookstore element
/bookstore/book[position()<3]	Selects the first two book elements that are children of the bookstore element
//title[@lang]	Selects all the title elements that have an attribute named lang
//title[@lang='eng']	Selects all the title elements that have an attribute named lang with a value of eng

(continued)

(continued)

Path Expression	Result
/bookstore/book[price>35.00]	Selects all the book elements of the bookstore element that have a price element with a value greater than 35.00
/bookstore/book[price>35.00]/title	Selects all the title elements of the book elements of the bookstore element that have a price element with a value greater than 35.00

SELECTING UNKNOWN NODES

XPath wildcards can be used to select unknown XML elements.

Table 13.5 XPath Wildcards

Wildcard	Description
*	Matches any element node
@*	Matches any attribute node
node()	Matches any node of any kind

In the following table, we have listed some path expressions and the result of the expressions.

Path Expression	Result
/bookstore/*	Selects all the child nodes of the bookstore element
//*	Selects all elements in the document
//title[@*]	Selects all title elements which have any attribute

SELECTING SEVERAL PATHS

By using the | operator in an XPath expression, you can select several paths.

In Table 13.6, we have listed some path expressions and the result of the expressions.

Table 13.6 Path Expressions and the Result of the Expressions

Path Expression	Result
//book/title | //book/price	Selects all the title AND price elements of all book elements
//title | //price	Selects all the title AND price elements in the document
/bookstore/book/title | //price	Selects all the title elements of the book element of the bookstore element AND all the price elements in the document

THE ROOT NODE

If we wanted to select the root node, we could use either the node's name or a forward slash. Both of these options are absolute location paths and select the root node.

Option 1—use the root node's name:albums
Option 2—use a forward slash:/

XPATH LOCATION PATH – RELATIVE

A relative location path is one where the path starts from the node of your choosing—it doesn't need to start from the root node. This can reduce the amount of code you need to write—especially if you need to select many nodes that share the same name.

EXAMPLE OF A RELATIVE LOCATION PATH

Consider the following XML document:

```
<albums>
 <rock>
  <title>Tool Box</title>
  <artist>Green Velly</artist>
 </rock>
```

```
<blues>
 <title>Summer Occasion</title>
 <artist>Marris Mano</artist>
</blues>
<country>
 <title> Atlas </title>
 <artist>Romi</artist>
</country>
</albums>
```

If we wanted to select the "title" node of all albums, we could use the following (relative) location:path:title.

Result

This single line of code has exactly the same result as the example in the previous lesson. The only difference is that, in the previous lesson, we needed 3 lines of code to provide the same result.

This line of code is selecting all title nodes within our XML document. We don't need to provide the full path—just the name of the node we need to work with. This makes our life easier and keeps our code nice and clean.

```
<albums>
 <rock>
  <title>Tool Box</title>
  <artist>Green Velly</artist>
 </rock>
 <blues>
  <title>Summer Occasion</title>
  <artist>Marris Mano</artist>
 </blues>
 <country>
  <title> Atlas </title>
  <artist>Romi</artist>
 </country>
</albums>
```

CHILDREN

We can also select a node's children using relative location paths.

Example 1: Select the two children of the "rock" node ("title" and "artist"). The context node is "rock," because that's where our relative path starts:

```
rock/title
rock/artist
```

Example 2: Using a wildcard to select all children of the "rock" node. This (single line of code) has the same result as the above two lines of code. Further, if another node was added to the XML document under the "rock" node, it would be automatically included using the wildcard:

```
rock/*
```

THE WILDCARD

The "wildcard" is represented by the asterisk (*). The wildcard represents any node that would be located where the wildcard is positioned. Therefore, using our example, it is representing any node that comes under the "rock" node.

Wildcards don't have to appear at the end of a location path—they can also appear in the middle of a location path. We aren't limited to just one either—we could use as many as we like within a location path.

XPATH ATTRIBUTES

To select an attribute using XPath, you prefix the attribute's name with a @ symbol.

Example 1

Consider the following XML document. Note that the "artist" node now has an attribute called "status:"

```
<albums>
 <rock>
  <title>Tool Box</title>
  <artist status="active">Green Velly</artist>
 </rock>
 <blues>
  <title>Summer Occasion</title>
  <artist status="active">Marris Mano</artist>
```

```
 </blues>
 <country>
  <title>Atlas </title>
  <artist status="disbanded">Romi</artist>
 </country>
</albums>
```

If we wanted to select the "status" attribute of the "artist" node under the "rock" node, we could use the following expression:

```
albums/rock/artist/@status
```

Example 2

Attributes, just like any other node, can be the subject of a conditional statement. For example, imagine we're using XSLT to transform our XML document, and we want to select all "artist" nodes where the "status" attribute is set to "active." We could use the XSL "if " element to test the value.

Here's what we would write:

```
<xsl:if test="@status ='active'">
 (content goes here)
</xsl:if>
```

XPATH – EXPRESSIONS

XPath can locate any type of information in an XML document with one line of code. These one liners are referred to as "expressions," and every piece of XPath that you write will be an expression.

An XPath expression is exactly that: it's a line of code that we use to get information from our XML document.

XPATH—OUR SAMPLE XML FILE

We have slightly modified our lemonade XML document to make it more interesting. Our new XML document is lemonade2.xml, and it has new attributes and elements added to it.

XML Code, lemonade2.xml:

```
<inventory>
      <drink>
           <lemonade supplier="mother" id="1">
                  <price>$2.50</price>
                  <amount>20</amount>
           </lemonade>
           <pop supplier="store" id="2">
                  <price>$1.50</price>
                  <amount>10</amount>
           </pop>
      </drink>
      <snack>
           <chips supplier="store" id="3">
                  <price>$4.50</price>
                  <amount>60</amount>
                  <calories>180</calories>
           </chips>
      </snack>
</inventory>
```

A SIMPLE XPATH EXPRESSION

An XPath expression describes the location of an element or attribute in our XML document. By starting at the root element, we can select any element in the document by carefully creating a chain of children elements. Each element is separated by a slash "/ ".

QUESTIONS FOR DISCUSSION

1. What is XPath?
2. What is New in XPath 2.0?
3. What is XLink?
4. What is XLL?

5. What is server-side XPointer?
6. What is a URL path?
7. What are non-XML resources?
8. How do we configure an XPointer processor?
9. Give some examples of XML DTDs or schemas.
10. What is SOAP and how does it relate to XML?
11. What is a Web application?
12. Write about XPath 2.0.

CHAPTER 14

XLINK, XQUERY, AND XPOINTER

INTRODUCTION TO XQUERY

XQuery for XML is like SQL for databases. XQuery is the language for querying XML data only. XQuery is to XML what SQL is to database tables. XQuery is designed to query XML data—not just XML files, but anything that can appear as XML, including databases. XQuery is supported by all the major database engines (Oracle, IBM, and Microsoft). XQuery is built on XPath expressions. XQuery is a language for finding and extracting the elements and attributes from XML documents.

XQUERY EXAMPLE

We will use the following XML document in the example below.

The XML Example Document

```
"bookdetails.xml":
<?xml version="1.0" encoding="ISO-8859-1"?>
<bookstore>
<book category="COOKING">
<title lang="en">Pizza & Pasta</title>
<author>Bill Smith</author>
<year>2019</year>
```

```
<price>30.00</price>
</book>
<book category="CHILDREN">
<title lang="en">The Internet</title>
<author>S. Banzal</author>
<year>2019</year>
<price>49.00</price>
</book>
<book category="WEB">
<title lang="en">MYSQL Queries</title>
<author>S. Jain</author>
<author>P. Agrawal</author>
<author>K. Rai</author>
<author>R. Ram</author>
<author>Vivek Banzal</author>
<year>2018</year>
<price>65.00</price>
</book>
<book category="WEB">
<title lang="en">Learning XML</title>
<author>Erik T. Ray</author>
<year>2019</year>
<price>79.00</price>
</book>
</bookstore>
```

Functions

XQuery uses functions to extract the data from XML documents.

The doc() function is basically used to open the "bookdetails.xml" file:

```
doc("bookdetails.xml")
```

Path Expressions

XQuery uses path expressions to navigate through elements in the XML document. The following path expression is used to select all the title elements in the "bookdetails.xml" file:

```
doc("bookdetails.xml")/bookstore/book/title
```

(/bookstore selects the bookstore element, /book selects all the book elements under the bookstore element, and /title selects all the title element under each book element).

The XQuery code above will extract the following result:

```
<title lang="en">Pizza & Pasta</title>
<title lang="en">The Internet</title>
<title lang="en">MYSQL Queries</title>
<title lang="en">Learning XML</title>
```

Predicates

XQuery uses predicates to limit the extracted data from the XML documents.

The following predicate is used as to select all the book elements under the bookstore element that have a price element with a value that is less than 30:

```
doc("bookdetails.xml")/bookstore/book[price<30]
```

The XQuery above will extract the following result:

```
<book category="CHILDREN">
<title lang="en">The Internet</title>
<author>S. Banzal</author>
<year>2011</year>
<price>200.00</price>
</book>
```

XQuery FLWOR Expressions

We will use the "booksdetail.xml" document in the example below.

FLWOR is an acronym for the "For, Let, Where, Order by, Return".

How to Select Nodes From "books.xml"

With FLWOR

Look at the path expression given below:

```
doc("bookdetails.xml")/bookstore/book[price>30]/title
```

The expression above will select all the title elements under the book elements that are under the bookstore element that have a price element with a value that is higher than 30. The following FLWOR expression selects exactly the same as the path expression above:

```
for $x in doc("bookdetails.xml")/bookstore/book
where $x/price>30
return $x/title
```

The result is

```
<title lang="en">MYSQL Queries</title>
<title lang="en">Learning XML</title>
```

With FLWOR, you can sort the result like this:

```
for $x in doc("bookdetails.xml")/bookstore/book
where $x/price>30
order by $x/title
return $x/title
```

The for clause is used to select all book elements under the bookstore element into a variable called $x.

The where clause selects only the book elements with a price element with a value greater than 30.

The order by clause defines the sort-order.

The return clause specifies what should be returned. Here, it returns the title elements.

The result of the XQuery expression above is as follows:

```
<title lang="en">Learning XML</title>
<title lang="en">MYSQL Queries</title>
```

XQuery FLWOR +HTML

Look at the XQuery FLWOR expression given below:

```
for $x in doc("bookdetails.xml")/bookstore/book/title
order by $x
return $x
```

The expression above selects all the title elements under the book elements that are under the bookstore element and returns the title elements in the alphabetical order. Now we want to list all the book-titles in our bookstore element in an HTML list. So we add <ul> and <li> tags to the FLWOR expression:

```
<ul>
{
for $x in doc("bookdetails.xml")/bookstore/book/title
order by $x
return
<li>{$x}</li>
}
</ul>
```

The result of the above code:

```
<ul>
<li><title lang="en">Pizza & Pasta</title></li>
<li><title lang="en">The Internet</title></li>
<li><title lang="en">Learning XML</title></li>
<li><title lang="en">MYSQL Queries</title></li>
</ul>
```

Now we want to eliminate the title element, and show only the data inside the title elements:

```
<ul>
{
for $x in doc("books.xml")/bookstore/book/title
order by $x
return <li>{data($x)}</li>
}
</ul>
```

The result will be in the form of an HTML list:

```
<ul>
<li>Pizza & Pasta</li>
<li>The Internet</li>
<li>Learning XML</li>
<li>MYSQL Queries</li>
</ul>
```

XQuery Terms

In XQuery, there are seven kinds of nodes: element, attribute, text, namespace, processing-instruction, comment, and document nodes.

Nodes

XML documents are treated as tree of nodes. The root of the tree is called the document node or root node.

Look at the XML document given below:

```
<?xml version="1.0" encoding="ISO-8859-1"?>
<bookstore>
<book>
<title lang="en">The Internet</title>
```

```
<author>S. Banzal</author>
<year>2011</year>
<price>200.00</price>
</book>
```

Example of nodes in the XML document above:

```
<bookstore> (document node)
<author>S. Banzal</author> (element node)
lang="en" (attribute node)
```

Atomic Values

Atomic values are nodes with no parent or children. Examples of the atomic values are as follows:

```
S. Banzal
"en"
```

Items

Items are the atomic values or nodes.

Relationship of the Nodes

Parent

Each element and attribute has one parent only. In the example given below, the book element is the parent of the title, author, year, and price:

```
<book>
<title>The Internet</title>
<author>S. Banzal</author>
<year>2011</year>
<price>200.00</price>
</book>
```

Children

Element nodes may have zero, one or more than one children. In the example given title, author, year, and price elements are all children of the book element:

```
<book>
<title>The Internet</title>
<author>S. Banzal</author>
<year>2011</year>
```

```
<price>200.00</price>
</book>
```

Siblings

Nodes that have the same parent is called siblings. In the example given below; the title, author, year, and price elements are all siblings:

```
<book>
<title>The Internet</title>
<author>S. Banzal</author>
<year>2011</year>
<price>200.00</price>
</book>
```

Ancestors

A node's parent and parent's parent are called ancesters. In the example that follows the ancestors of the title element are the book element and the bookstore element:

```
<bookstore>
<book>
<title>The Internet</title>
<author>S. Banzal</author>
<year>2011</year>
<price>200.00</price>
</book>
<bookstore>
```

Descendants

A node's children and children's children are called descendants. In the example given below; descendants of the bookstore element are the book, title, author, year, and price elements:

```
<bookstore>
<book>
<title>The Internet</title>
<author>S. Banzal</author>
<year>2011</year>
<price>200.00</price>
</book>
<bookstore>
```

XQUERY SYNTAX

XQuery is case-sensitive and XQuery elements, attributes, and variables must have valid XML names.

XQUERY BASIC SYNTAX RULES

Some basic syntax rules are as follows:

- XQuery is case-sensitive.
- XQuery elements, attributes, and variables must have valid XML names.
- An XQuery string value can be in single or double quotes.
- An XQuery variable is defined with a $ sign followed by a name, e.g., $bookstore.
- XQuery comments are always delimited by (: and :), e.g., (: XQuery Comment :).

XQuery Conditional Expressions

"If-Then-Else" expressions are allowed in XQuery.

```
for $x in doc("books.xml")/bookstore/book
return if ($x/@category="CHILDREN")
then <child>{data($x/title)}</child>
else <adult>{data($x/title)}</adult>
```

Note that on the "if-then-else" syntax, parentheses around the if expression are always required. For the else expression, it is required, but it can be just else (). The result of the example above

```
<adult>Pizza & Pasta</adult>
<child>The Internet</child>
<adult>Learning XML</adult>
<adult>MYSQL Queries</adult>
```

XQuery Comparisons

There are two ways of comparing values in XQuery.

1. General comparisons: =, !=, >, >=, <, <=
2. Value comparisons: eq, ne, gt, ge, lt, le

The differences between the two comparison methods are given below.

```
$bookstore//book/@q>10
```

The expression above returns true if any q attributes have values greater than 10.

```
$bookstore//book/@q gt 10
```

The expression above returns true if there is only one q attribute returned by the expression, and its value is greater than 10. If more than one q is returned, an error occurs.

XQuery Adding Elements and Attributes to the Result

We will use the "bookdetails.xml" document in the next example below.

As we have seen in a previous chapter, we may include element and attribute from the input document ("bookdetails.xml") in the result:

```
for $x in doc("bookdetails.xml")/bookstore/book/title
order by $x
return $x
```

The XQuery expression above will include both the title elements and the lang attribute in the result:

```
<title lang="en">Pizza & Pasta</title>
<title lang="en">The Internet</title>
<title lang="en">Learning XML</title>
<title lang="en">MYSQL Queries</title>
```

The XQuery expression above return the title elements the exact same way as they are described in the input document. We now want to add our own element and attribute to the result.

Add HTML Elements and Text

```
<html>
<body>
<h1>Bookstore</h1>
<ul>
{
for $x in doc("booksdetail.xml")/bookstore/book
order by $x/title
return <li>{data($x/title)}. Category: {data($x/@category)}</li>
```

```
}
</ul>
</body>
</html>
```

The XQuery expression above will generate the following output:

```
<html>
<body>
<h1>Bookstore</h1>
<ul>
<li>Pizza & Pasta. Category: COOKING</li>
<li>The Internet. Category: CHILDREN</li>
<li>Learning XML. Category: WEB</li>
<li>MYSQL Queries. Category: WEB</li>
</ul>
</body>
</html>
```

Add Attributes to HTML Elements

Next, we want to use the category attribute as a class attribute in to the HTML list:

```
<html>
<body>
<h1>Bookstore</h1>
<ul>
{
for $x in doc("bookdetails.xml")/bookstore/book
order by $x/title
return <li class="{data($x/@category)}">{data($x/title)}</li>
}
</ul>
</body>
</html>
```

The XQuery expression above generates the following output:

```
<html>
<body>
<h1>Bookstore</h1>
<ul>
```

```
<li class="COOKING">Pizza & Pasta</li>
<li class="CHILDREN">The Internet</li>
<li class="WEB">Learning XML</li>
<li class="WEB">MYSQL Queries</li>
</ul>
</body>
</html>
```

XQUERY SELECTING AND FILTERING ELEMENTS

Selecting and Filtering Elements

We select and filter elements with either a FLWOR expression or with a Path expression.

for $x in doc("bookdetails.xml")/bookstore/book where $x/price>30 order by $x/title return $x/title

for—(optional) binds the variable to each item returned by the in expression

let—optional

where—(optional) specify a criteria

order by—(optional) specify the sort-order of the result

return—specify what to return in the result

The for clause binds a variable to each item returned by the expression. The for clause results in iteration. There may be multiple for clauses in the same FLWOR expression.

To loop a specific number of times in a for clause, you may have to use the to keyword:

```
for $x in (1 to 5)
return <test>{$x}</test>
```

Result

```
<test>1</test>
<test>2</test>
<test>3</test>
<test>4</test>
<test>5</test>
```

The at keyword can be used to count the number of iterations:

```
for $x at $i in doc("bookdetails.xml")/bookstore/book/title
return <book>{$i}. {data($x)}</book>
```

Result

```
<book>1. Pizza & Pasta</book>
<book>2. The Internet</book>
<book>3. MYSQL Queries</book>
<book>4. Learning XML</book>
```

You can use more than one in expression in the for clause. Use a comma to separate the parts of the expression:

```
for $x in (10,20), $y in (100,200)
return <test>x={$x} and y={$y}</test>
```

Result

```
<test>x=10 and y=100</test>
<test>x=10 and y=200</test>
<test>x=20 and y=100</test>
<test>x=20 and y=200</test>
```

The Let Clause

The let clause allows variable assignments. The let clause does not result in an iteration.

```
let $x := (1 to 5)
return <test>{$x}</test>
```

Result

```
<test>1 2 3 4 5</test>
```

The Where Clause

The where clause is used to specify one or more criteria for the particular result:

```
where $x/price>30 and $x/price<100
```

The Order by Clause

The order by clause is used to specify the sort order of the results. Here, we want to order the result by the category and title:

```
for $x in doc("bookdetails.xml")/bookstore/book
order by $x/@category, $x/title
return $x/title
```

Result

```
<title lang="en">The Internet</title>
<title lang="en">Pizza & Pasta</title>
<title lang="en">Learning XML</title>
<title lang="en">MYSQL Queries</title>
```

The Return Clause

The return clause specifies what is to be returned.

```
for $x in doc("bookdetails.xml")/bookstore/book return $x/title
```

Result

```
<title lang="en">Pizza & Pasta</title>
<title lang="en">The Internet</title>
<title lang="en">MYSQL Queries</title>
<title lang="en">Learning XML</title>
```

XQUERY FUNCTIONS

XQuery includes over 100 built-in functions. There are functions for string values, numeric values, date and time comparison, node and QName manipulation, sequence manipulation, Boolean values, and many more. You can also define your own function in XQuery.

Examples of Function Calls

A call to the function can appear where an expression may appear. Look at the examples below:

Example 1: In an element

```
<name>{uppercase($booktitle)}</name>
```

Example 2: In the predicate of a path expression

```
doc("bookdetails.xml")/bookstore/book[substring(title,1,5)='Harry']
```

Example 3: In the let clause

```
let $name := (substring($booktitle,1,4))
```

XQUERY USER-DEFINED FUNCTIONS

If you cannot find the XQuery function you need, you can write your own functions. User-defined functions are always defined in the query or in a separate library.

Syntax

```
declare function prefix:function_name($parameter AS datatype)
AS returnDatatype
{
(: ...function code here... :)
};
```

Note that on user-defined functions,

- The user always declares the function's keyword.
- The name of the function must have a prefix.
- The data types of the parameters are mostly the same as the data types defined in the XML schemas
- The body of the function must be surrounded by curly braces only

Example of a User-defined Function Declared in the Query

```
declare function local:minPrice(
$price as xs:decimal?,
$discount as xs:decimal?)
AS xs:decimal?
{
let $disc := ($price * $discount) div 100
return ($price - $disc)
};
(: Below is an example of how to call the function above :)
<minPrice>{local:minPrice($book/price, $book/discount)}</minPrice>
```

XLINK AND XPOINTER INTRODUCTION

XLink is short for XML Linking Language. XLink defines a standard way of creating hyperlinks in XML documents. XLink is used to create hyperlinks in XML documents. With XLink, the links can be defined outside the linked files.

XPointer allows the hyperlinks to point to more specific parts (fragments) in the XML document.

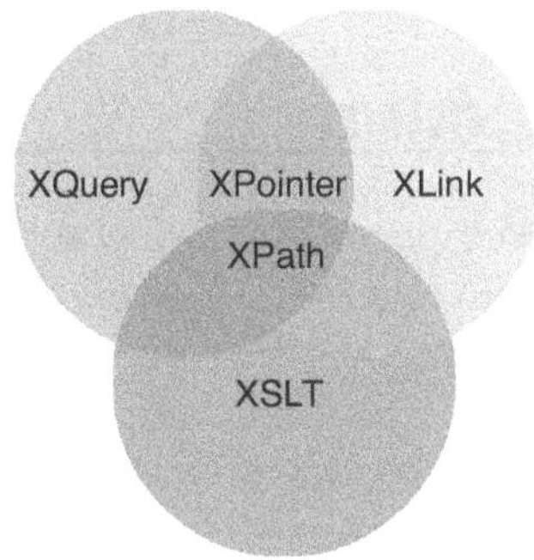

FIGURE 14.1 Relationship between XLink and XPointer

XLINK AND XPOINTER SYNTAX

In HTML, the <a> element defines a hyperlink. However, this is not how it works with XML. In XML documents, you can use whatever element names you want; therefore, it is impossible for browsers to predict what hyperlink elements will be called in XML documents.

The solution for creating links in XML documents is to put a marker on elements that should act as hyperlinks.

Below is a simple example of how to use XLink to create links in an XML document:

```
<?xml version="1.0"?>
<homepages xmlns:xlink="http://www.w3.org/1999/xlink">
<homepage xlink:type="simple"
xlink:href="http://www.abc.com">Visit Abc</homepage>
<homepage xlink:type="simple"
xlink:href="http://www.w3.org">Visit W3C</homepage>
</homepages>
```

To get access to the XLink attributes and features, we must declare the XLink namespace at the top of the document. The XLink namespace is *"http://www.w3.org/1999/xlink"*.

The xlink:type and the xlink:href attributes in the <homepage> elements define that the type and href attributes come from the xlink namespace. The xlink:type="simple" creates a simple, two-ended link (means "click from here to go there"). We will look at multi-ended (multidirectional) links later.

HTML, XML, AND LINKING

Similar to HTML Web pages, XML documents can also benefit greatly from links that connect them together. Knowing this, the architects of XML created a linking mechanism for XML that provides support for traditional one-way links, such as those you may be familiar with in HTML, along with more advanced links, such as two-way links. Links in XML considerably more powerful than HTML links, as you will learn in a moment when you begin exploring XLink and XPointer. Before getting into that, however, it's worth taking a moment to assess the role of links in HTML.

HTML links (hyperlinks) are based on the concept of connecting one resource to another resource source linked to a target. The source of an HTML link is typically displayed on a Web page (via text or an image) so as to call out the fact that it links to another resource. Text links are typically displayed with an underline, and the mouse pointer usually changes when the user drags it over a link source. Traversing a link in HTML typically involves clicking the source resource, which results in the Web browser navigating to the target resource. This navigation can occur in the same browser window, in which case the target resource replaces the current page or in a new browser window.

The important thing to understand about HTML links is that although they involve two resources, they always link in one direction. In other words, one side of the link is always the source and the other side is always the target, which means you can follow a link only one way. You might think that the Back button in a Web browser allows HTML links to serve as two-way links, but the Back button has nothing to do with HTML. The Back button in a Web browser is a browser feature that involves keeping a running list of Web pages so that the user can move back through them. There is nothing inherent in HTML links that supports backing up from the target of a link to the source; the target of a link knows nothing about its source. HTML links are somewhat limited in that they can link only in one direction.

If your only exposure to document linking is HTML, you probably regard link resources as existing completely separate of one another, at least in terms of how they are displayed in a Web browser. XML links shatter this notion by allowing you to use links to embed resources within other resources. In other words, the content of a target resource can be inserted in place of the link in a source document. Granted, images are handled much like this in HTML already, but XML links offer the possibility of embedding virtually any kind of data in a document, not just an external image. Traversing embedded links in this manner ultimately results in compound documents that are built out of other resources, which has some interesting implications for the Web. For example, you could build a news Web page out of paragraphs of text that are dynamically pulled from other documents around the Web via links.

Speaking of link traversal, HTML links are limited in that the user must trigger their traversal. For example, the only way to invoke a link on a Web page is to click the linked text or image, as shown in Figure 14.2.

In order to traverse an HTML link, the user must click on linked text or a linked image, which points to another document or resource.

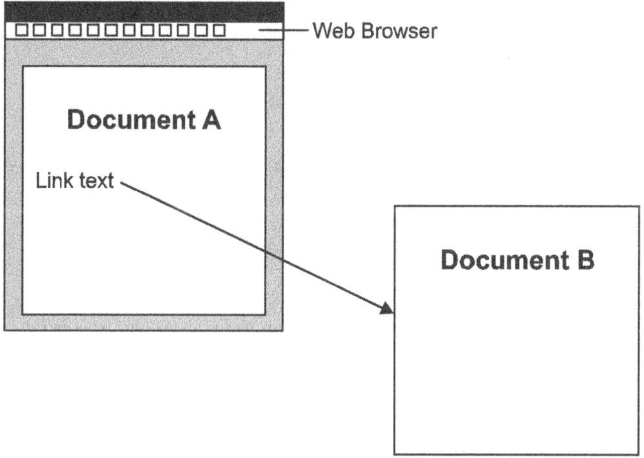

FIGURE 14.2 Document linking in HTML

You may be wondering why it would be desirable to have it any other way. Well, consider the situation where a linked resource is to be embedded directly in a document to form a compound document. You might want the embedding to take place immediately upon opening the document, in which case the user would have nothing to do with the link being invoked. In this sense, the link is serving as a kind of connective tissue for components of a compound Web document (see Figure 14.3), which is far beyond the role of links in HTML. Again, images already work like this in HTML via the img tag, but XML links open the door for many other possibilities with flexible linking.

XML links are flexible enough to allow you to construct compound documents by pulling content together from other documents.

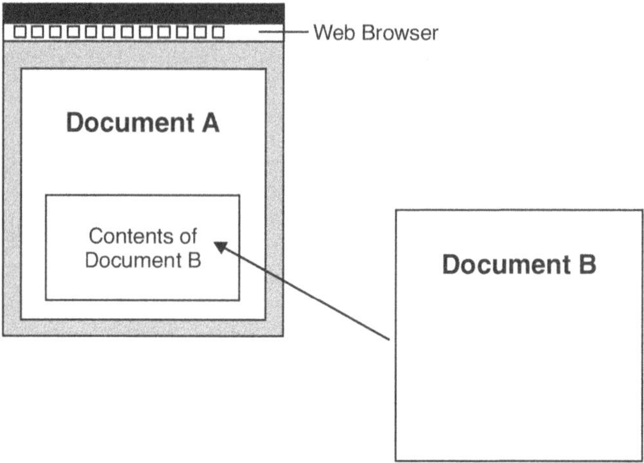

FIGURE 14.3 Document linking in XML

XML links, which are made possible by the XLink technology, are much more abstract than HTML links, and therefore can be used to serve more purposes than just providing users a way of moving from one Web page to the next.

Yet another facet of XLink is its support for creating links that reside outside of the documents they link. In other words, you can create a link in one document that connects two resources contained in other documents (see Figure 14.4). This can be particularly useful when you don't have the capability of editing the source and target documents. These kinds of links are known as out-of-line links and will probably foster the creation of link repositories. A link repository is a database of links that describe useful connections between resources on the Web.

XML links allow you to do interesting things, such as referencing multiple documents from a link within another document.

One example of a link repository that could be built using XLink is an intricately cross-referenced legal database, where court cases are linked in such a way that a researcher in a law office could quickly find and verify precedents and track similar cases. Though it's certainly possible to create such a database and incorporate it into HTML Web pages, it is cumbersome. XLink provides the exact feature set to make link repositories a practical reality.

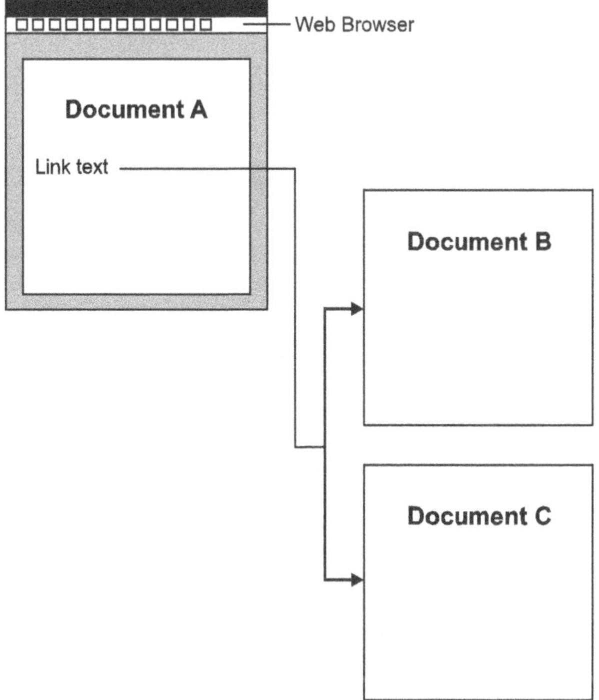

FIGURE 14.4 Multiple document linking of XML

XLink is designed to support simple one-way links similar to those in HTML, as well as a variety of different extended links that offer interesting new ways of linking documents. XLink is implemented as an XML language, which means that it can be easily integrated into XML applications. XPointer is a non-XML language based upon XPath that is used to address internal structures in XML documents. XPointer is an important part of XLink because it specifies the syntax used to create fragment identifiers, which are used to reference internal document constructs.

LINKING WITH XLINK

The whole point of XPointer (no pun intended) is to provide a means of referencing portions of XML documents for the purpose of creating powerful XML links. XLink ultimately makes links possible through linking elements, which are elements that describe the characteristics of links. The anchor element in HTML is a good example of a linking element. Although linking elements form the basis of XLink, there are no predefined linking elements in the XLink language. Although it may seem strange at first, you won't find any standard element in the XLink language. The reason is because XML is all about the creation of custom tags (elements), which precludes the use of a fixed linking element in XLink. In other words, you are encouraged to define your own linking elements specific to a particular XML-based language, as opposed to being locked into a fixed element, such as HTML's anchor element (a).

Even though HTML's anchor element is somewhat limiting in the context of XML, there still must be some kind of mechanism in XLink that identifies links. This mechanism comes in the form of standard linking attributes that can be associated with any element. There are several of these attributes, which you learn about in the next section. For now, just understand that the presence of XLink attributes is sufficient to identify an element as a linking element.

A linking element uses a construct called a locator to connect resources involved in a link. In both HTML and XML, the HRef attribute serves as the locator for links. Although HTML and XML share this attribute, links in XML are described in much more detail than their HTML counterparts. Perhaps the most important difference is the fact that XML links completely describe the resources involved, even if a target resource is just a document fragment. In HTML, it is necessary to place an anchor element in a target fragment resource and identify it using the id attribute. This is not the case in XML because XLink provides the necessary ingredients to fully describe the resources involved in a link. There are two types of linking elements supported in XLink:

- Inline links
- Out-of-line links

An *inline link* is a link whose content serves as one of the link's participating resources. Typically, an inline link has a linking element that contains content that serves as the source for the link. HTML anchor links are good examples of inline links because an anchor link contains text or an image that acts as the source for the link. Due to HTML's use of inline links, you may be curious as to how a link could work any other way. Out-of-line links extend the concept of linking in XML by allowing you to create links that are independent of the linked resources.

An *out-of-line link* is a link whose content doesn't serve as one of the link's participating resources. This means that out-of-line links are independent of their participating resources and therefore serve a very different purpose than inline links. Out-of-line links are useful for linking information in documents that you can't modify for one reason or another. For example, if you wanted to create a link between two resources that reside on other Web sites, you'd use an out-of-line link. Such a link is possible because out-of-line links are geared toward opening up interesting new opportunities for how links are used to connect documents. More specifically, it would be possible to create link databases that describe relationships between information spread across the Web.

Out-of-line links partially form the concept of extended links in XML. Extended links are basically any links that extend the linking functionality of HTML. Out-of-line links obviously are considered extended links because HTML doesn't support any type of out-of-line linking mechanism. Extended links also support the association of more than one target resource with a given link. With extended links, you could build a table of contents for a Web site that consists solely of extended links that point to the various pages in the site. If the links were gathered in a single document separate from the table of contents page itself, they would also be considered out-of-line links.

XLINK EXAMPLE

Let's try to learn some basic XLink syntax by looking at an example.

THE XML EXAMPLE DOCUMENT

Look at the following XML document, "bookstore.xml," that represents a few books:

```
<?xml version="1.0" encoding="ISO-8859-1"?>
<bookstore xmlns:xlink="http://www.w3.org/1999/xlink">
<book title="The Internet">
<description
xlink:type="simple"
xlink:href="http://book.com/images/HPotter.gif"
xlink:show="new">
As his fifth year at Hogwarts School of Witchcraft and
Wizardry approaches, 15-year-old.......
</description>
</book>
```

```
<book title="MYSQL Queries">
<description
xlink:type="simple"
xlink:href="http://book.com/images/XQuery.gif"
xlink:show="new">
MYSQL Queries delivers a concise introduction
to the XQuery standard.......
</description>
</book>
</bookstore>
```

In the example above the XLink namespace is declared at the top of the document (xmlns:xlink="*http://www.w3.org/1999/xlink*"). This means that the document has access to the XLink attributes and features.

The xlink:type="simple" creates a simple "HTML-like" link. You can also specify more complex links (multidirectional links), but for now, we will only use simple links.

The xlink:href attribute specifies the URL to link to, and the xlink:show attribute specifies where to open the link. xlink:show="new" means that the link (in this case, an image) should open in a new window.

In the example above, we only demonstrated simple links. XLink is more interesting when we want to access remote locations as resources, instead of standalone pages. The <description> element in the example above sets the value of the xlink:show attribute to "new." This means that the link should open in a new window. We could have set the value of the xlink:show attribute to "embed." This means that the resource should be processed inline within the page. When you consider that this could be another XML document and not just an image, you could, for example, build a hierarchy of XML documents.

With XLink, you can also specify WHEN the resource should appear. This is handled by the xlink:actuate attribute. xlink:actuate="onLoad" specifies that the resource should be loaded and shown when the document loads. However, xlink:actuate="onRequest" means that the resource is not read or shown before the link is clicked. This is very handy for low-bandwidth settings.

UNDERSTANDING XLINK ATTRIBUTES

XLink defines standard attributes that are used to establish linked elements in XML documents. The following are the XLink attributes that can be used to create linked elements:

- type A string, which specifies the type of link
- href A locator, which addresses a target resource using a URI
- from A string, which identifies the resource being linked from when describing an arc
- to A string, which identifies the resource being linked to when describing an arc
- show A string, which determines how a target resource is to be revealed to the user
- actuate A string, which determines how a link is initiated
- role: An application-specific string used to describe the function of a link's content
- title A string, which serves as a name for a link

The type attribute determines the type of a link and can have one of the following values: simple, extended, locator, resource, arc, or group. The href attribute is one with which you are already familiar, based on its use in HTML. The from and to attributes are used by arcs, which describe the traversal behavior of links. More specifically, an arc defines where a two-way link comes from and where it goes. Arcs could be used to establish Web rings, where Web pages are linked from one to the next using the from and to attributes to traverse the ring.

The show attribute determines how a target resource for a link is revealed to the user. There are three main values for the show attribute:

- replace the target resource: replaces the current document (default value).
- new: the target resource is shown in a new window.
- embed: the target resource is inserted into the current document in place of the link.

The functionality of the show attribute follows that of the HTML anchor links until you get to the last possible value, parsed. If you set the show attribute to parsed, the link will be replaced by the target resource. This type of link allows you to divide a document into sub-documents and then link them together to form a compound document, which can help improve the organization of the data.

The actuate attribute determines how a link is initiated and is typically set to one of the following values:

- onRequest: The link must be manually traversed by the user (default value).
- onLoad: The link is automatically traversed upon loading the source document.

Setting the actuate attribute to onRequest makes a link act like an HTML link, which means that you have to click the link in order to activate it. The onLoad value offers functionality not directly available in HTML by allowing a link to be traversed when a document is first loaded. The onLoad value is particularly useful when used in conjunction with the embed value for the show attribute; this results in a resource being automatically loaded and placed directly in a document.

The last two XLink attributes are role and title, which are used primarily for descriptive purposes. The role attribute describes the role of the content in a link, whereas title provides a human-readable title for the link that may be displayed in a browser.

CREATING LINKS WITH XLINK

You're now finally ready to put all of your XPointer and XLink knowledge to work and create some links that would never be possible in HTML. As an example, consider an element named employees that is used to identify a group of employees for a company. The following is an example of how you might create a simple link for the employees element:

```
<employees xmlns:xlink="http://www.w3.org/1999/xlink"
xlink:href="employees.xml">
Current Employees
</employees>
```

This example is the simplest possible link you can create using XLink, and it actually carries out the same functionality as an HTML anchor link, which is known as a simple link in XML. Notice in the code that the XLink namespace is declared and assigned to the xlink prefix, which is then used to reference the href attribute; this is the standard approach used to access all of the XLink attributes. What you may not realize is that this link takes advantage of some default attribute values. The following is another way to express the exact same link by spelling all of the pertinent XLink attribute values:

```
<employees xmlns:xlink="http://www.w3.org/1999/xlink"
xlink:type="simple"
```

```
xlink:href="employees.xml"
xlink:show="replace"
xlink:actuate="user"
xlink:role="employees"
xlink:title="Employee List">
Current Employees
</employees>
```

In this code, you can more clearly see how the XLink attributes are specified in order to fully describe the link. The type attribute is set to simple, which indicates that this is a simple link. The show attribute has the value replace, which indicates that the target resource is to replace the current document when the link is traversed. The actuate attribute has the value user, which indicates that the link must be activated by the user for traversal to take place. And finally, the role and title attributes are set to indicate the meaning of the link and its name.

The previous example demonstrated how to create a link that imitates the familiar HTML anchor link. You can dramatically change a simple link just by altering the manner in which it is shown and activated. For example, take a look at the following link:

```
<resume xmlns:xlink="http://www.w3.org/1999/xlink"
xlink:type="simple"
xlink:href="resume_e1.xml"
xlink:show="parsed"
xlink:actuate="auto"
xlink:role="employee1 resume"
xlink:title="Employee 1 Resume"/>
```

This code shows how to effectively embed another XML document into the current document at the position where the link is located. This is accomplished by simply setting the show attribute to parsed and the actuate attribute to auto. When a Web browser or XML application encounters this link, it will automatically load the resume_e1.xml document and insert it into the current document in place of the link. When you think about it, the img element in HTML works very much like this link except that it is geared solely toward images; the link in this example can be used with any kind of XML content.

XPointer impacts links through the href attribute, which is where you specify the location of a source or target resource for a link. All of the flexibility afforded by XPointer in specifying document parts can be realized in the href attribute of any link.

Although simple links such as the previous example are certainly important, they barely scratch the surface in terms of what XLink is really capable of doing. Links get much more interesting when you venture into extended links. A powerful use of extended links is the linkset, which allows you to link to a set of target resources via a single source resource. For example, you could use an extended link to establish a link to each individual employee in a company. To create an extended link, you must create child elements of the linking element that are set to type locator; these elements are where you set each individual target resource via the href attribute. The following is an example of an extended link, which should help clarify how they work:

```
<employees xmlns:xlink="http://www.w3.org/1999/xlink"
xlink:type="extended"
xlink:role="employees"
xlink:title="Employee List"
xlink:show="replace"
xlink:actuate="user">
<employee xlink:type="locator" xlink:href="employee1.xml">
Frank Rizzo
</employee>
<employee xlink:type="locator" xlink:href="employee2.xml">
 Sol Rosenberg
</employee>
<employee xlink:type="locator" xlink:href="employee3.xml">
Jack Tors
</employee>
</employees>
```

This example creates an extended link out of the employees element, but the most interesting thing about the link is that it has multiple target resources that are identified in the child employee elements. This is evident by the fact that each of the employee elements has an href attribute that is set to their respective target resources.

XPOINTER SYNTAX

In HTML, we can create a hyperlink that either points to an HTML page or to a bookmark inside an HTML page (using #).

Sometimes it is more useful to point to more specific content. For example, let's say that we want to link to the third item in a particular list, or to the second sentence of the fifth paragraph. This is easy with XPointer.

If the hyperlink points to an XML document, we can add an XPointer part after the URL in the xlink:href attribute, to navigate (with an XPath expression) to a specific place in the document.

For example, below we use XPointer to point to the fifth item in a list with a unique id of "rock:"

```
href="http://www.example.com/cdlist.xml#id('rock').child(5,item)"
```

ADDRESSING WITH XPOINTER

XPointer allows you to walk the tree of nodes that an XML document is comprised of to address a specific node or nodes. XPointer expands the syntax set forth by XPath to provide a means of creating fragment identifiers, which are used to specify parts of documents. XPointer provides considerably more control over the referencing of XML document data than the hyperlink approach employed by HTML. For example, XPointer allows you to do things such as address an element with a given value within a list of elements of a given type. You use XPointer expressions in XML links by appending them onto the end of URIs with a pound symbol (#), as in the separation between a URI and an XPointer expression. The next few sections break down XPointer into further detail and demonstrate exactly how to create XPointer expressions.

BUILDING XPOINTER EXPRESSIONS

The most important component of XPointer expressions is the *location path*, which is a construct used to describe the path that must be followed to arrive at a node within an XML document tree. Location paths are the building blocks of XPointer expressions, which are evaluated to arrive at a specific location within a tree. More specifically, location paths allow you to traverse siblings, ancestors, children, and descendants of nodes, not to mention attributes. Location paths are broken down into two basic types absolute paths and general paths.

Absolute location paths point to a specific location within an XML tree, and therefore aren't dependent on context. The following are the different absolute location paths defined in XPointer:

- / locates the root node, which is the parent node for the entire document tree
- id(Name) locates the element with an attribute ID value of Name

- here() locates the node containing the current XPointer expression
- origin() locates the sub-resource from which the user initiated a link (used with out-of-line links)

The most important absolute location paths are the root and id() paths. The root path is represented by a forward slash (/), and is often used at the start of an XPointer expression as the basis for absolute location paths. The id() location path is used to locate an element with a specific attribute value.

In addition to absolute location paths, XPointer also defines a rich set of relative location paths. Relative location paths are always relative to some node, which is known as the context node for the path. The following are the relative location paths available for use in XPointer expressions:

- child locates the child nodes of the context node
- descendant locates the nodes within the context node
- descendant-or-self is the same as descendant except the context node is also included
- parent locates the nodes one level above the context node that contain the context node
- ancestor locates all the nodes above the context node that contain the context node
- ancestor-or-self is the same as the ancestor except the context node is also included
- preceding-sibling locates the sibling nodes that precede the context node
- following-sibling locates the sibling nodes that follow the context node
- preceding locates the nodes that precede the context node
- following locates the nodes that follow the context node
- self locates the individual context nodes within a list of context nodes
- attribute locates the attributes of the context node

CREATING XPOINTERS

Seeing a few examples of XPointer expressions can make all the difference in understanding how XPointer is used to define document fragment identifiers. The following is an example of a simple XPointer expression:

```
child::factoid
```

This example uses the child relative location path to locate all of the children of the context node that are of element type factoid. Let me rephrase it in a different way: The sample expression locates element nodes of type factoid that are child nodes of the context node. Keep in mind that the context node is the node from which you are issuing the expression, which is like the current path of a file system when you're browsing for files. Also, it's worth clarifying that the XPointer expression child::factoid simply describes the fragment identifier for a resource and is not a complete resource reference. When used in a complete expression, you would pair this fragment identifier with a URI that is assigned to an href attribute, like this:

```
href="http://www.stalefishlabs.com/factoids.xml#child::factoid"
```

In this example, a URI is specified that references the XML document named factoids.xml. The XPointer expression is then provided as a fragment identifier, which is separated from the URI by a pound symbol (#). This is the typical way in which XPointers are used, although expressions can certainly get more complex than this. For example, the following code shows how to use location paths to create a more elaborate expression that carries out a more intricate reference:

```
child::factoid/following-sibling::legend
```

This example first locates all child elements that are of type factoid and then finds the second siblings following each of those element nodes that are of type legend. To understand how this code works, let's break it down. You begin with the familiar child::factoid expression, which locates element nodes of type factoid that are child nodes of the context node. Adding on the following-sibling::legend location path causes the expression to locate sibling elements of type legend. Granted, this may seem like a strange use of XPointer, but keep in mind that it is designed as an all-purpose language for addressing the internal structure of XML documents. It's impossible to say how different applications might want to address document parts, which is why XPointer is so flexible.

In addition to location paths, XPointer defines several functions that perform different tasks within XPointer expressions. One class of functions is node test functions, which are used to determine the type of a node. Of course, you can use the name of an element to check if a node is of a certain element type, but the node test functions allow you to check and see if a node contains a comment, text, or processor instruction. The following is an example of how to use one of these functions:

```
/child::processing-instruction()
```

This expression results in the location of any processing instructions that are children of the root element. The reason the expression results in children of the root element is because the root element (/) is specified as the basis for the expression.

As you can see in these few examples, XPointer is a comprehensive yet flexible technology that is capable of doing some interesting things.

XPOINTER EXAMPLE

In this example, we will show you how to use XPointer in conjunction with XLink to point to a specific part of another document.

The Target XML Document

The target XML document is called "dogbreeds.xml" and it lists a few different dog breeds:

```
<?xml version="1.0" encoding="ISO-8859-1"?>
<dogbreeds>
 <dog breed="Poodle" id="Poodle">
 <picture url="http://dog.com/Poodle.gif" />
 <history>The Poodle's ancestors were probably Roman
 drover dogs.....</history>
 <temperament>Confident, bold, alert and imposing, the Poodle
 is a popular choice for its ability to protect....</temperament>
</dog>
<dog breed="Boxer" id="Boxer">
<picture url="http://dog.com/Boxer.gif" />
 <history>One of the earliest uses of retrieving dogs was to
 help fishermen retrieve fish from the water....</history>
 <temperament>The flat-coated retriever is a sweet, exuberant,
 lively dog that loves to play and retrieve....</temperament>
 </dog>
</dogbreeds>
```

THE LINKING XML DOCUMENT

Instead of linking to the entire document (as with XLink), XPointer allows you to link to specific parts of the document. To link to a specific part of a page, add a number sign (#) and an XPointer expression after the URL in the xlink:href attributes.

The expression: #xpointer(id("Poodle")) refers to the element in the target document, with the id value of "Poodle." So the xlink:href attribute would look like this:

```
xlink:href="http://dog.com/dogbreeds.xml#xpointer(id('Poodle'))"
```

However, XPointer allows a shorthand form when linking to an element with an id. You can use the value of the id directly, like this:

```
xlink:href=http://dog.com/dogbreeds.xml#Poodle
```

The following XML document refers to information of the dog breed for each of my dogs :-), all through XLink and XPointer references:

```
<?xml version="1.0" encoding="ISO-8859-1"?>
<mydogs xmlns:xlink="http://www.w3.org/1999/xlink">
<mydog xlink:type="simple"
xlink:href="http://dog.com/dogbreeds.xml#Poodle">
<description xlink:type="simple"
xlink:href="http://myweb.com/mydogs/anton.gif">
Anton is my favorite dog. He has won a lot of.....
</description>
</mydog>
<mydog xlink:type="simple"
xlink:href="http://dog.com/dogbreeds.xml#Boxer">
<description xlink:type="simple"
xlink:href="http://myweb.com/mydogs/pluto.gif">
Pluto is the sweetest dog on earth......
</description>
</mydog>
</mydogs>
```

XPOINTER EXAMPLE

In this example, we will show you that how to use XPointer in conjunction with XLink to point to a specific part of another document.

The Target XML Document

The target XML documents is called "dogbreeds.xml" and it lists a few different dog breeds:

```
<?xml version="1.0" encoding="ISO-8859-1"?>
<dogbreeds>
<dog breed="Poodle" id="Poodle">
<picture url="http://dog.com/Poodle.gif" />
<history>
The Poodle's ancestors were probably Roman
drover dogs.....
</history>
<temperament>
```

Confident, bold, alert and imposing, the poodle is a popular choice for its ability to protect.

```
</temperament>
</dog>
<dog breed="Boxer" id="Boxer">
<picture url="http://dog.com/Boxer.gif" />
<history>
```

One of the earliest uses of retrieving dogs was to help fishermen retrieve fish from the water.

```
</history>
<temperament>
```

The flat-coated retriever is a sweet, exuberant, lively dog that loves to play and retrieve...

```
. </temperament>
</dog>
</dogbreeds>
```

THE LINKING XML DOCUMENT

Instead of linking to the entire document (as with XLink), XPointer allows you to link to specific part of the document. To link to a specific part of a page, add a number sign (#) and an XPointer expression after the URL in the xlink:href attribute.

The expression: #xpointer(id("Poodle")) refer to the element in the target document, with the id value of "Poodle."

So the xlink:href attribute would looks like this:

```
xlink:href="http://dog.com/dogbreeds.xml#xpointer(id('Poodle'))"
```

However, XPointer allows a shorthand form when linking to an element with the id. You can also use the value of the id directly, like this:

```
xlink:href="http://dog.com/dogbreeds.xml#Poodle"
```

The following XML document refer to information of the dog breed for each of my dogs:-), all through XLink and XPointer references:

```
<?xml version="1.0" encoding="ISO-8859-1"?>
<mydogs xmlns:xlink="http://www.w3.org/1999/xlink">
<mydog xlink:type="simple"
xlink:href="http://dog.com/dogbreeds.xml#Poodle">
<description xlink:type="simple"
xlink:href="http://myweb.com/mydogs/anton.gif">
Anton is my favorite dog. He has won a lot of.....
</description>
</mydog>
<mydog xlink:type="simple"
xlink:href="http://dog.com/dogbreeds.xml#Boxer">
<description xlink:type="simple"
xlink:href="http://myweb.com/mydogs/pluto.gif">
Pluto is the sweetest dog on earth......
</description>
</mydog>
</mydogs>
```

QUESTIONS FOR DISCUSSION

1. What is the primary difference in how XSLT and XQuery transform an XML document (in terms of schema)?
2. How you define atomic values?
3. How you define terms in XQuery?
4. What does it mean to select and filter elements in XQuery?
5. How do you define functions in XQuery?
6. How do you add elements and attributes with XQuery in XML data?
7. How do you perform comparisons in XQuery?

8. How do you perform conditional operations in XQuery?
9. Give the syntax rules of XQuery.
10. How do you use XQuery FLWOR with HTML?
11. What is server-side XPointer?
12. What is the difference between XLink and XPointer?
13. How do you transform XLink/XPointer into HTML using XSL?
14. Why don't you use XPath/XPointer?
15. What does the following XPointer link statement point to? href=?http://www.example.com/cdlist.xml#.
16. What types of IDs are currently supported for XPointers?
17. Does the XInclude processor support XPointer?
18. What's the concept of XPointer?
19. What are non-XML resources?
20. What is server-side XPointer?
21. What XPointer schemes are supported in this release?
22. How do you implement an application-specific XPointer scheme?
23. How do you integrate XPointer into my application?
24. How do you configure an XPointer processor?
25. What are XPointer resources?
26. What is server-side XPointer?
27. How the use XPointer?
28. What is XPointer?
29. How do you define do you syntax of XPointer?

CHAPTER 15

XFORMS

INTRODUCTION TO XFORMS

XForms is the next generation of HTML forms. XForms uses XML to create input forms on the Web. XForms is the next generation of HTML forms. It is richer and more flexible than HTML forms. XForms will be the forms standard in XHTML 2.0. XForms is platform- and device-independent. It separates data and logic from presentation. XForms uses XML to define form data. It stores and transports data in XML documents. It contains features like calculations and validations of forms. XForms reduces or eliminates the need for scripting.

Like an XHTML, SVG, and RSS, XForms is also an XML-based language written with the tags that can be identified by surrounding the angle brackets (the XML purists perfer to call these elements). Learning the XForms is largely a matter of understanding what an individual elements do, as well as how do they interrelate. XForms provides a more elements for forms than authors might be accustomed to. As a result, several tasks that would have otherwise required complicated scripting can be accomplished declaratively, just by putting a right elements in the place.

FEATURES OF XFORMS

- XForms are the successor of HTML forms

Forms are an important part of many Web applications today. An HTML form makes it possible for Web applications to accept input from a user.

Today, ten years after HTML forms became a part of the HTML standard, Web users do complex transactions that are starting to exceed the limitations of standard HTML forms.

XForms provides a richer, more secure, and device-independent way of handling Web input. We should expect future Web solutions to demand the use of XForms-enabled browsers (all future browsers should support XForms).

- XForms separate data from presentation

XForms uses XML for data definition and HTML or XHTML for data display. XForms separates the data logic of a form from its presentation. This way, the XForms data can be defined independently of how the end-user will interact with the application.

- XForms uses XML to define form data

With XForms, the rules for describing and validating data are expressed in XML.

- XForms uses XML to store and transport data

With XForms, the data displayed in a form are stored in an XML document, and the data submitted from the form, are transported over the internet using XML.

The data content is coded in, and transported as Unicode bytes.

- XForms is device independent

Separating the data from the presentation makes XForms device-independent because the data model can be used for all devices. The presentation can be customized for different user interfaces, like mobile phones, handheld devices, and Braille readers for the blind.

Since XForms is device independent and based on XML, it is also possible to add XForms elements directly into other XML applications like VoiceXML (speaking Web data), WML (Wireless Markup Language), and SVG (Scalable Vector Graphics).

PARTS OF XFORMS

Structurally, the form can be throught of having two parts: a specification of what it must do and a specification of how it must look. In the XForms these two parts are called the XForms Model and the XForms User Interface respectively.

1. *The XForms Model*

The XForms model defines a template for the data to be collected from a form.

The XForms Framework

The purpose of an HTML form is to collect data. XForms has the same purpose.

With XForms, input data is described in two different parts:

- The XForm model—defines what the form is, what it should do, what data it contains
- The XForm user interface—defines the input fields and how they should be displayed

The XForms model describes the data. The XForms model defines a data model inside a model element:

```
<model>
 <instance>
  <person>
   <fname/>
   <lname/>
  </person>
 </instance>
 <submission id="form1" action="submit.asp" method="get"/>
</model>
```

In the example above, the XForms model uses an instance element to define the XML-template for the data to be collected, and a submission element to describe how to submit the data.

The XForms model does not say anything about the visual part of the form (the user interface).

The Instance Element

The instance element defines the data to be collected. XForms is always collecting data for an XML document. The instance element in the XForms model defines the XML document. In the example above, the "data instance" (the XML document) the form is collecting data for looks like this:

```
<person>
 <fname/>
 <lname/>
</person>
```

After collecting the data, the XML document might look like this:

```
<person>
 <fname>Kshitij</fname>
 <lname>Banzal</lname>
</person>
```

The Submission Element

The submission element describes how to submit the data. The submission element defines a form and how it should be submitted. In the example above, the id="form1" identifies a form, the action="submit.asp" defines the URL to where the form should be submitted, and the method="get" attribute defines the method to use when submitting the form data.

2. *The XForms User Interface*

The XForms user interface defines the input fields and how they should be displayed. The user interface elements are called controls (or input controls):

```
<input ref="fname"><label>First Name</label></input>
<input ref="lname"><label>Last Name</label></input>
<submit submission="form1"><label>Submit</label></submit>
```

In the example above, the two <input> elements define two input fields. The ref="fname" and ref="lname" attributes point to the <fname> and <lname> elements in the XForms model.

The <submit> element has a submission="form1" attribute, which refers to the <submission> element in the XForms model. A submit element is usually displayed as a button.

Notice the <label> elements in the example. With XForms, every input control element has a required <label> element. This means that there must be a container.

XForms is not designed to work alone. There is no such thing as an XForms document. XForms has to run inside another XML document. It could run inside XHTML 1.0, and it will run inside XHTML 2.0.

If we put it all together, the document will look like this:

```
 <xforms>
<model>
 <instance>
  <person>
   <fname/>
    <lname/>
```

```
    </person>
 </instance>
 <submission id="form1" action="submit.asp" method="get"/>
  </model>
   <input ref="fname"><label>First Name</label></input>
  <input ref="lname"><label>Last Name</label></input>
  <submit submission="form1"><label>Submit</label></submit>
</xforms>
```

And the page will display like this:

Top of Form
First Name ----------
Last Name ----------
Bottom of Form

THE FORM CONTROLS

Individual user interface elements in the XForms are called the *form controls*, each of which are represented by the element. The two most commonly used elements are input and submit.

The user interface elements in XForms are called XForms controls. The most commonly used control elements are <input> and <submit>. Each control element has a ref attribute pointing back to the XForms data model.

Device Independent Controls

It is important to know that the XForms user interface does not describe exactly how to display the XForms controls. Because XForms is platform- and device-independent, XForms leaves it up to the browser to decide how to display the controls.

This way XForms can be used for all types of devices, personal computers, cell phones, and hand held computers. XForms is also the perfect solution for defining user interfaces for people with disabilities.

The Input Control

The input control is the most common XForms control. It can hold one line of text:

```
<input ref="name/fname"><label>First Name</label></input>
```

Most often, the input control will display as an input field, like this:

First Name: ----------

The <label> Element

The <label> element is a mandatory child element for all XForms input controls.

The reason for this is to secure that the form can be used for all types of devices (because labels can be treated in different ways). For voice software, the label has to be spoken, and for some hand held computers, the label has to follow the input, screen by screen.

The Secret Control

The secret control is designed to input passwords or other hidden information:

```
<secret ref="name/password"><label>Password:</label></secret>
```

Most often the secret control will display as an input field like this:

Password: * * * * * *

The Textarea Control

The textarea control is used for multi-line input:

```
<textarea ref="message"><label>Message</label></textarea>
```

The textarea control might display as an input field like this:

Message:

The Submit Control

The submit control is used to submit the data:

```
<submit submission="form1"><label>Submit</label></submit>
```

The Trigger Control

The trigger control is used to trigger an action:

```
<trigger ref="calculate"><label>Calculate!</label></trigger>
```

The Output Control

The output control is used to display XForms data.The example below will simply output the content of the <fname> and <lname> node in the XForms XML document (XForms instance):

Example

```
<model>
 <instance>
  <person>
   <fname>Hege</fname>
   <lname>Refsnes</lname>
  </person>
 </instance>
</model>
<output ref="fname"/>
<output ref="lname"/>
```

The Upload Control

The upload control is designed for uploading files to a server:

```
<upload bind="name">
   <label>File to upload:</label>
   <filename bind="file"/>
   <mediatype bind="media"/>
</upload>
```

THE FORM CONTROLS LISTED

The list of the form controls shown in Table 15.1 helps you to focus on the intent behind each of the form controls. After that, you will learn how to fine-tune the presentation of the form controls.

Table 15.1 A Form Controls

Form Control	Intent	Examples
input	Entry of free-form values	The edit box, The voice prompt
textarea	Entry of the large amounts of free-form text	An email body, Weblog entry
secret	Entry of sensitive information	The password prompt
select1	Choice of one-and-only-one item from the list	The radio buttons, drop-list

(continued)

(continued)

Form Control	Intent	Examples
select	Choice of one or more items from the list	The checkbox group, listbox
range	Selecting a value from the range	The slider, volume control
upload	Selecting the data source	The file picker, a digital camera interface
trigger	Activating the defined process	The button, hyperlink
submit	Activating submission of a form	The submit button
output	Display only of the form data	The inline text

Every form control has a required label child (except output, where it's optional). This enforces the good design habit of always associating a label with a form control. Other common child elements are help for a message at the user's request, hint for a message at the user agent's request, and alert, which is available for error messages.

THE XFORMS PROCESSOR

An XForms processor built into the browser is responsible for submitting the XForms data to a target. The data can be submitted as XML and could look something like this:

```
<person>
  <fname>Hege</fname>
  <lname>Refsnes</lname>
</person>
```

Or it can be submitted as text:

```
fname=Hege;lname=Refsnes
```

THE XFORMS NAMESPACE

The official namespace for XForms is: *http://www.w3.org/2002/xforms*

If you want to use XForms in HTML (or XHTML 1.0), you should declare all XForms elements with an XForms namespace. XForms is expected to be a standard part of XHTML 2.0, eliminating the need for the XForms namespace. This example uses the XForms namespace:

```
<html xmlns:xf="http://www.w3.org/2002/xforms">
 <head>
  <xf:model>
   <xf:instance>
    <person>
    <fname/>
 <lname/>
 </person>
 </xf:instance>
 <xf:submission id="form1" method="get" action="submit.asp"/>
 </xf:model>
</head>
<body>
<xf:input ref="fname"><xf:label>First Name</xf:label></xf:input><br />
<xf:input ref="lname"><xf:label>Last Name</xf:label></xf:input><br /><br />
<xf:submit submission="form1"><xf:label>Submit</xf:label></xf:submit>
</body>
</html>
```

In the example above, we have used the xf: prefix for the XForms namespace, but you are free to call the prefix anything you want.

XForms Example

You can test XForms with Internet Explorer (XForms will not work in IE prior version 5). Just click on the "Try it Yourself" button under the example.

```
<xforms>
<model>
 <instance>
 <person>
  <fname/>
  <lname/>
 </person>
 </instance>
 <submission id="form1" method="get"
 action="submit.asp"/>
```

```
</model>
<input ref="fname">
<label>First Name</label>
</input>
<input ref="lname">
<label>Last Name</label>
</input>
<submit submission="form1">
<label>Submit</label>
</submit>
</xforms>
```

First Name ----------
Last Name ----------
Submit

XFORMS AND XPATH

XForms uses XPath to address data. This is called *binding*.

XForms Binding

XForms uses two sections to define data: the XForms model and the XForms user interface.

The XForms model is an XML template (instance) for the data, and the XForms user interface is a description of the input and display of the data.

XForms uses XPath to define the connection between the two sections. This binding is defined differently above.

XPath

XPath is a W3C standard syntax for defining parts of XML documents.

XPath uses path expressions to identify nodes in an XML document. These path expressions look much like the expressions you see when you work with a computer file system. This XPath expression

```
/person/fname
```

addresses the fname node in the XML document:

```
<person>
 <fname>Hege</fname>
 <lname>Refsnes</lname>
</person>
```

Binding Using Ref

With an XForms model instance like this:

```
<instance>
 <person>
 <name>
 <fname/>
 <lname/>
 </name>
 </person>
</instance>
```

the XForms user interface can bind <input> elements using the ref attribute:

```
<input ref="name/fname"><label>First Name</label></input>
<input ref="name/lname"><label>Last Name</label></input>
```

The ref="name/fname" attribute in the example above is an XPath expression pointing to the <fname> element in the instance model. This binds the input field to the <fname> element in the XML document (instance) that is collecting data from the form.

The XForms user interface could also use a reference like this:

```
<input ref="/person/name/fname"><label>First Name</label></input>
<input ref="/person/name/lname"><label>Last Name</label></input>
```

In the example above, the slash (/) at the beginning of the XPath expression indicates the root of the XML document.

Binding Using Bind

With an XForms model instance like this:

```
<model>
 <instance>
 <person>
 <name>
 <fname/>
 <lname/>
 </name>
 </person>
 </instance>
 <bind nodeset="/person/name/fname" id="firstname"/>
 <bind nodeset="/person/name/lname" id="lastname"/>
</model>
```

the XForms user interface can bind <input> elements using the bind attribute:

```
<input bind="firstname"><label>First Name</label></input>
<input bind="lastname"><label>Last Name</label></input>
```

When you start using XForms in complex applications, you will find binding using bind to be a more flexible way to deal with multiple forms and multiple instance models.

XFORMS PROPERTIES

XForms uses properties to define data restrictions, types, and behaviors.

Examples

A required="true()" property means that the input field is required (cannot be empty on submit). A type="decimal" property will only allow a decimal value to be submitted. A calculate property can calculate a value.

Bind Properties to Data

XForms uses the bind element to bind XForms properties to XForms data:

```
<model>
 <instance>
 <person>
 <fname/>
<lname/>
 </person>
 </instance>
 <bind nodeset="person/lname" required="true()"/>
</model>
```

In the example above, the <bind nodeset="person/lname" required = "true()"> specifies that the lname input field is required (cannot be empty on submit).

XForms Properties Reference

Table 15.2 XForms Properties Description

Name	Description
calculate	Defines a calculation to be performed on the item
constraint	Defines a constraint for the item

(continued)

Name	Description
p3ptype	Defines a P3P data type for the item
readonly	Defines an edit restriction for the item (cannot be changed)
relevant	Defines how relevant the data is (for display or submission)
required	Defines that a data item is required (cannot be blank)
type	Defines the data type for the item

XFORMS ACTIONS

XForms actions handle response to events.

The message Element

The XForms message element defines a message to be displayed in the XForms user interface. Look at this simplified example:

```
<input ref="fname">
 <label>First Name</label>
 <message level="ephemeral" event="DOMFocusIn">
 Input Your First Name
 </message>
</input>
```

In the example above, the message "Input Your First Name" should be displayed as a tool tip when the input field gets focus.

```
The event="DomFocusIn" defines the event to trigger the message.
The level="ephemeral" defines the message to be displayed as a tool tip.
```

Other values for the level attribute are modal and modeless, defining different types of message boxes.

The setvalue Element

The XForms setvalue element defines a value to be set in response to an event. Look at this simplified example:

```
<input ref="size">
 <label>Size</label>
 <setvalue value="50" event="xforms-ready"/>
</input>
```

In the example above, the value 50 will be stored in the "size" input field when the form opens.

QUESTIONS FOR DISCUSSION

1. How you define data types in XForms?
2. How do you bind datatypes in XForms?
3. How do you perform actions in XForms?
4. How do you define functions in XForms?
5. Will XForms work on PDAs and mobile phones?
6. What servers (currently) support XForms?
7. Who is backing XForms?
8. Is XForms more complicated than HTML forms?
9. What can we do with XForms that we can't do with old HTML forms?
10. What are the advantages of XForms?
11. How do you define data types in XForms?
12. How do you perform selection control in XForms?
13. How do you define controls in XForms?
14. What is binding in XForms?
15. How do you define the XForms Namespace?
16. How do you define the XForms Processor?
17. How do you use both XForms Model and XForms User Interface together?
18. How do you define the XForms User Interface?
19. How do you define the XForms model?
20. How do you define the XForms Framework?

CHAPTER 16

XSL-FO

INTRODUCTION TO XSL-FO

XSL-FO is about formatting XML data for output. It is a language for formatting XML data. XSL-FO stands for Extensible Stylesheet Language Formatting Objects. It is based on XML. XSL-FO is now formally named XSL. XSL-FO describes the formatting of XML data for output to screen, paper, or other media. XSL-FO is formally named XSL.

XSL-FO is an XML-based markup language that describes the formatting of XML data for output to the screen. After several years of development, Extensible Stylesheet Language (XSL) Version 1.0 became a W3C Recommendation on October 15, 2001. It enhances the flexibility of the XML (Extensible Markup Language) standard. XSL draws on earlier specifications, including CSS and DSSSL.

XSL-FO is an XML language designed for describing all visual aspects of paginated documents. HTML is another language for specifying formatting semantics, but is more for documents that are presented on screen and less for materials created for printing because it does not support pagination elements like headers and footers, page size specifications, and footnotes. XSL-FO is part of the XSL language family:

- **XSLT:** (XSL Transformations) a language for transforming XML
- **XSL-FO:** (XSL Formatting Objects) a language that can be used in XSLT for the purpose of "presenting" the XML
- **XPATH:** A syntax for addressing parts of a document, a syntax which is also significant in XPointer and to the emerging XQuery, an XML query language

XSL Formatting Objects is a W3C standard used by XF Rendering Server 2008 to produce print ready documents in PDF, AFP, Postscript, TIFF, and other formats.

XF Designer can edit XSL-FO documents like an HTML editor can edit HTML pages.

Figure 16.1 depicts the steps required to produce a PDF document (or any other supported output format) using XSL.

FIGURE 16.1 Steps required to produce a PDF document using XSL

As you can see, the XML data is transformed together with the XSL stylesheet to produce an XSL-FO document, and the document is then converted to PDF.

XSL-FO DOCUMENTS

XSL-FO documents are XML files with output information. XSL-FO documents are stored in files with a .fo or a .fob file extension. You can also store XSL-FO documents with an .xml extension (to make them more accessible to XML editors).

XSL-FO documents contain two required sections. The first section details a list of named page layouts. The second section is a list of document data, with markup, that uses the various page layouts to determine how the content fills the various document pages.

The properties of the page are define by the page layout. They can define the directions for the flow of text, so as to match the conventions for the language in question. They define the size of a page as well as the margins of that page. Most important that they can define sequences of pages that allow for effects where the odd and even pages look different. Example one can define a page layout sequence that gives extra space to the inner margins for printing purposes; this allows more space to be given to the margin where the book will be bound.

The document data portion is brake up into a sequence of flow, where each flow is attached to a page layout. The flows contain a list of blocks and each contain a list of text data, inline markup elements, or a combination of the two. Content may also be added to the margins of the document, for page numbers, chapter headings and the like.

Blocks and inline element function are the same way as for CSS, though some of the rules for padding and margins differ between CSS and FO. The direction, relative to the page orientation, for the progression of inlines and blocks can be fully specified, thus allowing FO documents to function under languages that are read different from English. The language of the FO specification, unlike that of CSS 2.1, uses direction-neutral terms like start and end rather than left and right when describing these directions.

Comparisons are often made between XSL-FO and CSS, and for the most part they are valid. One critical distinction between the two technologies is that CSS styles are always attached to an existing document tree, whereas XSL-FO establishes its own document structure. In other words, you apply CSS styles to XML data, whereas XSL-FO represents a complete merger of data and styles. In practice, XML data is typically still maintained separately from its XSLT stylesheet, which is then used to combine the data and XSL-FO styles into a complete XSL-FO document.

XSL-FO's basic content markup is derived from CSS and its cascading rules. Many attributes in XSL-FO propagate into the child elements unless explicitly overridden.

XSL-FO DOCUMENT STRUCTURE

XSL Formatting Objects documents are XML documents but they do not have to conform to any schema. Instead, they conform to a syntax defined in the XSL-FO specification. XSL-FO documents have a structure like this:

```
<?xml version="1.0" encoding="ISO-8859-1"?>
<fo:root xmlns:fo="http://www.w3.org/1999/XSL/Format">
<fo:layout-master-set>
 <fo:simple-page-master master-name="A4">
 <!-- Page template goes here -->
```

```
 </fo:simple-page-master>
</fo:layout-master-set>
<fo:page-sequence master-reference="A4">
 <!-- Page content goes here -->
</fo:page-sequence>
</fo:root>
```

Explanation

XSL-FO documents are XML documents and must always start with an XML declaration:

```
<?xml version="1.0" encoding="ISO-8859-1"?>
```

The <fo:root> element is the root element of XSL-FO documents. The root element also declares the namespace for XSL-FO:

```
<fo:root xmlns:fo="http://www.w3.org/1999/XSL/Format">
 <!-- The full XSL-FO document goes here -->
</fo:root>
```

The <fo:layout-master-set> element contains one or more page templates:

```
<fo:layout-master-set>
 <!-- All page templates go here -->
</fo:layout-master-set>
```

Each <fo:simple-page-master> element contains a single page template. Each template must have a unique name (master-name):

```
<fo:simple-page-master master-name="A4">
 <!-- One page template goes here -->
</fo:simple-page-master>
```

One or more <fo:page-sequence> elements describe the page contents. The master-reference attribute refers to the simple-page-master template with the same name:

```
<fo:page-sequence master-reference="A4">
 <!-- Page content goes here -->
</fo:page-sequence>
```

The master-reference "A4" does not actually describe a predefined page format. It is just a name. You can use any name, like "MyPage" or "MyTemplate." XSL-FO uses rectangular boxes (areas) to display output.

Example: 1

```
<?xml version="1.0" encoding="ISO-8859-1"?><fo:
root xmlns:fo="http://www.w3.org/1999/XSL/Format">
<fo:layout-master-set>
<fo:simple-page-master master-name="A4">
<!-- Page template goes here -->
</fo:simple-page-master>
</fo:layout-master-set>
<fo:page-sequence master-reference="A4">
<!-- Page content goes here -->
</fo:page-sequence></fo:root>
```

Explanation

XSL-FO documents always start with an XML declaration:

```
<?xml version="1.0" encoding="ISO-8859-1"?>
```

The <fo:root> element is the root element of XSL-FO documents.

```
<fo:root xmlns:fo="http://www.w3.org/1999/XSL/Format">
<!-- The full XSL-FO document goes here -->
</fo:root>
<fo:layout-master-set> tag element contains one or more page
templates
<fo:layout-master-set>
<!-- All page templates go here -->
</fo:layout-master-set>
```

Each <fo:simple-page-master> tag element contains a single page template. Each template must have a unique name:

```
<fo:simple-page-master master-name="A4">
<!-- One page template goes here -->
</fo:simple-page-master>
```

One or more <fo:page-sequence> tag describe the page contents. The master-reference attribute refers to the simple-page-master template with the same name:

```
<fo:page-sequence master-reference="A4">
<!-- Page content goes here -->
</fo:page-sequence>
```

Example: 2

```
<?xml version="1.0" encoding="iso-8859-1"?>❶
<fo:root xmlns:fo="http://www.w3.org/1999/XSL/Format">❷
 <fo:layout-master-set>❸
 <fo:simple-page-master master-name="my-page">
 <fo:region-body margin="1in"/>
 </fo:simple-page-master>
 </fo:layout-master-set>
<fo:page-sequence master-reference="my-page">❹
 <fo:flow flow-name="xsl-region-body">❺
  <fo:block>Hello, world!</fo:block>❻
   </fo:flow>
  </fo:page-sequence>
</fo:root>
```

Explanation

1. This is an XML declaration. XSL FO (XSLFO) belongs to XML family, so this is obligatory.
2. Root element. The obligatory namespace attribute declares the XSLFO namespace.
3. Layout master set. This element contains one or more declarations of page masters and page sequence masters—elements that define layouts of single pages and page sequences. In the example, we defined a rudimentary page master with only one area in it. The area should have a 1 inch margin from all sides of the page.
4. Page sequence. Pages in the document are grouped into sequences; each sequence starts from a new page. The master-reference attribute selects an appropriate layout scheme from the masters listed inside <fo:layout-master-set>. Setting the master-reference to a page master name means that all pages in this sequence are formatted using this page master.
5. Flow. This is the container object for all user text in the document. Everything contained in the flow is formatted into regions on pages generated inside the page sequence. The flow name links the flow to a specific region on the page (defined in the page master); in our example, it is the body region.

6. Block. This object roughly corresponds to <DIV> in HTML and normally includes a paragraph of text. We need it here because text cannot be placed directly into a flow.

FONT AND TEXT ATTRIBUTES

Let us now enrich the text with character-level formatting. Several properties control font styles—family, size, color, and weight. Let's look at some examples:

```
<fo:block font-family="Times" font-size="14pt">
Hello, world!
</fo:block>
```

The font family is Times, and the font size is 14 points.

```
<fo:block font-family="Times" font-size="14pt" font-style="italic">
 <fo:inline color="red">H</fo:inline>ello,
 <fo:inline font-weight="bold">world!</fo:inline>
</fo:block>
```

Same as above, plus

- the text is italicized (font-style="italic")
- the first letter of the first word is written in red (color="red")
- the second word is written in bold (font-weight="bold")

Note a new formatting object—<fo:inline>. It corresponds to <SPAN> in HTML, and ascribes formatting to chunks of text within a block.

Font properties are inheritable. It means that, once defined for a formatting object, they apply to all formatting objects inside it. That's why the first inline sequence affects only the color of the font, leaving its family, size, and slant unmodified. Inheritable properties can be put almost everywhere on the formatting objects tree; as a rule, you specify default font for a document by applying these properties to <fo:flow>, <fo:page-sequence> or even <fo:root>.

To reduce typing, you can use a shorthand notation for setting font attributes as a group. For example, the above example can be rewritten as follows:

```
<fo:block font="italic 14pt Times">
 <fo:inline color="red">H</fo:inline>ello,
 <fo:inline font-weight="bold">world!</fo:inline>
</fo:block>
```

The font property has the following syntax:

[<style, weight, and/or variant>] <size>[/<line height>] <family>

It sets all mentioned attributes to specified values, and resets all other font-related attributes to their default values, overriding inherited values. Be careful when using this feature: font="14pt Times" is not equivalent to a conjunction of font-size="14pt" and font-family="Times"!

Let's now build a full XSL-FO (XSL-FO) example with the font attributes introduced above:

```
<?xml version="1.0" encoding="iso-8859-1"?>
<fo:root xmlns:fo="http://www.w3.org/1999/XSL/Format">
 <fo:layout-master-set>
  <fo:simple-page-master master-name="my-page">
   <fo:region-body margin="1in"/>
  </fo:simple-page-master>
 </fo:layout-master-set>
 <fo:page-sequence master-reference="my-page">
  <fo:flow flow-name="xsl-region-body" font="12pt Times"❶>
   <fo:block font="italic 24pt Helvetica">
    <fo:inline color="red">F</fo:inline>ont
   <fo:inline color="red">A</fo:inline>ttributes
  </fo:block>
 <fo:block>❷
```

The inherited font for this block is 12pt Times.

```
</fo:block>
<fo:block>
```

Font attributes:

```
<fo:inline color="red">colored</fo:inline>,
<fo:inline font-weight="bold">bold</fo:inline>,
<fo:inline font-style="italic">italic</fo:inline>,
<fo:inline font-size="75%">small</fo:inline>,
<fo:inline font-size="133%">large</fo:inline>.
</fo:block>
<fo:block>
```

Text attributes: ❸

```
<fo:inline text-decoration="underline">underlined</fo:inline>,
<fo:inline letter-spacing="3pt"> expanded </fo:inline>,
```

```
        <fo:inline word-spacing="6pt">
         text with extra spacing between words
        </fo:inline>,
        <fo:inline text-transform="uppercase">all capitals</fo:inline>,
        <fo:inline text-transform="capitalize">capitalized</fo:inline>,
        text with <fo:inline baseline-shift="sub"
        font-size="smaller">subscripts</fo:inline>
        and <fo:inline baseline-shift="super"
        font-size="smaller">superscripts</fo:inline>.
       </fo:block>
      </fo:flow>
     </fo:page-sequence>
    </fo:root>
```

1	A common font for the whole flow is specified.
2	This block inherits font attributes from the flow.
3	In this block, we introduce several other text-level properties: • text decoration • underline/overline/strikethrough • letter and word spacing • a positive value expands text, a negative value condenses it • text transformations • upper/lower case, capitalize • shifted text • subscripts and superscripts

XSL-FO AREAS

The XSL formatting model defines a number of rectangular areas (boxes) to display output. All output (text, pictures, etc.) will be formatted into these boxes and then displayed or printed to a target media. We now take a closer look at the following areas:

- Pages
- Regions

- Block areas
- Line areas
- Inline areas

XSL-FO Pages

XSL-FO output is formatted into pages. Printed output normally goes into many separate pages. Browser output often goes into one long page.

XSL-FO Pages contain Regions.

XSL-FO Regions

Each XSL-FO Page contains a number of regions:

- region-body (the body of the page)
- region-before (the header of the page)
- region-after (the footer of the page)
- region-start (the left sidebar)
- region-end (the right sidebar)
- XSL-FO regions contain Block areas.

XSL-FO Block Areas

XSL-FO Block areas define small block elements (the ones that normally starts with a new line) like paragraphs, tables, and lists.

XSL-FO Block areas can contain other Block areas, but most often they contain Line areas.

XSL-FO Line Areas

XSL-FO Line areas define text lines inside Block areas. XSL-FO Line areas contain Inline areas.

XSL-FO Inline Areas

XSL-FO Inline areas define text inside Lines (bullets, single character, graphics, and more).

XSL-FO OUTPUT

XSL-FO defines output inside elements.

XSL-FO Block, Flow, and Page

"Blocks" of content "Flow" into "Pages" and are transferred to output media.

XSL-FO output is normally nested inside <fo:block> elements, <fo:flow> elements, and <fo:page-sequence> elements:

```
<fo:page-sequence>
<fo:flow flow-name="xsl-region-body">
<fo:block>
<!-- Output goes here -->
</fo:block>
</fo:flow>
</fo:page-sequence>
```

XSL-FO Flow

XSL-FO pages are filled with data from <fo:flow> elements.

XSL-FO pages are filled with data from <fo:flow> elements. XSL-FO pages are filled with content from the <fo:flow> element. The <fo:flow> element contains all the elements to be printed to the page. When the page is full, the same page master will be used over (and over) again until all the text is printed.

The <fo:flow> element has a "flow-name" attribute. The value of the flow-name attribute defines where the content of the <fo:flow> element will go. The legal values are

- xsl-region-body (into the region-body)
- xsl-region-before (into the region-before)
- xsl-region-after (into the region-after)
- xsl-region-start (into the region-start)
- xsl-region-end (into the region-end)

PAGE LAYOUT

XSL-FO Page Sequences

XSL-FO uses <fo:page-sequence> tag to define output pages. Each Page output refers to a page master which defines the layout. Each output page has a <fo:flow> tag defining the output. Each output is displayed in a sequence.

Page Sequence Masters

So far, we have used only single page masters in examples. In this section, more complex cases are analyzed. To start, let's design a page sequence with two page masters: one for the first page, the other one for the rest of the document.

```
<?xml version="1.0" encoding="iso-8859-1"?>
<fo:root xmlns:fo="http://www.w3.org/1999/XSL/Format">
 <fo:layout-master-set>
  <fo:simple-page-master master-name="first-page">
   <fo:region-body margin="1in" border="thin silver ridge" ❶
          padding="6pt"/>
 </fo:simple-page-master>
<fo:simple-page-master master-name="all-pages">
  <fo:region-body margin="1in"/>
</fo:simple-page-master>
<fo:page-sequence-master master-name="my-sequence">❷
  <fo:single-page-master-reference master-reference="first-page"/>❸
  <fo:repeatable-page-master-reference master-reference="all-pages"/>❹
 </fo:page-sequence-master>
</fo:layout-master-set>
<fo:page-sequence master-reference="my-sequence"❺>
 <fo:flow flow-name="xsl-region-body" font="72pt Times">
  <fo:block space-before="2in" space-after="2in">❻
```

First Block

```
</fo:block>
<fo:block break-before="page" space-before="2in" space-after="2in">❼
```

Second Block

```
</fo:block>
<fo:block break-before="page" space-before="2in" space-after="2in">
```

Third Block

```
   </fo:block>
  </fo:flow>
 </fo:page-sequence>
</fo:root>
```

Explanation

1	In XSL-FO, you can specify borders, padding, and background on regions in exactly the same way as you do it on blocks. The first page in this example has a border around it, while the others remain borderless.
2	The page sequence master defines the chain of page masters to use for a page sequence.
3	<fo:single-page-master-reference> inserts a single page master in the chain.
4	<fo:repeatable-page-master-reference> makes the specified page masters repeat up to the end of the chain.
5	Note that master-reference attribute of a <fo:page-sequence> can refer to either <fo:page-sequence-master> or <fo:simple-page-master>. In the latter, all pages generated by this <fo:page-sequence> use the same page master.
6, 7	Spaces are not inheritable: you cannot specify them on a surrounding block. There's no alternative to specifying them explicitly on every block involved.

Where To Flow?

The <fo:flow> tag consist "flow-name" attribute. The value of the flow-name attribute describes where the content of the <fo:flow> element will go. These values are legal:

- xsl-region-body
- xsl-region-before
- xsl-region-after
- xsl-region-start
- xsl-region-end

XSL-FO Pages

To define the layout of pages, XSL-FO uses page templates called "Page Masters."

Page Templates

To define the layout of pages, XSL-FO uses page templates called "Page Masters" and each template must have a unique name. In the following example, three <fo:simple-page-master> elements define three different templates and each template has a different name.

The first template is called "intro" and it is used for the introduction pages.

The second and third templates are called "left" and "right" and used for even and odd page numbers.

```
<fo:simple-page-master master-name="intro">
<fo:region-body margin="5in" />
</fo:simple-page-master>
<fo:simple-page-master master-name="left">
<fo:region-body margin-left="2in" margin-right="3in" />
</fo:simple-page-master>
<fo:simple-page-master master-name="right">
<fo:region-body margin-left="3in" margin-right="2in" />
</fo:simple-page-master>
```

In the example above, three <fo:simple-page-master> elements define three different templates. Each template (page-master) has a different name.

The first template is called "intro." It could be used as a template for the introduction pages. The second and third templates are called "left" and "right." They could be used as templates for even and odd page numbers.

Page Size

To define the page size of a page XSL-FO page size, use the following attributes:

- page-width defines the width of a page
- page-height defines the height of a page

XSL-FO Page Margins

To define the margins of a page, XSL-FO page margins, use the following attributes:

- margin-top
- margin-bottom
- margin-left
- margin-right
- margin defines all four margins

XSL-FO Page Regions

To define the regions of a page, XSL-FO page regions use the following attributes:

- region-body: For the body region
- region-before: For the top region
- region-after: For the bottom region
- region-start: For the left region
- region-end: For the right region

The region-start, region-end, region-before, and region-after are part of the body region. To avoid text in the body region and to overwrite text in these regions, the body region must have margins set as the minimum size of these regions.

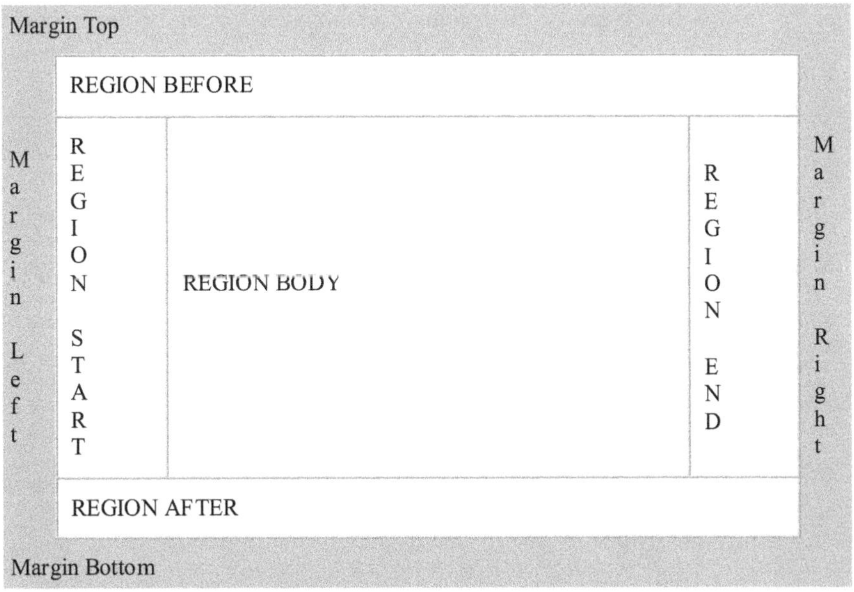

Margin Top
REGION BEFORE
Margin Left
REGION START
REGION BODY
REGION END
Margin Right
REGION AFTER
Margin Bottom

FIGURE 16.2 XSL-FO Page

XSL-FO BLOCKS

XSL-FO output goes into blocks. This output is normally nested inside <fo:block> elements. "Blocks" of content "Flow" into "Pages" of the output media. XSL-FO output is normally nested inside <fo:block> elements, nested inside <fo:flow> elements, nested inside <fo:page-sequence> elements:

Syntax

```
<fo:page-sequence>
<fo:flow flow-name="xsl-region-body">
<fo:block>
<!-- Output goes here -->
</fo:block>
</fo:flow>
</fo:page-sequence>
```

Block Area Attributes

Blocks are sequences of output in rectangular boxes.

Since block areas are rectangular boxes, they share many common area properties:

```
<fo:block
border-width="1mm">
```

This block contains a one millimeter border around it.

```
</fo:block>
```

Rectangular block area boxes share many common area properties:

- space before
- space after
- margin
- border
- padding
- font-weight
- font-style
- font-size
- font-variant

Text attributes:

- text-align
- text-align-last

- text-indent
- start-indent
- end-indent
- wrap-option (defines word wrap)
- break-before (defines page breaks)
- break-after (defines page breaks)
- reference-orientation (defines text rotation in 90" increments)
- XSL-FO Lists

STYLING TEXT IN XSL-FO

Finally, it's time to see where XSL-FO has some similarity with other technologies that you may be more familiar with. XSL-FO's text styling properties are very similar to those used in CSS. In XSL-FO, you set the font specifics for text using attributes on the <fo:block> and <fo:inline> tags. More specifically, the font-size, font-family, and font-weight attributes can all be used to set the font for a block or inline content. These attributes are set just like their CSS counterparts.

The following is an example of setting the font size and font family for a block in XSL-FO:

```
<fo:block text-align="end" font-size="10pt" font-family="serif"
background-color="black" color="white">
```

Great Sporting Events

```
</fo:block>
```

In this example, the text content Great Sporting Events is styled using a 10-point, serif font. Furthermore, the alignment of the text is set to end via the text-align attribute, which is equivalent to right-alignment in CSS. There is no concept of left or right in XSL-FO. Instead, you use start and end when referring to the alignment of content that you might otherwise think of as being left-aligned or right-aligned. Of course, center is used in XSL-FO when it comes to alignment.

The background-color and color attributes in this code are direct carry-overs from CSS. You can use them just as you would the similarly named CSS styles.

CONTROLLING SPACING AND BORDERS

There are a few spacing and border properties that you can set when it comes to XSL-FO content. The space-before and space-after attributes are used to control the spacing before and after a block. Because we're talking about blocks, the spacing applies vertically to the top (space-before) and bottom (space-after) of the block. In this way, the space-before and space-after attributes work sort of like top and bottom margins, except they apply outside of the margins.

The following is an example of setting the space after a block so that the next content is spaced a little further down the page:

```
<fo:block font-size="18pt" font-family="sans-serif" space-after="5pt"

background-color="black" color="white" text-align="center" padding-top="0pt">
```

Welcome to the Computer Center

```
</fo:block>
```

Notice in this code that the padding-top attribute is set, which controls the padding along the top of the block. All of the standard CSS margin and padding styles are available for you in XSL-FO as attributes of the <fo:block> tag. These attributes include margin, margin-left, margin-right, margin-top, margin-bottom, padding, padding-left, padding-right, padding-top, and padding-bottom. There are also several familiar border attributes that you can use with blocks: border, border-left, border-right, border-top, and border-bottom.

MORE COMPLEX STRUCTURES

Lists

Lists in XSL-FO are much more than just a bulleted sequence of paragraphs: they form a general-purpose mechanism to align two blocks adjacent to each other. They may be used to format ordinary lists, footnotes, image lists, and even to produce some table-like layout patterns.

A list is created by a <fo:list-block> object. Inside it, there are one or more <fo:list-item> elements. Each list item contains one <fo:list-item-label> followed by one <fo:list-item-body>. These two elements contain blocks that are aligned vertically and placed side-by-side. Let's start with an ordinary bulleted list:

```
<fo:list-block provisional-distance-between-starts="18pt"❶
        provisional-label-separation="3pt"❷>
 <fo:list-item>
  <fo:list-item-label end-indent="label-end()"❸)>
    <fo:block>&#x2022;❹</fo:block>
 </fo:list-item-label>
 <fo:list-item-body start-indent="body-start()"❺>
   <fo:block>First item</fo:block>
  </fo:list-item-body>
 </fo:list-item>
 <fo:list-item>
  <fo:list-item-label end-indent="label-end()">
 <fo:block>&#x2022;</fo:block>
 </fo:list-item-label>
 <fo:list-item-body start-indent="body-start()">
   <fo:block>Second item</fo:block>
  </fo:list-item-body>
 </fo:list-item>
</fo:list-block>
```

1	This property specifies how far the left side of the label is from the left side of the body.
2	This property specifies the separation between the right side of the label and the left edge of the body.
3	The end-indent attribute specifies the offset of the right edge of <fo:list-item-label> from the right edge of the reference area (i.e., page). A special label-end() function sets it to the value calculated from provisional-distance- between-starts and provisional-label-separation values. However, this is not a default value: you have to specify end-indent="label-end()" on each <fo:list-item-label> in the list. Alternatively, you can use an explicit value of end-indent.
4	This is a Unicode for a round bullet.
5	The start-indent attribute specifies the left offset of the <fo:list-item-body> from the left. A special body-start() function sets it to the value calculated from provisional-distance-between-starts. Like for the <fo:list- item-label>, this is not a default value; don't forget to specify it on each <fo:list-item-body>.

XSL-FO List Blocks

To create a lists there are four XSL-FO objects:

- o:list-block (it contains the whole list)
- fo:list-item (it contains each item in the list)
- fo:list-item-label (it contains the label for the list-item like number and character)
- fo:list-item-body (contains the body of the list-item—typically one or more <fo:block> objects)

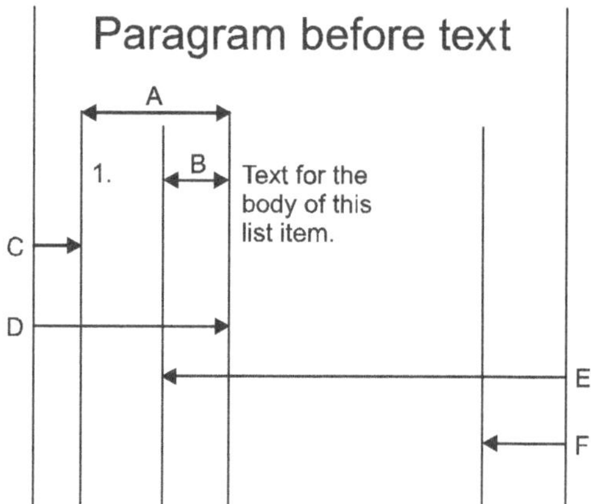

- provisional-distance-between-starts
- provisional-label-separation
- start-indent for list-item-label
- start-indent for list-item-body
- end-indent for list-item-label
- end-indent for list-item-body

```
<xsl:template match="ol">
<fo:list-block
space-before="0.25em" space-after="0.25em">
<xsl:apply-templates/>
</fo:list-block>
</xsl:template>
<xsl:template match="ol/li">
<fo:list-item space-after="0.5ex">
<fo:list-item-label start-indent="1em">
```

```
<fo:block>
<xsl:number/>.
</fo:block>
</fo:list-item-label>
<fo:list-item-body>
<fo:block>
<xsl:apply-templates/>
</fo:block>
</fo:list-item-body>
</fo:list-item>
</xsl:template>
```

XSL-FO Lists

XSL-FO uses the <fo:list-block> element to define lists.

XSL-FO Lists Blocks

There are four XSL-FO objects used to create lists.

- fo:list-block (contains the whole list)
- fo:list-item (contains each item in the list)
- fo:list-item-label (contains the label for the list-item—typically an <fo:block> containing a number and character)
- fo:list-item-body (contains the content/body of the list-item—typically one or more <fo:block> objects)

An XSL-FO list example is as follows:

```
<fo:list-block>
<fo:list-item>
 <fo:list-item-label>
 <fo:block>*</fo:block>
 </fo:list-item-label>
 <fo:list-item-body>
 <fo:block>Volvo</fo:block>
 </fo:list-item-body>
</fo:list-item>
<fo:list-item>
 <fo:list-item-label>
 <fo:block>*</fo:block>
```

```
 </fo:list-item-label>
 <fo:list-item-body>
 <fo:block>Saab</fo:block>
 </fo:list-item-body>
</fo:list-item>
</fo:list-block>
```

The output from the code above would be something like this:

- Volvo
- Saab

TABLES

Tables in XSL-FO resemble HTML ones: they are made of cells grouped into rows; rows are further grouped into row groups—table header, table footer, and table bodies (one or more). There are also column descriptors.

Tables are described in XSL-FO using the fo:table element. A table can have a header (fo:tableheader), a body (fo:table-body), and a footer (fo:table-footer). Each of these groups contain rows (fo:table-row), which in turn contain cells (fo:table-cell). The columns are described using the fo:table-column elements.

A basic 2x2 table is as follows:

```
<fo:table border="0.5pt solid black" text-align="center">
 <fo:table-body>
  <fo:table-row>
   <fo:table-cell padding="6pt" border="0.5pt solid black">❶
    <fo:block> upper left </fo:block>
   </fo:table-cell>
   <fo:table-cell padding="6pt" border="0.5pt solid black">
    <fo:block> upper right </fo:block>
   </fo:table-cell>
 </fo:table-row>
 <fo:table-row>
  <fo:table-cell padding="6pt" border="0.5pt solid black">
   <fo:block> lower left </fo:block>
  </fo:table-cell>
   <fo:table-cell padding="6pt" border="0.5pt solid black">
   <fo:block> lower right </fo:block>
```

```
    </fo:table-cell>
   </fo:table-row>
  </fo:table-body>
</fo:table>
```

Table Columns

A column can have a proportional width or a fixed width. A fixed width includes the length units (in, pt, cm; for example<fo:table-column column-width="3in"/>).

A proportional width is expressed via the proportional-column-width function (for example, <fo:table-column column-width= "proportional-column-width(20)"/>) or by using a percentage sign (<fo:table-column column-width="20%"/>). There is a third way to specify a column width: by omitting the column-width attribute, the column will size itself automatically, depending on its content.

A table can mix fixed, proportional, and automatic columns. When a table contains only proportional columns, XF will resize them even if the sum of percentages is not 100.

For example:

```
<fo:table>
<fo:table-column column-width="50%"/>
<fo:table-column column-width="50%"/>
..
</fo:table>
```

And

```
<fo:table>
<fo:table-column column-width="proportional-column-width(1)"/>
<fo:table-column column-width="proportional-column-width(1)"/>
..
</fo:table>
```

And

```
<fo:table>
<fo:table-column column-width="proportional-column-width(60)"/>
<fo:table-column column-width="proportional-column-width(60)"/>
..
</fo:table>
```

will produce the same result.

XSL-FO OBJECTS

There are nine XSL-FO objects used to create tables:

- fo:table-and-caption
- fo:table
- fo:table-caption
- fo:table-column
- fo:table-header
- fo:table-footer
- fo:table-body
- fo:table-row
- fo:table-cell

Example

The <fo:table-and-caption> element is used to define a table. It contains a <fo:table> and an optional <fo:caption> element.

The <fo:table> element contains optional element like <fo:table-column>, <fo:table-header>, <fo:table-body>, and <fo:table-footer>. Each of these elements has one or more <fo:table-row> elements, with one or more <fo:table-cell> elements:

```
<xsl:template match="ol">
<fo:list-block
space-before="0.25em" space-after="0.25em">
<xsl:apply-templates/>
</fo:list-block>
</xsl:template>
<xsl:template match="ol/li">
<fo:list-item space-after="0.5ex">
<fo:list-item-label start-indent="1em">
<fo:block>
<xsl:number/>.
</fo:block>
</fo:list-item-label>
<fo:list-item-body>
<fo:block>
<xsl:apply-templates/>
</fo:block>
</fo:list-item-body>
```

```
</fo:list-item>
</xsl:template>
```

Output

Car	Price
Volve	$50000
SAAB	$48000

GRAPHICS

There is a special inline element for including graphics into XSL-FO—<fo:external-graphic>. The source image is specified by the src attribute whose value is a URI. XEP handles HTTP, FTP, data and filesystem resource locators in URIs. An unqualified URI is treated as a path to a file in the local file system; if the path is relative, it is calculated from the location of the source XSL-FO document. Here's an example:

```
<fo:block>
```

This text includes a picture:

```
<fo:external-graphic src="url('smile.gif')"❶
          content-height="1em"❷ content-width="1em"❸/>
</fo:block>
```

1.	Note the url('...') function-like wrapper around the file name: this is required by the XSL 1.0 Recommendation. (XEP recognizes unwrapped URLs, too).
2.	In this example, the height and the width of the image are expressed in units relative to the nominal font size.
3.	This is a convenient technique to scale small inlined images proportionally to the text height.

XSL-FO PROCESSORS

XSL-FO processors are a type of software program for formatting XSL documents. Most XSL-FO processors output in PDF documents as well as HTML and other formats. Some well-known XSL-FO processors are FOP, PassiveTeX, and xmlroff.

XSL-FO processors are really typesetting engines. An XSL-FO file is a mixture of text from your XML source document and XSL-FO tags that suggest how the text should be formatted. It is the XSL-FO processor that actually creates the typeset lines of text and lays them out on pages. An XSL-FO processor typically generates a PDF or PostScript file which can be fed to a printer to produce hard-copy output.

Currently there are many XSL-FO processors, but few of them have completely implemented the standard. There are at least three reasons for this:

- The XSL-FO standard was finalized almost two years after the XSLT standard.
- The XSL-FO standard is big and complicated.
- Typesetting is hard.

The authors of the XSL-FO standard recognized how difficult it would be to implement, and so divided it into three levels of conformance: basic, extended, and complete. That way a processor can claim conformance to the lower conformance levels and produce useful output, while still being under development for the higher conformance levels.

XSL-FO SOFTWARE

Scriptura

Scriptura is a cross-platform document that generates solutions based on XSLT and XSL-FO. Scriptura has a WYSIWYG design tool and engine. The XSL-FO formatter used in the engine is no longer based on Apache FOP, but was written from scratch by inventive designers. The new features in this release are bulleted and numbered lists, break-after and break-before properties, extended bar code options, and improved number and currency formatting.

XSL-FO AND XSLT

XSL-FO and XSLT can help each other.

```
<fo:block font-size="14pt" font-family="verdana" color="red"
space-before="5mm" space-after="5mm">
```

```
 W3Schools
</fo:block>
<fo:block text-indent="5mm" font-family="verdana" font-size="12pt">
Welcome to the computer center !
</fo:block>
```

Result:

Welcome to the computer center!

QUESTIONS FOR DISCUSSION

1. What are XSL-FO processors?
2. What are XSL-FO Documents? Explain XSL-FO documents' structure.
3. What is XSL-FO?
4. Why do we need XSL-FO?
5. Write a comparative feature list for XSL-FO.
6. What are XSL-FO Block areas?
7. Explain XSL-FO areas.
8. How can XSL-FO and XSLT can help each other?
9. Write a short note on Scriptura software.

CHAPTER 17

XML WITH DATABASES

INTRODUCTION

This chapter gives a high-level overview of how to use XML with databases. It describes how the differences between data-centric and document-centric documents affect their usage with databases, how XML is commonly used with relational databases, and what native XML databases are and when to use them.

Although the information discussed in this chapter is (mostly) up-to-date, the idea that the world of XML and databases can be seen through the data-centric/document-centric divide is somewhat dated. It used to be a convenient metaphor for introducing native XML databases, which were then not widely understood, even in the database community. However, it was always somewhat unrealistic, as many XML documents are not strictly data-centric or document-centric, but somewhere in between. So while the data-centric/document-centric divide is a convenient starting point, it is better to understand the differences between XML-enabled databases and native XML databases and to choose the appropriate database based on your processing needs.

XML DOCUMENTS AS DATABASES

Before we start talking about XML and databases, we need to answer a question that occurs to many people: "Is an XML document a database?"

An XML document is a database only in the loosest sense of the term. That is, it is a collection of data. In many ways, this makes it no different from any other file—after all, all files contain data of some sort. As a "database" format, XML has some advantages. For example, it is self-describing (the markup describes the structure and type names of the data, although not the semantics), it is portable (Unicode), and it can describe data in tree or graph structures. It also has some disadvantages. For example, it is verbose and access to the data is slow due to parsing and text conversion.

A more useful question to ask is whether XML and its surrounding technologies constitute a "database" in another sense of the term—that is, a database management system (DBMS). The answer to this question is, "Sort of." On the plus side, XML provides many of the things found in databases: storage (XML documents), schemas (DTDs, XML Schemas, and RELAX NG), query languages (XQuery, XPath, XQL, XML-QL, and QUILT), programming interfaces (SAX, DOM, and JDOM), and so on. On the minus side, it lacks many of the things found in real databases: efficient storage, indexes, security, transactions and data integrity, multi-user access, triggers, and queries across multiple documents.

Thus, while it may be possible to use an XML document or documents as a database in environments with small amounts of data, few users, and modest performance requirements, this will fail in most production environments, which have many users, strict data integrity requirements, and the need for good performance.

A good example of the type of "database" for which an XML document is suitable is an .ini file—that is, a file that contains application configuration information. It is much easier to invent a small XML language and write a SAX application for interpreting that language than it is to write a parser for comma-delimited files. In addition, XML allows you to have nested entries, something that is harder to do in comma-delimited files. However, this is hardly a database, since it is read and written linearly, and then only when the application is started and ended.

Examples of more sophisticated data sets for which an XML document might be suitable as a database are personal contact lists (names, phone numbers, and addresses). However, given the low price and ease of use of databases like dBASE and Access, there seems little reason to use an XML document as a database even in these cases. The only real advantage of XML is that the data is portable, and this is less of an advantage than it seems due to the widespread availability of tools for serializing databases as XML.

WHY USE A DATABASE?

The first question you need to ask yourself when you start thinking about XML and databases is why you want to use a database in the first place. Do you have legacy data you want to expose? Are you looking for a place to store your Web pages? Is the database used by an e-commerce application in which XML is used as a data transport? The answers to these questions will strongly influence your choice of database and middleware (if any), as well as how you use that database.

For example, suppose you have an e-commerce application that uses XML as a data transport. It is a good bet that your data has a highly regular structure and is used by non-XML applications. Furthermore, things like entities and the encodings used by XML documents probably aren't important to you—after all, you are interested in the data, not how it is stored in an XML document. In this case, you'll probably need a relational database and software to transfer the data between XML documents and the database. If your applications are object-oriented, you might even want a system that can store those objects in the database or serialize them as XML.

On the other hand, suppose you have a Website built from a number of prose-oriented XML documents. Not only do you want to manage the site, you would like to provide a way for users to search its contents. Your documents are likely to have a less regular structure and things such as entity usage are probably important to you because they are a fundamental part of how your documents are structured. In this case, you might want a product like a native XML database or a content management system. This will allow you to preserve physical document structure, support document-level transactions, and execute queries in an XML query language.

DATA VERSUS DOCUMENTS

Perhaps the most important factor in choosing a database is whether you are using the database to store data or documents. For example, is XML used simply as a data transport between the database and a (possibly non-XML) application? Or is its use integral, as in the case of XHTML and DocBook documents? This is usually a matter of intent, but it is important because all data-centric documents share a number of characteristics, as do all document-centric documents, and these influence how XML is stored in the database. The next two sections examine these characteristics.

DATA-CENTRIC DOCUMENTS

Data-centric documents are documents that use XML as a data transport. They are designed for machine consumption and the fact that XML is used at all is usually superfluous. That is, it is not important to the application or the database that the data is, for some length of time, stored in an XML document. Examples of data-centric documents are sales orders, flight schedules, scientific data, and stock quotes.

Data-centric documents are characterized by fairly regular structure, fine-grained data (that is, the smallest independent unit of data is at the level of a PCDATA-only element or an attribute), and little or no mixed content. The order in which sibling elements and PCDATA occurs is generally not significant, except when validating the document.

Data of the kind that is found in data-centric documents can originate both in the database (in which case you want to expose it as XML) and outside the database (in which case you want to store it in a database). An example of the former is the vast amount of legacy data stored in relational databases; an example of the latter is scientific data gathered by a measurement system and converted to XML. For example, the following sales order document is data-centric:

```
<SalesOrder SONumber="12345">
 <Customer CustNumber="543">
  <CustName>ABC Industries</CustName>
  <Street>123 Main St.</Street>
  <City>Chicago</City>
  <State>IL</State>
  <PostCode>60609</PostCode>
 </Customer>
 <OrderDate>981215</OrderDate>
 <Item ItemNumber="1">
  <Part PartNumber="123">
   <Description>
    <p><b>Turkey wrench:</b><br />
     Stainless steel, one-piece construction,
     lifetime guarantee.</p>
    </Description>
   <Price>9.95</Price>
  </Part>
 <Quantity>10</Quantity>
```

```
</Item>
 <Item ItemNumber="2">
  <Part PartNumber="456">
   <Description>
    <p><b>Stuffing separator:<b><br />
     Aluminum, one-year guarantee.</p>
     </Description>
    <Price>13.27</Price>
   </Part>
  <Quantity>5</Quantity>
 </Item>
</SalesOrder>
```

In addition to such obviously data-centric documents as the sales order shown above, many prose-rich documents are also data-centric. For example, consider a page on Amazon.com that displays information about a book. Although the page is largely text, the structure of that text is highly regular, much of it is common to all pages describing books, and each piece of page-specific text is limited in size. Thus, the page could be built from a simple, data-centric XML document that contains the information about a single book and is retrieved from the database, and an XSL stylesheet that adds the boilerplate text. In general, any Website that dynamically constructs HTML documents today by filling a template with database data can probably be replaced by a series of data-centric XML documents and one or more XSL stylesheets. For example, consider the following document describing a flight:

```
<FlightInfo>
  <Airline>ABC Airways</Airline> provides <Count>three</Count>
  non-stop flights daily from <Origin>Dallas</Origin> to
  <Destination>Fort Worth</Destination>. Departure times are
  <Departure>09:15</Departure>, <Departure>11:15</Departure>,
  and <Departure>13:15</Departure>. Arrival times are minutes later.
</FlightInfo>
```

This could be built from the following XML document and a simple stylesheet:

```
<Flights>
 <Airline>ABC Airways</Airline>
 <Origin>Dallas</Origin>
 <Destination>Fort Worth</Destination>
 <Flight>
```

```
    <Departure>09:15</Departure>
    <Arrival>09:16</Arrival>
   </Flight>
   <Flight>
    <Departure>11:15</Departure>
    <Arrival>11:16</Arrival>
   </Flight>
   <Flight>
    <Departure>13:15</Departure>
    <Arrival>13:16</Arrival>
   </Flight>
  </Flights>
```

DOCUMENT-CENTRIC DOCUMENTS

Document-centric documents are (usually) documents that are designed for human consumption. Examples are books, email, advertisements, and almost any hand-written XHTML document. They are characterized by a less regular or irregular structure, larger grained data (that is, the smallest independent unit of data might be at the level of an element with mixed content or the entire document itself), and considerable amounts of mixed content. The order in which sibling elements and PCDATA occurs is almost always significant.

Document-centric documents are usually written by hand in XML or some other format, such as RTF, PDF, or SGML, which is then converted to XML. Unlike data-centric documents, they usually do not originate in the database. For example, the following product description is document-centric:

```
<Product>
 <Intro>
 The <ProductName>Turkey Wrench</ProductName> from <Developer>Full
 Fabrication Labs, Inc.</Developer> is <Summary>like a monkey wrench,
 but not as big.</Summary>
 </Intro>
<Description>
 <Para>The turkey wrench, which comes in <i>both right- and left-
 handed versions (skyhook optional)</i>, is made of the <b>finest
 stainless steel</b>. The Readi-grip rubberized handle quickly adapts
 to your hands, even in the greasiest situations. Adjustment is
 possible through a variety of custom dials.</Para>
 <Para>You can:</Para>
```

```
 <List>
 <Item><Link URL="Order.html">Order your own turkey wrench</Link></Item>
 <Item><Link URL="Wrenches.htm">Read more about wrenches</Link></Item>
 <Item><Link URL="Catalog.zip">Download the catalog</Link></Item>
 </List>
 <Para>The turkey wrench costs <b>just $19.99</b> and, if you
 order now, comes with a <b>hand-crafted shrimp hammer</b> as a
 bonus gift.</Para>
</Description>
</Product>
```

DATA, DOCUMENTS, AND DATABASES

In practice, the distinction between data-centric and document-centric documents is not always clear. For example, an otherwise data-centric document, such as an invoice, might contain large-grained, irregularly structured data, such as a part description. And an otherwise document-centric document, such as a user's manual, might contain fine-grained, regularly structured data (often metadata), such as an author's name and a revision date. Other examples include legal and medical documents, which are written as prose but contain discrete pieces of data, such as dates, names, and procedures, and often must be stored as complete documents for legal reasons.

In spite of this, characterizing your documents as data-centric or document-centric will help you decide what kind of database to use. As a general rule, data is stored in a traditional database, such as a relational, object-oriented, or hierarchical database. This can be done by third-party middleware or by capabilities built in to the database itself. In the latter case, the database is said to be XML-enabled. Documents are stored in a native XML database (a database designed especially for storing XML) or a content management system (an application designed to manage documents and built on top of a native XML database).

These rules are not absolute. Data—especially semi-structured data—can be stored in native XML databases and documents can be stored in traditional databases when few XML-specific features are needed. Furthermore, the boundaries between traditional databases and native XML databases are beginning to blur, as traditional databases add native XML capabilities and native XML databases support the storage of document fragments in external (usually relational) databases.

STORING AND RETRIEVING DATA

In order to transfer data between XML documents and a database, it is necessary to map the XML document schema (DTD, XML Schemas, and RELAX NG) to the database schema. The data transfer software is then built on top of this mapping. The software may use an XML query language (such as XPath, XQuery, or a proprietary language) or simply transfer data according to the mapping (the XML equivalent of SELECT * FROM Table).

In the latter case, the structure of the document must exactly match the structure expected by the mapping. Since this is often not the case, products that use this strategy are often used with XSLT. That is, before transferring data to the database, the document is first transformed to the structure expected by the mapping; the data is then transferred. Similarly, after transferring data from the database, the resulting document is transformed to the structure needed by the application.

MAPPING DOCUMENT SCHEMAS TO DATABASE SCHEMAS

Mappings between document schemas and database schemas are performed on element types, attributes, and text. They almost always omit physical structure (such as entities, CDATA sections, and encoding information) and some logical structure (such as processing instructions, comments, and the order in which elements and PCDATA appear in their parent). This is more reasonable than it may sound, as the database and application are concerned only with the data in the XML document. For example, in the sales order shown above, it doesn't matter if the customer number is stored in a CDATA section, an external entity, or directly as PCDATA, nor does it matter if the customer number is stored before or after the order date.

One consequence of this is that "round-tripping" a document—that is, storing the data from a document in the database and then reconstructing the document from that data—often results in a different document, even in the canonical sense of the term. Whether this is acceptable depends on your needs and might influence your choice of software.

Two mappings are commonly used to map an XML document schema to the database schema: table-based mapping and object-relational mapping.

RELATIONAL DATABASE PRIMER

Before you can learn about relating XML to databases, you need to learn about databases themselves. When most people think of databases, they're thinking specifically about relational databases. All of the popular database products (Microsoft SQL Server, Oracle, IBM DB2, MySQL) use the relational model. In turn, most Web and business applications use one relational database or another for data storage.

The relational database model is all about tables. All of the data is stored in a tabular format and relationships between tables are expressed through data shared among those tables. Tables in relational databases are just like tables in HTML or tables in this book. They consist of rows and columns. Each row represents a record in the database, and each column represents one field in each of the records.

A group of tables is generally referred to as a schema, which conceptually isn't all that different from an XML schema. In a schema, some or all of the tables are generally related to one another. Let's look at how those relationships work. Ordinarily, every table contains a column (or group of columns) that contains data that uniquely identifies that row in the table. In most cases, this is an ID field that simply contains a number that sets that row apart from the others in the table. This value is referred to as the *primary key*. In relational database design, the primary key is extremely important because it is the root of relationships between tables.

Here's a simple example. Let's say you have a table called students. The students table contains, among other bits of data, a column called id_students. The table might also include the student's name, address, and phone number. You might also have a second table, called majors. This table contains the major and minor for all of the students, under the assumption that no student has more than one major or minor.

This is what is referred to as a one-to-one relationship. Each record in the students table can have one corresponding row in the majors table. There are two other types of relationships between tables: one-to-many and many-to-many. The students table contains a column called id_students, which serves as its primary key. The majors table should contain a column that contains student IDs. This is referred to as a foreign key, because it's a reference to a primary key in another table. The foreign key is used to implement the one-to-one relationship between the records in the two tables.

In a one-to-many relationship, a record in one table can have a reference to many records in a second table, but each record in the second table can have a reference to only one record in the first table. Here's an example: Let's say you create a table called grades, which contains a column for student IDs as well as columns for class names and the grades themselves. Because a student can take multiple classes, but each grade applies to only one student, the relationship between students and grades is a one-to-many relationship.

In this case, id_students in the grades table is a foreign key relating to the students table.

An example of a many-to-many relationship is the relationship between students and classes. Each student is usually enrolled in several classes, and each class usually contains multiple students. In a relational database, such a relationship is expressed using what is sometimes referred to as a *joining table* a table that exists solely to express the relationship between two pieces of data. The schema contains two tables, students and classes. You already know about the students table; the classes table contains information about the classes offered the name of the professor, the room where the class is held, and the time at which the class is scheduled.

Before you can deal with integrating databases and XML, you need to understand both databases and XML. You've been learning about XML for a while now, so consider this a crash course in database theory.

To relate students to classes, you need a third table, called classes_students (or a similarly descriptive name). At a bare minimum, this table must include two columns, id_students and id_classes, both of which are foreign keys pointing to the students and classes tables, respectively. These two columns are used to express the many-to-many relationship. In other words, both of the other two tables have one-to-many relationships with this table. Using this table, each student can be associated with several classes, and each class can be associated with any number of students. It may also contain properties that are specific to the relationship, rather than to either a student or a class specifically.

THE WORLD'S SHORTEST GUIDE TO SQL

One term you can't go far into databases without encountering is SQL, which stands for Structured Query Language. SQL is the language used to retrieve, add, modify, and delete records in databases. Let's look at each of these features in turn.

Incidentally, the pronunciation of SQL is somewhat of a contentious issue. The official party line is that SQL should be pronounced "es queue el." However, many people opt for the more casual and also more efficient pronunciation, "sequel."

RETRIEVING RECORDS USING SELECT

Just about everything in SQL is carried out via a query, which is simply the act of communicating with the database according to an established set of SQL commands. The query used to retrieve data from a database is called the SELECT statement. It has several parts, not all of which are mandatory. The most basic SELECT statement is composed of two parts the select list and the FROM clause. A very simple SELECT statement looks like this:

```
SELECT *
FROM students
```

Table 17.1 shows the database records returned as the results of the query.

Table 17.1 Database Records as the Results of the Above Query

Id_Students	Student_ Name	City	State	Classification	Tuition
1	Franklin Pierce	Hillsborough	NH	senior	5000
2	James Polk	Mecklenburg County	NC	freshman	11000
2	Warren Harding	Marion	OH	junior	3500

In this case, the * is the select list. The select list indicates which database columns should be included in the query results. When a * is supplied, it indicates that all of the columns in the table or tables listed in the FROM clause should be included in the query results.

The FROM clause contains the list of tables from which the data will be retrieved. In this case, the data is retrieved from just one table, students. We now explain how to retrieve data from multiple tables in a bit.

Let's go back to the select list. If you use a select list that isn't simply *, you include a list of column names separated by commas. You can also rename columns in the query results (useful in certain situations), using the AS keyword, as follows:

```
SELECT id_students AS id, student_name, state
FROM students
```

As the results in Table 17.2 show, only the student name and state columns are returned for the records.

Table 17.2 Database Records as the Results of the Above Query

Id	Student_Name	State
1	Franklin Pierce	NH
2	James Polk	NC
2	Warren Harding	OH

The id_students column is renamed id in the query results using the reserved word AS. The other keyword you'll often use in a select statement is DISTINCT. When you include DISTINCT at the beginning of a select statement, it indicates that no duplicates should be included in the query results. Here's a sample query:

```
SELECT DISTINCT city
FROM students
```

The results are shown in Table 17.3.

Table 17.3 Database Records as the Results of the Above Query

City
Hillsborough
Mecklenburg County
Marion

Without DISTINCT, this query would return the city of every student in the students table. In this case, it returns only the distinct values in the table, regardless of how many of each of them there are. In this case, there are only three records in the table and each of them has a unique city, so the result set is the same as it would be if DISTINCT were left off.

The WHERE Clause

Both of the previous queries simply return all of the records in the students table. Often, you'll want to constrain the resultset so that it returns only those records you're actually interested in. The WHERE clause is used to specify which records in a table should be included in the results of a query. Here's an example:

```
SELECT student_name
FROM students
WHERE id_students = 1
```

As shown in Table 17.4, only the record with the matching ID is returned in the results.

Table 17.4 Database Records as the Results of the Above Query

Student_Name
Franklin Pierce

When you use the WHERE clause, you must include an expression that filters the query results. In this case, the expression is very simple. Given that id_students is the primary key for this table, this query is sure to return only one row. You can use other comparison operators as well, like the > or != operators. It's also possible to use Boolean operators to create compound expressions. For example, you can retrieve all of the students who pay more than $10,000 per year in tuition and who are classified as freshmen using the following query:

```
SELECT student_name
FROM students
WHERE tuition > 10000
AND classification = 'freshman'
```

Table 17.5 shows the results of this query.

Table 17.5 Database Records as the Results of the Above Query

Student_name
James Polk

There are also several other functions you can use in the WHERE clause that enable you to write more powerful queries. The LIKE function allows you to search for fields containing a particular string using a regular expression like syntax. The BETWEEN function allows you to search for values between the two you specify, and IN allows you to test whether a value is a member of a set you specify.

INSERTING RECORDS

The INSERT statement is used to insert records into a table. The syntax is simple, especially if you plan on populating every column in a table. To insert a record into majors, use the following statement:

```
INSERT INTO majors
VALUES (115, 50, 'Math', 'English')
```

The values in the list correspond to the id_majors, id_students, major, and minor columns, respectively. If you only want to specify values for a subset of the columns in the table, you must specify the names of the columns as well:

```
INSERT INTO students
(id_students, student_name)
VALUES (50, 'Milton James')
```

When you create tables, you can specify whether values are required in certain fields, and you can also specify default values for fields. For example, the classification column might default to freshman because most new student records being inserted will be for newly enrolled students, who are classified as freshmen.

UPDATING RECORDS

When you want to modify one or more records in a table, the UPDATE statement is used. Here's an example:

```
UPDATE students
SET classification = 'senior'
```

The previous SQL statement will work, but you can figure out what's wrong with it. Nowhere is it specified which records to update. If you don't tell it which records to update, it just assumes that you want to update all of the records in the table, thus the previous query would turn all of the students into seniors. That's probably not what you have in mind. Fortunately, the UPDATE statement supports the WHERE clause, just like the SELECT statement.

```
UPDATE students
SET classification = 'senior'
WHERE id_students = 1
```

That's more like it. This statement updates the classification of only one student. You can also update multiple columns with one query:

```
UPDATE students
SET classification = 'freshman', tuition = 7500
WHERE id_students = 5
```

As you can see from the example, you can supply a list of fields to update with your UPDATE statement, and they will all be updated by the same query.

DELETING RECORDS

The last SQL statement, the DELETE statement, is similar to the UPDATE statement. It accepts a FROM clause and optionally a WHERE clause. If you leave out the WHERE clause, it deletes all the records in the table. Here's an example:

```
DELETE FROM students
WHERE id_students = 1
```

You now know just enough about SQL to get into trouble! Actually, your newfound SQL knowledge will come in handy a bit later in the lesson when you develop an application that carefully extracts data from a database and encodes it in XML. But first, you find out how to export an entire database table as XML.

DATABASES AND XML

When you integrate XML with databases, the first question that you must look at is how you're using XML in your application. There are two broad categories of XML applications: those that use XML for data storage and those that use XML as a document format. The approach for database integration depends on which category your application falls into.

Although XML is commonly thought of as a document format, it's also very popular as a format for data storage. Many applications use XML files to store their configuration, as well as rely on remote procedure calling services like XML-RPC and SOAP to format the messages that they exchange using XML.

The fact that XML is highly structured and can be tested to ensure that it's both well-formed and valid in a standardized, programatic fashion takes a lot of the burden of reading and modifying the data file off of the application developer when he or she is writing a program.

Let's look at a couple of real world examples where XML might need to be integrated with a relational database. The structured nature of XML makes it a good choice to use as a data interchange format. Let's say that a company periodically receives inventory information from a supplier. That information might be stored in an Oracle database on a server in the supplier's system but might need to be imported into an Access database when the company receives it. XML would make a good intermediate format for the data because it's easy to write programs that import and export the data and because, by using XML, the data can be used in future applications that require it as well.

The news articles could be distributed via XML files so that they could easily be transformed for presentation on the Web, or they could be imported into a relational database and published from there.

RESOLVING XML DATA INTO DATABASE TABLES

The question you face when you integrate applications that use XML for data storage with relational databases is the degree to which you want to take advantage of the features of the relational database. If you simply insert entire XML documents into the database, you can't use advanced SQL features to retrieve specific bits of information from the XML documents.

Here's an XML document that is used to store information related to automobiles:

```
<dealership>
 <automobile make="Buick" model="Century" color="blue">
  <options>
   <option>cruise control</option>
   <option>CD player</option>
  </options>
 </automobile>
 <automobile make="Ford" model="Thunderbird" color="red">
  <options>
   <option>convertible</option>
   <option>leather interior</option>
   <option>heated seats</option>
  </options>
 </automobile>
</dealership>
```

Now, let's look at how you might design a database to store this information. As mentioned earlier, the path of least resistance is just to stick the whole XML document in a field. However, that probably isn't a good idea for this file because it contains more than one automobile "record."

As you can see, the XML document has been turned into two tables, automobiles and options. The automobiles table contains all the information stored in the attributes of the automobile tag in the XML document. Because automobiles have a one-to-many relationship to options, we created a separate table for them. In the options table, id_automobiles is a foreign key that relates back to a specific automobile in the automobiles table.

To make sure you understand why the automobile options were broken out into a separate database table, consider that the number of options for a single automobile can vary from one automobile to the next. This is a scenario where a single database field in the automobiles table can't account for a varying amount of data (hence the one-to-many relationship). Therefore, the solution is to break out the options into a separate table where each row is tied back to a specific automobile. Then you can add as many options as you want for one automobile as long as each option includes the appropriate automobile ID.

STORING XML DOCUMENTS IN A DATABASE

If you're storing entire XML documents in a database, you don't need to worry about translating the XML document format into a tabular database structure. Instead, you just need to extract the information from the document that you need to use in the relational database world and create columns for that. As an example, if you store newspaper articles as XML documents, the section, headline, author, body, and perhaps more information will all be included in the XML document within their own tags. It is then possible to process the XML code to access each portion of the document.

If you store those documents in a database and plan on publishing them on the Web from that database, you may want to consider breaking up the XML data so that it can be retrieved more easily. For example, you might want separate columns for the section and writer so that you can write simple SQL statements that retrieve the documents based on those values. Either way, you would be retrieving XML code from the database, which is far different than the earlier automobile example where the database data has been translated from XML into pure database content.

EXPORTING AN XML DOCUMENT FROM A DATABASE

If you need to pull data from a database for processing as XML on a onetime basis, or maybe periodically but not necessarily in real-time, you might consider just exporting the data manually. Most databases offer an "export as XML" option that converts a database table into a structured XML document with the database columns turned into XML tags. This is a very simple approach to quickly generating an XML document from a database that you might now otherwise be able to access without database tools.

MySQL is a very popular open source database that does a great job for small- to medium-scale applications. A nice front-end is available for MySQL called phpMyAdmin, which provides a Web-based user interface for interacting with a MySQL database. phpMyAdmin provides a very easy-to-use export feature that will export any MySQL database as an XML document.

To get started exporting an XML document from a MySQL database, open the database in phpMyAdmin, and select the table you want to export. Then click the Export tab. Within the Export options, click XML to indicate that XML is the output data format. If you want to generate an XML file that is stored on the Web server, click the Save Now. You can choose to save the XML file locally or otherwise use the XML code for further processing and manipulation. The key point to realize is that with one button click, you've converted an entire tabular database into a well-formed XML document.

ACCESSING DATA FROM A DATABASE AS XML

Although manually exporting an XML document from a database can be useful, it isn't quite the same as drilling into a database via a SQL query and extracting exactly the data you need. A more realistic example would involve generating XML code on the fly based upon a SQL query.

The example you're about to see extracts data from a real database created to manage the statistics for a recreational hockey team, Music City Mafia. The database is a MySQL database that stores statistics for both games and players. In this example, you're only concerned with game data, which is stored in a database table called games. To access the data and initiate a SQL query, we use PHP, which is an open source scripting language used to create dynamic Web pages. PHP has very good integration with MySQL, and is a great option for dynamic Web page development that involves MySQL databases and XML.

PHP is a recursive acronym that stands for PHP Hypertext Processer. Although the code you're about to see is written in PHP, you don't have to understand the PHP language in order to get the gist of what's going on. The key things to pay attention to are the SQL query being made on the database and the generation of the XML code. PHP is used to carry out these tasks but the code isn't too terribly difficult to decipher.

Listing 19.1 contains the code for the mcm_schedule.php sample Web page that uses PHP to dynamically generate an XML file based upon a MySQL database query.

Listing 17.1. The Hockey Game Schedule PHP Example Document

```
<?php
// Connect to the database
$mcm_db = mysql_connect("localhost", "admin", "password");
mysql_select_db("mcm_hockey", $mcm_db);

// Issue the query
$mcm_query = sprintf("SELECT date, time, opponent, location, type, outcome,
 gf, ga, overtime FROM games WHERE season=\"%s\" ORDER BY
 date", $season);
$mcm_result = mysql_query($mcm_query, $mcm_db);

// Format the query results as XML
if (mysql_num_rows($mcm_result) > 0) {
// Assemble the XML code
$xml ="<?xml version=\"1.0\" encoding=\"UTF-8\" ?>\r\n";
$xml.="<games>\r\n";
while (list($date, $time, $opponent, $location, $type, $outcome,
 $gf, $ga, $overtime) = mysql_fetch_array($mcm_result)) {
 $formatted_date = date("F j, Y", strtotime($date));
 $formatted_time = date("g:ia", strtotime($time));
 $xml.= sprintf(" <game date=\"%s\" time=\"%s\">\r\n",
  $formatted_date, $formatted_time);
 $xml.= sprintf(" <opponent>%s</opponent>\r\n", $opponent);
 $xml.= sprintf(" <location>%s</location>\r\n", $location);
 $xml.= sprintf(" <score outcome=\"%s\" overtime=\"%s\">
%s - %s</score>\r\n", $outcome, $overtime, $gf, $ga);
$xml.= " </game>\r\n";
}
$xml.="</games>";

// Write the XML code to the file mcm_results.xml
$file= fopen("mcm_results.xml", "w");
fwrite($file, $xml);
fclose($file);

echo "The XML document has been written - <a href=\"mcm_results.xml\">
 view the XML code.</a>";
} else {
 echo "Sorry, no matching records found.";
}
// Close the database
mysql_close($mcm_db);
?>
```

The first few lines of the page establish a database connection and open the Music City Mafia hockey database. A SQL query is then constructed based upon a parameter ($season) that is passed into the page via the URL. The point of this parameter is to allow you to limit the XML file to a particular season of data (*http://www.musiccitymafia.com/mcm_schedule.php?-season=Summer%202005*).

The %20 near the end of URL is just a separator to provide a space between the word Summer and the word 2005. The result of this URL is that the mcm_schedule.php Web page assigns the value Summer 2005 to the variable $season, which can then be used throughout the PHP code. And, in fact, it is when the SQL query is issued in lines 7 through 9 of the listing. More specifically, the date, time, opponent, location, type, outcome, goals for, goals against, and overtime database fields are selected from the games table but only for the Summer 2005 season. The result of this query is stored in the $mcm_result variable (line 10).

In PHP programming, all variable names are preceded by a dollar sign ($). The next big chunk of code goes through the results of the SQL query one record at a time, formatting the data into XML code. Notice that the XML processor directive is first generated (line 15), followed by a root tag, <games> (line 16). Each piece of pertinent game data is then further formatted into XML code in lines 17 through 28. The document is wrapped up with a closing </games> tag in line 29.

The last important step in the PHP code is writing the XML data to a file. The file is named mcm_results.xml, and the XML data is written to it with just a few lines of code (lines 32 to 34). A simple line of HTML code is then written to the browser so that you can access the XML file. More specifically, a link is generated that allows you to click and view the XML document (lines 36 and 37).

QUESTIONS FOR DISCUSSION

1. What is an XML database?
2. Why are XML databases interesting?
3. What is the XML:DB initiative for?
4. Who is behind the organization that developed the initiative?
5. What license is used for reference implementations?
6. What happens after the specifications are written?
7. How can you lay claim to the XML: namespace prefix?

CHAPTER 18

WEB SERVICES

WEB SERVICES

Web Services, in the general meaning of the term, are services offered via the Web. In a typical Web services scenario, a business application sends a request to a service at a given URL using the SOAP protocol over HTTP. The service receives the request, processes it, and returns a response. As example of this, consider a stock quote service, in which the request asks for the current price of a specified stock, and the response gives the stock price. This is one of the simplest forms of a Web service in that the request is filled almost immediately, with the request and response being parts of the same method call.

Another example could be a service that maps out an efficient route for the delivery of goods. In this case, a business sends a request containing the delivery destinations, which the service processes to determine the most cost-effective delivery route. The time it takes to return the response depends on the complexity of the routing, so the response will probably be sent as an operation that is separate from the request.

Technically, Web services are actually application components which communicate using open protocols. They are self-contained, self-describing and modular applications that can be published, located, and can be invoked across the Web. Web Services define a platform-independent standard based on XML to communicate within distributed systems. XML is used to tag the data.

Web services can convert an application into a Web-application, which can publish its function or message to the world.

THE WEB SERVICES PLATFORM

The basic platform is XML plus HTTP. HTTP is the ubiquitous protocol, which is running practically everywhere on the Internet.

XML provides the meta-language you use to write specialized languages to express the complex interactions between the clients and the services or between the components of a composite service. Behind the facade of the Web server, an XML message gets converted to the middleware request and the results are converted back to the XML.

A Web needs to be augmented with few other platform services, which can maintain the ubiquity and the simplicity of Web, to constitute more functional platform. A full-function Web services platform can be thought of as the XML plus HTTP plus SOAP plus WSDL plus the UDDI. At the higher levels, one may also add the technologies such as the XAML, XLANG, XKMS, and the XFS—services which are not universally been accepted as the mandatory.

WEB SERVICES PLATFORM ELEMENTS

Web Services have three basic platform elements:

- SOAP (Simple Object Access Protocol): SOAP is used to transfer the data.
- UDDI (Universal Description, Discovery, and Integration): UDDI is used for listing what services are available.
- WSDL (Web Services Description Language): WSDL is used for describing the services available.

TYPES OF WEB SERVICES

However, there are two types of Web applications:

Presentation-oriented: A presentation-oriented Web application generates interactive Web pages containing various types of markup language (HTML or XML) and dynamic content in response to requests. This is the form of Web application we are familiar with and we have covered practical implementations of such applications through the vast majority of this module.

Service-oriented: A service-oriented Web application implements the endpoint of a Web service. Presentation-oriented applications are often clients of service-oriented Web applications.

WEB SERVICE ARCHITECTURES

The diagram in Figure 18.1 shows a generic architecture for Web Services. The core element of this relates to the communication between the service requester and the service provider. This communication is handled via the Simple Object Access Protocol (SOAP).

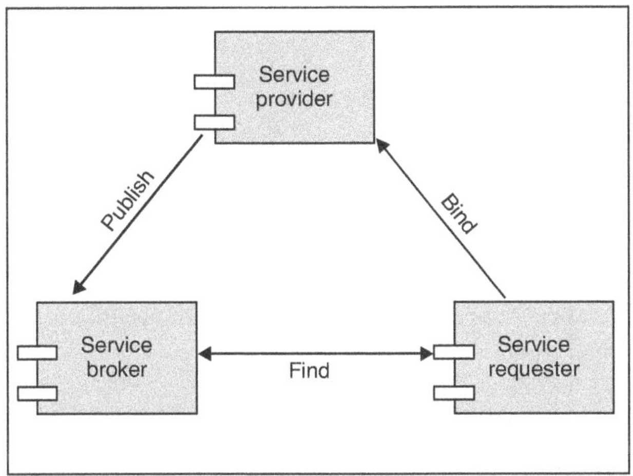

FIGURE 18.1 Web Services Architecture 1

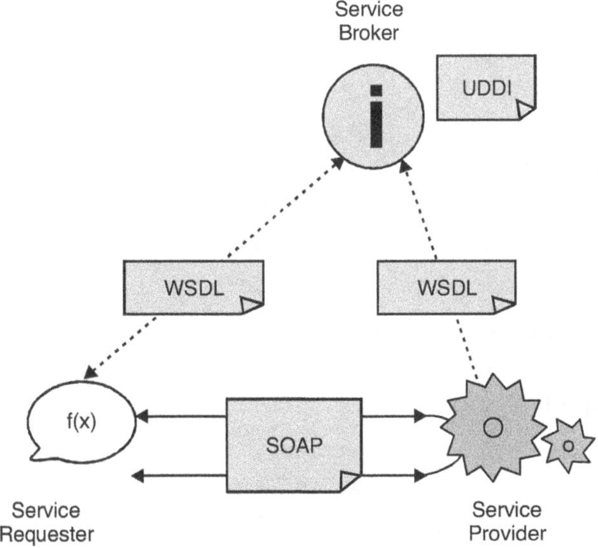

FIGURE 18.2 Web Services Architecture 2

WEB SERVICES EXAMPLE

Any application can have a Web Service component. Web Services can be created regardless of programming language. In the following example, we will use ASP.NET to create a simple Web Service that converts the temperature from Fahrenheit to Celsius and vice versa:

```
<%@ WebService Language="VBScript" Class="TempConvert" %>
```

Imports System

```
Imports System.Web.Services
Public Class TempConvert :Inherits WebService
<WebMethod()> Public Function FahrenheitToCelsius
(ByVal Fahrenheit As String) As String
 dim fahr
 fahr=trim(replace(Fahrenheit,",","."))
 if fahr="" or IsNumeric(fahr)=false then return "Error"
 return ((((fahr) - 32) / 9) * 5)
end function
<WebMethod()> Public Function CelsiusToFahrenheit
 (ByVal Celsius As String) As String
 dim cel
 cel=trim(replace(Celsius,",","."))
 if cel="" or IsNumeric(cel)=false then return "Error"
 return ((((cel) * 9) / 5) + 32)
end function
end class
```

This document is saved as an .asmx file. This is the ASP.NET file extension for XML Web Services.

The first line in the example states that this is a Web Service, written in VBScript, and has the class name "TempConvert:"

```
<%@ WebService Language="VBScript" Class="TempConvert" %>
```

The next lines import the namespace "System.Web.Services" from the .NET framework:

Imports System

```
Imports System.Web.Services
The next line defines that the "TempConvert" class is a WebService class type:
Public Class TempConvert :Inherits WebService
```

The next steps are basic VB programming. This application has two functions: one to convert from Fahrenheit to Celsius and one to convert from Celsius to Fahrenheit.

The only difference from a normal application is that this function is defined as a "WebMethod()". Use "WebMethod()" to convert the functions in your application into Web services:

```
<WebMethod()> Public Function FahrenheitToCelsius
(ByVal Fahrenheit As String) As String
 dim fahr
 fahr=trim(replace(Fahrenheit,",","."))
 if fahr="" or IsNumeric(fahr)=false then return "Error"
 return (((fahr) - 32) / 9) * 5)
end function
<WebMethod()> Public Function CelsiusToFahrenheit
(ByVal Celsius As String) As String
 dim cel
 cel=trim(replace(Celsius,",","."))
 if cel="" or IsNumeric(cel)=false then return "Error"
 return (((cel) * 9) / 5) + 32)
end function
Then, end the class:
end class
```

Publish the .asmx file on a server with .NET support, and you will have your first working Web Service.

HOW TO USE WEB SERVICES

The FahrenheitToCelsius() function can be tested here: FahrenheitToCelsius include link?

The CelsiusToFahrenheit() function can be tested here: CelsiusToFahrenheit include link?

These functions will send an XML response like this:

```
<?xml version="1.0" encoding="utf-8" ?>
<string xmlns="http://tempuri.org/">38</string>
```

Put the Web Service on Your Web Site

Using a form and the HTTP POST method, you can put the Web service on your site.

How To Do It

Here is the code to add the Web Service to a Web page:

```
<form action='tempconvert.asmx/FahrenheitToCelsius'
method="post" target="_blank">
<table>
 <tr>
  <td>Fahrenheit to Celsius:</td>
  <td>
  <input class="frmInput" type="text" size="30" name="Fahrenheit">
 </td>
 </tr>
  <tr>
  <td></td>
   <td align="right">
   <input type="submit" value="Submit" class="button">
 </td>
 </tr>
 </table>
</form>
<form action='tempconvert.asmx/CelsiusToFahrenheit'
method="post" target="_blank">
<table>
 <tr>
   <td>Celsius to Fahrenheit:</td>
   <td>
   <input class="frmInput" type="text" size="30" name="Celsius">
   </td>
 </tr>
<tr>
<td></td>
  <td align="right">
  <input type="submit" value="Submit" class="button">
  </td>
  </tr>
 </table>
</form>
```

Substitute the "tempconvert.asmx" with the address of your Web service like:

```
http://www.example.com/webservices/tempconvert.asmx
```

SOAP

SOAP is the protocol specification that defines a uniform way of passing the XML-encoded data. It also defines the way to perform the remote procedure calls (RPCs) using the HTTP as a underlying communication protocol.

SOAP arises from a realization that no matter how nifty a current middleware offerings are, they need the WAN wrapper. Architecturally, sending the messages as a plain XML has advantages in terms of ensuring the interoperability (and debugging). Middleware players seem willing to put up with costs of parsing and serializing the XML in order to scale their approach to wider networks.

UDDI (Universal Description, Discovery, and Integration)

The UDDI provides the mechanism for clients to dynamically find other Web services. Using the UDDI interface, a business can dynamically connect to the services provided by external business partners. The UDDI registry is similar to the CORBA trader, or it can be thought of as the DNS service for the business applications. The UDDI registry has two kinds of the clients: businesses which want to publish the service (and the usage interfaces) and the clients who want to obtain the services of certain kind and bind programmatically to them. Table 18.1 is the overview of what an UDDI provides. The UDDI is layered over the SOAP and assumes that the requests and the responses are UDDI objects sent around as the SOAP messages. A sample query is included.

WSDL (Web Services Definition Language)

WSDL defines the services as the collection of the network endpoints or the ports. In a WSDL, the abstract definition of the endpoints and the messages are separated from their concrete network deployment or the data format bindings. This allows the reuse of the abstract definitions of the messages, which are the abstract descriptions of the data being exchanged, and the port types, which are the abstract collections of the operations. The concrete protocol and the data format specifications for the particular port type constitute the reusable binding. The port is defined by associating the network address with the reusable binding; the collection of ports defines the service. And, thus, the WSDL document uses the following elements in a definition of the network services:

- Types—the container for data type definitions using some type of system (such as XSD)

- Message—the abstract, typed definition of the data being communicated
- Operation—the abstract description of the action supported by a service
- Port Type—the abstract set of the operations supported by the one or more endpoints
- Binding—the concrete protocol and the data format specification for a particular port type
- Port—the single endpoint defined as the combination of binding and the network address
- Service—the collection of related endpoints

So, WSDL is the template for how the services should be described and bound by the clients.

WSDL Documents

A WSDL document is just a simple XML document. It contains set of definitions to describe a Web service.

The WSDL Document Structure

A WSDL document describes a Web service using the major elements shown in Table 18.1.

Table 18.1 Web Service Elements Description

Element	Defines
<types>	The data types used by the Web service
<message>	The messages used by the Web service
<portType>	The operations performed by the Web service
<binding>	The communication protocols used by the Web service

The main structure of a WSDL document looks like this:

```
<definitions>
<types>
 definition of types........
</types>
<message>
 definition of a message....
</message>
<portType>
```

```
 definition of a port.......
</portType>
<binding>
 definition of a binding....
</binding>
</definitions>
```

A WSDL document can also contain other elements, like extension elements, and a service element that makes it possible to group together the definitions of several Web services in one single WSDL document.

WSDL Example

This is a simplified fraction of a WSDL document:

```
<message name="getTermRequest">
 <part name="term" type="xs:string"/>
</message>
<message name="getTermResponse">
  <part name="value" type="xs:string"/>
</message>
<portType name="glossaryTerms">
 <operation name="getTerm">
   <input message="getTermRequest"/>
   <output message="getTermResponse"/>
 </operation>
</portType>
```

In this example, the <portType> element defines "glossaryTerms" as the name of a port and "getTerm" as the name of an operation.

The "getTerm" operation has an input message called "getTermRequest" and an output message called "getTermResponse."

The <message> elements define the parts of each message and the associated data types. Compared to traditional programming, glossaryTerms is a function library, getTerm is a function with getTermRequest as the input parameter and getTermResponse as the return parameter.

WSDL AND UDDI

Universal Description, Discovery, and Integration (UDDI) is a directory service where businesses can register and search for Web services. UDDI is a platform-independent framework for describing services, discovering businesses, and integrating business services by using the Internet. UDDI is a directory for storing information about Web services. UDDI is a directory of Web service interfaces described by WSDL. UDDI communicates via SOAP. UDDI is built into the Microsoft .NET platform.

UDDI uses World Wide Web Consortium (W3C) and Internet Engineering Task Force (IETF) Internet standards such as XML, HTTP, and DNS protocols.

UDDI uses WSDL to describe interfaces to Web services. Additionally, cross platform programming features are addressed by adopting SOAP, known as XML Protocol messaging specifications on the W3C Web site.

UDDI BENEFITS

Any industry or businesses of all sizes can benefit from UDDI.

Before UDDI, there was no Internet standard for businesses to reach their customers and partners with information about their products and services. Nor was there a method of how to integrate into each other's systems and processes. Problems the UDDI specification can help to solve:

Making it possible to discover the right business from the millions currently online.

- Defining how to enable commerce once the preferred business is discovered.
- Reaching new customers and increasing access to current customers.
- Expanding offerings and extending market reach.
- Solving customer-driven need to remove barriers to allow for rapid participation in the global Internet economy.
- Describing services and business processes programmatically in a single, open, and secure environment.

HOW CAN UDDI BE USED

If the industry published an UDDI standard for flight rate checking and reservation, airlines could register their services in an UDDI directory. Travel agencies could then search the UDDI directory to find the airline's reservation interface. When the interface is found, the travel agency can communicate with the service immediately because it uses a well-defined reservation interface.

UDDI is a cross-industry effort driven by all major platform and software providers like Dell, Fujitsu, HP, Hitachi, IBM, Intel, Microsoft, Oracle, SAP, and Sun, as well as a large community of marketplace operators and e-business leaders.

QUESTIONS FOR DISCUSSION

1. Are there toolkits that automatically generate service proxy code from a WSDL service description?
2. Are there tools to test SOAP-based Web Services?
3. What are Web Services? What are the Web Services Standards?
4. Where can you find a sample SOAP client using Apache SOAP for Java?
5. What is UDDI?
6. What is WSDL?
7. How do you send attachment using soap? Where can you find article or example on how to send attachments using SOAP?
8. How can you find SOAP Services that other people/companies have developed?
9. Exception handling in Apache-SOAP—Is there a way of catching server exceptions in the client side?
10. Are there any Web sites that will validate the well-formed ness of an XML document?
11. What are the Web services in ASP.NET?
12. Does the W3C support any Web service standards?
13. How do you get started with Web Services?
14. What is the Web service protocol stack?
15. What is the use of SOAP (Simple Object Access Protocol) in .Net Web Services?
16. What is new about Web services?

APPENDIX A

XML BASICS

1. In the XML sample, we see that information is seeded over several lines. However, this was generated by the parser (Microsoft Internet Explorer). In general, an XML document is a continuous document without a carriage return or line feed characters in it.
2. Any XML document that meets the basic rules as defined by the XML specification is called a well-formed XML document. An XML document can be checked to determine whether it is well-formed—that is, whether the document has the correct structure (syntax).
3. When an XML document meets the rules defined in the DTD, it is called a valid XML document. (DTD: Document Type Definiton)
4. Schemas are similar to DTDs, but they use a different format. DTDs and schemas are useful when the content of a group of documents shares a common set of rules.
5. XML gives you the opportunity to create messages in standard forms.
6. XML separates data from presentation.
7. XML gives you the possibility to call methods behind firewalls and between different platforms.
8. XML describes the contents but not the layout.
9. XML is tagged-based: every tag begins with <descr> and an end tag </descr>, where descr is the name of the tag.
10. You can define the character encoding used by encoding = "UTF-8."

11. Tags should only be written in lowercase to be compatible with the XHTML definitions (upcoming format).

12. You have some predefined tokens that can't be used unless they actually are part of a CDATA section. These tokens are also referred to as Predefined.

    ```
    entieis
    Î &lt Î &gt Î &amp &
    Î &apos '
    Î &quot "
    ```

13. The most basic components of an XML document are elements, attributes, and comments.

14. Every tag should have an end-tag.

    ```
    Correct is: <tag> <element> … </element></tag>
    Incorrect is: <tag> <element> … </tag> </element>
    ```

15. All attribute values should be written between single or double quotes.

    ```
    i.e. <element id="myvalue">
    ```

16. The designer of the XML document defines the structure of the document and the mark-up elements.

17. XML must be properly written to get interpreted (not with HTML). This means that every tag must have an end tag.

    Elements can be nested, i.e.,

    ```
    <Patient>
    <PatientName>John Smith</PatientName>
    <PatientAge>108</PatientAge>
    <PatientWeight>155</PatientWeight>
    </Patient>
    ```

18. -Names consist of one or more "no space" characters. If a name has only one character, that character must be a letter, either uppercase (A-Z) or lowercase (a-z).

    -A name can only begin with a letter or an underscore.

    -Beyond the first character, any character can be used, including those defined in the Unicode standard.

    -Element names are case sensitive.

19. An attribute is a mechanism for adding descriptive information to an element.

```
<PatientWeight unit="KG">81</PatientWeight>
```

or

```
<PatientWeight unit="KG"/> (=empty element)
```

20. Comments are descriptions embedded in an XML document to provide additional information about the document. They are placed between the tags.

```
<!-- and -->
<!-- Comment text -->
```

21. An element without a value can be written as <sample/>, a.k.a., a singleton.

22. Some HTML tools can't interpret the singletons. Therefore, you might want to change the code towards <sample> ... </sample>. Another solution is to add a comment field.

The XML Tag and Namespaces

XML files begin with an <?xml> version tag:

```
<?xml version="1.0" encoding="UTF-8"?>
```

Following the version tag, markup consists of one or more elements. An audience file, for example, uses an <audience> element that contains all additional markup:

```
<?xml version="1.0" encoding="UTF-8"?>
<audience xmlns="http://ns.real.com/tools/audience.2.0"
xmlns:xsi="http://www.w3.org/2001/XMLSchema-instance"
xsi:schemaLocation="http://ns.real.com/tools/audience.2.0
http://ns.real.com/tools/audience.2.0.xsd">
...audience information...
</audience>
```

Each xmlns attribute shown above defines an XML namespace. This namespace tells RealProducer how to handle the markup contained within the file. The namespace identifier is in the form of a URL only to ensure uniqueness. RealProducer does not contact the URL.

Tags, Attributes, and Values

The elements within an XML file take the following form:

```
<tag type="type">value</tag>
```

The following are the basic parts to an XML element:

tag	The tag name comes just after a left angle bracket. Some tags may consist of just the name, as in the <stream> tag. Other tags may have attributes. Except for the XML version tag and the comment tag, all tags in an XML file have a corresponding end tag. For example, the <audience> tag has the end tag <Iaudience>.
type	The type attributes define the type of data that the element provides. For more information.
value	The value is a character string, integer, or time value, that defines the feature.

Lowercase or Camel Case for Tags and Attributes

In RealProducer markup, single-word tags and attributes are lowercase. When a tag, attribute, or predefined value consists of a compound word, the first letter of all words after the first word is generally capitalized, as in encodingComplexity. This is referred to as "camel case."

Attribute Values Enclosed in Double Quotation Marks

Attribute values, such as string in type="string", must be enclosed in double quotation marks. Do not add any blank spaces between the quotation marks and the value they enclose.

Data Type Values

Most XML elements within the RealProducer files must include a type attribute that indicates the type of value.

Value Types		
Type	**Value**	**Notes**
type="bag"	group	Indicates a group of properties
type="bool"	true|false	True or false values use this type, which stands for "Boolean." You can also use 1 for true and 0 for false.

(continued)

Value Types		
Type	**Value**	**Notes**
type="double"	decimal values	A double type is used for very large values, values that include a decimal point, and values that may be negative.
type="duration"	time value	A duration type indicates a time value in the format [d:][h:][m:]s[.xyz].
type="string"	text string	A string can include letters and numbers. Do not use double quotation marks within the value string. Maximum lengths may vary, but are typically at least 256 characters
type="uint"	unsigned integer	Values that are positive integers, including 0, use this type.
xsi:type="value"	customized value	An xsi: prefix allows for customized value types.

Value Type Examples

The following examples illustrate the use of the type attribute in RealProducer XML files:

```
<outputWidth type="uint">360</outputWidth>
<maxFrameRate type="double">15.000000</maxFrameRate>
<streamContext type="bag">
...stream context elements...
</streamContext>
<stream xsi:type="audioStream">
...audio stream elements...
</stream>
<deinterlace type="bool">true</deinterlace>
<pluginName type="string">rn-prefilter-deinterlace</pluginName>
```

Duration Syntax

The format for the value of a parameter that specifies a duration is the following:

```
[d:][h:][m:]s[.xyz]
```

Only the seconds value is required. If a value is omitted, it is assumed to be zero. You must specify intermediate values. To indicate hours, for example, you must include the minutes and seconds field. Here are some sample values:

30	30 seconds
45.5	45–1/2 seconds
5:35	5 minutes, 35 seconds
1:0.0	1 hour
1:22:30:0	1 day, 22 hours, 30 minutes

File Names and Paths Observe Letter Cases

In tags that specify files or other input, paths and file names can be uppercase, lowercase, or mixed case, corresponding to their actual names on the operating system. All of the following path and file name examples are allowable, for example:

```
<filename type="string">C:\media\video\video1.rm</filename>
<filename type="string">C:\media\video\Video1.rm</filename>
<filename type="string">C:\media\video\VIDEO1.rm</filename>
```

XML Recommendations

Although not strict rules, the following recommendations will help you keep your XML markup organized and understandable.

XML Comments

As in HTML, XML has a comment tag that starts with these characters:

```
<!--
```

and ends with these characters:

```
-->
```

There is no corresponding end tag:

```
<!-- This is a comment -->
```

A comment can be any number of lines long. It can start and end anywhere in a XML file. Multiple comments cannot be nested, though. Use comments to describe what various sections of your XML file are meant to do. This helps other people understand your file more easily.

Indentation Between Elements

Although indenting XML markup is not required, it helps you to keep track of the XML file's structure. You typically indent markup by pressing the Tab key once for each level of indentation. In a stream section, for example, the element tags are indented one level from the <stream> tag. The two tags that make up the stream context are indented one level from the <streamContext> tag:

```
<stream xsi:type="audioStream">
 <codecFlavor type="uint">25</codecFlavor>
 <codecName type="string">cook</codecName>
 <encodingComplexity type="string">high</encodingComplexity>
 <pluginName type="string">rn-audiocodec-realaudio</pluginName>
 <streamContext type="bag">
   <audioMode type="string">voice</audioMode>
   <presentationType type="string">audio-only</presentationType>
 </streamContext>
</stream>
```

APPENDIX B

WELL FORMED XML DOCUMENTS

Well-formed XML documents can be created by using elements, attributes, and comments. These components define content within the document. Using these definitions, applications can be created that will manipulate the content. To be well-formed, your XML document must meet the following requirements:

1. The document must contain a single root element.
2. Every element must be correctly nested.
3. Each attribute can have only one value.
4. All attribute values must be enclosed in double quotation marks or single quotation marks.
5. Elements must have begin and end tags, unless they are empty elements.
6. Empty elements are denoted by a single tag ending with a slash (/).
7. Isolated markup characters are not allowed in content. The special characters <, &, and > are represented as >, &, < in content sections.
8. A double quotation mark is represented as ", and a single quotation mark is represented as &apos in content sections.
9. The sequence <[[and]]> cannot be used.
10. If a document does not have a DTD, the values for all attributes must be of type CDATA by default.

XML Declaration

```
<?xml version="version_number" encoding="encoding_declaration"
standalone="standalone status"?>
```

The version attribute is the version of the XML standard that this document complies with. The encoding attribute is the Unicode character set that this document complies with. Using this encoding, you can create documents in any language or character set. The standalone attribute specifies whether the document is dependent on other files (standalone = "no") or complete by itself (standalone = "yes").

Document Type Definition

The DTD can be used to verify that a set of XML documents is created according to the rules defined in the DTD by checking the validity of the documents.

Every element used in your XML documents has to be declared by using the <!ELEMENT> tag in the DTD. The format for declaring an element in a DTD is shown here:

```
<!ELEMENT ElementName Rule>
```

The rule component defines the rule for the content contained in the element. These rules define the logical structure of the XML document and can be used to check the document's validity. The rule can consist of a generic declaration and one or more elements, either grouped or unordered.

The Predefined Content Declarations

Three generic content declarations are predefined for XML DTDs: PCDATA, ANY, and EMPTY.

1. **PCDATA:** The PCDATA declaration can be used when the content within an element is only text—that is, when the content contains no child elements. Our sample document- snippet contains several such elements, including title, a, h1, and b. These elements can be declared as follows (the pound sign identifies a special predefined name).

```
<!ELEMENT title (#PCDATA)>
<!ELEMENT a (#PCDATA)>
<!ELEMENT h1 (#PCDATA)>
<!ELEMENT b (#PCDATA)>
```

PCDATA is also valid with empty elements.

2. **ANY:** The ANY declaration can include both text content and child elements.The *html* element, for example, could use the ANY declaration as

   ```
   <!ELEMENT html ANY>
   ```

   The ANY declaration allows any content to be marked by the element tags, provided the content is well-formed XML. Although this flexibility might seem useful, it defeats the purpose of the DTD, which is to define the structure of the XML document so that the document can be validated. In brief, any element that uses ANY cannot be checked for validity, only for being well formed.

3. **EMPTY:** It is possible for an element to have no content—that is, no child elements or text. The img element is an example of this scenario. The following is its definition: <!ELEMENT img EMPTY>

   ONE or MORE elements: This (head, body) declaration signifies that the html element will have two child elements: head and body. You can list one child element within the parentheses or as many child elements as are required. You must separate each child element in your declaration with a comma. For the XML document to be valid, the order in which the child elements are declared must match the order of the elements in the XML document. The comma that separates each child element is interpreted as followed by; therefore, the preceding declaration tells us that the HTML element will have a head child element followed by a body child element.

   REOCCURENCE XML Element Markers:

Marker	Meaning
?	The element either does not appear or can appear only once (0 or 1).
+	The element must appear at least once (1 or more).
*	The element can appear any number of times, or it might not appear at all (0 or more).

   Putting no marker after the child element indicates that the element must be included and that it can appear only one time. The head element contains an optional base child element. Here are some sample markers.

To declare this element as optional, modify the preceding declaration as follows:

<!ELEMENT head (title, base?)>

The body element contains a basefont element and an *a* element that are also optional. In our example, the table element is a required element used to format the page, so you want to make table a required element that appears only once in the body element. You can now rewrite the Body element as follows:

<!ELEMENT body (basefont?, a?, table)>

The table element can have as many rows as needed to format the page but must include at least one row. The table element should now be written as follows:

<!ELEMENT table (tr+)>

The same conditions hold true for the *tr* element. The row element must have at least one column, as shown here:

<!ELEMENT tr (td+)>

The *a*, *ul*, and *ol* elements might not be included in the *p* element, or they might be included many times, as shown here:

<!ELEMENT p (font+, img, br, a, ul*, ol*)>*

Because the *br* element formats text around an image, the *img* and *br* tags should always be used together.

Grouping child objects

(1) You can also group child objects.

```
<!ELEMENT p (font*, (img, br?)*, a*, ul*, ol*)> or
<!ELEMENT p (font*, (img, br?)*, a*, ul*, ol*)+> or
<!ELEMENT p (font | (img, br?) | a | ul | ol)+>
```

(2) You can separate the elements by a comma (,) or with a pipe (|). If you use the pipe, it indicates that one or the other child element will be included, but not both. The latest sample defines an unsorted set of child elements.

The !ATTLIST Statement

Every element can have a set of attributes associated with it. The attributes for an element are defined in an !ATTLIST statement. The format for the !ATTLIST statement is shown here:

<!ATTLIST ElementName AttributeDefinition>

ElementName is the name of the element to which these attributes belong. *AttributeDefinition* consists of the following components:

AttributeName AttributeType DefaultDeclaration

AttributeName is the name of the attribute. *AttributeType* refers to the data type of the attribute.

DefaultDeclaration contains the default declaration section of the attribute definition.

Attribute Data Types

XML DTD attributes can have the following data types: CDATA, enumerated, ENTITY, ENTITIES, ID, IDREF, IDREFS, NMTOKEN, and NMTOKENS.

CDATA: The CDATA data type indicates that the attribute can be set to any allowable character value.

Enumerated: The enumerated data type lists a set of values that are allowed for the attribute. The declaration is case sensitive.

ENTITY and ENTITIES: The ENTITY and ENTITIES data types are used to define reusable strings that are represented by a specific name.

ID, IDREF, and IDREFS: Within a document, you may want to be able to identify certain elements with an attribute that is of the ID data type. The name of the attribute with an ID data type must be unique for all of the elements in the document. Other elements can reference this ID by using the IDREF or IDREFS data types. IDREFS can be used to declare multiple attributes as IDREF.

NMTOKEN and NMTOKENS: The NMTOKEN and NMTOKENS data types are similar to the CDATA data type in that they represent character values. The name tokens are strings that consist of letters, digits, underscores, colons, hyphens, and periods. They cannot contain spaces.

The Default Declaration: The default declaration can consist of any valid value for your attributes, or it can consist of one of three predefined keywords: #REQUIRED, #IMPLIED, or #FIXED.

The #REQUIRED keyword indicates that the attribute must be included with the element and that it must be assigned a value. There are no default values when #REQUIRED is used.

The #IMPLIED keyword indicates that the attribute does not have to be included with the element and that there is no default value.

The #FIXED keyword sets the attribute to one default value that cannot be changed. The default value is listed after the #FIXED keyword.

If none of these three keywords are used, a default value can be assigned if an attribute is not set in the XML document.

Associating the DTD With an XML Document

There are two ways to associate a DTD with an XML document: the first is to place the DTD code within the XML document and the second is to create a separate DTD document that is referenced by the XML document. Creating a separate DTD document allows multiple XML documents to reference the same DTD. We use the external DTD in our project connecting to the accounting package. All defined DTD's are stored in a DTD Base Container.

<!DOCTYPE DocName [DTD]>

or

<!DOCTYPE RootElementName SYSTEM|PUBLIC [Name]DTD-URI>

The SYSTEM keyword is needed when you are using an unpublished DTD.

We will use the second set of our own defined XML definitions. It guarantees we only send well formed and valid messages. We define it as PUBLIC with a reference to the DTD-container expressed as a UNC coded location.

Entities

Entities are like macros in the C programming language in that they allow you to associate a string of characters with a name. This name can then be used in either the DTD or the XML document; the XML parser will replace the name with the string of characters. All entities consist of three parts: the word ENTITY, the name of the entity (called the literal entity value), and the replacement text—that is, the string of characters that the literal entity value will be replaced with. All entities are declared in either an internal or an external DTD.

Internal General Entities

Internal general entities are the simplest among the five types of entities. They are defined in the DTD section of the XML document.

Declaring an internal general entity: The syntax for the declaration of an internal general entity is shown here:

```
<!ENTITY name "string_of_characters">
```

To reference a general entity in the XML document, you must precede the entity with an ampersand (&) and follow it with a semicolon (;).

Internal Parameter Entities

Internal parameter entities are interpreted and replaced within the DTD and can be used only within the DTD. While you need to use an ampersand (&) when referencing general entities, you need to use a percent sign (%) when referencing parameter entities.

Declaring an internal parameter entity

The syntax for declaring an internal parameter entity is shown here:

```
<!ENTITY % name "string_of_characters">
```

The XHTML Standard and Internal Parameter Entities

XHTML is currently out of the scope of this document. We just mention some key strokes. Whenever, applicable, consult a book concerning XHTML.

Inline entities and elements

The XHTML standard provides the following declarations for defining a series of internal parameter entities to be used to define the inline elements

```
<!ELEMENT p %Inline;>
```

Block entities and elements
The XHTML standard also declares a set of internal parameter entities that can be used in the declarations of the block elements

```
<!ELEMENT body %Block;>
```

APPENDIX C

XML OVERVIEW

C.1 Introduction to XML

XML is the most popular way to store data and exchange information over the Internet. Since so many languages can read and write XML files, use XML when you want to share data among different applications and platforms. One of XML's greatest features is its ubiquity.

XML also benefits from being easy to learn. Since XML looks like HTML, Web developers are familiar with its tag-based syntax. However, XML is not HTML. HTML has a fixed set of elements, such as <a>, <img>, and <h1>. With XML, you have the flexibility to use whatever element names best represent your data.

When choosing how to represent data, developers seem to fall into one of two camps. Some people think of XML as a record format, similar to comma-separated files. But instead of separating entries with newlines and fields with commas, XML provides rich classification options.

Other developers view XML as a document specification format. The online PHP Manual (*http://www.php.net/manual*) is produced from XML files. The PHP Documentation Team's documents use tags such as <function>, <parameter>, and <example>. This allows them to release the manual in multiple formats, including two versions of HTML, Windows CHM help files, and PDF.

C.2 Well-Formed XML

For an XML document to be considered valid, it must satisfy the following restrictions:

The document must have only one top-level element. This element is called the root element.

Every element must have both a start and an end tag.

All attributes must have values, and those values must be quoted.

Elements must not overlap. You cannot use <a><b></a></b>, because the ending </a> tag comes before </b>.

You must convert &, <, and > to their entity equivalents. You can use htmlentities( ) to solve this.

When a document meets these rules, it's valid, or well-formed, XML.

C.3 Schemas

When you validate HTML, your file is checked not only to see if it's well-formed, but also that your markup corresponds to the specification. While your application parses XML instead of HTML, it also expects data in a certain format. When it gets anything else, it can't work correctly.

Therefore, it's beneficial to create a data specification, or schema, that outlines the layout of the XML document your program requires. This allows you to check the input XML file against a specification to see if the XML is not only well-formed, but also valid. There are three different schema formats: DTDs, XML Schema, and RelaxNG.

DTD: DTDs, short for Document Type Definitions, are the old way to write a schema. They come from SGML and have a more limited syntax than other formats. They're not written in XML, so they can be difficult to read. Try to avoid DTDs when you can.

XML Schema: The XML schema is the W3-approved document specification format. XML schemas are written in XML, so your XML parser can also validate the schema.

C.4 Transformations

One of XML's great advantages is that you can easily manipulate an XML document into another format. It could be HTML, PDF, or even another XML document. For instance, you could create an RSS feed for the articles in your XML-based CMS.

XSLT, short for Extensible Stylesheet Language Transformations, is a W3C-defined language for modifying XML documents. With XSLT, you can create templates (written, of course, in XML) that act as a series of instructions for how an XML document provided as input should end up as output.

If you're unfamiliar with XSLT, check out *XSLT*, by Doug Tidwell, or Sal Mangano's *XSLT* Cookbook (both published by O'Reilly). *XSLT* assumes no knowledge of XSLT, while *XSLT* Cookbook is more useful for programmers who want a grab bag of recipes to solve commonly encountered XSLT tasks, such as renaming attributes and elements. The complete specification is located at *http://www.w3.org/TR/xslt*.

C.5 XML Namespaces

XML Namespaces let you place a set of XML elements inside a separate "area" to avoid tag name clashes. This is an important feature because it allows XML documents to be extended and combined. Unfortunately, using XML namespaces is tricky. For something that initially seems very straightforward, there's a surprising amount of explanation required.

C.5.1 Why Use Namespaces?

Using XML Namespaces, developers can work together to define a common set of markup for different sets of data, such as RSS items, meta-information about pages on the Internet, or books. When programmers everywhere represent related information using the same set of elements in the same namespace, then everyone can create powerful applications based on a large set of shared data.

On a more practical side, avoiding tag name clashes is still an issue because it's useful to modify XML documents. Clashes aren't a problem when everyone is working with a fixed set of elements. However, you can run into trouble if you allow others to extend a document by adding their own elements.

For example, you may decide to use <title> to refer to the title of a Web page, but your friend used <title> as the title of a person, such as Mister or Doctor. With XML Namespaces, you can keep <html:title> distinct from <person:title>.

Some languages have a similar concept, where functions and objects belonging to a package can be namespaced together. PHP does not support namespaces, which is why you may see the PHP function and class names prefixed with a unique string. For example, the PEAR::DB MySQL module is named DB_mysql. The leading DB_ means that this class will not conflict with a class named simply mysql.

Another example of namespaces is the domain name system: columbia.com is the Columbia Sportswear company, while columbia.edu is Columbia University. Both hosts are columbia, but one lives in the .com namespace and the other lives in .edu.

C.5.2 Syntax

In XML, a namespace name is a string that looks like a URL, for example, *http:// www.example.org/namespace/*. This URL doesn't have to resolve to an actual Web page that contains information about the namespace, but it can. A namespace is not a URL, but a string that is formatted the same way as a URL.

This URL-based naming scheme is just a way for people to easily create unique namespaces. Therefore, it's best only to create namespaces that point to a URL that you control. If everyone does this, there won't be any namespace conflicts. Technically, you can create a namespace that points at a location you don't own or use in any way, such as *http:// www.yahoo.com*. This is not invalid, but it is confusing.

Unlike domain names, there's no official registration process required before you can use a new XML namespace. All you need to do is define the namespace inside an XML document. That "creates" the namespace. To do this, add an xmlns attribute to an XML element. For instance:

```
<tag xmlns:example="http://www.example.com/namespace/">
```

When an attribute name begins with the string xmlns, you're defining a namespace. The namespace's name is the value of that attribute. In this case, it's *http://www.example.com/ namespace/*.

C.5.3 Namespace Prefixes

Since URLs are unwieldy, a namespace prefix is used as a substitute for the URL when referring to elements in a namespace (in an XML document or an XPath query, for example). This prefix comes after xmlns and a :. The prefix name in the previous example is example. Therefore, xmlns:example="*http:// www.example.com/namespace/*" not only creates a namespace, but assigns the token example as a shorthand name for the namespace.

Namespace prefixes can contain letters, numbers, periods, underscores, and hyphens. They must begin with a letter or underscore, and they can't begin with the string xml. That sequence is reserved by XML for XML-related prefixes, such as xmlns.

When you create a namespace using xmlns, the element in which you place the attribute and any elements or attributes that live below it in your XML document are eligible to live in the namespace. However, these elements aren't placed there automatically. To actually place an element or attribute in the namespace, put the namespace prefix and a colon in front of the element name. For example, to put the element title inside of the *http:// www. example.com/namespace/* namespace, use an opening tag of <example:title>.

The entire string example:title is called a qualified name, since you're explicitly mentioning which element you want. The element or attribute name without the prefix and colon, in this case title, is called the local name.

Note that while the xmlns:example syntax implies that xmlns is a namespace prefix, this is actually false. The XML specification forbids using any name or prefix that begins with xml, except as detailed in various XML and XML-related specifications. In this case, xmlns is merely a sign that the name following the colon (:) is a namespace prefix, not an indication that xmlns is itself a prefix.

C.5.4 Examples

Example: This code snippet updates the address book from Example C-1 and places all the elements inside the *http://www.example.com/address-book/ namespace*.

Example: Simple address book in a namespace

```
<ab:address-book xmlns:ab="http://www.example.com/address-book/">
 <ab:person id="1">
   <ab:firstname>Rasmus</ab:firstname>
   <ab:lastname>Lerdorf</ab:lastname>
   <ab:city>Sunnyvale</ab:city>
   <ab:state>CA</ab:state>
   <ab:email>rasmus@php.net</ab:email>
 </ab:person>
<!— more entries here —>
</ab:address-book>
```

If two XML documents map the same namespace to different prefixes, the elements still live inside the same namespace. The URL string defines a namespace, not the prefix. Also, two namespaces are equivalent only if they are identical, including their case. Even if two URLs resolve to the same location, they're different namespaces.

Therefore, this document is considered identical to Example C-2:

```
<bigbird:address-book xmlns:bigbird="http://www.example.com/address-book/">
  <bigbird:person id="1">
   <bigbird:firstname>Rasmus</bigbird:firstname>
   <bigbird:lastname>Lerdorf</bigbird:lastname>
   <bigbird:city>Sunnyvale</bigbird:city>
   <bigbird:state>CA</bigbird:state>
   <bigbird:email>rasmus@php.net</bigbird:email>
```

```
</bigbird:person>
<!— more entries here —>
</bigbird:address-book>
```

The ab prefix has been changed to bigbird, but the namespace is still *http:// www.example.com/address-book/*. Therefore, an XML parser would treat these documents as if they were the same.

C.5.5 Default Namespaces

As you can see, prepending a namespace prefix not only becomes tedious, it clutters up your document. Therefore, XML lets you specify a default namespace. Wherever a default namespace is applied, nonprefixed elements and attributes automatically live inside the default namespace.

A default namespace definition is similar to that of other namespaces, but you omit the colon and prefix name:

xmlns="http://www.example.com/namespace/"

This means there's yet another way to rewrite the example:

```
<address-book xmlns="http://www.example.com/address-book/">
  <person id="1">
    <firstname>Rasmus</firstname>
    <lastname>Lerdorf</lastname>
    <city>Sunnyvale</city>
    <state>CA</state>
    <email>rasmus@php.net</email>
</person>
<!— more entries here —>
</address-book>
```

It is not uncommon to find a document that uses multiple namespaces. One is declared the default namespace, and the others are given prefixes.

C.6 XPath

XPath is a W3C standard (*http://www.w3.org/TR/xpath*) for locating portions of an XML document that match a set of criteria. Use XPath to find the names of all the people in your XML address book who live in New York, all the URLs for articles written on PHP in a Meerkat RSS feed, or the most recent entry into your XML-based content management system.

Think of XPath as SQL for XML documents. You can do all kinds of advanced queries using XPath, such as finding items with a certain parent, attribute, or location in the tree. XPath uses the same syntax as XSLT, so you might be familiar with parts of it, even if you're not an XPath expert.

There are two parts to an XPath query: the portion of the XML document you wish to retrieve and the restrictions you want to place upon your query. This is analogous to SQL SELECT and WHERE clauses.

For example, you can search the XML address book in Example C-1 for all the email addresses:

```
/address-book/person/email
```

Levels in an XML document are separated by a /, similar to the separators for folders in a directory path. When the query begins with a slash, it tells XPath to start looking at the top-level element. Therefore, /address-book/person/email means gather all the email elements under a person element under an address-book element.

This is like a SQL SELECT without a WHERE. However, if you're planning a trip to Manhattan and just want to find all your friends who live in New York, NY, use this:

```
/address-book/person[city = "New York" and state = "NY"]/email
```

The text inside square brackets refines the XPath query. [city = "New York" and state = "NY"] restricts the search to entries where the city element under person is New York and the state is NY. To check attributes instead of elements, prepend an @:

```
/address-book/person[@id = "1"]
```

This finds all persons with an id attribute of 1.

GLOSSARY

DEFINITIONS OF STANDARD XML TERMS

Attributes

Attributes are a name/value pairings that sit inside element tags. For example, an attribute for an inventory listing might include a date the product became available.

```
<lamps date="01/01/2010"> - lamps is the element and date is the attribute
```

Child Element

A child element sits inside of the parent and further itemizes the tags within the file. In an inventory listing of lamps, the element tag "desktop," might be a child element of both "lamps" and "inventory."

```
<inventory> - root/parent element
<lamps> - parent element
<desktop> - child element
```

Comments

Comments are data strings not meant to be seem by those visiting a Web page. Comments are intended to define or explain a coding section to anyone who must update or review the XML file.

```
<!--this is a comment -->
```

CDATA

Character data. CDATA is text in a document that should not be parsed by the XML parser. Any entities included in the CDATA block will not be replaced by their value and markup (such as HTML tags) will not be treated as markup.

CDF (Channel Definition Format)

CDF is a push technology based on XML syntax (submitted to W3C by Microsoft and Marimba). CDF is an XML vocabulary designed to specify metadata about Web pages which will enable filtering to create "Web Push Channels." With CDF, we can describe content ratings, scheduling, logos, and abstract information. Today, the channels we see in the IE4.0 browser are powered by XML and the CDF vocabulary. An XML-based data format is used in Microsoft® Internet Explorer 4.0 and later to describe Active Channel™ content and desktop components.

Character

A character is an atomic unit of text as specified by ISO/IEC 10646. A character is a single alpha, numeric, or punctuation mark.

Character Set

A mapping of a set of characters to their numeric values. For example, Unicode is a 16-bit character set capable of encoding all known characters; it is used as a worldwide character-encoding standard.

Component

An object that encapsulates both data and code, and provides a well-specified set of publicly available services.

Content

Content is all data between the start tag and end tag of an element. Content may be made up of markup characters and character data.

Content Model

The content model in XML is the expression specifying what elements and data are allowed within an element.

CSS (Cascading Style Sheets, Level 1)

CSS is a formatting description that provides augmented control over the presentation and layout of HTML and XML elements. CSS can be used for describing the formatting behavior of simply structured XML documents, but does not provide a display structure that deviates from the structure of the source data. See also Extensible Stylesheet Language. It is an earlier specification of a W3C Recommendation.

CSS2 (Cascading Style Sheets, Level 2)

(supersedes CSS1); a W3C Recommendation.

Document Type Definition (DTD)

A DTD provides the legal structure of the core XML file for validation.

Declaration Statement

The declaration statement gives the browser information to recognize the language and syntax of the file. Without a declaration statement, the Internet processor is unable to compute the code. This is the first line of any XML document and defines the language, version, specifies encoding, and declares the standalone status of the file. Only the language definition and version are required for a declaration statement. Encoding and standalone are optional attributes.

```
<?xml version="1.0" encoding="UTF-8" standalone="yes">
```

Data Strings

A data string is the information you want the viewer to see. For example, a description of an inventory item would be a data string. Data strings sit between the opening and closing tags of element.

```
<description> - element tag
```

This lamp sits on top of a table. - data string viewable on a Webpage

```
</description> - closing tag
```

Data Island

Data islands are a proposed format for putting XML-based data inside HTML pages (<XML> or <SCRIPT language="XML">). HTML is used as the primary document or display format, and XML is used to embed data within the document.

Data Type

The type of content that an element contains such as a number or a date. In XML, an author can specify an element's data type.

Delimiter

A delimiter is a special character that marks the beginning and end of a string or text field.

DHTML (Dynamic HTML)

DHTML, is a term introduced by Netscape and Microsoft, but not accepted by W3C; "the combination of HTML, style sheets and scripts that allows documents to be animated" is how W3C describes DHTML; see also DOM, CSS2, and ECMAScript.

Document Element

Document element is the top-level element of an XML document. Only one top-level element is allowed. The document element is a child of the document root.

Document Root

Document root is the top-level node of an XML document. Its descendants branch out from it to form the XML tree for that document. The document root contains the document element and can also contain a set of processing instructions and comments.

DSO (Data Source Objects)

Provides data, embedded by use of data binding, into an HTML page. Users can then sort and filter the data as they would in a database, without needing to return to the server. DSOs supply data asynchronously to the page, similar to the way GIF images are displayed incrementally as they are transmitted.

DSSSL (Dynamic Style Semantics and Specification Language)

DSSSL It is a powerful formatting language, more so than CSS and XSL (not a W3C standard).

EBNF (Extended Backus-Naur Form)

A formal set of production rules that comprise a grammar defining another language, such as XML.

ECMA Script

ECMA Script is W3C's evolving scripting specification (based on JavaScript). ECMA is an international, Europe-based industry association founded in 1961 and dedicated to the standardization of information and communication systems.

Empty Declaration

Empty declaration in XML is the DTD declaration for an empty tag. For example, if <xyz/> is an empty tag, the empty declaration looks like: <!ELEMENT xyz EMPTY>.

Empty Element

Not all elements have content. Those elements that do not have content are empty elements and in XML may be noted with a special empty element tag that ends with a slash directly preceding the closing angle bracket of the tag, so an XML parser can immediately recognize it as an empty tag and not bother looking for a matching end tag. If "xyz" is an empty tag, it looks like <xyz/>.

Entity

Entity in XML is a virtual storage unit. It is often a separate file, but may be a string or even a database record. In XML, an entity declaration provides the ability to have constants or replacement strings, which are expanded by a pre-processor. An entity declaration maps some token to a replacement string. Later the token can be prefixed with the & character and the replacement string is put in its place. An entity is a XML structural construct. It is a character sequence or well-formed XML hierarchy associated with a name. The entity can be referred to by an entity reference to insert the entity's contents into the tree at that point. The function of an XML entity is similar to that of a macro definition. Entity declarations occur in the DTD.

Entity Reference

XML structural construct. Refers to the content of a named entity. The name is delimited by the ampersand and semicolon characters; for example, &bookname; and <. It is used in much the same way as a macro.

Event Handler

The code that is executed when an event occurs.

Element Tags

Element tags are created by the author and establish a hierarchical syntax to the code. When designing elements for an XML information file, supply names to tags that are recognizable and easily managed. For example, when creating an inventory file, you might use key names, such as "table" to supply structure to the code. Within the element "table" you might list more tags the further identify the inventory, such as "desktop" or "floor." The simplicity of XML lies is this process of naming the element tags. XML does not have static tags that you must memorize in order to write valid code. All element tags must have closing tags.

```
<table> - element tag
</table> - closing tag
```

Generic Identifier

Generic identifiers, often called the "GI" is the XML tag name. So <head> has a generic identifier equal to "head." A generic identifier is unique in its namespace.

Grammar

The syntax of a language. It is expressed formally by a set of production rules, such as the EBNF rules.

Granular Updating

Changing only an element of a page, rather than rebuilding the entire page. The new element is sent from the server to the client, which replaces the old element while leaving the rest of the page intact.

Graphing

A very generalized way to represent certain data relationships.

HGML (Hyper Graphics Markup Language)

HGML is a graphically-oriented alternative to HTML specifically designed for use in wireless contexts.

HTML (Hypertext Markup Language)

Hyper Text Markup Language (HTML) is the pervasive data format for the World Wide Web. While HTML provides an outstanding mechanism to deliver simple documents over the Web, its simplicity imposes limitations that significantly raise the cost of deploying complex Websites. Currently, version HTML 4.0 is the official W3C Recommendation, but many authors and browsers are still using HTML 3.2.

ICE (Information and Content Exchange)

ICE is an XML vocabulary that provides an exchange protocol for content on the Web. ICE defines the roles and responsibilities of syndicators (data providers) and subscribers (data consumers). While ICE was initially developed to support commercial publishing applications on the Web, it is expected to prove useful in automating content exchange and reuse in both traditional publishing environments and in business-to-business relationships.

ID

A special attribute type within the XML language. The ID attribute on the XML element provides a unique name, enabling links to that element using the IDREF attribute type. The value associated with the ID attribute must be unique within that XML document. IDs are currently declared with a DTD or schema.

Java Script

Java Script is Netscape's scripting language; current version is 1.2.

JScript

JScript is Microsoft's scripting language derived from JavaScript.

Markup

Markup is a text character that identifies the storage and logical structures of the data. Tags and entities are markup characters of an XML document. It is the text in an XML document that does not represent character data: start tags, end tags, empty-element tags, entity references, character references, comments, CDATA section delimiters, DTDs, and processing instructions.

MathML (Mathematical Markup Language)

MathML is an XML vocabulary for describing mathematical notation and capturing both its structure and content. MathML is designed to enable mathematics to be served, received, and processed on the Web. MathML can be used to encode both mathematical notation and mathematical content.

Twenty-eight of the MathML tags describe abstract notational structures, while another seventy-five provide a way of unambiguously specifying the intended meaning of an expression.

MCF (Meta Content Framework)

MCF is a data model for metadata.

Metadata

Metadata is generally a machine understandable information about data, specifically for data describing Web resources.

Mixed Content

An element type has mixed content when elements of that type can contain character data, optionally interspersed with child elements. In this case, the types of the child elements can be constrained, but not their order or their number of occurrences.

Namespace

A namespace is a set of unique identifiers. It is a mechanism to resolve naming conflicts between elements in an XML document when each comes from a different vocabulary. It allows the commingling of like tag names from different namespaces. A namespace identifies an XML vocabulary defined within a URN. An attribute on an element, attribute, or entity reference associates a short name with the URN that defines the namespace; that short name is then used as a prefix to the element, attribute, or entity reference name to uniquely identify the namespace. Namespace references have scope. All child nodes beneath the node that specifies the namespace inherit that namespace. This allows nonqualified names to use the default namespace.

NDATA

The literal string "NDATA" is used as part of a notation declaration.

Normalize

To collapse two or more adjacent text nodes in the document tree into one text node. This ensures that the tree structure will match the tree structure generated when the document is stored and reloaded. The element object offers a normalize method.

Notation

Usually refers to a data format, such as BMP. A notation identifies by name the format of unparsed entities, the format of elements that bear a notation attribute, or the application to which a processing instruction is addressed.

Notation Declaration

A notation declaration provides a name and an external identifier for a notation. The name is used in the entity and attribute-list declarations and in attribute specifications.

The external identifier is used for the notation, which can allow an XML processor or its client application to locate a helper application capable of processing data in the given notation.

OFX (Open Financial Exchange)

(from Microsoft, Intuit and CheckFree; not W3C); supports banking, bill payment, bill presentment and investments. A data format used by personal-finance applications to communicate with financial institutions over the Web. Although it is currently described using SGML, OFX will soon be based on XML.

OSD (Open Software Description)

OSD is for platform-independent software installation and updates. It is an XML-based data format for advertising and installing software components over the Internet (from Microsoft and Marimba; not W3C).

Parent Element

A parent element holds other related element tags. For example, a file that lists inventory might have a parent tag called lamps, and contain tags the list the individual lamps available in the product line. The root element is the parent tag for all other elements in the XML file.

```
<inventory> - parent element
<lamps> - element tag
```

Prolog

An XML prolog consists of a declaration of the version of XML being used as well as the DTD that the document will validate against.

XML documents do not have to have the DTD to be well-formed, but it is required to be valid. Examples:

```
<?xml version="1.0">
```

html PUBLIC "-//W3C//DTD XHTML 1.0 Transitional//EN" "http://www.w3.org/TR/xhtml1/ DTD/xhtml1-transitional.dtd">

P3P (Platform for Privacy Preferences)

Websites state their privacy practices which user agents match against the preferences defined by the user (giving the user better control) based on RDF, which is based in turn on XML syntax. The W3C Platform for Privacy Preference Project Vocabulary Working Group presents a basic model for the P3P privacy conversation between a user agent and a service. P3P provides a grammatical model for expressing P3P service practices and user preferences over data in the semantic framework of RDF and a data design model for expressing and referencing data elements, classes, and categories.

PGML (Precision Graphics Markup Language)

PGML is a 2D scalable graphics useful for precision graphics as well as for simple vector graphics; it is based on XML syntax and the object model of PostScript and Portable Document Format (PDF).

PI (Processing Instruction)

PIs are instructions that are passed through to the application. The target is specified as part of the PI. The syntax for a PI is <?pi-name content?>.

PICS (Platform for Internet Content Selection)

PICS is an infrastructure for associating labels (metadata) with Internet content. PICS 2.0 is based on RDF which is based in turn on XML syntax (the earlier PICS version 1.1 pre-dates XML and therefore uses a different syntax).

RDF (Resource Description Framework)

RDF is a language for writing metadata. It is useful for defining sitemaps, content ratings (see), search engine data collection (resource discovery), intelligent agents, etc. An object model similar in function to an application programming interface (API), RDF can be used by developers to access the logical meaning of designated content in XML documents.

RDF Namespace

RDF namespace is a specialized XML syntax designed to provide a limited form of RDF on the Web.

Reference Node

The reference node for a search context is the node that is the immediate parent of all nodes in the search context. Every search context has an associated reference node.

Root Element

The root element is the first named tag of every XML file and is a container for all other elements.

```
<inventory> - root element
<lamps> - element tag
```

SGML (Standard Generalized Markup Language)

In 1986, the Standard Generalized Markup Language (SGML) became an international standard for the format of text and documents. SGML has withstood the test of time. Its popularity is rapidly increasing among organizations with large amounts of document data to create, manage, and distribute. However, various barriers exist to delivering SGML over the Web. These barriers include the lack of widely supported stylesheets, complex software because of SGML's broad and powerful options, and obstacles to the interchange of SGML data because of varying levels of SGML compliance among SGML software packages. The international standard for defining descriptions of structure and content of electronic documents. XML is a subset of SGML designed to deliver SGML-type information over the Web.

SMIL (Synchronized Multimedia Integration Language, SMIL 1.0, pronounced "smile")

SMIL, a W3C Recommendation, is an XML vocabulary that allows integrating a set of independent multimedia objects into a synchronized multimedia presentation. With SMIL you can describe the temporal behavior of the presentation, describe the layout of the presentation on a screen, and associate hyperlinks with media objects.

SOAP

SOAP is an acronym that stands for Simple Object Access Protocol.

SOAP is an XML-based protocol that allows you to activate an application or object within an application across the Internet. SOAP is used for distributed computing and Internet applications. It was developed by a group of vendors, including Microsoft, to revolutionize how Web applications are developed.

Outside of Web development, SOAP stands for Symbolic Optimal Assembly Programming.

SAX

Stands for Simple API for XML. An event driven method of dealing with an XML file.

Instead of containing the entire hierarchy in memory at one time, it presents elements as events which can then be exploited by your code. SAX has the advantage of less memory consumption for large files, but has the disadvantage that the programmer must write code to save anything he wants saved and must write changes to the XML file in sequential order. DOM allows random changes to elements. Because it doesn't need to keep entire files in memory all at once, SAX is universally useful, whereas DOM is not useful for truly large XML files.

Tags

Tags are text structures that mark the beginning and end of elements within the XML document. Tags are markup characters.

Target

The application to which a processing instruction is directed. The target names beginning with "XML" and "xml" are reserved. The target appears as the first token in the PI. For example, in the XML declaration <?xml version="1.0"?>, the target is "xml."

Text Markup

Inserting tags into the middle of an element's text flow to mark certain parts of the element with additional meta-information.

Tokenized Attribute Type

Each attribute has an attribute type. Seven attribute types are characterized as tokenized: ID, IDREF, IDREFS, ENTITY, ENTITIES, NMTOKEN, and NMTOKENS.

TEI (Text Encoding Initiative)

TEI it is not a W3C Standard and predates the Web.

UCLP (Universal Commerce Language and Protocol)

The Universal Commerce Language and Protocol (UCLP) is an XML vocabulary for tagging metadata that can be used in identifying and retrieving commerce data residing across the Internet. UCLP presents a tagging schema which captures the relevant parameters describing an object, but is not bound to a prescriptive DTD. UCLP is designed to evolve to capture changes in the marketplace in the same time frame in which these are occurring. The system using these tags would have to be flexible in incorporating changes, would have to provide the industry domain with means to monitor and regulate changes according to their own policies, and must be sufficiently general so that advances made in one domain can be transferred to others. UCLP is intended to introduce a new paradigm for dynamic data tagging for which data typing is only a required tool.

Unicode

Unicode is a standard for representing characters from languages around the world. Unicode standards are synchronized with UCS-2 subset of ISO 10646.

Updategram

XML generated by agents to notify the client of changes to data on the server, or vice versa; the agents could run on the middle tier to access multiple existing database management systems (DBMSs) and output XML.

URI (Uniform Resource Identifier)

URI is the system used for naming all the resources on the Web. This includes URL (Uniform Resource Locators) and all future resource categories. It is defined in Berners-Lee, T., R. Fielding, and L. Masinter, Uniform Resource Identifiers (URI): Generic Syntax and Semantics - 1997. The Layman-Bray proposal for namespaces makes every element name subordinate to a URI, which would ensure that element names are always unambiguous.

URL (Uniform Resource Locator)

The set of URI schemes that have explicit instructions on how to access the resource on the Internet.

URN (Uniform Resource Identifier)

A Uniform Resource Name identifies a persistent Internet resource.

Valid

An XML document is valid if it conforms to the vocabulary specified in a DTD or schema. In other words, an XML document with an associated document type declaration that follows all the rules of that declaration is valid.

VML (Vector Markup Language)

VML defines markup formatting for vector graphics along with style information to assist in display and editing.

Well Formed

A well-formed XML document follows all the rules of the XML specification but is not necessarily valid according to an associated document type declaration. A well formed XML document contains one or more elements; it has a single document element, with any other elements properly nested under it; each of the parsed entities referenced directly or indirectly within the document is well-formed. A well-formed XML document does not necessarily include a DTD.

WIDL (Web Interface Definition Language)

WIDL is an XML vocabulary that that implements a service-based architecture over the document-based resources of the World Wide Web. WIDL allows interactions with Web servers to be defined as functional interfaces that can be accessed by remote systems over standard Web protocols, and provides the structure necessary for generating client code in languages such as Java, C/C++, COBOL, and Visual Basic. WIDL enables a practical and cost-effective means for diverse systems to be rapidly integrated.

XLL (Extensible Link Language)

XLL, now called XLink, is a simple and extended linking mechanism. XLL provides links in XML similar to those in HTML but with more functionality.

Linking could be multidirectional, and links could exist at the object level rather than just at a page level.

XMI (XML Metadata Interchange)

Format, IBM, and Unisys response to the OMG's request for proposals for a stream-based model interchange format for UML (Unified Modeling Language) models.

XML Aware

Any software application that recognizes the XML data format and understands XML concepts. Often XML aware software contains an embedded XML parser.

XML Data

XML data is a proposal, submitted by Microsoft and others to the W3C, to define a number of common scalar data types that can be applied to elements. The XML-Data proposal includes the concept of XML schemas.

XML Declaration

An XML declaration is an optional declaration at the top of an XML document that specifies the version of XML and an encoding declaration. The first line of an XML file can optionally contain the "xml" processing instruction, which is known as the XML declaration. The XML declaration can contain pseudo-attributes to indicate the XML language version, the character set, and whether the document can be used as a standalone entity.

XML Document

A data object that is well-formed, according to the XML recommendation, and that might (or might not) be valid. The XML document has a logical structure (composed of declarations, elements, comments, character references, and processing instructions) and a physical structure (composed of entities, starting with the root, or document entity).

XML Engine

Software that supports XML functionality on the client; Internet Explorer 4.0 and Internet Explorer 5 include XML engines.

XML OM (XML Object Model)

An API that defines a standard way in which developers can interact with the elements of the XML structured tree. The object model controls how users communicate with trees, and exposes all tree elements as objects, which can be accessed without any return trips to the server. The XML OM uses the W3C standard Document Object Model.

XML Vocabulary

An XML vocabulary is an XML tag set with a specific functionality. SMIL, WIDL, MathML, and ICE are all examples of XML vocabularies. The actual elements used in particular data formats. Channel Definition Format, for example, is a format for describing collections of pages and when these pages should be downloaded. Vocabularies, along with the structural relationships between the elements, can be defined in a DTD or a schema.

XML (Extensible Markup Language)

A subset of ISO 8879, Standard Generalized Markup Language (SGML). The XML subset of SGML has been specifically designed to function on the Web. A subset of SGML that provides a uniform method for describing and exchanging structured data in an open, text-based format, and delivers this data by use of the standard HTTP protocol. At the time of this writing, XML 1.0 is a World Wide Web Consortium Recommendation, which means that it is in the final stage of the approval process.

XML-QLA (Query Language for XML) - XQL

XML with similarities to SQL.

XSL Pattern

Part of XSL that provides simple querying capability against an XML document. Internet Explorer 5 supports XSL Patterns with some of the extensions described in XML Query Language.

XML DOM

XML DOM provides a standard for structure and navigational properties of all XML files.

XSL (Extensible Stylesheet Language)

XSL is a family of languages designed to render XML to an output stream readable on various platforms.

XSL Transformations (XSLT)

XSLT is an XSL document that transforms the data of an XML file into XHTML to be read by a parser and displayed on a browser.

XPath

XPath is a language that provides navigation through XML using path expressions.

XQuery

XQuery is a language that provides a way to search and extract elements and attributes within an XML document.

XML Linking Language (XLink)

XLink creates hyperlinks within XML documents.

XML Pointer Language (XPointer)

XPointer serves as a partner to XLink that allows links to the individual parts of an XML document.

XML Schema

Schemas are XSL documents designed to provide structure to the linked XML file for validation and output.

Extensible Stylesheet Language Formatting Objects (XSL-FO)

XSLO-FO is a language that formats XML data for output for various media platforms.

XForms

XForms provides a way to display forms within XML to create interactive pages.

XML Editor

An XML editor is a software application that facilitates coding in the XML markup language. There are many levels of XML editors. Some programmers prefer a basic text editor, such as Notepad, to write XML documents. When creating a platform that utilizes XML for Web design, a savvy author will look to more advanced XML editors, such as Oxygen XML Editor. This package provides not only text files to create a core data file, but also XSL formatting and an HTML output stream. With the right editor, a designer can organize the data and create the page all in one place.

XML Validator

XML is easy to create, but unwavering in the rules. Syntax must be followed in order to provide pages on the internet. A validator will examine an XML document and certify that all tags are closed and properly nested. XML makes demands on the designer. It requires structure and proper format. Unlike HTML, elements without closing tags or misplaced in the hierarchical stage will generate an error. A validator will look closely at the file and help develop well-formed XML. It is a valuable tool for both novices and veterans alike.

XML DOM

Document Object Model (DOM) is the interface that defines how data is accessed. This is the place that allows programmers to create dynamic content that will display the same basic way on any browser. The DOM is a standard interface that enable all languages to work cohesively. It is not a language on its own, but a mechanism that allows programming languages to exist. All structured documents work within a DOM system. Without the DOM, parsers would not be able to identify and processes any part of a file. It works to locate and move the information. The DOM supplies a method for the ever growing list of browsers to read and process code.

XML Parser

An XML parser is a module that reads the code and converts it into the XML DOM. From this point, the file can be manipulated into presentable form. Without a parser, computers would not understand the meaning of the files. A parser reads the code within the XML file, determines it is well-formed, and then assigns meaning to it. You cannot display information on a Web page without a parser to read it.

INDEX

E

F

J

K

L

M

N